The Roots of Modern English

The Roots of Modern English

SECOND EDITION

L. M. Myers
Arizona State University (Emeritus)

Richard L. Hoffman
Virginia Polytechnic Institute and State University

with a chapter on Contemporary Developments in America by Samuel R. Levin and Constantine Kaniklidis

Little, Brown and Company
Boston Toronto

Library of Congress Catalog Card No.: 78–70454

ISBN 0-316-59316-8

10 9 8 7 6 5 4 3

MV

Published simultaneously in Canada
by Little, Brown & Company (Canada) Limited

Printed in the United States of America

Preface

The first edition of this book (1966) was by Myers alone. Six years later it was supplemented by *Companion to the Roots of Modern English,* by Hoffman with minor assistance from Myers. Now we have extensively revised both books in a joint effort. We have transferred some material from *Companion* to *Roots* and replaced the badly outdated final chapter on current developments in linguistic theory with an entirely new one by Samuel R. Levin and Constantine Kaniklidis.

The preface to the first edition began with the following sentence: "Our profession is deeply committed to the idea that every English teacher (and preferably every citizen) should take a course in the history of the language, but our opinions of what material should be covered vary enormously." We cannot pretend to be all things to all men; but in this new edition of the two books we have tried to provide adequate material for at least three emphases: (1) the purely historical; (2) (our own preference) direct experience with various stages of the changing language; (3) attempts to analyze the nature of linguistic structure. There is no attempt to cover "current English usage," a subject which deserves at the very least a course and a text of its own. Even with this omission it does not seem likely that any one instructor will attempt a uniformly thorough coverage of all the material in the two books. There is room for choice.

A further word about our new Chapter 10 "Contemporary Developments in America." Professors Levin and Kaniklidis have provided a highly concentrated survey of transformational-generative theory and variation as they have developed over the last ten years. Their linguistic terminology is, necessarily, different from that of the traditional grammar explained in Chapter 9 and used throughout the rest of our book. Consequently, most of this material may be foreign and potentially intimidating to many students. Very close reading(s) under gentle instructional guidance may be necessary here. The review questions and exercises in *Companion* should offer some assistance.

We have had the advantage of an unusual number of reviews of the first edition, for which we are most grateful. We must extend our particular gratitude (accompanied by the usual exculpation) to Professor Jack Conner of California State University at Hayward and Professor Francis G. Greco of Clarion State College. Professor Wayne H. Phelps of Virginia Polytechnic Institute and State University has very generously assisted in assembling the illustrations which are a new feature of this edition.

L. M. Myers
Richard L. Hoffman

Contents

The Roots of Modern English

1

What Is a Language?

Some Confusion about Language

The word *language,* like every other word in any language, is used for a number of more or less related meanings. No one of these is exclusively right, but some of them can be dangerously misleading, so that it is quite possible to spend years studying or even teaching various languages without ever having a very firm or useful notion of what a language is. This lapse in understanding is probably the principal reason why so many Americans say "Of course I don't really know any French — I just had it in college." It is also at least one of the reasons why the enormous effort that goes into teaching the English language in our schools and colleges often seems to have little effect beyond making most students hate the subject in class and feel guilty about it for the rest of their lives.

It would be arrogant to attempt to cure this condition by offering, at last, the one true definition. It would also be futile, because if we adopted any definition as uniquely true we would continually find that we were either stretching the definition to cover some aspect that we had not previously considered, or narrowing our idea of language to fit the definition.

What most students need is not a sacred definition to defend, but information about how a few languages have developed and how they work; some discussion of what we actually know about languages and what we can still only guess at; and (perhaps most of all) a demonstration that some of our most widely cherished beliefs about language are inaccurate to the point of superstition. Of course some sort of working definition is needed, and a tentative one is offered on page 5 below. Memorizing it is unlikely to do anybody much good; but considering it carefully may save a good deal of misdirected effort. It will be well, however, to clear a few things out of the way before attempting it.

To begin with the obvious, language is what human beings talk with. Those who wish to may define the word so as to include the noises made by crows or the wing-signals of bees, but these things are not considered here. Nor are the "real language" of philosophy, "body language," Indian sign language, or the concept that mathematics is a kind of language. No disrespect for any of these is intended — they simply lie beyond the scope of this book. Without language the human race would hardly be human in any very important sense. We could not even think as we now do, because most of our thinking is done in language and could not be done without it; and it seems unlikely that we could have developed even the simplest kind of stone-age culture.

Why Did We Choose to Talk?

The wing-signals of bees have been mentioned, and we all know that some of the social life of dogs seems to be carried on by sniffing. That our main system of signals is composed of sounds is therefore a matter of choice rather than necessity, but there is little doubt that our ancestors made a wise choice. If we consider each of the five senses we can see at once that a really extensive set of signals based on smell or taste would be rather hard to organize or transmit. We might use touch, but not at a distance; and sight has disadvantages as a *basic* system. It won't work in the dark or in thick brush or under many other conditions; and it interferes too much with other activities. Hearing seems to be much the most promising, and it is the one that our ancestors somehow selected. Maybe they tried all five before discovering which one worked best.

Sounds are made in many ways. Crickets rub their legs together and ruffed grouse drum on hollow logs, but neither method seems to permit of much variety. By using their mouths and some nearby organs our ancestors developed a much more flexible system.

Some Theories about the Origin of Language

Most of the theories about how the first steps in language building were made have been scornfully rejected. One very old one is that some sounds just naturally represent some things, so that man had merely to recognize, not invent. This idea has been expressed metaphorically by saying that when early man first saw a large milk-producing animal "a bell rang" in his brain and he said *cow*. There is no evidence at all for this explanation, and it takes no account of the great differences between languages. People who do not care for the explanation have called this the *ding-dong theory*. Another guess is that language began by imitation of natural sounds, so that the first words were the ancient equivalents of *bow-wow, gurgle, swish,* and others. Certainly we have words of this sort, which may be called "echoic" or "onomatopoetic," but no one can prove that they are among the earliest words, and they are too few to make a satisfactory base for all language. Unbelievers have therefore dismissed this as the *bow-wow theory*.

A third theory is that vocal sounds were at first merely accidental accompaniments to gestures. A man who was disgusted might make a face to indicate his disgust, perhaps rounding and pushing out his lips. If he did this forcefully enough some breath might escape, and he would make a noise. At first it was only the face that had the meaning; then the sound that accompanied it began to take on a share of the meaning; and finally, the sound being more convenient, it took over the job of conveying the meaning all by itself. If you try making such a face and noise you may guess that people who didn't like it called this the *pooh-pooh theory*.

Another is a *yo-he-ho theory,* which argues that men engaged in heavy shared labor automatically made grunts that gradually became symbols of the activities that called them forth; and there are others, none widely accepted. We just don't know how language began, and have no sound reason to suppose that we ever shall.

The Structural Levels of Language

However they began, the early speakers of a language had to take several steps, though presumably not in such a clear-cut and logical order as here indicated:

1. Select, from the innumerable possibilities, a few dozen sounds as the building blocks of their speech. No two of them could possibly pronounce the sounds exactly alike; in fact, no one of them could always pronounce the "same" sound in exactly the same way. But the variations had to fall within recognizable limits, so that the selected sounds could be reliably told from each other. These elements, now called *phonemes,* are actually sound-classes rather than precise sounds. *They are not pronunciations of letters.* Letters are indications or signs, often very ambiguous, of sounds.

2. Arrange these phonemes, which have no meanings of their own, into some thousands of meaningful units, now called *morphemes,* which may be either complete words or significant parts of words. *Fire* contains only one morpheme; *fireman* contains two, each of which could occur alone; and *fireman's* contains three, one of which occurs only in combination. Though the morpheme indicated by *'s* is not a word, it is an important unit in the structure of the language.

3. Develop a *syntax,* consisting of some habitual patterns for combining the morphemes into longer utterances, such as sentences. Three elements in these patterns are most obvious in writing:

   a. Word order.
   b. "Inflectional" morphemes, such as those which distinguish among *walk, walks, walked,* and *walking,* or *big, bigger,* and *biggest.*
   c. "Function words," such as prepositions and auxiliary verbs, which are often more important as structural elements in a sentence than for any exact meaning of their own. Thus we may say "in honor of John" instead of "in John's honor"; and "will walk" puts *walk* into the future just as the *-ed* in *walked* puts it into the past.

Equally real, and quite as important in speech, are musical pitch, comparative stress, and "juncture" or transition between sounds or sound and silence, which can give several sentences containing the same words in the same order entirely different meanings. These elements may be suggested on paper by punctuation, italics, underlining, or other devices; but they are not usually indicated as regularly or as reliably as the first three, so that their importance is often inadequately recognized and sometimes denied. Most of us have been disastrously misquoted by kind friends who have repeated our "exact words" while giving them a completely different meaning by changing their intonation.

The three levels — phonemic, morphemic, and syntactic — are completely interwoven in every utterance of a language; it is only in analysis that it is sometimes advisable to keep them strictly separate.

A Tentative Definition of Language

The preceding section is obviously the barest outline of what had to be done in developing a language. The actual procedure must have been incredibly complicated, explaining why no group ever managed to make the necessary steps with complete uniformity. We have no reason to believe that even two people can either speak exactly alike or understand each other perfectly and consistently. When the communicating group consists of hundreds of millions of people spread over millions of square miles and developing through fifteen centuries of an ever-changing world, a complete and tidy analysis of their language is an impossibility. It is, however, now appropriate to offer a tentative definition:

> *A language is composed of a limited selection of vocal sounds, meaningless in themselves but capable of being combined into symbolic units to which the speakers somehow agree to give the same range of arbitrary meanings, and a systematic but flexible method of arranging these units to make extended communication possible.*

A few notes on this definition:

1. Phonemes, as such, have no meaning, though a language may have a very few morphemes consisting of a single phoneme apiece.

2. Morphemes are the smallest *symbolic* units. Without symbols we could communicate in a limited way about things actually present by handling them, pointing to them, and so forth; but we would have no way of referring to anything not at hand. Moreover, symbols can often be manipulated much more easily than the things for which they stand, and easy manipulation may not only help us understand relations but make it possible to develop new ones.

3. The dream of making language reliable by giving each word one fixed meaning and forcing everybody to use that one alone is based on a hopeless misunderstanding. Because we can have only a limited number of words to apply to an infinite number of things, actions, and relations, one word *must* be used for things that are similar but not identical; and people with different interests and points of view see different similarities. It is of course admirable to use words carefully and with the meanings appropriate to particular discussions. But any one who insists that the meaning he prefers is the only true one is displaying ignorance as well as arrogance.

4. A few words in any language may be considered to have "natural" meanings, because they imitate nonlinguistic sounds. But unless most meanings were arbitrary, languages could not be so different, and would be much easier to learn. Moreover, even the "echoic" words have an arbitrary element. Thus we have somehow agreed to *whisper,* but the French have decided to *chuchoter;* and when our dogs say *bow-wow* theirs reply *gnaf-gnaf.*

5. Though a language is never perfectly regular, it must have enough regularity to limit the strain on intelligence and memory. We can manage quite a few irregular verbs; but without a dependable system for all the rest we would be utterly lost.

6. If a language were not flexible we could never say anything new in it, but only repeat fixed, memorized bits, as parrots do. As it is, we continually create brand new sentences, and understand without trouble ones we have never heard before.

7. A main system may be reflected in one or more derived systems. We can represent a sequence of spoken sounds by a corresponding sequence of written letters; and the correspondence may be either one-to-one, as in phonetic transcriptions, or conventional, as in ordinary spelling. Writing often has, for specific purposes, great advantages over speech, and it would be silly to belittle its importance. But we should remember that it is a secondary system, and not try to make speech conform to it.

We can go further and represent letters by "dots and dashes" transmitted electrically — a tertiary system. Or we may use signal flags, either with a position for each letter (another tertiary system) or to represent dots and dashes — a quaternary one.

8. Before leaving this subject, note that some scholars hold that even the sound system is secondary, and that the primary linguistic activity takes place quietly in human nervous systems. They have a good deal of evidence to support them. We can all think silently; deaf-and-dumb people can be

taught to read and write capably; and the deaf, dumb, and blind Helen Keller mastered English by purely tactile signals. There is therefore a sound argument for distinguishing between *internal language* — a sense-free neural activity — and *external language,* the expression of that activity by auditory, visual, or other signals.

We refrain from discussing internal language on the simple grounds of incompetence — we don't know enough about neurology. But although it does not seem to be bound to any sense, it can apparently be acquired only by using one or another. And as soon as it is transmitted from one person to another it becomes external language; for most of us its primary form is speech.

Speech and Writing

Language developed for a good many thousand years, and apparently became as complicated as it ever got to be before any way of writing it down was invented. The old and apparently logical idea that uncivilized and illiterate people must speak a very simple kind of language has been completely destroyed by modern investigation. Linguists have found that African Bushmen and Amazonian Indians speak languages of a grammatical complexity that would make most of us shudder. The spoken form of language is therefore primary, and the written form, however important it may be, is secondary. Most of us realize this — in a way, and part of the time. It seems perfectly obvious when we think of history. But when it comes to our everyday use of language we often think of the written form as the true one, and of speech as an often very imperfect reflection. Our usual pronunciations are often considered careless or sloppy when they do not contain all the sounds that seem to be indicated by the established spelling. It seldom occurs to most people that when writing and speech differ, the simplest explanation is that writing is falling down on its job of reflecting speech.

Of course the simplest explanation may be a little too simple to be entirely accurate. Writing began simply as a secondary representation of speech, but for many purposes it has clear advantages, especially in its comparative permanence; and among literate people it always develops independent characteristics of its own, and exerts some influence on the original spoken form. Even the English spoken by a man who is illiterate is very different from what it would have been if our society had no tradition of literacy. It is therefore natural — as most things that happen consistently are — that the comparative importance of the written form should often be exaggerated in schools. When the teacher writes a sentence on the blackboard or calls attention to one in a textbook, it is there for all to consider uniformly and at leisure. It seems both more real and more important than a spoken sentence that disappears as soon as it is uttered; and it is certainly more convenient to consider and discuss. Therefore the teacher uses it as a model for rather than a record of speech, and says things like, "Danny, don't say *ol' knight,* say *old knight*. Can't you see the *d?* You must learn to pronounce words the way they are written." That even the teacher does not pronounce the *k,* the *g,* or the *h* in *knight* is seldom considered.

The importance given to the written form of language, in schools and in many other situations, is an undeniable fact, and not necessarily a shameful one; but we will find it very useful to remember that the spoken form is not only the earlier, but for most purposes still the primary one.

Some Writing to Look Through

This last point is easy enough to accept in theory, but quite hard to grasp firmly as a working principle; and the better educated we are, and the more our education has concentrated on English, the more likely we are to feel that the language really lives in books and is only imperfectly reflected in speech. Perhaps the best way to see this tendency is to examine a passage that was printed before our conventions of writing had become comparatively uniform:

> And certaynly our langage now vsed varyeth ferre from that whiche was vsed and spoken whan I was borne; for we Englysshe men ben borne vnder the domynacyon of the mone, whiche is neuer stedfaste, but euer wauerynge, wexynge one season, and waneth and dyscreaseth another season. And that comyn Englysshe that is spoken in one shyre varyeth from a-nother in so moche, that in my dayes happened that certayn marchauntes were in a shippe in Tamyse, for to haue sayled ouer the see into Zelande; and for lacke of wynde thei taryed atte forlond, and wente to lande for to refreshe them. And one of theym, named Sheffelde, a mercer, cam in-to an hows, and axed for mete; and

> specyally he axed after eggys. And the goode wyf answerde, that she coude speke no Frenshe. And the marchaunt was angry, for he also coude speke no Frenshe, but wolde haue hadde egges; and she vnderstode hym not. And thenne at laste a-nother sayd, that he wolde haue eyren. Then the good wyf sayd that she vnderstod hym wel! Loo, what sholde a man in thyse dayes now wryte, egges or eyren? Certaynly it is harde to playse euery man by cause of dyuersite and chaunge of langage.[1]
>
> [From Caxton's Preface to his *Eneydos,* 1490.]

It is really amazing how differently people of approximately equal intelligence will react to such a passage. One will read it almost at sight, possibly pausing for a second or so at *vsed* and *wauerynge,* but adapting himself almost immediately, and quickly recognizing every word except perhaps *forlond* and *mercer*. Another will find it almost unintelligible at first glance, and almost intolerable even after a good deal of study. For anybody who finds it difficult, these steps are suggested:

1. Make up your mind that there is not a misspelled word in the passage. Never mind whether this statement is true — it is useful. The man who wrote the passage was simply using the letters he knew to indicate the sounds of the words he used, and he is fairly, though far from perfectly, consistent. If he happened to spell a word two ways — *eggys* and *egges* — he had no way of finding out which was right, because no dictionary of the language had been published, and he could find plenty of practice on both sides.
2. Notice that he uses some conventions quite different from ours. If we reversed his *u*'s and *v*'s the passage would look far more normal, and if we reversed his *i*'s and *y*'s we should gain about as much as we lost.
3. Use your ears to help your eyes. A number of words that seem strange to the sight are immediately clear to the ear, especially if they are pronounced in context and with no excess of precision. *Comyn* alone might suggest nothing, but if you read aloud and rather casually "that comyn Englysshe" it could hardly be anything but "that common English."

We have here, in other words, a spoken language represented somewhat inadequately, but not hopelessly, in print; and the way to understand this language is to look through the groups of letters for the sounds that lie

[1] Rolf Kaiser, *Medieval English* (Berlin-Wilmersdorf, 1961), p. 567, lines 195–211.

behind them. (Semiliterate people sometimes seem to understand this better than the thoroughly educated.) In studying Modern English it is possible, if not reasonable, to think of a word as a group of letters that should be pronounced in a specific way; but in studying the earlier stages it is absolutely necessary to remember that a word is a group of sounds, which the spelling suggests but does not control.

The Variations of Language

This passage of Caxton's is interesting for another reason. Over five hundred years ago the man who brought printing to England was worried by the "dyuersite & chaunge of langage." He would have had just as much reason for worry if he had lived five hundred or a thousand years earlier; and he has successors who are as much worried now. Uniformity and stability in language would certainly have their advantages, but before we yearn for them too passionately perhaps we should consider whether they are even theoretically possible.

To begin with, nobody talks simply language — we have to talk English or Spanish or German. Several hundred millions of us talk English, in one way or another. The Americans don't talk just like the British, and the Americans in South Carolina don't talk just like the Americans in Cleveland. In fact, nobody talks simply English — we have to talk one dialect or another. Of course there are snobbish people who think that what they talk is pure English, and anything different is a dialect; and there are humble people who realize that they talk a dialect, but credit more fortunate people with talking the language pure. All qualified students of the subject now seem to agree, however, that the language is composed exclusively of dialects. They also agree that we are on pretty slippery ground if we argue that some dialects are *intrinsically* better than others, though some certainly have more prestige, and may therefore be worth learning.

If we go one step further we will realize that no two speakers of a dialect talk exactly alike. Each has his own *idiolect,* or individual language, which differs at least a little from all others. And if we consider our own idiolects we realize that no one of us talks exactly the same way all the time. Language then is really languages, which are really collections of dialects, which are really collections of idolects — and even these aren't quite uniform and dependable.

The Chicken or the Egg?

We are now faced with a very difficult question. Are the dialects and idiolects merely group and individual departures from the true language? Or is a language simply the sum total of what the idiolects that compose its dialects happen to add up to? Unfortunately, each answer looks quite reasonable from one point of view, but entirely impossible from another. We are then reminded of the ancient puzzle of which came first, the chicken or the egg; the situation seems completely paradoxical. No solution so far proposed squares with all the evidence, or satisfies all competent linguists. Probably the best way to approach the question is to remove the word *merely* from the second sentence of this paragraph, and the word *simply* from the third. Anybody who wants to keep either word in and answer *yes* to the question in which it occurs is interested in defending a dogma rather than forming an opinion. And anybody who really wants to learn anything about the subject will find it profitable to devote most of his effort to understanding the point of view he finds least attractive. There really is important evidence on both sides.

Langue and Parole

About seventy years ago the great Swiss linguist, Saussure,[2] attempted to clarify the problem by dividing human speech into two components — *langue,* an impersonal set of conventions to which all members of a speech community must (subconsciously) subscribe in order to understand and make themselves understood; and *parole,* a collective term for individual acts of speaking. Parole would be utterly meaningless if it were not based on langue; but it never reflects langue quite perfectly, and it inevitably involves physical phenomena that are no more a part of langue than the chalk mark with which a circle may be represented on a blackboard is

[2] Ferdinand de Saussure, *Cours de Linguistique Générale* (Paris, 1916). Unfortunately, this book was not actually written by Saussure, but was compiled by two of his students from notes on his three series of lectures, delivered between 1906 and 1911. It is impossible to determine whether contradictions that mar an exceedingly valuable book are due to changes in his thinking or to inaccurate reporting and editing. The book has been translated into English by Wade Baskin as *Course in General Linguistics* (New York, 1959). The quotations and references in this chapter are all from pages 14 to 20 of the English version.

part of the circle it represents. Saussure says that langue is "the social side of speech, outside the individual who can never create or modify it by himself; it exists only by virtue of a sort of contract signed by the members of a community." A little later he adds that it "exists in the form of a sum of impressions deposited in the brain of each member of a community, almost like a dictionary of which identical copies have been distributed to each individual." [3]

Saussure says that one might, if really necessary, apply the term "linguistics" to each of the two branches, and speak of a linguistics of *parole;* but that such a science must not be confused with linguistics proper, whose sole object is *langue*. Since his time most European linguists have followed his lead, while until quite recently American linguists have emphasized *parole,* denying with considerable vigor his statement that it was no part of "linguistics proper." During the past two decades many American linguists have adopted the Saussurean attitude, but we postpone discussion of this development to Chapter 10.

The True-Language Theory

To a nonlinguist the Saussurean emphasis on *langue* is likely to seem merely a more precise statement of a theory that all sensible people have always (if rather vaguely) taken for granted. According to this theory a language is a set of conventions, an agreement that certain combinations of sounds (or letters) stand for certain things and activities and ideas; and that these combinations must be arranged in a limited number of grammatical patterns. Whether we believe that these conventions are ultimately based on logic or are purely arbitrary makes, for the moment, little difference. At any rate our ancestors have somehow decided that Rags is to be called a *dog,* and not a *chien* or a *cane* or a *perro* (as other ancestors have decided

[3] *Langue* is often translated as *language,* and some of Saussure's most zealous followers seem to think that this settles the question of what language really is. It seems unlikely that he would have agreed with them, because he says:

> Note that I have defined things rather than words; these definitions are not endangered by certain ambiguous words that do not have identical meanings in various languages. . . . No word corresponds exactly to any of the notions specified above; that is why all definitions of words are made in vain; starting from words in defining things is a bad procedure.

Language is used here (and in many other books) to include both components, so that we use the French terms to avoid confusion.

elsewhere). They have likewise decided that we should say *a black dog,* and not *a dog black,* which would be the normal word order in some other languages. This is not merely a matter of style, but an important signaling device. We recognize at once the difference between *business college* and *college business;* but a Frenchman, whose language has the opposite conventions, would be likely to get the two reversed. Countless other decisions of the same general kind were made before we were born, and as children we could neither understand nor talk to our elders until we somehow began to be aware of their conventions, and to imitate them — at first pretty crudely. After a few years of steady effort, imitation, practice, and correction much of the crudeness disappeared, and we eventually learned to reflect the conventions in our own speaking with some accuracy. Whenever we failed we simply made a mistake; the language was already there, and we had neither the right nor the power to modify it. The mistake might be purely personal, or it might be picked up from our parents and other elders who had already departed from the true path, and spoke a dialect rather than the pure language.

Obviously, the more closely we adhere to the established conventions, the more dependable our communication will be. Every conceivable effort should therefore be made to encourage uniformity, and to discourage departures in pronunciation, word forms, patterns of arrangement, meaning assigned to each word, or any other variations from the established system. And whenever a group of people, whether from geographic isolation, social submergence, foreign influence, or any other reason, develops a system noticeably different from the pure and original one, their kind of language should be considered an inferior dialect, and they should be penalized (not nastily, of course, but firmly) for speaking it.

The trouble with this theory is that there is no such thing in nature as that intrinsically pure, good, or correct English that we would like so much to teach; and there never has been. Neither can we find a uniquely pure form of French, German, or Latin, though it is easy enough to talk as if we could. Nothing can prevent Harris from talking about "pure, Parisian French" if he wants to; but likewise nothing will prevent Clarke from replying, "What do you mean, pure Parisian? They speak with a horrible twang in Paris. If you want to hear really good French you should go to Tours." Meanwhile Reade is thinking how silly they both are, because he has known for years that the only *really* good French is spoken in Geneva, the entire French nation having lost the true way some generations back. And of course if we went to Paris (or Tours or Geneva) we would find that its inhabitants speak with much variety and argue about some points, that the older ones accuse the younger ones of corrupting the language, and so forth.

A linguist — even one who concentrates on *langue* — knows all this, and has no theories at all about how people ought to use a language. His approach is purely descriptive; and he wants to describe not the infinitely varied acts of *parole,* but the underlying system of conventions that these acts imperfectly reflect. His basic theory is that all members of a speech community must have the same "set of impressions deposited in the brain" in order to communicate. Their performance may vary enormously, but their "competence" — their mastery of the system — is identical.

This is a very useful hypothesis, freeing him from having to take account of all the physical irregularities of *parole,* and it has resulted in important advances in our knowledge. Its chief defect is that there is no precise way of determining the exact membership of a speech community sharing identical conventions. Probably no two adults anywhere in the world know exactly the same list of words, and certainly no two people know exactly the same things about them, or pronounce, arrange, and react to them identically. Some of the differences can be dismissed as matters of *parole,* but others seem to be based on a difference in the *langue* itself. This *langue* certainly varies from one dialect to another; and there is satisfactory evidence that it varies in a smaller degree within each dialect. Language, like everything else, is always and necessarily changing. No speaker ever reflects his underlying conventions (whatever they are) quite perfectly, and of course speakers are influenced to some extent by each other. Each act of speech carries at least the possibility of a tiny modification in a group's conventions, and a good many of these possibilities eventually take obvious effect, so that in time the whole set of conventions changes beyond easy recognition.

The Sum-of-Parts Theory

Until recently most American linguists paid little attention to the theories of Saussure, but followed the "structural" approach of Leonard Bloomfield.[4] They started with the assumption that language is simply people talking, and that if we want to study it scientifically we should not (at least in the beginning) try to look *behind* the talking for some system assumed

[4] *Language* (New York, 1933).

to underlie it. We should look directly *at* the talking, and describe it as accurately and completely as possible. Like other scientists we should begin by observing the phenomena, and we should do so with absolute impartiality. When we have made enough observations we may try to arrange them into a system; but our procedure must be purely inductive, and we can neither make value judgments nor discard inconvenient evidence to make it so. We cannot say that *ellum* is a mispronunciation of *elm,* but only that two pronunciations of this word occur. Similarly, we must record that some people say "He don't like them apples" where others would say "He doesn't like those apples" without permitting ourselves to make any prejudiced comment about "bad grammar."

This inductive, objective approach was devised in studying previously unwritten languages, such as those of American Indians, and proved extremely fruitful for the purpose. It reduced the temptation for an investigator to distort his description to make it fit any preconceived theory about how the language ought to be constructed. Anything a native speaker said had to be accepted as part of the data. A pronunciation might be comparatively unusual, but it simply could not be wrong, any more than a pebble can be of a wrong shape.

Attempts to apply this approach to English immediately run into two difficulties. It seems reasonable to postulate that any three Papago Indians who consent to act as informants can give us a satisfactory sample of their language. After all, there are not very many of them, and they are a fairly homogeneous group. But English is spoken by hundreds of millions of people, and spoken with such variety that it is hard to find a sample small enough to study intensively, and at the same time widely acceptable as typical of the whole. Moreover, we may not suppose that any Papago is dissatisfied with his own use of his language, or contemptuous of his neighbor's use. His *langue,* to the best of our knowledge, is completely subconscious. He knows what words and grammatical patterns mean, and uses them accordingly. But an American usually has two kinds of *langue,* one as subconscious as the Papago's, the other quite explicit, though perhaps not completely mastered. He knows perfectly well what *ain't* means, whether or not he himself uses it. But even if he does use it, he is conscious that it is often regarded as wrong. Whether he tries to conform or decides to go on living comfortably in a state of grammatical sin, he seldom quarrels with the idea that the explicit conventions are somehow right.

A few structural linguists want to treat English exactly like Papago, and take the stand that anything a native speaker says (except a slip that he would himself correct) must be right because he says it — a language is simply what its speakers talk, and all attempts to legislate about it are illegitimate. Most structuralists, however, are willing to admit that "standard English" has so much social importance that we are justified in teaching it in our schools. They insist only that such instruction should be based on careful observation of how selected speakers do talk, and not on any theories about how they should. Such an attitude immediately arouses the fury of a good many people. To anybody who feels outraged we can say only that we are not advocating it as *the* true approach; but that we do most urgently suggest that the more it annoys him, the harder he should try to understand its possible value for some purposes, because it simply cannot be tossed aside as worthless. The pronunciation of English has changed a good deal since Anglo-Saxon times, and quite noticeably even since the time of Dr. Johnson, and the structure has changed along with it. It would probably be impossible to find one correct sentence today that would not have been wrong once. Take such an innocent-looking one as "Those little girls are very nice." If the repeated mistakes of our ancestors had not somehow come to be sanctified as "good grammar," *those* should be *tho* — the *s* got in by mistaken analogy with other plurals; *little* should have a special ending to agree with the noun it modifies; *are* should be *be* — nobody knows just how the past tense of an entirely different verb came to be used as the present tense of *to be;* and *very,* having started life as an adjective, should not be permitted to modify another adjective without adding *-ly*. Perhaps we should add that *nice* meant "ignorant" before it meant "foolish," "foolishly precise," and "precise" on its way to its current meaning of something like "mildly admirable"; and that *girls* formerly meant something like "teenagers" — young people of either sex.

In short, all the evidence we have tells us that any language is always changing, and never quite uniform at any one time. It seems a little naive to assume that all the changes that took place up to about Aunt Emma's day were improvements and that all those which have been taking place since are calamities.

A Suggested Compromise

Neither the "chicken first" nor the "egg first" theory being entirely satisfactory, some sort of compromise seems necessary. We have seen that no two people can possibly *use* a language in exactly the same way. The critical question is, do they differ merely in *performance* — the accuracy with which their *parole* reflects the *langue* that has been built into their nervous systems and is identical for them all? Or is the *langue* itself a little different for each speaker? Saussure chose the first answer, which has a large advantage, allowing us to investigate the underlying system without being distracted by insignificant physical differences. But it is of course an assumption, not a demonstrable fact; and its adherents are likely to shy away from the question of exactly how widely a *langue* is spread. They admit differences in dialects, but (like everybody else) have found it impossible to give the precise boundaries of a homogeneous dialect group.

It seems more reasonable to assume that all speakers differ somewhat in their *langue* as well as their *parole*. We can say then that each speaker of a language must somehow have in mind a chart of that language which his acts of speech must approximately reflect, or they would have no meaning at all, even to him. And each of the neighbors with whom he talks must also have a chart, somewhat similar to his, or they could not interchange ideas; but not quite the same, because all men are different. In any group of speakers the charts must overlap considerably to make some communication possible; but they are never quite identical, and the possibilities of variation in the overlap are practically infinite. In other words, our idiolects do not differ from each other simply as imperfect reflections of one perfect chart. Rather, each is based on its own chart — imperfectly constructed in imitation of other charts already imperfect. When we speak of the chart for a whole language, or even a widely disseminated dialect, we are using a fiction, useful for some purposes, very troublesome for others. We have to choose between overgeneralization and interminable qualification. Speakers of "Standard English" agree unanimously on some points, such as a preference for *I saw* over *I seen.* They disagree rather casually on many others, such as *different from* or *than* or *to;* and quite bitterly on some others, such as *he don't* or the meaning of *disinterested*. Some of the uses they usually condemn can be shown to be sounder, either historically or logically, than the ones they prefer; but these usages will remain nonstandard unless and until enough standard speakers take them up.

So far we have been concentrating on one level of a language, the words that are its most obvious units. Much more can be said about these, but much of it cannot be said intelligibly until we have looked both down and up — down at the assortment of sounds that the speakers of a language somehow manage to select as the building blocks with which they will make their words, and up at the structural patterns by means of which they combine the words into meaningful utterances.

Caxton's language is so close to our own that we can approach it without bothering much about these two levels. Once we learn to look through the spelling we can find recognizable words, and treat them almost as if they were our own. But in the earlier stages of the language we shall meet not only quite unrecognizable words but sounds and sound combinations that may at first seem impossible; and we shall sometimes find, as we do with foreign languages, that even after we have looked up the meaning of every word in a sentence we are unable to read it because we do not understand its structure.

2

The Sounds We Talk With

Selection of Sounds

The human voice can make hundreds, perhaps thousands, of recognizably different sounds, but no language uses more than a few dozen of these, and probably no two languages make exactly the same selection. If you listen to a Frenchman or a German talking his own language you will hear sounds that native Americans do not make in speaking English, and cannot make at all without long and careful practice or special training. If you listen to more remote languages you may feel at first that the sounds you hear are scarcely human. This is a natural reaction, because we are almost inevitably inclined to take our own familiar habits as normal, and to consider all conflicting habits as inferior, if not downright ridiculous. But like many natural reactions this one is worse than inaccurate, it is expensive. As long as we keep it we will be handicapping ourselves in learning any foreign language, and even in learning many important things about our own. It is a big step forward to decide firmly that the sounds we happen to be accustomed to are neither better nor more natural than those we encounter in other languages or dialects. Then we can consider both old and new sounds with the idea of seeing just what they are and how they are made and used.

Phonetics

Many students have a strong resistance to phonetics because they don't see beyond the transcriptions, which they think of as a sort of misguided spelling reform. Having more or less mastered conventional spelling, they see little to gain by learning another system that they know is not generally used, even if it is theoretically better. But transcription is merely an incidental technique, not an end in itself. The basic subjects of phonetics[1] are:

1. The gymnastics by which speech sounds are produced.
2. The ways in which neighboring sounds may modify one another.
3. The ways in which sounds may, under various conditions, change to other sounds.

It is a difficult and complex study, but a few of its findings can be explained quite simply, and are useful even to beginners.

The sounds represented by any alphabet are traditionally divided into vowels and consonants. This division is not wrong, but it is so rough that it does not tell us much. Most of us probably have a vague idea that a vowel is a vowel because — well, because it has a vowel-like nature; and a consonant is a consonant because it is somehow consonantal. We may not even realize that some consonants have much more in common with vowels than others do. A slightly closer look may therefore be helpful.

Our vocal apparatus makes up a sort of complicated musical instrument. At the top of the windpipe are a pair of bands called vocal cords, which serve like the reeds in a wind instrument. When they vibrate, our normally almost inaudible breath takes on the sound of speech. During speech the vibrations may be briefly interrupted for some consonant sounds, but without them we couldn't talk above a whisper.

The inside of the mouth acts as a very flexible resonance chamber. Its shape can be modified by the position of the lips, and especially by the movements of the tongue. Our vowel sounds vary according to which part of the tongue is raised and how close it comes to the roof of the mouth. Other movements can affect their quality, but in Modern English these are incidental.

[1] We are here interested only in articulatory phonetics, not in studying how speech sounds are heard. The diagram of the vocal apparatus facing this page may be of some help in understanding what follows. Notice particularly that the tongue is much larger than most people think, and shaped quite differently. The small part that occasionally protrudes misleads us.

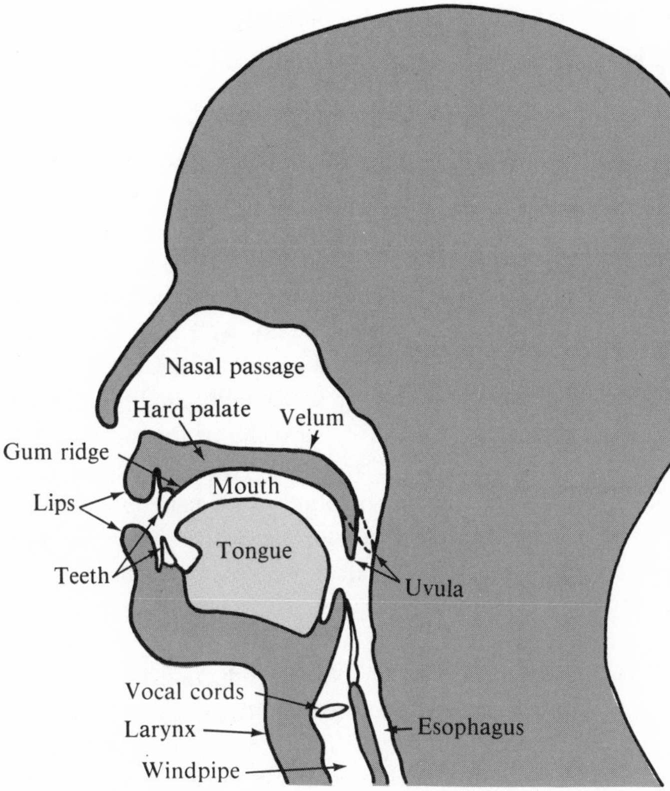

The air passage left for pronouncing different vowels varies in size, but it must not be small enough to cause audible friction, or the sound produced will be a consonant of the type called *fricative* rather than a vowel. If the passage is, for an instant, completely stopped, the resultant sound will be a consonant of the type called *plosive* or *stop*. (This division is rough, but it will do for the present.)

All English speech sounds are made as we are breathing out[2] — a limitation that is not true of some languages. All are made by definite muscular movements of various organs, from the diaphragm to the lips. For instance, /t/ is made when we stop the vocal cords from vibrating and briefly

[2] Some noises indicated by such spellings as *tsk-tsk* or *tut-tut* may be made on an indrawn breath; but these are generally regarded as substitutes for rather than parts of English.

interrupt the breath stream by pressing the tip of the tongue just behind the upper front teeth; and /k/ is made by bringing some part of the tongue up hard against the roof of the mouth, the exact place of contact depending on the neighboring vowels. We learned to make the appropriate movements by long-drawn-out trial-and-error practice when we were very young, and most of us have very little idea of how we do make them. This ignorance does not handicap us in normal speech, but it interferes deeply when we want to learn something about another language or a different variety of our own. The common belief that early childhood is the only time when a second language can be learned really well is based on a half-truth. By the time we are twelve or fifteen most of us have muscular habits of speech so strong that we can no longer successfully modify them by simple imitation of strange sounds. But if we are shown the mechanics of producing a French *u* or a German *ch,* and then given an opportunity to listen and imitate intelligently instead of blindly, we can do much better. We may still retain some "accent," but we can learn to use the language fluently and accurately much faster than we could as children — assuming that our mental development did not stop completely before we got out of elementary school.

Knowing the mechanics of speech production will also help us to understand how sound changes occurred in different areas and at different periods in the development of English. The new sound is always formed by a variation of the gymnastics used to produce the old one. Once we know what the gymnastics are we can see how some sound changes occur easily, and others are quite impossible.

Phonemes

The statement we made at the beginning of this chapter that no language uses more than a few dozen sounds now requires further explanation. Because no two of us have exactly the same pronunciation, the number of truly different sounds that millions of us can and do make is enormous, even though it is only a fraction of those we could make. But to communicate at all we have somehow come to an agreement to group all the sounds we make into a few dozen *contrasting classes* of sounds, technically called *phonemes.* When two sounds are recognized as significantly different, so that substituting one for another will change or destroy the identity of a word, they are said to belong to different phonemes. Thus the word *till* consists of the three phonemes /t/, /i/, and /l/ (the slashes — also called virgules — indicate that the symbols between them are used to indicate phonemes, not ordinary letters). If you substitute a /p/ for the /t/ or an /e/ for the /i/, you get a different word; and if you substitute a /z/ for the /t/, you get no word at all. All these are therefore different phonemes. But differences in pronunciation that, though quite audible, do not change the identity of a word are considered variations of the same phonemes. Even if we disregard personal and dialectal differences in pronunciation, we make some variations under the influence of neighboring sounds, though most of us are entirely unconscious of them. The sounds represented by the letter *t* in the words *till* and *still* are definitely different, because they are made in different ways. If you hold the palm of your hand about an inch in front of your mouth and pronounce the two words, you will find that *till* is uttered with a strong puff of breath — strong enough to blow out a lighted match if you have one handy. *Still* is uttered with no such puff. The *t* in *till is* therefore said to be "aspirated" and the *t* in *still* to be "unaspirated." The difference in sound made by the aspiration is audible, *but only to people who are used to listening for it.*

In some languages the difference between an aspirated and an unaspirated *t* is distinctive — that is, sufficient to distinguish two words that are otherwise identical. If we used the symbol *t* for the unaspirated sound, and the special symbol *t‘* for the aspirated one, we might have such pairs of words as *till* and *t‘ill* or *still* and *st‘ill,* with entirely different meanings. Native speakers of such languages, being trained to notice the difference, could tell *till* and *t‘ill* quite as easily as we can tell *till* and *dill* apart (though these two words would sound alike to the speakers of some languages in which aspiration is significant but voicing[3] is not). But most native speakers of English cannot readily hear the difference between *till* and *t‘ill* even after it has been explained and demonstrated to them. They fail to do so not simply because they have not been trained to hear it. They have been very definitely (though informally and subconsciously) trained *not* to hear it. We can understand each other only by disregarding the differences in pronunciation that are not, in our language, significant, and concentrating on those which are. *It is exactly as important not to notice some differences as it is to notice others.* Only by doing both, for example, can we recognize that words pronounced quite differently by people from different regions are somehow the same.

When two sounds are demonstrably but not significantly different they are

[3] The difference between voiced and voiceless consonants is explained on p. 28 below.

called *allophones* of the same phoneme. It may be helpful to compare non-significant differences in sound to differences in typefaces or in handwriting. Davis and Cassidy may make their capital *A*'s quite differently, or Davis may make an *r* that looks like Cassidy's *v*, but we soon learn to disregard these peculiarities. Both of them use exactly twenty-six letters that we interpret as the same; and we read by identifying the intended letters through any irregularities that may occur in the handwriting. In other words, to be able to read a number of handwritings, or kinds of type, we must look through specific physical differences to find the underlying similarities of intention; and the same is true in understanding pronunciations. *Spoken language is not composed of exact and invariable sounds any more than written language is composed of exact and invariable shapes.* We recognize a spoken word when we (subconsciously) identify the phonemes of which it is composed, and to do this we must disregard many details of the sounds produced. It is rather like recognizing the same musical phrase when played on different instruments in different keys. The sounds heard are quite different, but the significant relations are identical.

Origin and Distortion of the Ordinary Alphabet

We must be careful not to push the analogy between letters and sounds too far, because our erratic spelling by no means permits a one-to-one correspondence between the two. Presumably our ordinary alphabet was originally devised on principles we now call phonemic, as an attempt to find a symbol to represent each significant and contrasting sound wherever it occurred. We have no way of knowing how accurately it did this in Phoenician (if it *was* the Phoenicians who invented it). It was probably not perfect, because it is hard to believe that the Phoenicians had solved all the problems that are still bothering us; but it was good enough to be reasonably effective, and it was certainly one of the most durable inventions of all time. The Greeks borrowed it, directly or indirectly, from the Phoenicians, but had to make changes to fit their somewhat different sound system. The Romans borrowed it from the Greeks, making more adjustments; and hundreds of other languages have borrowed, adjusted, and modified it ever since. Many of the letters have changed form, and letters of the same form may now indicate entirely different sounds in different languages. Our *p* comes from the Greek *rho,* which was an *r* sound, as it still is in Russian;

and our *x* comes from the Greek *chi,* which had the value of *ch* in German words like *nicht* and *doch.*

Considering how many languages this alphabet has been stretched to fit, who can wonder that it does not always work equally well? In Spanish the results are very good, for the spelling represents the pronunciation accurately and efficiently. A Spaniard therefore seldom has trouble either in spelling correctly any word that he can pronounce or in pronouncing any unfamiliar word that he sees in print. But the relation between sound and symbol in English is notoriously irregular. Our alphabet contains a few characters that it could well spare, and lacks a number that it could well use, so that some must do at least double duty. But these deficiencies only partly account for its versatility: more than half the letters can represent distinctively different sounds in different words, and many sounds can be spelled in a bewildering number of ways. Another reason is that our spelling conventions were crystallized some centuries ago, and therefore do not reflect important sound changes that have occurred during the last few hundred years. A third, and probably the most important, is that these conventions were derived from a curious mixture of conflicting traditions, including those of French scribes and Dutch printers, and a wild assortment of odd bits of theories, often misguided.

All this is confusing enough when we are dealing only with Modern English, but when we try to trace the development of the language the difficulties are compounded. For instance, if we look at the two old English words *cƿic* and *leaf* and compare them to their modern derivatives *quick* and *leaf,* it seems that the first changed a good deal while the second has remained constant; but if we hear the words pronounced we get the opposite impression. *Cƿic* sounds exactly like *quick,* but the Old English *leaf* sounds much more like *layoff* than the modern *leaf.* Both sound and spelling changes are real; but as we saw in the first chapter, it is the sounds rather than the symbols for them that we care about most. The basic parts of our language are not the twenty-six letters of the alphabet, but the sounds that these letters rather inconsistently and ambiguously represent. To discuss them intelligibly on paper we therefore need a special alphabet.

The IPA

The International Phonetic Alphabet, hereafter called the IPA, was devised about a hundred years ago by the International Phonetic Association. It is still being improved and expanded in the attempt to indicate clearly and dependably all the speech sounds used in all known languages. It therefore includes symbols for many sounds not used at all in English, and others indicating minor differences in sound (such as that between aspirated and unaspirated [t]) which do not happen to be phonemically significant in English, though they are in some other languages. Because of the enormous number of languages it has been stretched to fit and the varied uses to which it can be put, it is no longer really an alphabet, but a storehouse of symbols, meticulously classified, from which materials for alphabets may be drawn as needed.

An expert phonetician may have occasion to indicate not simply how an utterance "is pronounced," but precisely how one speaker pronounced it on a particular occasion. This is as "narrow" a transcription as possible, and is intelligible only to other experts. Successively broader are transcriptions of the "usual" pronunciations in the speaker's idiolect, subdialect, dialect, and language. But the more area you include, the more detail you leave out — and the more phoneticians you leave behind you muttering disgustedly "this is no longer phonetics." The symbols used in narrow transcriptions are regularly enclosed in square brackets like the [t] in the paragraph above, to distinguish them from ordinary letters. In "broad" transcriptions they may be enclosed in slashes (/ /) instead; but here usage varies.

Can broad transcriptions properly be called phonemic? Opinions differ strongly, primarily because of disagreement about whether the name *phoneme* should be limited to vowel and consonant sounds, as in this chapter, or should be stretched to cover musical *pitch,* syllabic *stress,* and *juncture* (roughly, the transition — rising, level, or falling — between sounds or between sound and silence). A good many American linguists believe firmly that these elements simply *are* phonemes, and that no transcription that does not include them can be called phonemic.[4] Most European linguists, without questioning the importance of these elements, prefer to call them something else.[5] Whichever side we take, we do not know enough about the way these elements were used in early English to justify including them in transcriptions.

[4] They regularly use the special augmented alphabet devised by George L. Trager and Henry Lee Smith, Jr., *An Outline of English Structure* (Norman, Okla., 1951), even though many of them question the analysis on which it depends and dislike the alphabet itself, which was designed for convenience in typing and offset printing, not on any theoretical principles. But this system is neither intended for nor suited to transcriptions of Old or Middle English.

[5] For the difference between typical American and European attitudes see Daniel Jones's monograph, *The History and Meaning of the Term "Phoneme"* (London, University College, 1957), especially pages 19–21.

There is no one obligatory set of IPA symbols for transcribing Modern English. The number you need depends on how much ground you want to cover and how much detail you want to show. Students of dialects need many more symbols than compilers of dictionaries for general use, who assume that a reader might want to know that *heath* and *heather* rhyme with *wreath* and *weather* rather than with *breath* and *breather,* but would probably not care how or whether the inabitants of Kansas City pronounce a final *r.* And even when writers agree on the number of sounds to be distinguished they may legitimately disagree on the best ways to indicate some differences. See page 33 for examples.

The transcriptions in this book are not intended to change anybody's habitual pronunciation, or to show exactly how the language "was pronounced" at an earlier period. We have no reason to believe that pronunciation in Chaucer's time, for instance, was any more uniform than in our own, or even that his own habits were entirely consistent. But we do know that his "long vowels" were quite different from ours; that he stressed many words on different syllables; and that his poetry sounds much better if we approximate his pronunciation than if we simply impose our own.

In the interest of sanity rather than logic we will begin our phonemic analysis with the sounds of contemporary English, which most readers can make but have never examined systematically. We will then have some foundation for later treatment of differences in the sound systems at earlier stages of the language.

The Two Extremes of Our Sound System

We may begin by analyzing the simple word *pa,* which is composed of two phonemes and may be transcribed as /pɑ/. The one indicated by /ɑ/ is as complete a vowel as we can manage. We open our mouth as wide as we ever do, keep the tongue low, set our vocal cords to vibrating, and the result is /ɑ/. When a doctor wants to look down our throat he tells us to say "ah" just because we have to make a wide-open passage to say it. If we said "ee" we should not open our mouth so wide, the front part of the tongue would be close to the roof of the mouth, and the doctor would not get much of a view. And if the tongue got so close as to touch the roof of the mouth the breath would be interrupted, the vowel would slide into a neighboring consonant, and the result would be something like "eek!"

Furthest removed from /ɑ/ is the sound indicated by /p/, which might be called the extreme consonant. To make it we close our lips completely and do not allow the vocal cords to vibrate. This is as far as we can get from the sound of /ɑ/ and still be talking. The sounds indicated by all the other phonemic letters are somewhere between /ɑ/ and /p/, though not all in one straight line.

The Consonant Phonemes

Twenty-four consonant phonemes are generally recognized in Modern English. Because the symbols of the phonemic alphabet have no established order to correspond to the "a b c" order of the ordinary one, they are listed in a way which may at first seem peculiar, but which has the advantage of grouping the symbols for sounds with features in common.

p	t	k	s	ʃ	tʃ	l	r	m	n	ŋ	j	w	h
b	d	g	z	ʒ	dʒ								
f	θ												
v	ð												

The Voiceless Stops

The phonemes /p/, /t/, and /k/ are the only *voiceless stops* in English. "Voiceless" means that the vocal cords do not vibrate, and "stop" refers to stopping the breath stream. In /p/ the stopping is done by closing the lips, and this phoneme is called the voiceless *labial* stop from the Latin word for *lip*. In /t/ the stopping is done by pushing the tip of the tongue so firmly against the gum ridge behind the upper front teeth that no air can escape over it. This stop is now usually called *alveolar* from the anatomical name for the gum ridge. In /k/ the stopping is done by raising some part of the tongue against the roof of the mouth, the exact position of contact depending on the neighboring vowel sound. If you pronounce the two words /kik/ (*kick*) and /kuk/ (*cook*) slowly, you can feel that the contact is farther forward in /kik/ than in /kuk/, and if you practice long enough you can hear a difference between the resulting sounds. In some languages this difference is phonemic — sufficient to distinguish between otherwise identical words. But in English it is negligible, because these two sounds of /k/ are allophones of the same phoneme, their variation being both automatic and nonsignificant. This phoneme is now usually called the voiceless *velar* stop, from the *velum* or soft palate, even when, as in /kik/, the point of contact is actually forward on the hard palate.

The Voiced Stops

The next three sounds, /b/, /d/, and /g/, are similar to /p/, /t/, and /k/ respectively except that they are "voiced" — that is, the vocal cords vibrate when they are pronounced. You can test this sounding in two steps. First, grasp the very top of your Adam's apple between the thumb and forefinger of either hand and pronounce a prolonged "ahhh." When you get the right position you will feel the vibration that is characteristic of voicing. Then, retaining your grasp, pronounce the two words *gob* and *cop*. As you pronounce *gob* the vibration will continue throughout the word, because the consonants as well as the vowel are voiced; but when you pronounce *cop* the vibration is shorter, because both consonants are voiceless. Moreover, the presence or absence of voicing at beginning and end is the only reliably significant difference between the two words. It is probable that you put your tongue in a very slightly different position for /k/ and /g/; but if you voice /k/ you get /g/, and if you unvoice /g/ you get /k/; and the same relation holds true for /p/ and /b/ and /t/ and /d/.[6]

Fricatives and Affricates

The next four sounds, /f/, /v/, /θ/, and /ð/, are not stops but fricatives. The passage of the breath is restricted but not cut off. You breathe through a narrow opening, and the friction at that point makes a characteristic sound. To make /f/ and /v/ you press your lower lip, not against your upper lip as for /p/ and /b/, but against your upper front teeth, and exhale. Without voicing the result is an /f/, with voicing a /v/. These four phonemes make up the labial group. (More precisely, the two stops are *bilabial* and the two fricatives are *labiodental.*)

To make /θ/ and /ð/ you put the tip of your tongue near the position used for /t/ and /d/, but not quite so high. Instead of pressing firmly against the gum ridge and blocking the air, the tip presses more lightly against the bottom of the upper front teeth, allowing some air to escape. Unvoiced, the result is /θ/ (*theta*) as in *thin*. Voiced, it is /ð/ (*eth* or *edh*) as in *this*. The four phonemes in this group are often called *dentals,* though the two stops are more precisely *alveolar*. You will notice that they

[6] That we can understand whispered speech proves that voicing is not the *only* difference between such pairs; but in interpreting whispers we rely heavily on context and often require repetition.

parallel the labials — voiced and voiceless stops, voiced and voiceless fricatives. (Modern English has no fricatives to correspond to the /k/ and /g/ stops, though earlier English had them.)

The next two pairs of fricatives are formed by placing the tip of the tongue farther back in the mouth than for /θ/ and /ð/. Voiceless /s/ and voiced /z/ are made by forming a very narrow passage between the tip of the tongue and the gum ridge. Voiceless /ʃ/ (*esh*) and voiced /ʒ/ (*ezh*) are made by forming a passage still farther back. The closeness of the three positions accounts for the difficulties some people have with these sounds. If you attempt to make /s/ with the tongue just too far forward, you will lisp and make /θ/. On the other hand, a foreigner who keeps his tongue too far back in attempting /θ/ will make /s/. And anybody who attempts /s/ with tongue still farther back will make /ʃ/.

The sounds indicated by /tʃ/ and /dʒ/ are known as *affricates*. As the symbols indicate, an affricate may be regarded as composed of two successive sounds — a stop and its corresponding fricative. Some phoneticians do so regard them; but it is convenient (and usual) to consider them as single phonemes. Because six of the seven unfamiliar symbols for consonant phonemes are discussed in this section, their pronunciations are listed below, and you are advised to notice carefully the positions your tongue takes when you pronounce them.

/θ/	as in	*thin* /θin/	or	*myth*	/miθ/
/ð/	"	*then* /ðen/	"	*bathe*	/beið/
/ʃ/	"	*ship* /ʃip/	"	*fish*	/fiʃ/
/ʒ/	"	*vision* /viʒən/			
/tʃ/	"	*chip* /tʃip/	or	*pitch*	/pitʃ/
/dʒ/	"	*gem* /dʒem/	"	*edge*	/edʒ/

The Liquids and Nasals

It is impossible to describe simply how the *liquid* sounds /l/ and /r/ are pronounced, because they vary so much both among speakers of different dialects and in different phonetic environments. Moreover, some ways of making the two are quite similar. The difference between them is usually clear to native speakers of English, who have been trained to react to it, but not to speakers of some other languages. It is well known, for instance, that a Chinese may pronounce *very* as /veli/, but a Japanese is likely to go the other way and pronounce *hello* as /hero/.

It is worth special emphasis that English has three, not two, nasal phonemes, and that these are related to the three voiced stops. That is, /m/ is pronounced with the lips in the same position as for /b/, /n/ with the tongue in the same position as for /d/, and /ŋ/ (called *eng*) with the tongue in the same position as for /g/. The nasals are distinguished from the corresponding stops because the passage from mouth to nose, which is closed by the uvula when the stops are pronounced, is left open so that air escapes by the alternate route and the sounds can be continued. (You may have noticed that when a head cold closes the nasal passage an attempted /m/ sounds very much like /b/, and so forth.) That you can "hold" /ŋ/ as well as /m/ or /n/ shows that it really is a single sound, not a combination. So too does the pronunciation of *singer* /siŋər/ compared with that of *finger* /fiŋgər/. If you say *fishin'* rather than *fishing* you are not "dropping a *g*" but substituting a consonant.

Both the liquid and two of the nasal phonemes are capable of being complete syllables, but our spelling habits make this obvious only in the combination /sm/. We pronounce /prizm/ and spell *prism,* but pronounce /prizn/ and spell *prison.* In words like *meter* and *theater* we can put the vowel symbol *e* on either side of the *r,* but don't feel free to leave it out. And a German name like Hempl will probably be changed to Hemple or Hemphill so that it will "look natural." There is no sound reason why /ŋ/ should not also serve as a full syllable, but that does not seem to happen.

Consonant Summary

The phoneme /j/ does not resemble the English letter of the same shape, but has the value of *y* in *yet* /jet/. The phonemes /w/ and /h/ do have the normal values of the corresponding letters when these occur in initial position.

To master the consonantal part of the phonemic alphabet it is necessary to learn five symbols not in the regular alphabet: /θ/ (theta), /ð/ (eth), /ʃ/ (esh), /ʒ/ (ezh), and /ŋ/ (eng) — two of these in special combinations, /tʃ/ and /dʒ/; and to remember that /j/ is used in a different way from the letter of the same shape. The other symbols have the most usual values of the corresponding letters.

The Vowel Phonemes

Because vowel sounds depend mostly on the positions taken by the extremely flexible tongue, a very large number can be made. The number that can be distinguished varies with the acuteness and training of our ears. Even the number that are used phonemically, to distinguish one word from another, is not settled. Some variation is found among speakers, and a good deal more among linguists, not only about the number to be recognized but about how they should be symbolized. The system used here is offered as convenient for this book, but with no argument as to its superiority.

The usual schoolroom way of applying the terms "short vowels," "long vowels," and "diphthongs" may be useful in spelling rules about when to double consonants, but it is inaccurate and misleading in the description of sounds. In discussing phonemes they must be used very differently.

When a vowel sound is prolonged without movement of the tongue (consequently without change in quality) the result is a long vowel. Though any number of gradations in length are possible, only two — short and long — are phonemically distinct. But if the tongue changes position during the prolongation, the result is not a long vowel, but a *diphthong*. We emphasize that a diphthong is a sequence of two vowel sounds, not of two letters. You cannot pronounce the word *I* while holding your tongue in the same position throughout. You begin by saying "ah" with tongue low, and then move it up and forward to the position required for "ee." You may, if you like, prolong the first half and say "ahhhh-ee," or the second half and say "ah-eeee"; but you cannot prolong the whole complex sound. The word is therefore physically a diphthong, and is so transcribed — /ɑi/. It is spelled with a single letter by an unfortunate and deceptive historical accident — it was pronounced differently some centuries ago, before the "great vowel shift" discussed on pages 158–160. On the other hand, the word *bread* contains a single short vowel and can be transcribed /bred/. The *ea* used to spell the simple sound is a *digraph,* not a diphthong.

The Short Vowels

	FRONT	CENTRAL	BACK
High	i *pit* /pit/	(ɨ)	u *put* /put/
Mid	e *pet* /pet/	ə *putt* /pət/	o *pony* /poni:/
Low	æ *pat* /pæt/	ɑ *pot* /pɑt/ (in most areas)	ɔ *pot* /pɔt/ (in Boston area)

The terms *high, mid,* and *low* describe the height of the tongue in pronouncing these sounds, and *front, central,* and *back* mean the part of the tongue that is highest. It may not be graceful, but it is very instructive to sit in front of a mirror with your mouth wide open and pronounce the vowel sounds so that you can see that these terms have a phonetic reality.

The illustrative words should make most of the pronunciations clear, but a few need further explanation.

1. The word *pot* is pronounced in most parts of the country with a short version of the vowel sound in the first syllable of *father* /ɑ/. In eastern New England it is pronunced with a short version of the vowel in *paw* /ɔ/. Because most people use one or the other of these sounds, but not both, it is impossible to find two words that differentiate them clearly for everybody.
2. The high central vowel ɨ (called *barred i*) has a clear-cut phonetic existence, but its phonemic status is both complicated and debatable. You probably use it if you pronounce *pen* in such a way that ignorant strangers accuse you of saying *pin;* or if you pronounce *pretty* so that it does not quite rhyme with *pity, petty,* or anything else; and many people use it in the unstressed syllables of such words as *depend* and *senate,* where others use /ə/ or /i/. On the other hand, you are probably not conscious of it as a phoneme — a sound sufficiently distinct to contrast one word with another. Most people who say /pɨn/, for instance, firmly believe that they are saying /pen/. The sound is therefore real, and the symbol is useful in comparing dialects or idiolects, but it is not needed in transcriptions as broad as those used in this chapter, and there is no evidence that it was phonemic in earlier English.

Let us emphasize that *any* analysis of our vowel system is partly arbitrary, and the selection of symbols is more so. We have to distinguish between the vowel sounds in *pit* and *peat* (not shown above), but we do not have to tell all about them every time we use a symbol. The one in *peat* is not only longer than the other but pronounced with the tongue higher in the mouth and tenser — at least at the end of the sound; some speakers raise and tighten the tongue during the sound, making it a diphthong. Many users of the IPA show *pit* as /pit/ and *peat* as /pi:t/, selecting length as the critically distinctive feature. Many others show *pit* as /pɪt/ and *peat* as /pit/, selecting either tongue height or tensity, whichever they consider more important (notice that /i/ is used with different values by the two groups). And followers of Trager and Smith, who insist that vowel length is *never* phonemic in Modern English, show *peat* as /piyt/, emphasizing the diphthongization that may, though it certainly does not always, occur. In this book the colon is used because it is needed in transcriptions of Old and Middle English, and it seems sensible to keep the transcriptions as uniform as possible. But if you already know and prefer to use /ɪ/ and /i/, we see no objection.

Long Vowel and Diphthong Symbols

The long vowels are:

i: as in	*peat*	/pi:t/	u: as in	*pool*	/pu:l/
ɑ:	*palm*	/pɑ:m/	ɔ:	*pawn*	/pɔ:n/

The diphthongs in general use are:

ei as in	*pate*	/peit/	ɔi as in	*point*	/pɔint/
ɑi	*pike*	/pɑik/	ou	*pose*	/pouz/
ɑu	*pout*	/pɑut/	ju	*puke*	/pjuk/

Those users of IPA who choose /ɪ/ and /i/ for *pit* and *peat* also choose /ʊ/ and /u/ for *put* and *pool,* a parallel treatment. But they agree with the other group on transcribing /pɑ:m/ and /pɔ:n/. Followers of Trager and Smith show all four of the long vowels as diphthongs.

We pointed out on page 32 that /ɑi/ is an inevitable diphthong. You cannot even approximate the normal pronunciation by holding a single vowel sound. The same is true of /ɑu/ and /ɔi/, and almost true of /ju/, though here the diphthong consists of a semivowel plus vowel rather than two vowels. It is not quite so easy to hear that "long a" and "long o" are also diphthongs. But if you pronounce them carefully you will notice that in *pate* the tongue rises from an /e/ to an /i/ position, and in *pose* it rises from an /o/ to a /u/ position. This movement is not inevitable. You could simply hold the /e/ and /o/ sounds and be understood, but you would sound a little foreign. Notice that no colon is used after diphthongs, which are necessarily long.

Diphthongs in "R-Less" Dialects

In some varieties of both British and American English the usual /r/ sound does not occur in some positions. Words spelled with the letter *r* in final position (*tour*), before a silent *e* (*here*), or before another consonant (*fort*) are pronounced with an allophone of /r/ that lengthens or diphthongizes the preceding vowel. Some linguists therefore use such transcriptions as /tuə/, /hiə/, and /fɔət/ rather than /tur/, /hir/, and /fɔrt/. But in this book /r/ is used simply because it is easier for, say, a Georgia student to recognize /pɔrtər/ than for an Iowa student to recognize /pɔətə/.

Phonemic Transcription

Before studying this transcription you should get two things firmly in mind:

1. It is *necessarily* arbitrary in some details. We do not argue that transcribing *sit* and *seat* as /sit/ and /si:t/ is more accurate than transcribing them as /sɪt/ and /sit/ or /sit/ and /siyt/. Any of these three methods will indicate the difference between the two words, once you get used to it. We choose (perhaps unwisely) the one that our students seem to find it easiest to get used to.

2. It is not an attempt to indicate "correct" pronunciation, but only the most usual one. Though no two of us pronounce exactly alike, we are pretty uniform in using all the consonant phonemes except /r/ in specific positions; but we vary a good deal in using the vowel phonemes, especially when they are not stressed. If you pronounce *not* as /nɔt/ rather than /nɑt/, or *sounds* as /sæundz/ rathen than /sɑundz/, you may transcribe accordingly if you wish to. And it is not worth worrying about whether the best way of transcribing *senate* is /senət/, /senit/, or /senɨt/. All three pronunciations are widely used, and it would take a good deal more counting than it is worth to decide which is most frequent among educated people.

After studying the interlinear transcription you should be able to decipher the unaccompanied one with a moderate effort. It will then be useful to make a few transcriptions of your own until you can do it without too much trouble. If you are already familiar with some other method of transcription you may not find it necessary to make active use of this one. We don't feel very strongly about alphabets, and if any one were in general use we would gladly conform to it, whether we liked it or not. Unfortunately, anybody who reads many books on the language must at present be prepared to encounter a large number of variations. As long as he realizes this, however, and is in firm control of one system into which he can translate the others, he can manage to get along.

There are certain limitations on this transcription. In the first
/ðer ɑr sərtən limiteiʃənz ɔn ðis trænskripʃən in ðə fərst

place, it gives only the "alphabetical" sounds. Stresses, pitches,
pleis it givz onli: ði: ælfəbetikəl saundz stresiz pitʃiz

and junctures are not marked, simply because it seems
ænd dʒəŋkʃərz ɑr nɑt mɑrkt simpli: bi:kɔ:z it si:mz

advisable not to bring up too many difficulties at once. In the
ædvaizəbəl nɑt tu briŋ əp tu: meni: difikəlti:z æt wəns in ðə

second place, each word is transcribed in what is called its
sekənd pleis i:tʃ wərd iz trænskraibd in hwɑt iz kɔ:ld its

citation form — that is, as if it were pronounced rather
saiteiʃən fɔrm ðæt iz æz if it wər pronɑunst ræðər

carefully by itself, and not as it would be pronounced in
kerfəli: bai itself ænd nɑt æz it wud bi: pronɑunst in

natural, connected speech, where it would often be affected by
nætʃərəl kənektid spi:tʃ hwer it wud ɔfən bi: æfektid bai

the neighboring words in the sentence. For instance, if you say
ðə neibəriŋ wərdz in ðə sentəns fɔr instəns if ju: sei

"*And* is a conjunction," you pronounce *and* distinctly; but if
ænd iz ə kəndʒəŋkʃən ju: pronɑuns ænd distiŋktli: bət if

you talk of "ham and eggs" your *and* probably shrinks to
ju: tɔ:k əv hæm n egz jɔr ænd prɑbəbli: ʃriŋks tu

"n." This is not, as some of us used to be taught in school,
n ðis iz nɑt æz səm əv əs ju:st tu bi: tɔ:t in sku:l

a vicious habit — it is something that occurs naturally and
ə viʃəs hæbit it iz səmθiŋ ðæt əkərz nætʃərəli: ænd

inevitably in many, if not all, languages.
inevitəbli: in meni: if nɑt ɔ:l læŋgwidʒiz/

(When the French run their words together we speak admiringly of their *elision* and *liaison,* and carefully try to imitate them. When we do the same thing in our own language we are often accused of "sloppy English." Of course the blending of sounds *can* be overdone.)

/ðis trænskripʃən lɑik ðə wən əbəv iz nɑt intendid æz i:ðər ə ful ɔr ə riəli: ækjərit rendiʃən əv nɔməl spi:tʃ bət æz æn egzæpəl əv hɑu veriəs siləbəlz kæn bi: indikeitid leitər ɔ:n wi: ʃæl si: ðæt in its ərliər steidʒiz ðə læŋgwidʒ hæd səm foni:mz hwitʃ wi: hæv nɑu lɔ:st ænd feild tu meik səm foni:mik distiŋkʃənz ɔ:n hwitʃ wi: nɑu regjulərli: di:pend ði: eim əv ðis tʃæptər iz simpli: tu provɑid æn ænælisis əv fəmiljər məti:riəl səfiʃənt tu sərv æz ə fɑundeiʃən fɔr stədi:iŋ ði: ərliər steidʒiz əv ðə læŋgwidʒ/

3

The Pre-History of English

Reconstructing Languages

Scholars have been able to reconstruct a good deal of the pre-history of English and some other languages, in spite of the inconvenient absence of written records, complete with reliable dates. Like other searchers into the distant past they have had to depend heavily on various kinds of circumstantial evidence, and some of their conclusions may be mistaken — in fact some of them must be, because there are some conflicting theories. Nevertheless, the general picture of what must have happened is on the whole reasonably clear. The processes by which this picture was constructed are too complicated to be explained completely here, but some simple examples will give a general idea of the methods.

Some Romance Languages

We can begin with a development that took place late enough to be supported by a good deal of written evidence, though a number of sizable gaps disturb the record. It is well known that the Romance languages, including French, Spanish, and Italian (as well as some others), developed from Latin. If we didn't know it already, we could prove it by comparisons. Let's look at the numbers from one to ten in each of the four.

Latin	*French*	*Spanish*	*Italian*
unum	un	uno	uno
duo	deux	dos	due
tres	trois	tres	tre
quattuor	quatre	cuatro	quattro
quinque	cinq	cinco	cinque
sex	six	seis	sei
septem	sept	siete	sette
octo	huit	ocho	otto
novem	neuf	nueve	nove
decem	dix	diez	diece

Whenever two languages have similar words with the same or closely related meanings, three explanations are possible:

1. *Pure coincidence.* This certainly happens occasionally. There is no connection between the Latin *dies* and the English *day.* But we cannot accept too many coincidences, especially in a consistent pattern. When the same sort of resemblance occurs between many pairs of words in two languages there must be some other explanation.

2. *Direct borrowing.* This can occur whenever two languages are in contact with each other, and it often does happen on a very large scale. English has borrowed great numbers of words from Latin, Scandinavian, French, and Greek, and smaller numbers from a great many other languages; and other languages are now borrowing many words from English. Moreover, borrowing may be quite systematic in some ways. English has borrowed many musical terms from Italian — *adagio, andante, aria,* and others. This is understandable. In the eighteenth century the Italians were recognized leaders in developing musical theory, and when we began to learn from them it was natural to take their technical vocabulary along with their technical knowledge. But it would have been amazing if we had borrowed their words for *one, two, three,* for *hand* and *foot,* for *brother* and *sister.* We simply had to have our own words for these before we ever encountered the Italians, and we were very unlikely to give up ours for theirs.

3. *Common descent.* This is the obvious explanation for the resemblances in the numbers listed above. In this instance we have all sorts of evidence that the obvious explanation is the true one. But even if we knew nothing

of the history of these languages we could see that the resemblances were far too great to be accidental; and it would strain our imaginations to believe that three peoples had had to borrow the same set of such essential words from a fourth. Moreover, if we extend the list of words to be compared, we can see that the resemblances are not haphazard. Eventually we should be forced to conclude that Latin changed in rather different ways in France, Spain, and Italy, but that its changes in each country were amazingly regular.

Let us emphasize that it was the *sounds* in which the changes originally occurred. The three Romance languages were scarcely written at all until they had been spoken for centuries and had become quite distinct. And even the Latin from which they developed was not the literary language of Cicero and Vergil, but the spoken language of soldiers, peddlers, and workmen, mostly illiterate. The speech of these people differed from Classical Latin about as much as the speech of some comic strip characters differs from Standard English. If you heard the four lists instead of seeing them the resemblances would not be quite so obvious; but they would be there, and they would become clearer and clearer with further study. The French *cinq* is pronounced approximately /sæŋk/, and the Italian *cinque* approximately /tʃiŋkwe/. No reasonable man, hearing these two words in isolation, would suspect that they were related. The spelling, of course, gives us an immediate hint that they are; but even without this hint we might eventually discover the relation by studying other pairs of French and Italian words. If we did it carefully enough we would eventually find two important principles.

Mechanics of Sound Change

1. A sound change is always from one sound to another that is phonetically similar in at least one way, but different in another. Thus /b/ may change to /v/ because both are labials and both are voiced, though one is a stop and the other a fricative. Or /θ/ may change to /f/ because both are voiceless fricatives, though one is dental and the other labial. In both cases a comparatively slight variation in the muscular movements of the speech organs results in the new sound. But /b/ cannot suddenly change to /θ/, because the motions required to produce these two phonemes are so different that one could not possibly slide into the other.

2. When any sound change occurs in a language it occurs with great regularity *in the same phonetic environment;* that is, when the sound affected is in the same position relative to neighboring sounds. But this regularity may not appear on the surface, because some words may be affected by more sound changes than others.

Let's look first at some very simple examples. In Spain, where *octo* became *ocho, noctem* (night) became *noche;* but in Italy, where *octo* became *otto, noctem* became *notte.*[1] In other words, the *ct* /kt/ combination regularly changed to *ch* /tʃ/ in Spanish, but to *tt* /tt/ in Italian (in which language double consonants are a phonetic reality, not merely a spelling convention). We should therefore expect Latin *lactem* (milk) to develop into Spanish *lache* and Italian *latte;* but here the first complication sets in. The Italian word is in fact *latte,* but the Spanish one is *leche* instead of *lache.* If we happen to know such Latin-Spanish pairs as *sanctum-santo* (saint) or *mare-mar* (sea) we are at first surprised at the vowel change in *leche,* but perhaps it occurs only in the neighborhood of certain consonants. We first try another pair beginning with *l,* but *latronem-ladrón* (thief) shows no such change. If we then think of *lacum-lago* (lake) we seem to have come to a blind alley. But there is one more chance; what follows *a* in *lactem* is not simply *c,* but the combination *ct.* If this is the influence at work, then Latin *factum,* which becomes *fatto* in Italian, should become *fecho* in Spanish.

Now we have another complication, for the Spanish word turns out to be not *fecho* but *hecho.* At least part of our expectation has been fulfilled, however, so that we now wonder if the shift from Latin *f* to Spanish *h* can also be a regular occurrence. A search for additional examples turns up such pairs as *facere-hacer* (make), *famem-hambre* (hunger), *formoso-hermoso* (beautiful), and *filium-hijo* (son). The shift does seem to be regular, and if we pronounce such a pair of English words as *fit* and *hit,* exaggerating the initial consonants, we can see that it is phonetically quite a possible one. Of course the *br* in *hambre,* the *e* in *hermoso,* and the *j* in *hijo* leave still further questions to be resolved, but we shall not go into them here, because we are merely giving a few examples of the sort of evidence linguists use in finding relations among languages. The process

[1] For students familiar with Latin who may be puzzled by the choice of this form, it should be explained that nouns in the Romance languages were regularly derived from the accusative, not the nominative, case of their Latin originals. Often this makes no difference, but for many nouns it does. *Notte,* for example, could not possibly have come from *nox.*

does get a little complicated, and it is easy to sympathize with Voltaire's complaint that "philology is the science where the vowels count for nothing and the consonants for very little." Nevertheless, the forces at work are quite regular, and scholars who know enough about them can get very dependable results.

Nobody really knows why Latin changed in such different ways in the different countries, and the guesses are too complicated to go into now. But it seems to have been an invariable rule in the past that when the speakers of any language split into groups that lost contact with each other the changes that took place were never quite parallel, and the languages of the groups grew further and further apart. During recent times more and more unifying forces, from the printing press and public school to the radio, movie, and television, have to some extent counteracted this tendency, though they have by no means entirely stopped it.

English and German

English is not, like the Romance languages, descended from Latin. It belongs to another group, called Germanic, discussed on pp. 53–54. If we compare the same set of numbers in German and English we again find a relation between them.

German	*English*
eins	one
zwei	two
drei	three
vier	four
fünf	five
sechs	six
sieben	seven
acht	eight
neun	nine
zehn	ten

There is clearly enough resemblance to indicate a relation, and the evidence becomes much stronger if we notice that many other words that begin with *t* in English begin with *z* in German (*to, zu; twig, Zweig*); and many that begin with *th* in English begin with *d* in German (*then, dann; think, denken*).

The Great Language Families

Now suppose we compare the English and German numbers with the Latin ones. Still some obvious resemblances appear, but others are well hidden. It takes a rather elaborate demonstration to show that *quinque* and *five* are regular developments from a common original form, and we won't go into it here, but it can be shown quite conclusively; and altogether there is no doubt at all that the Germanic languages are related to the Romance ones, though much more distantly than these are to each other.

It is now time to step back a few hundred thousand years. We have already said that we do not know how language began. We do not even know whether it began just once and spread all over the world, or began independently in a number of places at different times. In other words, we don't know whether or not all languages are related to each other, but we do know that some of them are. It is therefore usual to speak of families of languages; and this metaphor is convenient if not taken too seriously. Strictly speaking, Italian is not a descendant of Latin, but simply a late and localized form; and the enthusiastic statement that any language is "a living, breathing organism with a life of its own" is not one of the happier misapplications of the theory of biological evolution. All the same, the metaphor is useful as a concise way of indicating relations. We can therefore say that French, Spanish, and Italian are sister languages, born of spoken Latin. English and German are cousins, descended from sister branches of a lost language which we may call primitive Germanic or Teutonic. This precursor was never written, but we have enough evidence to reconstruct a good deal of it, though of course some guesswork is involved. Latin and English are something like third cousins twice removed; and all the languages mentioned in this paragraph, along with a number of others, make up the family now usually called Indo-European.

Choosing other areas, we can show that Hebrew and Arabic and some others are related to each other as members of the Semitic family; that some American Indian languages are related in the Algonquian family, and so forth. But whether the Indo-European and the Semitic and the Algonquian families are ultimately related to each other we simply do not know. If they are they have changed so much that the proof of their common origin has been lost. There are occasional resemblances, which some scholars take as evidence of common ancestry; but others consider them as either late borrowings or pure coincidence. At any rate, we shall not go beyond the Indo-European family in this book.

Origin of the Indo-European Family

About five thousand years ago our Indo-European ancestors were living more or less together somewhere in Europe or western Asia, or maybe both. Because they had not developed writing, and did not leave much for archaeologists to dig up and investigate, we have very little definite and direct evidence about them, and the indirect evidence we do have can often be interpreted in different ways. Without going into various learned arguments, we can say that they seem to have been a nomadic people, depending more on their herds and on game than on settled farming. Some scholars are quite sure that their homeland was as far west as Lithuania; others think it was way over across the Ural Mountains in Asia. Quite possibly both theories are partly true. Because the Indo-Europeans were occupying an enormous territory not very long after they were first heard of, it isn't necessary to assume that they all came from one small district in the beginning. We do not really know either that they all came from the same stock or that they spoke a "pure" and original language. Maybe both they and their speech were already mixtures. We do know that a lot of things can be traced back to them and no further.

We have good reason for thinking that on the whole they were tall, blond, fertile, and energetic, because within a few hundred years after 2000 B.C. groups of them went out in various directions and took over most of what they found, all the way from India and Persia to the Scandinavian Peninsula. The dispersion required both fertility and energy, and in many places the earlier inhabitants (some of whom were much more civilized) referred to them as the tall, blond invaders. We don't know how accurate this generalization was, however. Some Germans still like to think of themselves as a tall, blond race, and consider the millions of short, dark Germans as exceptions who shouldn't be counted.

At any rate, each wave that went out soon lost touch with the others and began a new development of its own. Some of the waves, especially in northern Europe, seem to have driven out or killed off most of the earlier inhabitants of the areas they settled. Other waves conquered but did not eliminate. Beginning as ruling minorities, they soon mingled and intermarried with the native inhabitants, and eventually lost their distinctive physical traits. Their languages were also modified, some more and some less, by the native ones. Sometimes the modification was so great that it is debatable whether the result of the mixture can reasonably be called Indo-European.

Although we cannot pinpoint the area from which all these waves went out, we think it was inland and not too far south. In the various languages we find related words for such animals as wolves and bears, but no such related words for lions, tigers, or camels. In the same way we find common words for trees of the temperate zone, but not for tropical ones. And there are no common words for the sea or anything closely connected with it. It therefore seems very nearly certain that the area was well inland and too far north for subtropical flora and fauna.

Many scholars have tried to locate the area more specifically, but they run into conflicting evidence. So many languages have words related to our *beech* that it seems on the surface that the homeland must have been in the limited area where beech trees grew. Unluckily, it turns out that although all these words have a common origin, they do not all refer to the same kind of tree — and we can't be sure which of their quite different meanings was the original one — beech, oak, elm, or elder. In a very similar way a good many American trees have been given names once applied to quite different trees in Europe. People like to use the words they have grown up with; and if they move to an area where the objects to which they originally applied are not found, they are likely to use them for the nearest equivalents — which are not always very near. When trout fishermen moved to Alabama they went right on catching trout, even though they had to rechristen the large-mouthed black bass to do it. In the same way, quail hunters keep on shooting quail, though the birds they call by this name vary remarkably.

The Branches of Indo-European

On page 46 is a chart of the Indo-European family of languages. Many of the details are open to argument, but fortunately they do not have much to do with the history of English. Of the Asiatic branches only Sanskrit interests us, and that for scholarly rather than organic reasons. It is the language of ancient Hindu religious texts, and was analyzed and codified long before any other branch. Consequently it has been preserved in a form apparently much closer to the original Indo-European than anything else that has survived. The ordinary spoken languages of India have changed about as much as those elsewhere, but Sanskrit has been frozen in an early form — like classical Latin, but for a much longer time.

THE INDO-EUROPEAN FAMILY OF LANGUAGES

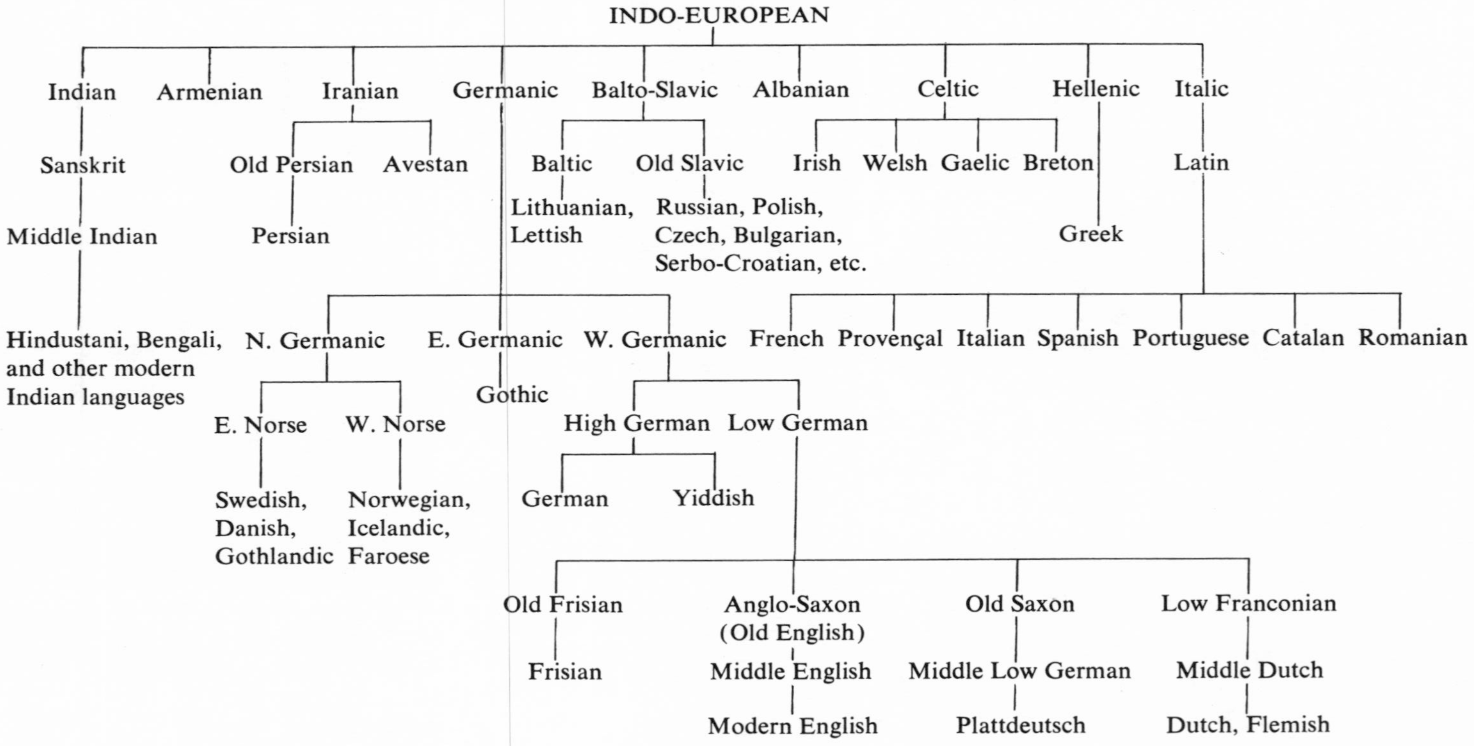

Adapted from *Webster's New World Dictionary of the American Language, College Edition,* Copyright 1966 by The World Publishing Company, Cleveland, Ohio.

Persian, Armenian, and Albanian are not very important for English. Neither is Balto-Slavic, with which English had very little contact before the twentieth century. More surprisingly, neither is the Celtic (or Keltic) branch, with which English has been in contact throughout its existence.

The three branches of most importance in the development of English are, in ascending order, Hellenic (Greek); Italic, which includes Latin and its Romance descendants; and Germanic. From the first two we derive well over half of the English vocabulary. From the third we get most of our everyday words and almost all the structural devices by which we combine them into sentences.

The Modern Discovery of Indo-European

In discussing the words for the first ten numbers we have already seen that, though the Germanic forms are related to Latin ones, the relation is sometimes not at all obvious on the surface. Such closer resemblances as those between English and German, among the Romance languages, and even between Latin and Greek had been noticed for centuries, but it was less than two hundred years ago that a comprehensive theory on a much larger scale was first developed. The decisive clue was the discovery by Sir William Jones, an English official in India, that Sanskrit, the classical language of the Hindus, contained such extensive and systematic similarities to Greek, Latin, and other European languages that it was obviously related to them; and that it was preserved in a much earlier form than any of the others. The result was that many words, which had developed so differently in various languages that they no longer bore a recognizable resemblance to each other, were found to resemble, each in its own way, a form nearer to the original source.

To take one example, the old English word for *am* is *eom,* and the Latin word is *sum.* They share only one phoneme, and neither look nor sound any closer together than, say, *eat* and *dot.* There is absolutely no reason to suspect a common origin. If we add the Greek equivalent, *eimi,* we can see that it might be related to the English word; however, the resemblance might be a pure coincidence, and there is still no sign of relation with Latin. But the Sanskrit equivalent, *asmi,* changes the whole picture. We know from such pairs as *prism* and *prismatic* that when a combination like /zm/ or /sm/ occurs at the end of a word it is necessary to insert a vowel sound in order to pronounce it. If the ancestors of the Romans happened to drop the /i/ ending, they would get /ásm/, with two syllables. If they shifted the stress to the second syllable they'd get /asúm/. Then if they dropped the unstressed syllable, they'd get /sum/. A little complicated, but all perfectly natural — and apparently exactly what happened.

On the other hand, anybody who knows much about French realizes that at one stage the speakers of that language found the combination of /s/ plus any following consonant hard to pronounce, and simply dropped the /s/, so that they have *bête* compared to our *beast, châtiment* compared to our *chastisement,* etc. (plain laziness is the obvious explanation for many sound changes). And so the Greek *eimi* might have developed by dropping the /s/, and the Old English *eom* by dropping both the /s/ and the /i/ ending. We have learned that we have to be broadminded (unless we want to work very hard) about early vowel changes.

This still looks pretty wild, but when we turn to the words for *is* we get some strong confirmation — Old English *is,* Latin *est,* Greek *esti,* and Sanskrit *asti.* Three of these are very close, and the absence of the *t* in *is* needn't bother us — we have all heard *best* and *last* pronounced as *bes'* and *las'*. Moreover, the Modern German form is *ist,* and we know English and German are related. Now if we look at the two sets together, we see something else. If *eom* originally had an /s/ in it, it was closer to *is* than it now looks. In Sanskrit the forms are *asmi* and *asti.* The only difference is the /m/ in the first person and the /t/ in the third. Could these sounds be related to the/m/ and /t/ in the English words *me* and *it?* Maybe these "personal endings" were originally pronouns of a sort.

If we had time we could examine many other sets of related words, but here we need say only that the evidence for a "family" of languages is overwhelming. For a while it was believed that Sanskrit was the parent of all the others. This theory soon had to be given up, but nothing has come up to change the belief that it is the earliest recorded form. It was described in precise detail about 500 B.C., and the description was based on religious texts that had carefully preserved the forms of a thousand years earlier. As we might expect under the circumstances, the inflectional system is more fully preserved than elsewhere. Nouns have eight cases, all quite distinct in form. It is highly probable that the sound system had changed somewhat since the migration to India; but when we trace back the other related languages, which had diverged in various directions, we find by a sort of triangulation that their common source cannot have been very different from Sanskrit.

The Germanic Group and Grimm's Law

The Germanic group seems to have been one of the last to push out from the Indo-European homeland, probably somewhere about 1600 B.C. During the next two thousand years or so it multiplied in size, divided into subgroups, and spread out over an enormous territory. The Burgundians, Franks, Goths, Lombards, and Vandals were only a few of the better known tribes whose languages have now died out. The most important modern languages that can be traced to this group are English, German, Yiddish, Dutch, Flemish, and the Scandinavian tongues.

Either before or shortly after the migration, but before the tribes had separated, the Germanic branch of the language developed several important characteristics that set it apart from the other Indo-European branches, and obscured its relation to them. The most remarkable was displacement of a number of the consonant phonemes. Even before the western discovery of Sanskrit it was obvious that some Germanic words bore some resemblance to Latin and Greek ones. If we compare English *mother, father,* and *brother* to Latin *mater, pater,* and *frater,* for instance, it seems clear that the two sets have something in common, but it is not easy to see exactly what it is; and the discovery of Sanskrit did not immediately clarify the matter. Early in the nineteenth century, however, the German Jacob Grimm and the Dane Rasmus Rask succeeded independently in finding a regular pattern. Because Rask wrote in Danish, Grimm got most of the credit; and though his statement has been considerably modified since, it is still known as Grimm's Law.

The uncovering of a whole set of systematic resemblances that had escaped notice for centuries was naturally very complicated. In considering the development of some Spanish-Italian pairs of words we have seen a bare hint of how involved tracing of relations even between two closely related languages can be, and Grimm and Rask were attempting to cover an enormously wider field, and one with much greater gaps in the evidence. It would therefore be worse than useless to try to trace the whole course of their investigations. Instead, we shall present merely a partial picture of what they and their successors eventually found, in a form that can be useful even to a student who knows no language but English. Below are listed Latin and English pairs of words that we can derive from the same Indo-European roots. We emphasize, shout, and reinforce with a flourish of trumpets that *in no case did the English word come from the Latin one.*

Biologists do not say that man was descended from monkey, but that man and monkey apparently had a common ancestor. English *has* borrowed a great many words from Latin — among others, *paternal* and *piscatorial.* But these words preserve much of their Latin form. *Father* and *fish* are cousins rather than children of *pater* and *piscis.*

pater	father	tu	thou	caput	head
piscis	fish	tres	three	cornu	horn
frater	brother	[2]thugater	daughter	[3]hortus	garden
fero	bear (carry)	[2]thura	door	hostis	guest
[3]bursa	purse	duo	two	genus	kin
[3]bucca	pouch	duco	tug	gelidus	cold

You will notice that in each subgroup the relation between the initial consonants is regular, but that the degree of resemblance between the rest of the words varies considerably. This is because the shift of the initial consonants is independent, but any of the other sounds may have been affected by one or more additional influences. All these could be systematically explained, but it would take a good many pages.

If you examine the whole group you will find that the initial consonants of the Latin words in the first column are labials, those in the second are dentals, and those in the third are velars. Dividing them horizontally, those at the top are voiceless stops, those in the middle are fricatives, and those at the bottom are voiced stops. In other words, the same sorts of changes have happened to consonants with something in common. These changes can be summarized by statements like these:

Indo-European voiceless stops, preserved as such in Latin (and most other Indo-European languages), *shifted to become fricatives in Germanic. At the same time, fricatives shifted to voiced stops, and voiced stops shifted to voiceless stops.*

This explanation is deliberately oversimplified. If you want to go into comparative linguistics seriously you will have to learn it in a somewhat more accurate and very much more complicated form. For instance, we believe that some of the Latin consonants, though nearer to the (hypotheti-

[2] These examples are from Greek rather than Latin, because the phoneme /θ/ disappeared from Latin by another sound shift that had nothing to do with this one.

[3] Some linguists are not sure that these pairs are cognate, but their sounds are in the proper relationship, and no other explanation has been found.

cal) original Indo-European sounds than the English ones are, had already changed somewhat in a manner that will not even be mentioned here. But most students of English will probably find this explanation adequate; and they may even find it useful. Even if you do not know any Latin, you know thousands of English words borrowed from Latin, and you are likely to encounter others at any time. It is quite often possible to recognize one by noticing that the appropriate consonant shift would make it close to an English word of Germanic origin. And if you are studying any Germanic language you can often recognize a strange word by applying the sound shift in the opposite way.

The shift (still in its oversimplified form) can be shown schematically as in this diagram.

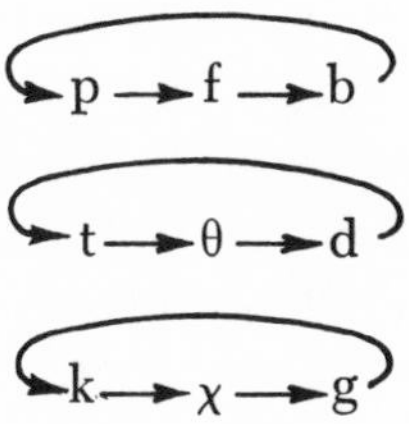

Several points need explanation.

1. It is convenient to think of these shifts as simultaneous, because otherwise the logical result would be to leave only one sound in each series. In a fuller explanation a chronological order of shifting could be shown.

2. /χ/ stands for a sound like that in German *doch.* It appears in our spelling as *h,* but this letter formerly represented a velar fricative that bears the same relation to /k/ as /f/ does to /p/ or /θ/ to /t/.

3. If you try simply to memorize this diagram, you may easily get mixed up. But if you understand the phonetic relations you can reconstruct it completely from any pair of Latin and English words to which it applies. If you remember *pater* and *father,* you have *p* → *f.* The only other labial sound to which *f* can go is *b,* and *b* must go back to *p.* It doesn't matter whether you put the velars or the dentals next, but you must be sure to put the voiceless stops under *p,* the fricatives under *f,* and the voiced stops under *b.*

The list of cognate words above is sufficient to prove a systematic relation between the sound systems of English and Latin. This list could be extended greatly, and a more extensive analysis would show clearly a fact that we need only state — the shift occurred in Germanic before that language broke up into branches. Unfortunately, the list could not be extended so much that we could simply apply the principles discovered to a passage of Latin and come up with anything like a complete English translation.

There are a number of reasons for this. We have mentioned that all languages are always changing, and one of the kinds of change is in the makeup of the vocabulary. Some words drop out and are replaced by others. Just why all languages drop some perfectly good words and replace them with others that seem no better cannot be explained by any general theory, though reasons are clear enough in some individual cases. At any rate, we do not find exactly the same pairs of cognates if we compare English and Latin, English and Greek, or Latin and Greek. Each language has dropped some items from the common heritage that both the others have retained.

Another difficulty is that even though the initial consonants in our cognates show a dependable relationship, the later ones have a good deal of apparent irregularity. For one thing, a consonant that occurred after an unstressed syllable sometimes shifted differently from one that occurred initially or after a stressed one.[4] Almost all the apparent irregularities can be confidently explained as really regular when we take into account all the forces at work; and the few that cannot now be explained may yield to later investigation. But it takes more than an elementary knowledge to handle such complications, and we shall not go into them here.

Heavy Germanic Stress

In some languages all the syllables are pronounced with nearly equal force, and the primary stress — such as it is — may shift from one syllable to another in different inflected forms of the same word. In the present indicative active of the Latin verb *vocō,* the forms *vocō, vocās, vocat,* and *vocant* all have the stress on the first syllable, but the forms *vocātis* and *vocāmus* have it on the second. In the Germanic languages the stress was both heavier and less variable. It regularly fell on the first syllable of a word unless that syllable was a mere prefix. The other syllables were pronounced so lightly that it was easy for them to weaken or drop off entirely, and a great many of them did. Most of our old Germanic words have been reduced to monosyl-

[4] Many years of classroom experience have convinced us that discussing Verner's Law at this stage adds more confusion than enlightenment.

lables in this way. We do have a good many polysyllables of Germanic origin, but they are mostly the result of combining several roots. Thus *hlafweard* (guardian of the loaf) went through such stages as *hlaford* and *lavord* on its way to becoming *lord;* but we combine the short form with other elements to make such newer words as *warlord, lordship,* and *lordliness.*

English words borrowed from non-Germanic languages very early are likely to be shortened in exactly the same way. Thus we get *priest* from *presbyteros.* More recent borrowings may keep all their syllables, but some of them will be pronounced much more lightly than their cognates in other languages. The Spanish *extraordinario* has seven full syllables. In the English *extraordinary* only two have a full pronunciation with clear vowel sounds. The others are either somewhat slurred or omitted entirely. In extreme cases the pronunciation becomes /strɔnri/.

The Three Branches of Germanic

Sometime after Germanic broke off from Indo-European it divided into three main branches, known as North, East, and West Germanic. From the first of these we get the Scandinavian languages, with the exception of Finnish, which is not of the Indo-European family. There is now no active survivor of the second, but Gothic lasted long enough to leave a written record that is of great linguistic importance because it preserves specimens of the language in a considerably earlier form than has come down for any of the other branches. Aside from its importance to linguists, Gothic is recommended to anyone who would like to attain complete mastery of a literature, because all that remains is part of a translation of the Bible by Bishop Ulfilas or Wulfila, for which ponies are readily available.

The West Germanic branch in turn split into two main divisions known, from the comparative altitudes of the regions in which they developed, as High and Low German. The official language of modern Germany is a High German dialect, though many of the spoken dialects in the northern part of the country are Low German (Plattdeutsch). Yiddish is also basically High German, though it contains many Hebrew words, and is usually written and printed in Hebrew characters — perhaps the most striking example we have of the fact that spoken language is affected comparatively little by the way it happens to be written. High German is distinguished from the Low principally by the second or High German sound shift, which occurred much later than the one covered by Grimm's Law. It will not be discussed in detail here, but it is the explanation of such correspondences as those mentioned earlier in this chapter between English *two* and German *zwei,* English *three* and German *drei,* and so forth. A working knowledge of it is extremely useful to any English speaker learning German.

The Genealogy of English

Low German split still further into a number of dialects, from which are descended the Plattdeutsch mentioned above, Dutch-Flemish, Frisian and — in at least three strands — Old English. Two of these are Anglian and Saxon. The third may or may not be Jutish, but it is the dialect of the Germanic settlers in Kent, parts of Hampshire, and the Isle of Wight, which definitely differed in a number of ways from both of the others. Of the three, Anglian has had the strongest influence on the development of standard Modern English, but neither of the others is negligible. It is healthy to realize that even at its very beginning as a national language English did not have one correct form, but several overlapping and competing forms, each "best" in its own area. The interworkings of these three during the past fifteen centuries are enormously complex, and our evidence is so fragmentary that we shall never know all the details; but we can attempt to trace the main lines.

It should be clear by now that fitting Modern English into our language chart is no simple matter. Its basic grammatical patterns and most of its commonest words have developed from three interweaving strands of Old English, but it has also borrowed a good deal from Scandinavian, Latin, French, and Greek, and odds and ends from many other languages. If we considered the whole vocabulary, giving the same value to rare words as to common ones, we would have to classify English with the Romance languages, because the words we have borrowed from Latin and French considerably outnumber the ones we have inherited from Old English. But both the basic structure and the core of the vocabulary have developed from Germanic origins, so that the classification used here seems on the whole most reasonable, and is generally accepted.

4

Old English

The Beginnings of English

Until the middle of the fifth century the part of Britain now called England was inhabited by the Britons, who spoke a variety of the Celtic rather than the Germanic branch of Indo-European. Some four hundred years earlier this territory had been conquered by the Romans, organized as part of the Roman Empire, and supplied with several legions of Roman troops. At first the legions were used principally to keep the native Britons in order. When they had achieved this purpose their mission was changed to protecting the inhabitants from raids and invasions from many directions, but especially from the northern part of the island, which is now Scotland. The Scots had not yet come over from Ireland, and this territory was then occupied by the Picts, a probably non–Indo-European people who had inhabited the whole island before the Britons came in and pushed them north. Because the Romans never conquered Pictland, they built a protective wall across the island and manned it with their legions, meanwhile discouraging the Britons from any military activities of their own.

But about 409 the whole Roman Empire was in such trouble that the legions were withdrawn for service nearer home. This left the Britons, whose military traditions had lapsed for centuries, at a disadvantage against the northern raiders. They struggled without much success for some forty years; then they had to face new, and eventually calamitous invasions. Some Germanic tribesmen from the west coast of the European continent had been raiding Britain even during the Roman occupation, and archaeologists have found evidence of a few small and apparently peaceful permanent settlements. The withdrawal of the legions and the disorganization that followed opened the way to much more extensive settlement, and three tribes soon conquered much of England. The two larger ones were the Angles and the Saxons, but the identity of the third group has never been settled. Bede called them Jutes, and this name will be used here, because no more satisfactory one has been found; but we simply do not know who they were or exactly where they came from. The Angles took possession of about the northern two-thirds of what is now called England (from Anglaland) after them. The Saxons took over most of the southern third, leaving only Kent, part of Hampshire, and the Isle of Wight to the Jutes. All three tribes spoke Low West Germanic dialects so much alike that they could understand each other, and Old English might be described as the result of a gradual fusion of the three. The fusion was by no means complete. Considerable regional differences remained for centuries, and at times increased. Even today many of them persist in popular speech. But the language of the whole country soon came to be known as English, and developed increasing differences from the dialects of the continent.

The history (or rather the collection of conflicting theories) of relations between the Germanic invaders and the earlier Celtic inhabitants of Britain is an interesting subject in itself, but it does not have much connection with the development of the language, and there is enough confusion within our own subject to make it inadvisable to borrow trouble from elsewhere. Whether the Angles, Saxons, and Jutes slaughtered, enslaved, or simply drove out the Britons, they borrowed only some place-names and a very small handful of ordinary words from their victims.

The very tiny Celtic influence on English is really an amazing fact, especially when we consider how enormously English has borrowed from other languages. Not only the Britons were Celts; so too were the Scots (though probably not the Picts) who had been harassing them. For many centuries varieties of Celtic were the normal languages of Wales, Ireland, and most of Scotland, not to mention Cornwall in southern England and Brittany just across the channel in France. Even now only the Cornish variety has com-

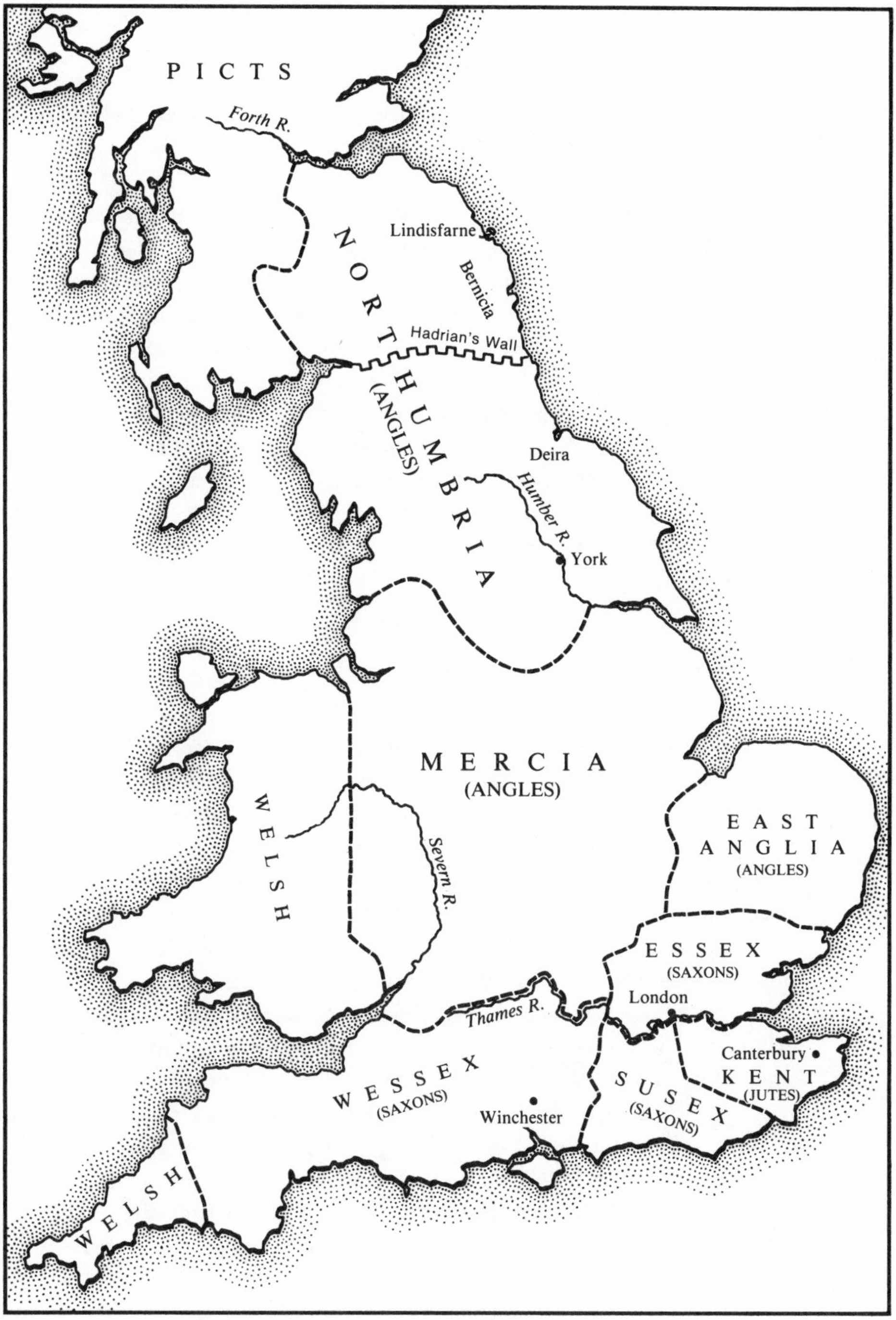

The Anglo-Saxon Heptarchy

pletely died out, though the other languages are now decidedly secondary — even in Eire, which is making a strenuous effort to be as un-English as possible. Yet in all this time English has borrowed scarcely more from Celtic than it has from Chinese.

There is, of course, an explanation of sorts. The English were converted to Christianity by missionaries steeped in the Graeco-Roman tradition, which was reinforced by their education for centuries. They were invaded, oppressed and sometimes ruled by the Danes, conquered and administered by the French. Their borrowings from these sources can be attributed to both pressure and need. Some words were literally forced into their language, and others were needed to fill out gaps in English. Still others were internationally current, and thus often seemed preferable to purely local words. Probably some were adopted out of simple snobbery. Neither necessity, international currency, nor snobbery gave the English any reason to borrow much from their Celtic neighbors; so they didn't. But it still seems curious.

Pre-Christian England

We know amazingly little about fifth- and sixth-century England, and that little is pieced together from various kinds of indirect evidence. No histories have survived, and there is not the slightest reason to suppose that any were written during this period. Archaeology gives us a little evidence of how the early English lived, but our strongest impressions come from the Germanic traditions, mostly continental, which were handed down (with continual modifications) for generations before they were put in writing. These contain all sorts of exaggerations and distortions, but we can take a brief look, for whatever it is worth, at the picture they present.

On this evidence the early English, like the continental tribesmen, were an able and vigorous group of people, but they seem to have gone on for some time within a fairly narrow range of ideas and ambitions. They lived by hunting, fishing, and farming, relaxed by eating, drinking, and listening to songs, and devoted most of their serious expenditures of energy to fighting. Sometimes they fought for gain, and sometimes for one emotional reason or another; but always in the background was a firm, even religious belief that fighting was the proper business of man, and that the only respectable way to die was in battle.

Their religion, like their language, was obviously a part of their Indo-European heritage. If we compare their gods to those of the Greeks and

Romans we of course find many differences, but the resemblances are far too great to be attributed to mere coincidence. Woden and Frigga were not exactly like the Greek Zeus and Hera, but then neither were the Roman Jupiter and Juno; and if you read enough Greek mythology you soon find that Zeus and Hera were not always like themselves. When stories are handed down for centuries they inevitably change as the interests and beliefs of the tellers and the audience change; and the Indo-European peoples, spreading over millions of square miles through thousands of years, developed some really remarkable changes. But behind them all are the signs of a common origin that cannot be hidden. There are the gods, neither all-good nor all-powerful, but worthy (on the whole) of worship, and certainly worth propitiating. And behind them are the three fates, whom the Romans called Parcae and the Germanic tribes Norns — old women beyond passion or personal interest, somehow laying out the lines of the future with which even the gods cannot tamper.

There is, in general, nothing comparable to the Christian idea of heaven. In the Germanic accounts, especially, not even the gods can look forward to an eternity of peace (which would certainly bore them) or happiness. They are temporarily ahead of their equally powerful enemies, the Giants, but the final battle — Ragnarok or Götterdämmerung — is still to come. For this battle Woden will need all the human heroes that he can get, though he knows that even with their help he cannot win. Accordingly he keeps a corps of beautiful (but rather hefty) young female recruiting officers. These are the Valkyrie — a word that means "choosers of the slain." It is their duty to watch over battles; and whenever they see a worthy champion at the very peak of his valor and performance, they arrange for an enemy weapon to kill him. Then they take his spirit to Valhalla — the Hall of the Slain — where he goes into training for Ragnarok. Each day he fights gloriously with his peers. Each night, his wounds healed, he feasts with his companions, with plenty of ale and appropriate song. And in the end the great fight against the Giants will come, and it will really be the end, for neither side can win. They will destroy each other and the very earth on which they have lived, and nothing will remain but utter chaos.

Neither such a life nor such a vision of the future would appeal to everybody, but the Germanic tribesmen seem to have found them adequate for some centuries. At least those who settled in Britain apparently found nothing in either the life or the ideas of the Romanized Britons (by most standards a considerably more advanced people) that they cared enough about to adopt. Whatever they did with the Britons, they went on living their own habitual lives in the new space they had acquired. They did not even bother to take over the towns and villas they found, but destroyed them or left them to rot while they built their own farm houses as they had on the continent.

It took the English about a hundred and fifty years to gain control of most of England. They did not accomplish it as a unified national movement, but as a tangle of local efforts, frequently interrupted by fighting among themselves; and we know very little about the details. But the very large Anglian territory was soon divided into two major areas — Northumbria from the river Humber north to well beyond the modern Scottish border, and Mercia from the Humber south to the Thames. There were marked dialectal as well as political differences between the two, so that during the Middle English period Northumbrian developed into Northern English and Mercian split into East and West Midland. Just south of the Thames and east of London the originally Jutish territory came to be called Kent, and retained dialectal characteristics of its own even after it came to be controlled by the West Saxon kings, who ruled (when they could manage it) all the southern fifth of the country.[1]

Not a single piece of writing either in English or by an Englishman has survived from this period, and we don't even know of any that have been lost. Our ignorance is highlighted by the attention historians have paid to the one surviving Latin account, by a Welshman named Gildas. This is a Jeremiad rather than a history, and is so obviously unreliable that it would be completely neglected if there were any other contemporary source. Possibly a few details of this account are more or less true.

In an age so committed as our own to the keeping of records this blank may seem incredible, but it is quite typical of the pre-Christian Germanic peoples. They had an alphabet — the Runic one — which they used for magic spells and for inscriptions on wood, stone, or metal, but not for extended compositions of any kind. Their literature was transmitted orally, and they had no interest in history as we conceive it — a systematic account of exactly what happened, and when, and where. They were vitally interested in the exploits of their heroes, but cheerfully unconcerned with either geography or chronology. Everything beyond living memory had simply happened "way back then," in a location that was either unspecified or subject to change according to taste.

[1] Cornwall, in the southwest corner, resisted until the ninth century; and some of its inhabitants continued to speak Cornish (a Celtic language close to Welsh) until the eighteenth.

The Introduction of Christianity

Toward the end of this period of expansion, in 597, Roman missionaries landed in Kent and began the systematic conversion of England to Christianity. The Welsh had been Christians since Roman times, but had shown no interest in converting their heathen oppressors, who would probably not have been very receptive to anything they had to offer. Also, Irish missionaries had converted most of Scotland, and there were certainly some individual Christians farther south. But the movement that changed the country from a pagan to a Christian one began when St. Augustine of Canterbury, sent by Gregory the Great, landed at Thanet with thirty-nine companions and received official permission to spread the new religion. There was of course some opposition, but progress was surprisingly fast.

Among other things that the Christian missionaries introduced was the habit of extended writing. Most of the people were still illiterate, but within the church an amazing tradition of scholarship developed, so that in little more than a century England had become one of the centers of learning for the entire western world. Bede (673–735) was probably the ablest and most learned scholar of his time, and has been called "the teacher of the Middle Ages." To us the most interesting of his encyclopedic writings is his *Ecclesiastical History of the English People*. He shows only occasional interest in purely secular affairs, and when he does deal with them he has to depend almost entirely on oral tradition; but he sifted this so carefully and intelligently that he is by far our best authority for the early Old English period.

Probably most of the writing that was done, and certainly most that has survived, was (like Bede's) in Latin. We have, however, a fair amount of English poetry from about 650 on. Most of this was written in the north of England, and consequently in the Anglian dialect, but it has come down to us only in much later West Saxon manuscripts. Because the idea of copying with letter-by-letter accuracy almost never occurred to a medieval scribe, it is only occasionally that a typical Anglian form has been preserved.

The Coming of the Danes

The explanation for this indirect preservation is that from about 787 on Scandinavian raiders, especially Danes, began to harry the north of England, and from about 850 they made permanent settlements there, until they con-

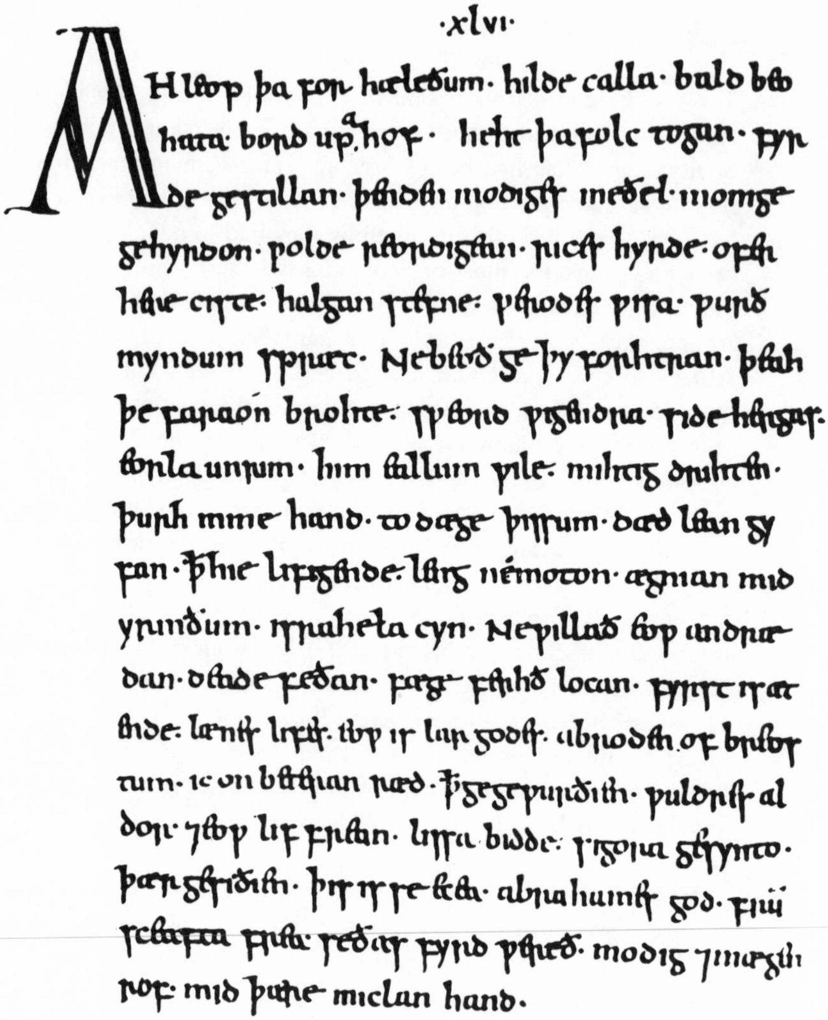
·xlvi·
AHleop þa for hæleðum· hilde calla· bald beo
hata· bord up ahof· heht þa folc togan· fyr
de gestillan· þenden modiges meðel monige
gehyrdon· wolde reordigean rices hyrde· ofer
here ciste· halgan stefne· werodes wisa· wurð
myndum spræc· Ne beoð ge þy forhtran· þeah
þe faraon brohte· sweord wigendra· side hergas·
eorla unrim· him eallum wile· mihtig drihten·
þurh mine hand· to dæge þissum· dæd lean gy
fan· þæt hie lifigende· leng ne moton· ægnian mid
yrmðum· israhela cyn· Ne willað eow andræ
dan· deade feðan· fæge ferhð locan· fyrst is æt
ende· lænes lifes· eow is lar godes· abroden of breos
tum· ic on beteran ræd· þæt ge gewurðien· wuldres al
dor· 7 eow lif frean· lissa bidde· sigora gesynto·
þær ge siðien· þis is se ecea· abrahames god· frum
sceafta frea· se ðas fyrd wereð· modig 7 mægen
rof· mid þære miclan hand·

Folios 156 and 166 of the Old English poem *Exodus*. These folios are reproduced with the kind permission of the British Academy from *The Caedmon Manuscript of Anglo-Saxon Biblical Poetry, Junius XI in the Bodleian Library*, with introduction by Sir Israel Gollancz (1927). An edition of the passage is given in the *Companion* to this book, page 16.

[1] This plate and the next (folio 166) are reproduced with kind permission of the British Academy from *The Cædmon Manuscript of Anglo-Saxon Biblical Poetry, Junius XI in the Bodleian Library*, with introduction by Sir Israel Gollancz (1927).

·xlviiii·

FOLC wæs afæred· flodegsa becwom· gas
tas geomre· geofon deaðe hweop· wæron beorh
hliðu· blode bestemed· holm heolfre spaw· hream
wæs on yðum· wæter wæpna ful· wælmist astah·
wæron egypte· eft oncyrde· flugon forhtigende·
fær ongeton· woldon herebleaðe· hamas findan·
gylp wearð gnornra· him ongen genap· atol yða ge
wealc· neðær ænig becwom· herges to hame· ac behin
dan beleac· wyrd mid wæge· þær ær wegas lagon·
mere modgode· mægen wæs adrenced· streamas
stodon· storm up gewat· heah to heofonum· here
wopa mæst· laðe cyrmdon· lyft up geswearc· fægum
stæfnum· flod blod gewod· rand byrig wæron rofe
ne· rodor swipode· meredeaða mæst· modige swul
ton· cyningas oncorðre· cyre swiðrode· wæs æt en
de wig bord scinon· heah ofer hæleðum· holm
weall astah· mere stream modig· mægen wæs on
cwealme· fæste gefeterod· forð ganges weard· sear
wum æsæled· sand basnodon· witodre wyrde
hwonne waðema stream· sin calda sæ· sealtum
yðum· æf lastum gewuna· ece staðulas· nacud
nyd boda· neosan come· fah feðe gast· se ðe
feondum geneop· wæs seo hæwene lyft· heolfre
geblanden· brim berstende· blod egesan hweop·
sæ manna sið· oð þæt soð metod· þurh moyses

trolled the whole Anglian territory. The procedure of the early raiders was simple: whatever they wanted, they took; whatever they could not use, they killed or destroyed. They were particularly thorough in destroying books, which were not only useless to them, but suspected of containing magic spells that might be dangerous in the hands of their enemies. In the latter half of the ninth century it seemed probable that the Danes would take over the whole country; but Alfred the Great, king of Wessex, managed to stop their expansion and keep the southern part of England free. Thereafter the Danes, even in the territory they continued to control, were gradually absorbed into the more numerous English people.

Alfred and English Prose

The place of Alfred is as important in a history of the English language as it is in a political history of England. He was distressed by the decay of learning in England since the great days of the eighth century, and did his best to remedy it by having the books he considered most essential translated into English. He himself translated Pope Gregory's *Pastoral Care,* though he tells us that he had to have two priests, a bishop, and an archbishop help him to understand the Latin; and he took at least some part in translating the general history of Orosius and Boethius' *Consolation of Philosophy*. It is generally believed that he also at least inspired the English version of Bede's *Ecclesiastical History* and the compilation of the group of annals collectively known as *The Anglo-Saxon Chronicle,* which was begun during his reign.

Obviously, English prose would have had to start some time, with or without King Alfred, and we need not here go into the argument about exactly how much of the work associated with his name should actually be attributed to him, or how much influence it had in encouraging the use of prose during succeeding generations. But we can be perfectly sure that without these works we would know much less about Old English than we do. Our knowledge of what may be called Alfredian prose is particularly important because in Old English manuscripts the vocabulary of prose differs from that of poetry much more than it does in most languages, or in most later periods of English. Considered as literature, the poetry is much more impressive; but it is in the prose that we find the roots of later English.

Alfred's successful resistance to the Danes was not the end of the trouble with them. Throughout the tenth century there was a great deal of raiding of

England by Danes from the continent, and in the early years of the eleventh century Danish kings actually reigned in England. But during this time the descendants of the earlier Danish invaders had become so mixed with the English that they usually joined them in the struggles with the newer raiders.

In 1066 England was conquered by the Normans under William, and the effect on the language was as great as on other sides of life. Perhaps the simplest way to explain what happened is to say that with Frenchmen in control of almost everything, nothing written in English could be very important or effective. Apparently very little was written in English, and certainly very little has survived, between the conquest and the beginning of the twelfth century. When we begin to find again a considerable body of native material, the language has changed so much that we call it Middle rather than Old English.

The Diversity of Old English

From its beginnings in the middle of the fifth century Old English was never a single language with anything like a uniform standard, but a group of Low German dialects that on the whole seem to have grown less rather than more alike during the six and a half centuries from the invasion to 1100, the date usually chosen as the beginning of the Middle English period. Because the manuscripts that have survived are mostly in West Saxon of the tenth and eleventh centuries, what we call Old English is actually Late West Saxon, enriched (or confused, according to taste) by bits from some of the other varieties. Most of the best poetry was originally composed in Anglian, but medieval scribes did not have our tradition of letter-by-letter accuracy; they normally wrote down the words they copied in the forms that seemed natural to them. The few distinctly Anglian forms that appear in the Beowulf manuscript, for instance, are probably there from carelessness rather than conscientiousness.

By using the few available scraps of written evidence, several kinds of indirect evidence, and enormous patience and industry (not to mention occasional flashes of pure revelation), scholars have built up a fairly detailed picture of the sound systems and a few other features of the Anglian and Kentish (originally Jutish) dialects. These are valuable to advanced students; but because they are merely confusing to beginners, we refer to them seldom in this book. The fact that Modern English eventually devel-

The Dialects of Old English

oped mostly from an Anglian rather than a Saxon base may lead us to grumble that history chose to preserve the wrong body of evidence, but we have to get along with what we have.

An Approach to the Old English Sound System

A student approaching a new modern language will do well to master the sound system by ear before giving the spelling a chance to mislead him. It is quite easy to learn that the German word for *and* is pronounced as if it were spelled *oont;* and not hard, though perhaps surprising, to learn later that the Germans have decided to spell the word *und.* But if you learn the written word first and start pronouncing it as if it were the first part of the English word *under* — and do the same sort of thing with many other words — you may find it hard to correct your habits. A great many people never recover from taking this first wrong step.

Approaching a stage of language no longer spoken is another matter. No tenth-century Saxons are handy either to serve as native informants or to be shocked at our accent. We might conceivably begin by listening to synthetic tapes in a language laboratory, but actually we look at printed texts and try to learn approximately how to pronounce them. Our knowledge of Old English pronunciation depends on various kinds of indirect evidence. The way English sounds were usually spelled in a basically Latin alphabet tells us something. The ways in which Old English writers spelled occasional foreign words helps a little, and so do the ways foreign writers spelled English words. We can learn something by observing gradual changes in spelling habits, by working back from what we know of later developments in various dialects, from recorded puns, and from the rhymes and meters of obviously careful poets. We may wish we had more, and more consistent, evidence, but let us summarize the effect of what we have:

1. We can be quite sure of some things, such as the pronunciation of most of the consonants.
2. There is room for difference of opinion about others, such as the values of the "long vowels."
3. About some things, such as the "intonation patterns," we don't know much and probably never will.

Writers are responsible for keeping these levels of knowledge in mind, and not mixing them irresponsibly; but most readers would be more confused than enlightened by meticulous reservations on every point. Because we don't really know how to fool a native speaker even if we could find one, it is not worthwhile to spend too much class time developing a synthetic "native accent"; but it is worth a reasonable effort to understand and approximate the general sound systems of Old, and (later) Middle, English. We will begin by examining the relation between the Old English alphabet and the phonemes it represented — not with complete consistency, but much more reliably than our alphabet represents our stage of the language.

The Consonants

The Old English alphabet had seventeen consonant letters, most of which give a modern reader little trouble. Ten of these — *b, d, l, m, n, p, r, t, w,* and *x* — regularly represent the same sounds as in modern English, though the *r* was stronger, and such initial combinations as *cn* and *hl,* which we are likely to regard as unpronounceable, were fully pronounced. Four others — *f, s,* and the interchangeable pair *þ* and ð, have two values apiece, but these are governed by dependable rules. Each could represent a voiceless fricative when it occurred initially, finally, or before another voiceless consonant, or a voiced one when it occurred between two voiced sounds. The voiced and voiceless fricatives were not yet separate phonemes, but allophones whose pronunciation varied with their phonetic environment. This accounts for such modern pairs as *wife-wives, calf-calves, house-houses,* and *cloth-clothes.* (The final *e*'s in *wife* and *house* are the result of a later spelling convention, and do not represent an Old English sound; the original forms were *wīf* and *hūs.* On the other hand the Old English dative form *wīfe* was pronounced /wi:və/.)

A good many people have thought, and some have written, that one member of the *þ*-ð pair *must* represent the voiced and the other the voiceless sound, but the evidence is dead against them. They are simply independent additions to the Latin alphabet, which had no symbols for these fricatives because the sounds did not occur in Latin. The *þ* (thorn) was borrowed from the Runic alphabet, and ð (eth or edh) was an Irish modification of *d.*

The letters *c, g,* and *h* are much more ambiguous because they represent a group of sounds that are particularly likely to be changed by neighboring sounds — and represent them both before and after the changes occur. The earlier sounds were the voiced and voiceless velar stops made by pressing the back of the tongue against the velum (soft palate), and the corresponding fricatives made by putting the tongue close enough to the velum to cause audible friction. But because the tongue is extremely flexible, the exact point of contact is not fixed. We explained on page 28 that a neighboring front vowel tends to move this point forward, so that the /k/ sounds in /kik/ are rather different from the /k/ sounds in /kuk/, though we do not ordinarily notice the difference. But if the forward movement is so marked that the difference in sound is inescapably evident, the new sounds are said to be *palatalized*. Many languages have gone through stages of palatalization, with curiously varied results.[2] The new sounds may come to be spelled differently from the old ones, or they may, as in Old English, retain the same spellings.

To understand how, if not why, such changes happen, pronounce first /kuk/, then /kik/, noticing that the point of contact moves forward, whether you can hear the difference or not. Then if you keep on pronouncing /kik/ with the contact farther and farther forward you will eventually run out of room for the /k/ sound and make some other sound, probably one of those mentioned in the note about the developments of *Cicero*.

Old English *c* keeps the original /k/ sound whenever it occurs before a consonant or a back vowel, as in *cwic* (quick) and *col* (cool). Next to a front vowel it *usually* changes to /tʃ/, as in *cinn* (chin). The front vowels in some words had originally been back vowels, however, and had not been brought forward until *after* the palatalizing had ceased to operate in English. Their fronting was caused by an entirely different kind of phonetic change called *mutation* or *umlaut*.[3] Consequently we have some words like *cēne* (keen) and *cyning* (king) in which the original velar sound

[2] We are taught in Latin classes that the Romans pronounced the name Cicero /kikero/; but outside the classroom the English and French pronounce it (with some minor differences) as /sisero/, the Germans as /tsitsero/, the Italians as /tʃitʃero/ and the Castilian Spanish as /θiθero/. The English pronunciation was apparently affected by French influence, because the usual development of palatalized /k/ is like that in Italian.

[3] Mutation was the moving forward of a back vowel because a front vowel or semivowel occurred in the following syllable (see pp. 102–103). The Germans call it umlaut, and record its occurrence by a spelling convention. They print the original vowel with a dieresis to show that it no longer has the original pronunciation, as in *höflich* (courtly) from *Hof* (court). English has no comparable convention.

remained. Some printed texts (including the first two passages in the *Companion* to this book) use a dotted *c* to indicate the palatalized /tʃ/ sound, and reserve the plain *c* for the velar /k/ one.

The letter *c* also occurs in two digraphs for sounds for which English has never had a single letter: *cg* for /dʒ/ as in *ecg* (edge), and *sc* for /ʃ/ as in *scunian* (shun).

The pronunciation of *g* is roughly parallel to that of *c,* with one additional complication. In the earliest-preserved Old English writing it stood not only for the voiced velar stop /g/, but for the voiced velar fricative for which our phonemic alphabet has no symbol, because most Americans are sure they couldn't possibly pronounce it.[4] Old English *g* had this value (but most instructors will accept /g/ as a substitute) when it occurred between two vowels of which at least one was a back vowel, or between a liquid consonant and a back vowel. In such positions it later changed to a /w/ sound, which eventually appeared in spelling. This is handy to know, because you can often identify an unfamiliar word by seeing what it suggests if you substitute *w* for *g*. Examples are *dagian* (dawn), *lagu* (law), and *folgian* (follow).

In other positions *g* was pronounced /g/ before consonants; initially before back vowels and such front vowels as had developed by mutation of back ones; and in the combination *ng,* which was always pronounced as in *finger,* not as in *singer.* Examples are *græs* (grass), *guma* (man), *ges* (geese), and *lang* (long).

It was pronounced /j/ (the symbol for the *y* sound in *yet,* not the *j* sound in *jet*) initially before front vowels not resulting from mutation; between two front vowels; and as the final sound in a word or syllable when it followed a front vowel. Examples are *gēar* (year); *fæger* (fair); *dæg* (day) and *dægtīma* (daytime). In this last position *g* was not simply the /i/ sound into which it later developed. *Dæg,* for instance, must have been pronounced /dæjə/, with the final schwa sound very light.

In some texts the palatalized pronunciation of *g,* like that of *c,* is indicated by printing it with a dot over it, as *ġ*. And as the examples just given show, substituting a *y* for a palatalized *g* will often identify an Old English word.

[4] Actually it is not very hard, though it takes a little practice. Say *wagon,* and notice how and where your tongue touches the roof of your mouth. Now try to say the same word with your tongue not quite touching in the same place, and listen carefully. The IPA symbol for the sound is [ɣ].

The letter *h* originally represented the voiceless velar fricative /χ/ (chi), which is found in such German words as *noch.* You can make it if you first say /nɔk/, and then try to say the same thing with your tongue not quite touching the roof of your mouth as you pronounce the final consonant. When it occurred finally, or medially before consonants, this sound persisted until long after the Old English period, and generally came to be spelled *gh.* Eventually it either disappeared, as in *bough* (from Old English *boh*) and *daughter* (from *dohtor*), or changed to the labial fricative /f/ as in *tough* (from *tōh*) and *laughter* (from *hleahtor*).

Before vowels it weakened to the modern /h/ sound. It had the same value initially before certain consonants, as in *hlaf, hring,* and *hnappian,* though here it later disappeared completely, giving us the modern *loaf, ring,* and *to nap.* In the combination *hw* the /χ/ (later /h/) sound persisted, but the spelling came to be reversed in the Middle English period.

The Vowels

The Old English alphabet had seven letters for vowels, each of which could represent either a "long" or a "short" sound, and length was phonemic — that is, sufficient to distinguish between otherwise identical words, such as *col* (modern *coal*) and *cōl* (modern *cool*). Vowel length is occasionally, but not usually, indicated in manuscripts by a macron, as in *cōl.* Until quite recently it was generally accepted that the long vowels were simply prolongations of the short ones. Some scholars still hold this view. Others think the significant difference was not one of length but of quality — that *col* was pronounced /kɔl/, and *cōl* /kol/. Still others think that some diphthongization was involved. Because it is impossible to prove any of the competing theories, a reasonable solution is to aim at pronouncing the long vowels like prolongations of the short ones, but not to worry if you slip a little. The transcriptions in this chapter show a colon after all "long" vowels, and (because it seems likely, though it can't be proved) assume that the "short *o*" was open and the "long *o*" closed, but that in all the other vowels length was the most obvious difference, though there may well have been also the same sorts of differences in quality that we find in long and short /i/ and /u/ in Modern English.

SHORT VOWELS		LONG VOWELS	
Letters	*Phonemic symbols*	*Letters*	*Phonemic symbols*
a	/ɑ/	ā	/ɑ:/
æ	/æ/	ǣ	/æ:/
e	/e/	ē	/e:/
i	/i/	ī	/i:/
o	/o/	ō	/o:/
u	/u/	ū	/u:/
y	/y/	ȳ	/y:/

A few observations:

1. The macrons over the long vowels are usual in dictionaries and glossaries but rarely appear in texts.

2. The pronunciation of the phonemic symbols for the first six vowels is shown on page 32.

3. The symbol /y/ represents a rounded high front vowel that does not occur in most dialects of Modern English. It can be pronounced by rounding the lips as if to pronounce *oo* and then trying (but not straining) to pronounce *ee* without changing their position. It occurs in other languages (French *u* and German *ü*), and is represented by [y] in the IPA. In English the sound unrounded to /i/ about the end of the Old English period, and the letter *y* came to be used first as an optional variant of *i* in any position, later as a required substitute for it in some positions.

The Diphthongs

Early Old English had four short diphthongs, *ea, eo, ie,* and *io,* and four long ones, *ēa, ēo, īe,* and *īo,* all of which apparently were pronounced simply as sequences of the vowels of which they were composed, with the stress on the first. But in the Late West Saxon with which we are working, the ones beginning with *i,* long or short, had virtually disappeared, and the second vowel of the ones beginning with *e* was becoming less distinct, so that /eə/ will do for both *ea* and *eo,* and /e:ə/ for *ēa* and *ēo.*

Summary of Old English Sounds

Briefly, and with some oversimplification:

1. Old English had four sounds that have since been lost: a rounded high front vowel, short and long, and the voiced and voiceless velar frica-

tives. It also contained four initial combinations from which the first element has now been dropped; /hl/, /hn/, /hr/, and /kn/, though in the last of these the lost element still appears in spelling. Thus Old English *hlaf* has come down to us as *loaf,* but *cniht* as *knight.*

2. The phoneme /ʒ/ for the medial consonant sound in *measure* had not yet developed; and the voiced and voiceless pairs of fricatives represented by *f, s,* and (interchangeably) *þ* and ð were not yet separate phonemes, but allophones. The tendency of unstressed vowels to blur toward the /ə/ sound had apparently begun, but there is no evidence of a stressed /ə/.

3. Next to back vowels and consonants *c* is pronounced /k/ and *g* is pronounced /g/, but next to front vowels they are usually pronounced /tʃ/ and /j/ respectively.

4. Though there is some disagreement about how long vowels were pronounced, they were certainly *not* pronounced like the "long vowels" of modern spelling rules.

A Specimen of Old English

Before going on to the other areas of grammar we will consider a short passage in Old English, partly for practice in the sound system just outlined, and partly because close examination of even a tiny amount of text is a useful preliminary to meeting a display of inflectional forms. If we carefully copied a bit from an old manuscript, making no changes except to modernize the punctuation and capitalization, we might get something like this:

> Fæder ure þu þe eart on heofonum, si þin nama gehalgod; to-becume þin rice; geƿurþe þin ƿilla on eorðan sƿa sƿa on heofonum; urne gedæghƿamlican hlaf syle us to dæg; and forgyf us ure gyltas sþa sƿa ƿe forgyfað urum gyltendum; and ne gelæd þu us on costnunge, ac alys us of yfele, soþlice.[5]

Maybe you recognize it, and if it were read aloud by somebody who understood it you almost certainly would; but it surely looks strange. Much of the strangeness, however, is caused simply by the forms of a few of the letters. If we substitute modern characters for the unfamiliar ones, we get the following, with a very rough phonemic transcription:

[5] Kaiser, p. 6.

Fæder ure thu the eart on heofonum, si thin nama gehalgod;
fæder u:re θu: θe eart ɔn heɔvɔnum si: θi:n nama jehalgɔd

to-becume thin rice; gewurthe thin willa on eorthan swa swa on
to bekume θi:n ri:tʃe jewurðe θi:n wila ɔn eɔrðan swa: swa:ɔn

heofonum; urne gedæghwamlican hlaf syle us to dæg; and
heɔvɔnum u:rne jedæjχwamli:kan hla:f syle u:s to dæj and

forgyf us ure gyltas swa swa we forgyfath urum gyltendum;
fɔrjyf u:s u:re gyltas swa: swa: we: fɔrjyvaθ u:rum gyltendum

and ne gelæd thu us on costnunge, ac alys us of yfele,
and ne jelæ:d θu: u:s ɔn kɔstnuŋge ac aly:s u:s ɔf yvele

sothlice.
so:ðli:tʃe

Here the text is a transliteration — that is, a transcription into a different (in this case only partly different) alphabet. The Old English ƿ (wynn) has been replaced by its modern equivalent, *w;* and both ð (*eth*) and þ (*thorn*) have been replaced by *th*. The phonemic transcription is in the same basic alphabet as that used in Chapter Two, but has the additional characters /χ/ and /y/ for the lost sounds explained on pages 70–72. A number of points remain debatable, but if you read the passage aloud with reasonable conviction and pronounced the words as indicated, you would probably be understood by any carefully preserved West Saxon you happened to meet — which is perhaps as much as you could hope for this early in the study.

To know that this passage is an Old English version of the Lord's Prayer is interesting, but not in itself very enlightening. To learn anything really useful from it we must examine it very carefully; and we must make a special effort to see whether any of the changes that have taken place in the language since the manuscript was written are *systematic*. The importance of looking for systematic developments cannot be overemphasized; it makes the difference between having to learn every detail as a separate item and learning a much smaller number of principles that can be applied again and again. No system works perfectly, and we have to make many adjustments, but the gain is still enormous. If we look at the passage in this way, here are some of the things we shall find:

1. A number of endings and other unstressed syllables that have since weakened or dropped off entirely.

a. *Endings.*

Old English	*Modern English*
ure	our
heofonum	heaven
nama	name
thin	thy
willa	will
eorthan	earth
urne	our
gyltas	guilts
forgyfath	forgive
urum	our

Notice particularly the different forms of the possessive adjective — *ure, urne,* and *urum* — as it agrees with different nouns. Because some weakening had already taken place, the same form is used in the nominative singular (*fæder ure*) and accusative plural (*ure gyltas*), but *urne* is used in the accusative singular and *urum* in the dative plural.

b. *Other unstressed syllables.*

Old English	*Modern English*
gehalgod	hallowed
to-becume	come
gedæghwamlican	daily
gelæd	lead
alys	loose

2. Certain changes in word order.

Old English	*Modern English*
Fæder ure	our Father
to-becume thin rice	Thy kingdom come
urne gedæghwamlican hlaf syle us	give us our daily bread

We need not worry about whether these changes were the causes or the results of the dropping of endings, or a little of both, but when endings no longer reliably indicate how words are related, we need a dependable word order to take their place.

3. Notice that the fricatives are voiced when they occur between two voiced sounds as in *heofonum, gewurthe, eorthan, forgyfath, yfele,* and

sothlice, but voiceless elsewhere. We don't really know why the originally voiceless initial /θ/ sound in the words that developed into the modern *thou, the, that* and a few other common ones later became the voiced /ð/. It remained voiceless in many others, including such common ones as *thick, thin, think,* and *three,* and is voiceless in all later additions to the language.

4. Notice that the pronunciation of all the *c*'s and most of the *g*'s clearly follows the rules on pages 69–70.[6] In *gehalgod* the compromise /g/ pronunciation is shown medially in the transcription, but the *w* in the modern form of the word is evidence that this sound was actually the voiced velar fricative discussed on page 70 above.

The sort of analysis we have just indicated may at first seem impossibly slow and cumbersome. You may think it would be much simpler just to get a translation to show you what the original means. Certainly a translation can be helpful, but it will seldom do the whole job. If it is in normal Modern English it often fails completely to show how the original was put together. If it is aimed at reflecting the original exactly it is always clumsy, and sometimes almost meaningless. Whichever it is, it must be supplemented by some analysis to be of any value.

Let's take another look at the clause "urne gedæghwamlican hlaf syle us to dæg." If you saw it alone without knowing where it came from it would probably convey absolutely nothing to you. When a translation tells you that all together it means "Give us this day our daily bread" you collect an odd bit of information, but you haven't really learned anything of value — certainly nothing that is likely to help you with other passages. The important question is, how and why does it mean what it does? To get at the answer to this question you must examine, compare, use your reason, guess, check your guesses, and (but only when nothing else works) memorize.

Once you know the gross meaning, it is obvious that *us to dæg* means *us today*. With this clue you should be able to disentangle *daily* from *gedæghwamlican*. Notice that in both these words a *g* has changed to a *y*.

[6] In the next to last full line *gyltas* and *forgyfath* make an interesting pair. Our general rules indicate a /j/ pronunciation for both *g*'s before the front vowel *y*, but modern pronunciation would suggest /g/ for both. We can be sure that /j/ is right for *forgyfath*, and that Modern English *forgive* does not come from the West Saxon form (as Chaucer's *foryeve* does), but from Anglian, with perhaps a Danish influence. But we can find no evidence that *guilt* ever had a /j/ sound, so that the *y* in *gyltas* is apparently the result of mutation. Unfortunately we have no trace of an earlier form without mutation either in English or any other Germanic language.

Because it may happen often, concentrate on the fact for a moment. If you don't remember it after these first occurrences, you will after a few more, if you keep your mind alert for such things. And do other long Old English words lose some of their less important syllables? (We have just seen that some of them do.) Next, there must be some word for *our,* and *urne* seems to be the obvious one. It does look a little like *our,* and it looks even more like *ourn.* Could it be that that "ignorant" form is really the survival of a perfectly good Old English form that has somehow been lost in the Standard language? This seems likely — and now you'll never forget *urne.*

That leaves *syle* and *hlaf* to mean *give* and *bread.* Doesn't seem probable. "Give us our bread — syle us our hlaf." Can't be the same words, but they do sound a little like something. Could it be "sell us our loaf"? *Loaf* looks all right, especially with *daily.* A little change in meaning, but it must be the same word. Could *sell* ever have meant *give?* It means "give for something" instead of "give for nothing." But does *give* always mean "give for nothing?" You have certainly heard a clerk say "I can give you some nice apples today," and he didn't mean that they were free. Maybe *sell* was used that way so often that it changed its meaning permanently. And there you have it.

If you study the passage thoroughly you will find that only four of the words have completely disappeared from the language: *ac, costnunge, gewurthe,* and *si. Rice,* cognate with German *Reich,* has almost gone, but we do have the compound form *bishopric.* All the others are still in the language in some form or other. They may look utterly strange at first, but it is possible to get at them when you know how to go about it.

In short, there are a number of steps to take in the early stages of reading any unfamiliar language.

1. Examine a passage carefully to see what you can get from it directly.
2. Figure out, look up, ask, or otherwise discover what each of the "hard" parts means, and, as nearly as possible, why it means that. Anything that you can connect with something you already know is much more likely to stay with you.

This step — a really thorough translation — is as far as even most thoroughly conscientious students ever get. It is a very silly place to stop, because you have done most of the work and got very little of the reward. Therefore:

3. While your information is fresh in your mind, *read* the passage —

that is, look at it and react to it directly. Do not allow yourself to say, or even to think, that *syle* means *give*. You have found out what *syle* meant to the Saxons. Let it mean the same thing to you. Then and only then will you actually be reading the passage.

This last step is not hard, but because a great many people never think of it as even possible, they never attempt it. And a fair number of students actively resist the idea that translation should be merely an intermediate step. They seem to be held back by a mixture of conscientiousness, insecurity, and a curiously limited imagination. They think that knowing a passage in a different language really means knowing its English equivalent. Well, that's translating, and it would be immoral not to do it. Pretending to understand it without translating would not be really honest, and they want to be honest. And besides, if you don't always think of the English word when you look at the French or German one, you might forget it while writing a test, and then where would you be? And they don't *really* believe it is possible to *think* in a different language — rapid and accurate translation is the limit of their dreams.

But it *is* possible to do a little thinking in a language even when you know only two or three of its words. You can eat *Brot* or drink *vin* on first acquaintance. It may pay you to analyze *auf wiedersehen* or *qu'est-ce que c'est?* just once; but when their structure is clear to you, you should realize that their meaning is precisely *auf wiedersehen* and *qu'est-ce que c'est?* and that calling them anything else is a step backward. If you will just allow such automatic responses to build up in your mind, they will do so much faster than if you insist on translating them again and again and again. And once you get to the point of translating only what you have to, you will often find that the known words tell you what the unknown ones must mean, so that you can read a sentence at once, without bothering about the preliminary translation at all. Of course you will sometimes make mistakes; but you will learn to read better as well as faster.

The "Synthetic" Structure of Old English

Old English differs from Modern English not only in its sounds and vocabulary (we have lost a few thousand words and gained a few hundred thousand), but in the ways the words are put together to form sentences.

The difference is often summarized by saying that English has changed from a synthetic to an analytic language. A synthetic language is one in which the relations of words are shown primarily by their inflectional forms. An analytic language is one in which most differences in form have disappeared, and relations are shown primarily by word order, supplemented by such "function words" as prepositions and auxiliary verbs.

The shift from one type to the other has been a matter of changing emphasis rather than of absolute conversion. Word order had some importance in Old English, and inflections have some communicative importance now (quite apart from the question of "correct usage"). Often the two supplement each other. But when they conflict we have to decide which one to believe. Consider such a sentence as "Him saw I." From the synthetic point of view it obviously means "I saw him," because *I* is in the normal form for the subject, *him* in the normal form for an object, and the order of the words is a secondary matter. An ancient Saxon would interpret it (with the words in a slightly different form) in this way without the slightest hesitation. But the natural reaction of almost any contemporary American would be that the sentence meant "He saw me," and that the speaker was either very ignorant or indulging in baby talk. An unusually fanatical grammarian might insist that the sentence "really" means "I saw him," but even he probably would not carry his theories very far. If he saw a sentence like "Sally and him invited my wife and I to breakfast," he would accept the obvious meaning and simply say that the sentence contained a couple of errors.

The drift toward analytic structure had begun even before the Germanic tribes left the continent, and was continuing all during the Old English period. That is, more and more inflectional forms that had once been different were coming to be identical and therefore losing much of their signaling power. The heavy Germanic stress on the root syllables made it easy to slur the endings. More or less simultaneously a reliable word order was developing. We could argue indefinitely about whether the new word order had to develop when the inflections dropped out, or whether the inflections were lost because the new word order made them unnecessary. It seems simpler to say that both tendencies were at work, and we don't know which was more important. But the dropping of inflections was happening a little faster than the development of a word order to replace them. That is, people sometimes depended on inflectional differences that were no longer there to depend on, and ambiguous sentences often resulted.

A student cannot be expected to master Old English grammar without far greater experience with the language than this book provides; but even a very sketchy outline of it can be useful in showing how some of the features of Modern English originated. Many points of usage that seem utterly unreasonable when considered in isolation can be readily understood when recognized as survivals from an earlier system. Moreover, it is obviously impossible to study the development of a language intelligently without having a firm, if not particularly detailed, idea of what it was like at the beginning.

Even late West Saxon shows a good deal of variation in the forms, which is no surprise. We have no evidence at all that English grammar was ever studied during either the Old or Middle English periods. So far as we know, people learned English by simple absorption, and had no accepted standards to keep their practices uniform. In this chapter the paradigms (sets of inflectional forms) have been simplified by leaving out most of the variants.

Students who are not thoroughly familiar with the terminology of traditional grammar may find it useful to read the first part of Chapter Nine before continuing with this one. In that chapter grammatical theory is considered in much more detail than is included here.

Nouns

Old English nouns, like Latin ones, occurred in a number of declensions with different endings; we do not know why. Possibly the "original Indo-European" was already a mixture of languages with different characteristic declensions. At any rate, some of the Old English declensions can be shown to be related to those in such languages as Greek and Latin, while others are either of purely Germanic origin or were borrowed by the Germanic peoples from some other language they encountered after separating from the other Indo-Europeans.

In Old English nouns the separate ablative case had already disappeared, and the running together of other originally distinct forms had gone further than in Latin. The paradigms for five nouns are given below. They should all be examined carefully, but only the *stān* declension is worth memorizing, as the one from which the modern pattern developed.

	stone (m.)	*word* (n.)	*gift* (f.)	*ape* (m.)	*foot* (m.)
Singular					
Nominative	stān	word	giefu	apa	fōt
Genitive	stānes	wordes	giefe	apan	fōtes
Dative	stāne	worde	giefe	apan	fēt
Accusative	stān	word	giefe	apan	fōt
Plural					
Nominative	stānas	word	giefa	apan	fēt
Genitive	stāna	worda	giefa	apena	fōta
Dative	stānum	wordum	giefum	apum	fōtum
Accusative	stānas	word	giefa	apan	fēt

Notice that two of the declensions do not have the *-s* ending in the genitive singular, and that only the *stān* declension has it in two cases of the plural. Since then the *stān* declension has been simplified in form and extended in use, so that it now takes in most of the nouns that originally belonged to others. But both the *-en* plural of *ox* and the unchanged plural of such words as *sheep* and *deer* go back to other declensions. Notice also that in the *fōt* declension the variation between the two vowels is not simply between singular and plural. In such expressions as "He was six foot tall" *foot* does not come from the singular, but from the genitive plural *fōta,* which could mean (all by itself) "to the extent of ___ feet."

There are several declensions besides the ones illustrated above, and all had subclasses with phonetic peculiarities. As we might reasonably expect, a number of irregular forms (not indicated above) are found, because the competing analogies put a considerable strain on the memory.[7] When irregular forms occur very rarely, they are considered to be mistakes. When they occur frequently, they are considered legitimate variants.

The nominative case is used primarily for a word that is, or refers to, the

[7] Some linguists object vigorously to the suggestion that the melting together of inflections could have been caused by any limitations of memory, preferring to attribute all clipping and slurring to speed of speech and changes in stress patterns. They hold that the multiplicity of forms which seems difficult to outsiders would present no problem to native speakers, who would make the appropriate choices routinely and accurately without ever having to think about them. It seems a trifle doctrinaire to insist that a whole speech community could lose a considerable number of forms without its members ever having had a lapse in memory. However, it does seem likely that very homogeneous speech communities would be more conservative than others. If so, the far from homogeneous English community might well be forgiven for letting some details escape.

subject of a sentence. The genitive is primarily the case of possession, but (as in Modern English) may also indicate other relations, such as control, kinship, authorship, and membership in a group. The accusative is primarily the case of the direct object, but also has a few other functions. The dative, which was originally used principally as the indirect object, had taken on most of the functions of several lost cases. It is used after many prepositions, and is often also used alone where Modern English would require a prepositional phrase.

The opening four lines of "The Battle of Brunanburh" not only show some uses of all four cases but illustrate the freedom of word order, often very effective, which inflections make possible:

Hēr Æþelstān cyning   eorla dryhten,
he:r æðelstɑn kyniŋ   eɔrlɑ dryχtən

beorna bēahgifa,   and his brōþər ēac,
beɔrna be:ɑχjivɑ   ɑnd his bro:ðɔr e:ɑk

Eadmund æþeling,   ealdorlangne tir
e:ədmund æðeliŋ   eɑldɔrlɑŋne ti:r

geslōgon æt sæcce   sweorda ecgum
jəslo:gɔn æt sække   sweɔrdɑ edʒum

If we translate the first seven words in order, paying no attention to inflections, we get:

Here Æthelstan king earl lord warrior ring giver . . . .

But the *-a* ending of both *eorla* and *beorna* shows that they are in the genitive plural. (The *-a* ending of *beahgifa* shows no such thing, because that word happens to be in a different declension.) The meaning is therefore:

Here King Æthelstan, lord of earls, ring-giver of warriors . . . .

The next five words need little adjustment:

and his brother also, Edmund prince . . .

although we would now either reverse the last two or put *the* between them. The last seven words, disregarding case endings, give:

lifelong honor won at battle sword edge . . . .

But *tir is* accusative, *sæcce* dative singular, *sweorda* genitive plural, and *ecgum* dative plural. The meaning is therefore:

won lifelong honor at battle with the edges of swords . . . .

It is true that you could not tell from the form of *tir* alone whether it was nominative or accusative, and it might therefore sometimes be ambiguous. But here it is modified by the adjective *ealdorlangne,* and if you peep ahead to page 87 you will see that *-ne* is an accusative ending. Meanwhile you should notice that although the dative form *sæcce* comes after the preposition *æt,* the dative form *ecgum* means, all by itself, "with the edges." If you now read the four lines again, knowing what they mean, you may get a little of the feel of the verse.

In *stān* and *word* the nominative and accusative forms are alike in both the singular and the plural. If they were alike in all declensions Old English would have only three cases. But in *giefu* and *apa* differences between nominative and accusative have been preserved, though some other original differences have been lost. We therefore have to recognize four cases in Old English nouns, and it is on the whole convenient to show each one in every paradigm, though no one noun keeps the forms for all four distinct.

Even at the risk of monotony we repeat that all the forms were originally distinct; in fact there were twice as many to be distinct as are shown above. The Indo-European nouns had eight cases — vocative, locative, ablative, and instrumental, as well as the four shown above. This made a good many forms to remember and keep separate, so that it was easy to make mistakes, either by using wrong forms or by slurring pronunciation so that originally different forms came to be pronounced alike. When the same mistakes were made often enough and long enough they stopped being mistakes — after all you can't blame a baby for not making a distinction that his great-grandfather forgot to pass along to his grandfather.

We can still find all eight cases in Sanskrit. Russian has six; but Latin nouns usually have only five, and Greek and German nouns, like Old English ones, only four. Modern English has only two, and French and Spanish only one. Nobody knows why the rate of change has been so different, but then nobody really knows how the cases started in the first place. One guess is that the various endings were originally separate words used to show special relations — something like prepositions except that they came after the words to which they pointed, so that they might be called "postpositions."

The Personal Pronouns

The personal pronouns have retained more of their original inflections than any other class of words in the language simply because people hear and use the forms so often that they are less likely to forget them or get them mixed up. Even in this group, however, there have been some losses and some changes, as you can see by examining the paradigms below.

		First person	Second person	Third person		
				Masc.	*Fem.*	*Neut.*
Sing.	*Nom.*	ic	ðū	hē	hēo	hit
	Gen.	mīn	ðīn	his	hiere	his
	Dat.	mē	ðē	him	hiere	him
	Acc.	mē	ðē	hine	hīe	hit
		(earlier mec)	(ðec)			
Dual	*Nom.*	wit (*we two*)	git (*ye two*)			
	Gen.	uncer	incer			
	Dat.	unc	inc			
	Acc.	unc	inc			
		(earlier uncit)	(incit)			
Plur.	*Nom.*	wē	gē		hīe	
	Gen.	ūre	ēower		hiera	
	Dat.	ūs	ēow		him	
	Acc.	ūs	ēow		hīe	
		(earlier ūsic)	(ēowic)			

The dual number disappeared so long ago that most people are amazed to learn that it ever existed, yet it had a very reasonable origin and has left a few traces in other parts of the language. As a matter of logic it is curious that we consider the difference between singular and plural — one and more than one — so important that it has to be indicated every time we use a noun or pronoun, while the difference between two and millions can be neglected. The series one, two, and more than two (which is still found in many languages) at least has an anatomical basis, going back to a stage when people counted on their hands rather than their fingers. Children still seem to go through this stage quite regularly. When they are very young *one* and *two* are distinct numbers, but *three, seven,* and *twenty* are synonyms — interchangeable terms for that confusing number that is too large to be grasped by either hands or mind. Our habit of saying "the *younger*" of two but "the *youngest*" of three or more is clearly a leftover from the same classification. Another occurs in the phrase "every *other* one" for "every *second* one." *Other* originally meant either "second" or "different" — these are identical if you can't count higher than two. To avoid confusion we eventually had to borrow *second* from French.

The old distinction between dative and accusative cases has now been completely lost; generally the dative form has survived. The old accusative forms *mec, ðec, ūsic,* and *ēowic* were dropping out in favor of the corresponding dative forms even in Old English times. Since then *him* and *hiere* (her) have driven out *hine* and *hīe*. The only old accusative form that has remained is *hit,* in the form *it.*

In the third person the number of forms has actually increased. In Old English all the forms began with *h,* and some were ambiguous. This ambiguity was increased in late Old and early Middle English when some of the originally distinct forms came to be pronounced (and therefore spelled) alike. Even the masculine and feminine singular forms became identical in some dialects — obviously an intolerable situation. Accordingly *she* was developed, probably by borrowing from the demonstrative pronoun (see below), and the plural forms that developed into *they, their,* and *them* were taken over from the Scandinavians who had settled in England.

If you pronounce the Old English forms carefully you will see that those which remain in the language have changed less than the spelling would seem to indicate. Even *gē* and *ēow* are less strange than they look if you remember that *g* before a front vowel regularly came to be pronounced as *y;* and *ēow,* when pronounced with the stress on the *o,* sounds a good deal like *you.*

Demonstrative and Interrogative Pronouns

The only other Old English pronouns that need be mentioned in a brief survey are demonstrative and interrogative. Not all the forms that occur in manuscripts are given here, and even those listed need not be memorized, but they are worth careful examination because of later developments; for though the inflection has since been much simplified, some of the forms that have been lost as cases of pronouns have been retained in the function of adverbs — *then, there, when,* and *why.* The modern *that-those* had (with additional variants) these forms:

	Masculine	*Feminine*	*Neuter*
Singular			
Nominative	sē	sēo	ðæt
Genitive	ðæs	ðære	ðæs
Dative	ðæm	ðære	ðæm
Accusative	ðone	ðā	ðæt
Instrumental	ðȳ		ðȳ

	Feminine
Plural (all genders)	
Nominative	ðā
Genitive	ðāra
Dative	ðǣm
Accusative	ðā

This word had a number of uses. As an adjective it was sometimes equivalent to modern *the,* sometimes to the stronger *that.* As a pronoun it was originally demonstrative: "Ðæt wæs god cyning" — "That was a good king." But it soon came to be used also as a relative: ". . . ðā sceolde cuman ðǣre helle hund ongēan hine, *ðæs* nama wæs Ceruerus, *sē* sceolde habban þrīo hēafdu" — "then (they say) came the hound of that hell to meet him *whose* name was Cerberus, *who* (they say) had three heads." The habit of using *that* for all genders now seems convenient, but the disappearance of a genitive form for *that* is a real loss. The use of the interrogative *who* and *which* as relatives did not develop until much later.

You will notice that in the masculine and neuter singular there is a fifth case, the *instrumental.* This case, originally used to designate the thing by means of which something was done, had extended its uses until it was generally equivalent to the Latin ablative; then it disappeared as a separate form in all nouns, in some pronouns, in the weak declension of adjectives, and in the feminine gender and plural number everywhere. Some grammarians list every dative form in the language as "dative and instrumental"; but it seems simpler to limit its mention to the places where it demonstrably occurs — in a few pronouns and in strong adjectives. (Weak and strong declensions of adjectives will be discussed on the next page.)

The other demonstrative pronoun, *ðēs, ðēos, ðis* (modern *this*) was inflected just as completely, and with even more variations in its forms, but has left fewer traces in Modern English.

The interrogative pronoun had lost its separate feminine forms, and has no plural. It is declined as follows:

	Masculine	*Neuter*
Nominative	hwā	hwæt
Genitive	hwæs	hwæs
Dative	hwǣm	hwǣm
Accusative	hwone	hwæt
Instrumental	hwī	hwī

The modern forms *who, whose, whom,* and *what,* plus the now separate words *when* and *why* can be traced to this pronoun. In Old English times *hwǣr* (*where*), *hwȳ* (*why*), and *hū* (*how*) had already broken off. The first of these was apparently an otherwise lost feminine form, and the others may have been.

Adjectives

In Old English the adjective was the most highly inflected of all the parts of speech. It had the same cases as the noun, plus the instrumental. It had forms for all three genders, singular and plural, because it had to agree with the noun it modified. Like Modern German, it had a "weak" declension for use whenever it was preceded by a limiting word, such as the definite article or a possessive or demonstrative pronoun; and a "strong" declension whenever it was not preceded by such a word. (You are hereby advised to accept this as a fact and not worry about why. We don't know — though we could say so in a more long-winded way.) And of course there are the three degrees — positive, comparative, and superlative — though the comparative was (mercifully) always weak.

	STRONG DECLENSION			WEAK DECLENSION		
	Masc.	*Fem.*	*Neut.*	*Masc.*	*Fem.*	*Neut.*
Sing.						
N.	gōd	gōd	gōd	gōd-a	gōd-e	gōd-e
G.	gōd-es	gōd-re	gōd-es	gōd-an	gōd-an	gōd-an
D.	gōd-um	gōd-re	gōd-um	gōd-an	gōd-an	gōd-an
A.	gōd-ne	gōd-e	gōd	gōd-an	gōd-an	gōd-e
I.	gōd-e		gōd-e			
Plur.						
N.	gōd-e	gōd-a	gōd		gōd-an	
G.	gōd-ra	gōd-ra	gōd-ra		gōd-ena	
D.	gōd-um	gōd-um	gōd-um		gōd-um	
A.	gōd-e	gōd-a	gōd		gōd-an	

Naturally enough our ancestors had begun to find these too many to keep straight even before the time of the earliest manuscripts that have come down. Many of the other endings had become identical, especially in the weak declension. But we may be devoutly thankful that in Middle English times speakers developed the habit of showing the relation of an adjective to its noun by position rather than agreement in form, so that the only trace of all these complications that remains is *-er, -est* endings for comparative and superlative degrees of short adjectives.

Verbs

None of the other parts of speech has changed as much between Indo-European and Modern English as the verb. The Latin verb *vocō,* which preserves the original system fairly well, has more than a hundred physically different forms, not counting duplications. Eighty-five of these are "finite" — each with a special, limited function that cannot be explained by fewer than five terms specifying *person, number, tense, mood,* and *voice.* By contrast, the English equivalent *call* has only the four forms *call, calls, called,* and *calling,* and of these only *calls* is finite, and thus the equivalent of a particular Latin form. The other three have various uses.

We have made up for the lost inflections by several devices. To indicate subjects we use a combination of more pronouns and a consistent word order instead of personal endings; and in place of inflections for tense, mood, and voice we have developed an extensive system of auxiliary verbs, supplemented by adverbial expressions of time and such conjunctions as *if* and *though.* Thus *vocārētur* may be translated *if he were to be called.*

The changes, which will be discussed in more detail in Chapter Nine, began even before Germanic split into its component groups. The number of inflected tenses was reduced to two, compared to the Latin six. By the time of the earliest English records the inflected passive voice had disappeared, and so had differences of person in the plural of both moods and in the singular of the subjunctive. As the conjugation of *bītan* on page 89 shows, only twenty-four theoretically different finite forms were left; and when we eliminate duplications, only nine. But the development of verb combinations had not kept pace with the disappearance of inflections.

Strong and Weak Verbs

But although the conjugation of each individual verb had greatly simplified, the variations between verbs remained extremely complex. There were two types of verbs, known as *strong* and *weak,* each divided into several classes.

In the strong verbs the past tense was formed by a change in the root vowel, as in the modern *sing, sang*. This is the normal development of a general Indo-European characteristic. The weak verbs were a special Germanic invention. They indicated the past tense by a "dental suffix" (see page 92). Eventually this became the general or "regular" way of forming past tenses, and many verbs that had originally had vowel changes were remade on the new model. Those which did not were credited by some philologists with a sturdy independence of character — hence the name "strong verbs." But it doesn't seem fair that the class that did on the whole win out should be called weak.

The Strong Verbs

The strong verb *bītan* (*bite*) is conjugated as follows:

	Indicative		*Subjunctive*
	present		*present*
ic	bīt-e	ic	bīt-e
ðū	bīt-st (-est)	ðū	bīt-e
hē	bīt-ð (-eð)	hē	bīt-e
wē	bīt-að	wē	bīt-en
gē	bīt-að	gē	bīt-en
hīe	bīt-að	hīe	bīt-en
	Past		*Past*
ic	bāt	ic	bit-e
ðū	bit-e	ðū	bit-e
hē	bāt	hē	bit-e
wē	bit-on	wē	bit-en
gē	bit-on	gē	bit-en
hīe	bit-on	hīe	bit-en

Several things are worth noticing about this paradigm.

1. Short vowels are not indicated by doubled consonants — this spelling convention developed much later. Instead, long vowels are here indicated by a line over them. Unmarked vowels are short. Also, long vowels are simply prolongations of the short ones, not the quite different diphthongs sometimes called long vowels in Modern English.

In addition to its finite forms, the Old English verb had a present participle (*bītende*), a past participle (*biten*), and an infinitive (*bītan*). Both participles were used like adjectives much more often than in such constructions as *was biting* and *had bitten,* and both could be declined like adjectives. The infinitive was a separate form, as in other inflected languages.

2. The difference between the long and short *i* is important. From the long *i* we get such modern forms as *bite;* from the short *i, bit.*

3. The past indicative shows two different vowel stems, one for the first and third persons singular, the other for all other persons. This distinction is not preserved in any Modern English verb, but it has resulted in much confusion. In some verbs the vowel of the plural has been generalized, so that we now say not only *they bit* but *he bit.* In other verbs it is the singular form that has been generalized, so that we now say either *he* or *they wrote* (which is the regular phonetic development of the old singular *hē wrāt*). It is simply a matter of chance that we haven't preserved the other forms, *writ* and *bote.* Actually, *writ* competed with *wrote* in Standard English for several centuries, and is still used in some dialects. *Bote* can be found in place of *bit* in earlier literature, but seems to have died out completely. In a few verbs, like *sink* and *shrink,* the two possible forms are still competing.

4. In both tenses and in both moods one form had already been generalized to serve for all three persons in the plural, and in both tenses of the subjunctive one form had come to serve for all three persons in the singular. Some forms (*ic bīte, ðū bite*) had already become identical in the indicative and subjunctive, and others (*wē biton, wē biten*) needed only a little slurring to become so.

Classes of Strong Verbs

Old English had more than three hundred strong verbs, divided into seven classes, as shown by these examples:

	Infinitive	*Preterite singular*	*Preterite plural*	*Past participle*
Class I	bītan	bāt	biton	biten
Class II	crēopan	crēap	crupon	cropen
Class III	drincan	dranc	druncon	druncen
Class IV	stelan	stæl	stǣlon	stolen
Class V	tredan	træd	trǣdon	treden
Class VI	bacan	bōc	bōcon	bacen
Class VII	crāwan	crēow	crēowon	crāwen

The first five of these classes show a vowel variation based on *ablaut,* which may be defined briefly (if not clearly) as an independent vowel change. In Indo-European, differences in pitch were more important than they are today, and different inflected forms of a word might have different pitches on the root syllable. The most important result is that we often find related forms containing an /e/ when the pitch was high, and an /o/ when the pitch was low.[8] As far as we can tell, neither of these vowels developed from the other. The "original" vowel has been lost, and we can trace the words back only to the stage where /e/ and /o/ appear.

These five classes all had an /e/ as the root vowel in the infinitive and an /o/ in the past singular; but these sounds had a different phonetic environment in each, and therefore developed differently. For instance, in Class I the /e/ or /o/ was followed by an /i/, and the resulting diphthongs developed in one way. In Class II the second element in the diphthongs was /u/, and in Class III there were no diphthongs, but the development of the vowels was influenced by the following /n/. The details of all the steps of change are too complicated to go into here; but, wild as the changes may look, they are both regular and predictable if you know all the phonetic forces at work. Our sounds inevitably influence each other, as you can see if you will try to pronounce the phoneme /e/ in exactly the same way in the five words *bet, bell, bent, berry,* and *bay*. In Class VI the original vowel of the infinitive was /a/ rather than /e/.

The changes in Class VII have a different origin. The verbs in this group were originally reduplicating. That is, they formed their preterites by doubling the root syllable. The repeated syllables were first somewhat differentiated, as in the Latin verbs *fallō-fefellī* and *parcō-peperci̅*. Later, in Germanic, the extra syllable was dropped. The vowel in the repeated syllables was then changed to /e/.

It would be a rather silly exercise to memorize the vowel changes in the seven classes of strong verbs — especially because these classes all have subclasses not here indicated. But some useful things can best be understood by considering some of the differences here displayed. As we noticed in *bītan,* the vowel of the preterite singular is usually different from that of the preterite plural, either in quality or length. Another thing to notice is that the /on/ ending of the preterite plural has now been completely lost, but that the /en/ ending of the past participle has been treated very irregularly. In some verbs, such as *rise, rose, risen,* it has been completely pre-

[8] This seems mildly improbable, but less so than competing theories.

served in Standard English. In some, such as *find, found,* it has been completely lost — nobody now says *founden.* And in many it is preserved only in specific uses, principally adjectival, as in *a drunken man* and *his bounden duty,* compared to *he had drunk* and *he had bound.*

We should also notice that such verbs as *bake* and *crow* have completely lost their older inflections, and are now regular weak verbs.

The Weak Verbs

The weak verbs originally formed their preterites by the addition of /ode/, /ede/, or /de/, endings that have come down to us (though not respectively) as /d/ (*earn-earned*), /t/ (*look-looked*), and /id/ (*wound-wounded*). Usually the root vowel did not change, but sometimes it did, as in the verbs from which we get *buy-bought* and *tell-told.* Thus all the regular verbs in Modern English are weak, but not all the weak verbs are regular. Any verb that adds /d/, /id/, or /t/, or changes /d/ to /t/ (*send-sent*) is called weak, whether or not there is also a vowel change.

When vowel changes do occur in weak verbs, they are not the independent or ablaut changes of the strong verbs, but are caused by the influence of neighboring sounds. A number of influences are possible, and when several of them happen to be at work on the same word the development can be very complicated and the results may seem most peculiar; but the working of each influence is amazingly regular, and if we know enough about the earlier forms we can see that the evolution of such apparently erratic pairs as *think-thought* is exactly predictable.

Weak verbs had the same vowel in the singular and plural of the preterite, and almost always had this same vowel in the past participle. The past participle ended in /ed/ rather than /en/, so that when personal endings disappeared in the preterite the two past forms became identical.

Changes in Classification

Of the 312 strong verbs recorded in Old English, slightly more than a third have completely disappeared from the language. Of those which remain, two-thirds have become weak. Thus we now say *crowed* instead of *crew, helped* instead of *holp,* and *washed* instead of *wesh* or *woosh.* This shift toward a regular pattern is comparable to the shift of most nouns to the *stān* declension. But as so often happens in the development of a language, a strong current in one direction is accompanied by a much smaller eddy in the other. A few originally weak verbs, such as *dig* and *fling,* have developed strong forms that have driven out the weak ones; others, like *chide* and *thrive,* now have strong forms competing with the weak ones; and still others, though weak in Standard English, have such forms as *brang* and *squoze* in some dialects. Each of these developments is simply a matter of incorrect analogy, and it would be impossible to prove that forms now scorned are essentially any worse than those which have become correct simply because everybody has made the same mistakes.

Adverbs

In Old English, adverbs are not discoverably a separate part of speech. But certain prepositions and conjunctions and some case forms of certain nouns, pronouns, and adjectives came to be used in one or more of the ways covered by the familiar definition — "a word that modifies a verb, adjective, or other adverb." Grammarians committed to this definition later called these words and forms adverbs when they were so used.

The *-ly* ending now so characteristic of adverbs was originally a noun, *līc,* meaning *body* or *shape.* From it we get the word *like* — "of the same shape." It then came to be used to make adjectives from nouns, usually in the weakened form of *-ly.* Thus *manlike* and *manly* are of identical origin. When the original meaning had been more or less forgotten, the ending was also used to make secondary adjectives from existing adjectives. Thus we find *glædlic* along with *glæd* (glad), and even *fæstlic* along with *fæst.* The Anglo-Saxons often used the instrumental cases of these words — either the simple or the compound ones — to modify verbs and adjectives as well as nouns. They could thus say either "Hē sang *glæde*" or "Hē sang *glædlice.*" Grammarians often say that this case form "developed into an adverb," but there was no perceptible development; our ancestors were simply broadminded about their modifiers.

During the Middle English period the feeling somehow arose that the *-ly* ending was the natural way to form adverbs, and the general pattern for such pairs as *beautiful-beautifully* was firmly set. Some old adjectives in *-ly* remained, and still do — *manly, friendly, goodly,* and so forth; and the adverbial use of some of the short forms, such as *fast* and *hard,* continues to be recognized. But other "flat adverbs" such as *quick* and *slow* are often condemned as incorrect, though they have been in continuous respectable use ever since Old English times.

Prepositions, Conjunctions, and Interjections

These three classes of words were uninflected in Old English, as they are now. The first two have considerably increased in number, so that we can show connections more precisely than used to be possible. We can think of no other useful generalizations to make about them.

Summary of Old English Inflections

Old English nouns, pronouns, and adjectives were inflected to indicate gender, number, and case. The adjectives were also inflected for comparison (*big, bigger, biggest*). Verbs were inflected for person, number, tense, and mood, and there were a few traces (too slight to be worth discussing in this chapter) of inflection for voice. These are the only kinds of form changes that are recognized as inflections. Such endings as *-ish, -ly, -ment,* and the *-er* in *baker* (as distinguished from the *-er* in *bigger*) are called *derivational suffixes* rather than inflections. There is positively nothing to gain by wondering whether such endings are "really" inflections or not. The classification is arbitrary.

We have now lost the inflections for gender, person, mood, and voice so thoroughly that the few remaining traces can be (and sometimes are) treated as isolated idioms, without ever mentioning these grammatical concepts. The other four kinds of inflection are still active, though not nearly so necessary for communication as they used to be.

"The Creation"

Here is a somewhat longer passage to investigate, taken from a sermon by Ælfric, Abbot of Eynsham, usually considered the greatest writer of Old English prose. It is followed by a quite literal translation, and a recommended way of studying it is indicated below.

> Ealle gesceafta, heofonas and englas, sunnan and monan, steorran and eorðan, ealle nytenu and fugelas, sæ and ealle fiscas God gesceop and geworhte on six dagum; and on ðam seofoðan dæge he geendode his weorc, and geswac ða and gehalgode ðone seofoðan dæg, forðan ðe he on ðam dæge his weorc geendode. And he beheold ða ealle his weorc ðe he geworhte; and hie wæron ealle swiðe gode. Ealle ðing he geworhte buton ælcum antimbre. He cwæð: "Geweorðe leoht!" And ðærrihte wæs leoht geworden. He cwæð eft: "Geweorðe heofon!" And ðærrihte wæs heofon geworht, swa swa he mid his wisdome and mid his willan hit gedihte. He cwæð eft, and het ða eorðan ðæt heo sceolde forðlædan cwicu nytenu. And he ða gesceop of ðære eorðan eall nytencynn and deorcynn, ealle ða ðe on feower fotum gað: ealswa eft of wætere he gesceop fiscas and fugelas, and sealde ðam fiscum sund and ðam fugelum fliht; ac he ne sealde nanum nytene ne nanum fisce nane sawle, ac heora blod is heora lif, and swa hraðe swa hie beoð deade, swa beoð hie mid ealle geendode. Forðy is se man betera, gif he gode geðihð, ðonne ealle ða nytenu sindon; forðan ðe hie ealle gewurðað to nahte, and se man is ece on anum dæle, ðæt is on ðære sawle; heo ne geendeð næfre.[9]

The text is here slightly normalized, to avoid a few unrewarding complications; the punctuation is modernized; and so is the alphabet except for the character ð. It has been translated as follows:

> All creatures, heavens and angels, sun and moon, stars and earth, all beasts and birds, the sea and all fishes God created and wrought in six days; and on the seventh day he ended his work and ceased, and hallowed the seventh day, because on that day he ended his work. And he beheld then all his works that he had wrought, and they were all exceedingly good. All things he wrought without any matter. He said, "Let there be light," and instantly there was light. He said again, "Let there be heaven," and instantly heaven was made, as he with his wisdom and his will had appointed it. He said again, and bade the earth bring forth living cattle, and he then created of earth all the race of cattle, and the brute race, all those which go on four feet; in like

[9] Kaiser, p. 1.

manner of water he created fishes and birds, and gave the power of swimming to the fishes, and flight to the birds; but he gave no soul to any beast, nor to any fish; but their blood is their life, and as soon as they are dead they are totally ended. Therefore is man better, if he grow up in good, than all the beasts are; because they will all come to naught, and man is in one part eternal, that is in the soul; that will never end.

Analyzing "The Creation"

No one method of studying language works best for everybody, but many students have found it profitable to follow the steps indicated here:

1. Go over the original twice, rather slowly but without strain, to see how much you can get from it with no outside help and no great effort. Probably it won't be very much — a number of words, a few phrases that are clear, and perhaps a few more that you feel you almost understand. It will of course help a good deal if you are familiar with the Bible.
2. Read the translation twice, rather carefully.
3. Go over the original again, without referring to the translation, and see how much more you can now understand. Certainly some words that meant nothing at the first approach will now be clear. You will get much better results if you try to *read* it this time, pronouncing the words, at least mentally, and grouping them for rhythm as the punctuation suggests. Most important, don't let yourself translate anything you don't have to. By now, for instance, you will certainly know what "heofonas and englas, sunnan and monan" are — let them be that, and don't blight your progress by calling them something else.
4. Now — and only now — go back and forth between the original and the translation. At this stage a pencil can be very useful. (But *not* a pen — by no means a pen.) Under each word that still seems either meaningless or arbitrary draw a line. In the first three lines you might have to mark *gesceafta, nytenu, fugelas,* and *gesceop*. Look at the words for each of these in the translation, and see if you can find any clue as to how the Old English words can mean what they do. *Fugelas* is not too hard. Try *ou* instead of *u* as in *ure-our,* and a *w* instead of *g* as in *gehalgod-hallowed*. That gives you *fouwelas,* and it is not hard to believe that our word for barnyard birds could have once meant birds of all kinds.

Then there is *nytenu* for *beasts*. If you have never heard of neat's foot oil you may have to give up on this one. But if you have, and know that *neat* once meant *cattle,* you will realize that still earlier it could have had a broader meaning. *Gesceafta* and *gesceop* are definitely harder, but they do offer some clues. First, they look as if they might be related, and the fact that they are translated as *creatures* and *created* confirms this. You should remember from the Lord's Prayer that an initial *ge-* regularly disappeared later, so that you can disregard this element. You then have *sceafta* and *sceop*. You will soon find out that you have to be a little broadminded about Old English vowels; but if the words are related the consonants must be either identical or related. Now *p* and *f* are both labials, so that a relation is at least possible. You can't be sure, but it looks promising. And *fiscas* for *fish* shows that *sc* can change to *sh,* so that the words must be pronounced something like *shaft* and *shop*. You can't make anything directly from *shaft,* so try *shop*. "God created everything, God shop everything." No. Let's be broadminded about vowels. "God created everything, God *shap* everything, God *shape* everything"—that's it. God *shaped* everything. So then the *sceafta* must be the *shapings* — "the things he created or shaped."

You may now think we are making it sound much easier than it really is, and perhaps you are right. Certainly you will miss some relations that seem obvious after they are pointed out, and you will sometimes go off on a false track. This sort of examination takes a good deal of effort, and some of the effort is wasted, but on the whole it is much more effective than simply trying to memorize equivalents.

Now you may want to see how many other words you can figure out for yourself before examining the clues given below; but here are some more things you should, sooner or later, consider. The words are given in the order of their appearance rather than alphabetically.

· *englas* · This word, originally Greek, but borrowed into English from Latin, became so thoroughly a part of the language that it is treated exactly like a native word, both in the change of *a* to *e* and in the form of its inflectional ending. It is the only word in the passage of foreign origin.

· *geworhte* · Our two words *worked* and *wrought* go back to this source. If you remember that *h* was pronounced $/\chi/$, you can see that the form *work* is an easy development. *Wrought* is an example of *metathesis,* which means the shift of a vowel sound to the other side of a consonant sound. This change is particularly likely to happen when the consonant is a "rolled r." There is a tendency for an extra vowel to develop on the other side. Then the new vowel may get the stress that was originally on the old one. Finally, the old vowel drops out. A clear example is the Old English ð*urh,* which developed first into *thorough* (preserved in a special meaning), then into *through.* In *third,* from older *thrid,* the movement was the other way.

· *seofoðan* · The *n* of *seventh,* which is missing here, was probably preserved in Anglian, though it may have been restored by analogy.

· *weorc* · Notice that *weorc* has the same form in the accusative singular and plural. Sometimes the form of the modifying adjective will tell which it is. Sometimes you have to guess from the context.

· *forðan* · This word, and *forðy,* which occurs a few lines further along, are both compounded of the word *for* and a case form of the word ð*æt.* It may seem curious that one is translated *because* and the other *therefore,* but consider these sentences: He sat down because he was tired.
He was tired; therefore he sat down.

· ð*e* · The word *the* originated as an unstressed form of *that.* The unstressed ð*e* is often used after a stressed form (here ð*an*), apparently to give a little extra flexibility. It need not be translated.

· *hie* · We have now differentiated the initial sounds of *he, she, it,* and *they,* but in Old English all forms of the third-person pronoun began with *h.* Compare *heora* for *their,* and the feminine form *heo,* used to refer to the feminine noun *sawle.*

· *antimbre* · The prefix *an-* can be disregarded.

· *cwæð* · The spelling with *qu* was introduced during the Middle English period by French scribes, who had no *w* in their alphabet.

· *forðlædan* · Notice that this compound is exactly equivalent to *produce,* which literally means "lead forward."

· *nytencynn* · The kin (race) of domestic animals.

· *deorcynn* · *Deor* meant any wild animal before it was specialized to mean a specific kind.

· *sealde* · The past tense of *syle,* which occurs in the Lord's Prayer.

· *ne* · This was the original word for *not.* It could be made more emphatic by expanding to the phrase *ne a wiht — not a bit* (*whit*). This later contracted, first to *naught,* later to *not. Ne* also can mean *nor.*

· *hraðe* · *H* later dropped out of the initial combinations *hl, hn,* and *hr.* Nothing is *rathe* nowadays except a poetic primrose, but we still have *rather,* which is exactly equivalent to *sooner,* though used in a more limited way.

· *beoð* · Our modern verb "to be" is a mixture of four verbs, *aren, beon, sindan,* and *wesan,* each of which was once complete.

· *dæle* · The meaning *part* is preserved in the phrase "a good deal of," and in the term for giving each card player his share of the cards.

There remain, of course, a number of words that have left no traces in the language, such as *geswac* and *gedihte;* and a few others, such as *ælcum* (modern *each*) which have changed so much in meaning that recognizing the relation is of no particular help. But a very large part of the Old English prose vocabulary will yield to this sort of examination. You will not, of course, remember permanently everything that has been said about every word discussed above; but you won't forget it all, either. If you make a serious attempt to learn Old English (or any other language) it is very economical to spend a good deal of extra time at first in a close examination of this sort. If you do, your knowledge will soon snowball, and you'll save a great deal more time than you have used up.

Once you have made the examination, go back to Ælfric's original, and see how many of the underlinings you can now afford to erase, because the words now mean something to you. And if you have written in the meanings of any of the words, erase them, too. You can't really read the original if your eye is attracted by a translation. If you have no interest in learning a language, and desire only to avoid embarrassment in case your instructor asks you to translate something in class, you can afford to gloss freely and indelibly with a pen. Otherwise not.

You will notice also that some words appear in different forms, for instance *fiscas* as a direct object, but *fiscum* as an indirect object; but these inflectional endings are not as much needed as they would be in Latin, because there has already been a good deal of development toward a standard word order — which is, of course, one reason why they soon disappeared. There are, however, many sentences in Old English that are misleading unless you pay close attention to the significance of the endings.

Vocabulary Replacements

A closer look at the translation will also show some interesting things about the difference in vocabulary between Old and Modern English. (The translation is not ours, because we did not want to take any chance of either exaggerating or minimizing the difference.) Here it is again, this time with every word that is not of Old English origin in italics:

> All *creatures,* heavens and *angels,* sun and moon, stars and earth, all *beasts* and birds, the sea and all fishes God *created* and wrought in six days; and on the seventh day he ended his work and *ceased,* and hallowed the seventh day, *because* on that day he ended his work. And he beheld then all his works that he had wrought, and *they* were all *exceedingly* good. All things he wrought without any *matter.* He said, "Let there be light," and *instantly* there was light. He said again, "Let there be heaven," and *instantly* heaven was made, as he *with* his wisdom and his will had *appointed* it. He said again, and bade the earth bring forth living *cattle,* and he then *created* of earth all the *race* of *cattle,* and the *brute race,* all those which go on four feet; in like *manner* of water he *created* fishes and birds, and gave the *power* of swimming to the fishes, and flight to the birds; but he gave no soul to any *beast,* nor to any fish; but *their* blood is *their* life, and as soon as *they* are dead *they* are *totally* ended. Therefore is man better, if he grow up in good, than all the *beasts* are; *because they* will all come to naught, and man is in one *part eternal,* that is in the soul; that will never end.

In the original the only borrowed word is *angels,* which expresses a concept that simply did not exist in English until it was introduced by Christianity; but in the translation a seventh of the words are from Danish, French, or Latin sources. There is nothing fancy about these borrowings. Ælfric's sermon was clearly addressed to rather simple people, and the translator has apparently tried to reflect the directness and naturalness of the style. He has to say *beasts* or *animals* (also from French) instead of *nytenu,* because no Old English synonym has survived. He could of course have translated *ðærrihte* as *right then* instead of *instantly,* but some readers would find that almost humorously chummy. In short, all the borrowed words are familiar, and most of them are so much a part of our everyday thinking that it is rather hard to believe we could ever have managed without them. Our language has been greatly enriched by such borrowings, but we have lost something, too. *Swiðe,* once you are used to it, is more direct and forceful than the rather artificial *exceedingly;* and though we can still say *flight* for *fliht,* we now have to say *the power of swimming* where Ælfric could say simply *sund.*

"Caesar's Invasion"

It naturally requires reading of a good deal more material than can be included in this book to develop anything like a mastery of Old English; but the prose, at least, is not as hard as it is sometimes made to seem, if it is approached by analysis, not as a mechanical exercise in memory. One more selection is offered, with no clues other than a few glosses, as a sort of aptitude test.

> Æfter þæm þe Romeburg getimbred wæs syx hunde wintra and seofon and syxtig, Romane gesealdon Gaiuse Juliuse seofon legan, to þon þæt he sceolde fif winter winnan on Gallie. Æfter þæm þe he hie oferwunnen hæfde, he for on Britannie þæt iglond, and wiþ þa Bryttas gefeaht, and gefliemed wearþ on þæm londe þe mon hæt Centlond. Raþe þæs he gefeaht eft wiþ þa Bryttas on Centlonde, and hie wurdon gefliemede. Heora þridde gefeoht wæs neah þære ie þe mon hæt Temes, neah þæm forda þe mon hæt Welengaford. Æfter þæm gefeohte him eode on hond se cyning and þa burgware þe wæron on Cirenceastre, and siþþan ealle þe on þæm iglonde wæron.[10]

legan, legions
winnan, to make war
geflieman, to put to flight
raþe, soon after
eode on hond, surrendered
burgware, citizens

The Latin Element in Old English

It is easy to find examples of Old English that show more foreign influence than the passage from Ælfric. A few dozen words had been borrowed from Latin even before the tribesmen left the continent. These mostly reflected Roman activities in war, road building, and trade, along with their considerably more advanced cuisine. Thus we find *camp* (battle), *pil* (javelin), *weall* (wall), *stræt* (road), *mil* (mile), *pund* (pound), *mynet* (coin), *win* (wine), *cytel* (kettle), *cycene* (kitchen), *cuppa* (cup), *disc* (dish), *ciese* (cheese), *and pise* (pea). One reason that we know many

[10] From King Alfred's translation of Orosius, Kaiser, p. 56.

of these words are borrowings from Latin rather than Germanic cognates is that they have not undergone the consonant shift covered by Grimm's Law. If they had come straight down from Indo-European, *camp, ciese, cuppa,* and *cytel* would begin with *h* rather than *c, pise* and *pund* with *f* rather than *p,* and so forth. And even if they did not occur in surviving manuscripts we could tell that some were early borrowings because their vowels have changed in exactly the same way as the vowels of native words in the same relative positions, whereas words borrowed much later have been preserved in a form much closer to their Latin originals. When related forms appear in a number of other Germanic dialects as well as English, we assume a continental origin.

Between their coming to England and their conversion to Christianity the English borrowed no more from the Latin than from the Celtic vocabulary of the Romanized Britons. The word *castra,* which meant first a military camp, later any walled and inhabited place, is about the only one we can be sure of. This occurs in a great many place names, usually as *-caster* in the north (*Lancaster*) and as *-cester* or *-chester* in the south (*Worcester, Winchester*).

After the conversion to Christianity began, borrowings from Latin were naturally increased. We cannot always be sure whether a word was borrowed before the move from the continent or in the early part of the seventh century, and a few of the words in the list on p. 101 may belong to this period. Others include many words connected with the new religion and with the living habits of the missionaries and their successors, who obviously imported a few characteristic garments and household furnishings and a great many vegetables, herbs, shrubs, and even trees.

How much the form of a Latin word changed after getting into English depends on three things. First, the sounds of which it was composed, because some sounds are, during any period, more stable than others. An extreme example is the Indo-European word for *mouse,* which came down in Latin and in English in the identical form *mūs,* because none of the three phonemes of which it is composed underwent any change in either the Italic or the Germanic branch during this period. More generally, during the development of English, short vowels have been far more stable than long ones, and both the dental and the labial consonants have been more stable than the velar ones.

Second in importance is the date of entry. During the seventh century the change known as *umlaut,* a kind of vowel-attraction, was active in

English. In its most important form, a front vowel in the second syllable of a word has the effect of changing the vowel in the first syllable from a back to a front position. Because the vowel in the second syllable later disappeared in English, and other changes occurred to complicate the picture, umlaut is rather too complex to discuss intelligibly here, but we can mention three things about it: it is the cause of such irregular plurals as *men, mice,* and *feet,* and the irregular past tenses of some weak verbs; it explains why the vowels in all forms of some words are farther forward than those in cognate words in other languages (*bench,* compared to *bank* borrowed from French); and it affected only those Latin words that came in before the end of the seventh century.

The third factor is the kind of usage into which words come. Those used by everybody tend to change much more than those known only to the educated minority. The effect of this difference is particularly obvious in pairs of words from the same root, one with a tangible reference known to everybody, the other a more abstract word that most people had no occasion to use. Such pairs as *deacon* and *diaconate, bishop* and *episcopal, pope* and *papacy* are examples.

It is often impossible to tell whether a conservative form is the result of late borrowing or learned use, because the question of just when a foreign word becomes a part of English is by no means simple. Lexicographers can often date the earliest appearance of a word in a surviving manuscript; but a word may have been used for centuries before it happens to appear in writing that has been preserved. On the other hand, a writer may at any time use a foreign word that does not really become a part of the language until much later, if ever.

At any rate, between four and five hundred words of Latin origin appear in Old English manuscripts. About a hundred of them do not seem to have been completely naturalized, and a good many others — like many native words — later went out of use; but most of them have been part of the language ever since. Because we have continued to borrow from Latin, some of them have been reintroduced in a form nearer the original. Thus we have *monastery,* whose unchanged vowel shows that it is a later borrowing than *minster* — both from *monasterium.* Such pairs as these are called *doublets. Mint* from *moneta* has the doublet *money,* originally from the same source, but coming into English through French, where the sound changes were quite different. Still later we based *monetary* directly on the Latin word.

The Scandinavian Element

Another language that had an important influence on Old English was Scandinavian, although most of the evidence of that influence does not appear in writing until the Middle English period. The Danes and Norwegians who first raided and then settled in England during the latter half of the Old English period spoke North Germanic dialects that had much the same basic vocabulary as the West Germanic dialects of the Angles and Saxons, though they differed considerably in their inflectional endings and in the development of a few of the phonemes. Moreover, the Scandinavians had much in common with the English in ancestry, traditions, and way of life. Once they adopted Christianity — which they agreed and began to do after their defeat by Alfred in the battle of Ethandun in 878 — there was no major obstacle to prevent their blending with the English far more completely than the English had ever mingled with the British.

The amalgamation of the two groups was far from peaceable. There were periods of bitter fighting between the English and the Danes almost until the time of the Norman conquest; but then there had always been bitter fighting among the English themselves, and no doubt would have been more if the Danes had never come. We should not forget that loyalties during this period were primarily personal rather than national. In the later battles between the Danes and the English the "Danish" armies from the northeast undoubtedly included a good many Englishmen; and if the English armies from the southwest did not include Danes, it was only because there were not many Danes in that part of England.

Under these circumstances it was inevitable that the two languages should modify each other. Before they died out completely (which was not until well into the Modern English period) the Scandinavian dialects were undoubtedly influenced by English, though they left no written records to prove this; and English — at first locally and then nationally — was greatly influenced by Scandinavian.

It is hard to measure this influence with anything like precision, for several reasons. For one thing, such classifications as North and West Germanic are arbitrary, and the language of the Angles was in some ways more like that of the Scandinavians than that of the Saxons. Moreover, it was Anglian territory that the Danes settled in, and manuscripts preserved from any part of this territory are extremely scarce. It is therefore often impossible to tell whether a word or form that does not appear in writing until much later was originally Scandinavian, Anglian, or a combination of both, and there is naturally some disagreement among scholars about the probabilities. The complete accuracy of the word lists and statistics given below cannot, therefore, be guaranteed, and it would not be useful to attempt here a minute examination of all the evidence; but the picture presented seems to be approximately correct.

First, more than 1,400 Scandinavian place-names appear in England, of which the most easily recognizable contain such endings as *-by, -thorpe,* and *-thwaite.* Then the general standard vocabulary has about nine hundred words almost certainly of Scandinavian origin, and about as many more which are probably Scandinavian or which clearly show some Scandinavian influence. And finally, nonstandard dialects hold some thousands of Scandinavian words that are certainly English to the speakers of these dialects. In general, the Scandinavian coloring is stronger the farther north we go. It is particularly strong in Lowland Scottish, as we can see from the poetry of Robert Burns. And of course it is always possible for a word in any dialect to move into the standard language, so that we have probably not seen the last of importations yet. Moreover, the mere number of borrowed words, even if we count everything possible, does not indicate the full strength of the Danish influence. The nature of these borrowings must also be considered.

In general the English borrowed from Latin only words that they needed to indicate new things or new ideas introduced by the Romans. They are all from the "open" parts of speech — nouns, verbs, adjectives, and adverbs. We are still borrowing words of these kinds from many languages, and inventing new ones, mainly from Greek and Latin roots. They are important additions to our language; but they do not greatly affect its structure, and they do not very often drive native words out of the language.

The Danish influence was quite different and much more intimate. There were comparatively few new words for new things and ideas, such as technical war, shipping, and legal terms, and most of these have not survived, though *law* and *outlaw* are interesting exceptions. Most of the borrowings were of everyday terms, and many of them drove out established English words. The nouns *egg, fellow, freckle, garden, guess, leg, root, skin,* and *sky;* the verbs *call, get, give,* and *take;* the adjectives *flat, loose, low, odd,* and *weak* — these are only a few of the more surprising importations.

Even more remarkable are the words *they, their,* and *them, both* and *same, till,* and *with.* These are not mere items in the vocabulary, but parts of the basic structure of the language. It is true that they are not many, but it is almost incredible that there should be any at all, because such words are just not borrowed from one language by another. Even the form *are* is often attributed to Danish influence, though it can also be traced to Anglian.

In form we may divide the Danish borrowings into three classes: those identical, except for their inflectional endings, with their English equivalents; those recognizably related to their equivalents, but with some difference of sound; and completely unrelated synonyms. Of the third class there is not very much to say. It is certainly surprising that the English gave up *niman* for *take* and *welkin* for *sky,* but they did. With words of the first class we can prove a borrowing only when we know (from later Old Norse literature) that the Scandinavian meaning was different from the English one. Thus *with* is common to both languages, but in Old English it meant *against,* a meaning preserved in the combinations *withstand* and *notwithstanding.* In Scandinavian it had the sense of accompaniment, a meaning expressed in Old English by *mid.* If we say, about the two world wars, that we fought *with* the British, we are using the word in its Scandinavian sense; but if we say that we and the British fought *with* the Germans we are using it in its original English sense. Probably the most important effect of words that were identical in the two languages except for their endings is that they increased the tendency to drop these endings almost entirely.

The most interesting Scandinavian borrowings are those of the second class, consisting of obviously related words with some difference in their sounds. The principal correspondences are these:

1. Germanic /g/ remained /g/ in all positions in Scandinavian, but changed to /j/ (usually spelled *y*) before a front vowel and to /i/ (usually spelled *i* or *y*) after one in English. Chaucer's normal form of *give* is *yive* or *yeve,* but the modern form is of Scandinavian origin. So too is the form *egg,* of which the normal English development was *ei,* which is found in Chaucer, and was still competing with *egg* in Caxton's time.

2. The other velar stop, /k/, also remained in Scandinavian, but changed to /tʃ/ in English. Thus *cyrice,* borrowed from Greek through Latin, has given us the two words *kirk* and *church.*

3. The combination /sk/ remained in Scandinavian but changed to /ʃ/ in English. If you drop a porcelain cup on a hard floor, the cup will probably *shatter* while the pieces of it *scatter.*

4. The Germanic diphthong /ɑi/ developed differently in the two languages, eventually resulting in /ei/ (spelled in various ways) in our words from Scandinavian, and /ou/ (usually spelled *o*) in our words from Old

English. Examples are *nay* along with *no* and *hale* along with *whole* (the *w* in this word is a late spelling convention). There were some other differences in vowel development, but they are too complicated to be discussed here.

When both the Scandinavian and the Old English form survived we may get either a regional difference like that between *kirk* and *church,* or a semantic difference like that between *scatter* and *shatter* or between *hale,* with its more limited meaning, and *whole.* The Old English *scyrte* and its Scandinavian equivalent both meant a long, smocklike garment. The time came when it might be called either a skirt or a shirt — a rather wasteful pair of synonyms. Somehow both terms became specialized, *skirt* for the lower half and *shirt* for the upper. The same sort of thing happened with *dike* and *ditch,* both of which used to mean both the trench and the long mound formed alongside it by the earth removed. Here the Scandinavian form has been specialized to mean the upper part, and the Old English one the lower. Other comparable pairs, now specialized, are *yard* (which comes from *geard,* so that the change to /y/ is normal) and *garden, shrub* and *scrub* (in its botanical sense), and probably *shell* and *scale* (of a fish).

With the scarcity of written evidence that has come down to us it is impossible to know just when each of these words came to be habitually used in English; and it is sometimes impossible to be sure whether a word with such a typically Scandinavian beginning as /sk/ was actually borrowed from Scandinavian, or was merely a Scandinavian mispronunciation (which eventually became established as correct) of an Old English word beginning with /ʃ/. When two sounds compete there is bound to be some confusion. We have the two words *screech* and *shriek.* Obviously they ought to be *shreech* and *scriek,* each a respectable descendant of its own tradition. Instead we have two hybrid forms.

Even before the Norman Conquest some French words began to appear in Old English, but they were so few in comparison with those which came in during the Middle English period that it is not worthwhile discussing them here. And because the greater number of Latin borrowings occur rather seldom, most of the writing that has come down to us is so thoroughly Germanic that a German or Scandinavian student can learn to read it with rather less effort than an English or American one; many of the words that have completely disappeared in Modern English have cognates still in use in the other Germanic languages. It seems unfair; but the tables are turned with Middle English, in which a native speaker can recognize innumerable words that have no meaning in Scandinavian or German.

5

The Middle English Period

The Norman Conquest

The pivotal event in English history, linguistically as well as otherwise, was the conquest by the Normans in 1066. The Anglo-Saxon invasion had been simply a movement of Germanic tribes to a new territory. These tribes pretty well cleared out all traces of what had preceded them, and went on living very much as they had on the continent. Their conversion to Christianity of course modified many of their values and attitudes, and for a while they added a considerable development of learning to their ordinary pursuits of fighting and farming. When the Danes conquered much of England the result was a setback rather than a forward step; these invaders wiped out most of the progress that had been made, and had very little new to contribute. In the six centuries before the Conquest England had been a unified kingdom for only two brief periods — about forty years in the middle of the tenth century, and about twenty years under the Dane, Cnut, in the early part of the eleventh. It had never really been an organized country. The Normans not only unified it quickly and more or less permanently, but brought in a very different language and culture. By the time they were finally absorbed by the English both the country and the language were unlike anything else in the world.

The kingdom of Cnut collapsed under his successor in 1042. Edward the Confessor, a legitimate English claimant who had grown up in exile in Normandy, was called to the throne, and was nominal king for the next twenty-four years. Actually the country was ruled by a number of independent and highly competitive earls, the most important of whom was Harold of Wessex. Edward was much admired (by interested people) for his piety and generosity to the church. There was not much else to admire him for, and he was a very ineffectual king. His sympathies and interests remained French rather than English, and he brought French favorites to take important positions at his court. Being childless, he also seems to have promised to make his second cousin, William, Duke of Normandy, his heir. He had no right whatever to do this, but it gave William a claim of sorts. The natural heir was Harold; but he had once been a prisoner of William's and (according to William) had promised, for the sake of his freedom, not to contest the latter's claim.

When Edward died in 1066 Harold was elected king and immediately faced trouble on two sides. The Norwegians had raised an army to invade England from the north, and William was preparing to cross the Channel. Harold defeated the Norwegians, but in the same year William defeated him at the Battle of Hastings. The fight was close, but when it was over the English had no organization with which to continue an effective resistance. In a remarkably short time William not only gained control of all England but organized it so thoroughly that it has been essentially one country ever since.

A little must be said about his background. Shortly after Alfred's victory in 878 had stopped the Danish expansion in England (and possibly for this reason), Scandinavian bands began taking over a part of northern France. They were called *Northmen* (*North-manni* or *Nortmanni* in contemporary manuscripts), and in a later contraction, *Normans*. Their history in Normandy was quite different from that of the Germanic conquerors of England. They took over the political and military control of their new territory both more rapidly and more efficiently than the English did; but they adopted the language as well as many of the customs of the people they had conquered. We can only guess why. Maybe they married more of the native women, and paid more attention to them. Maybe they, unlike the English, were impressed by the higher civilization they found. None of the explanations offered really seems adequate, but the fact remains that within a surprisingly short time they were speaking a sort of French and had apparently dropped their old language entirely.

The Feudal System

They also adopted the system of feudal tenure that had been developing in the continental remains of the Roman Empire — a system that, with all its disadvantages, had the seeds of a stronger and more effective central government than was likely to come out of the loose and almost tribal organization in use among the other Germanic peoples. In theory feudalism was a neat pyramidal structure rising from the broad base of the peasantry through the levels of the nobility to the monarch at the top. The underlying principle was that nobody owned any land outright, but that each of the levels had rights in it, and duties connected with those rights. A king was lord of his whole realm, but because he obviously couldn't be everywhere at once, either to farm or protect it, he divided it into fiefs, each controlled by a vassal in chief. These owed the king a share of their crops, financial contributions on specified occasions, and above all a specified amount of military service. As long as they faithfully fulfilled these obligations they were lords within their own territories. The king could not legally take the land from them, and he had very little to say about how they managed it or how they ruled their subjects. Moreover, their rights passed to their heirs, and the king could not revise the original distribution even though he might see that it was not working out at all well.

In a similar way the large holdings of a vassal in chief would be divided among lesser noblemen, down to the simple knights, who were the lowest members of the ruling class. A knight's holding was parceled out to peasants, who did the actual farming and other physical work. They were bound to the land; that is, they could not leave to find a better place, nor could the knight take their holdings from them. They had to work and fight for him, but he had to protect them, just as his lord owed him protection in return for service. Except for the king at the top and the peasant at the bottom, everybody had duties extending both up and down, and could count on help from both above and below. It was a beautifully symmetrical and strongly interlaced structure.

But when we turn from theory to recorded practice we find that the symmetry has pretty well disappeared, and that its solidity and efficiency are delusive. To consider only a few of the more obvious distortions, fiefs changed hands by marriage, inheritance, and conquest. A nobleman who had collected a few might owe allegiance to several overlords, who might well be at war with one another, leaving an interesting question of where his true allegiance lay. A duke, or even a count, who had collected enough might become more powerful than his royal master. And it was perfectly possible for two nobles to owe feudal allegiance to each other for different parts of their holdings. Altogether, the possibilities of chaotic disturbances were plentiful, and the history of medieval Europe indicates that they were abundantly realized.

From humanitarian and democratic viewpoints there are all sorts of objections to the feudal system, but from the viewpoint of a reigning monarch the chief one was that a vassal might become sufficiently powerful to rise against the king. William had had enough experience on the continent to be well aware of this danger, and when he set up his own system in England he took appropriate precautions. Inevitably, he parceled out the kingdom among his followers, in proportion to their rank and value to him; but as far as possible he avoided giving them large, unified holdings. Instead, he gave them scattered fiefs which would be less likely to provide centers of power. He also took the unusual, though not original, precaution of insisting that each minor vassal should take an oath of allegiance directly to him, which took precedence over his duties to any intervening lord. And he reinforced his authority by instituting a system of royal courts throughout the kingdom, which further limited the powers of the nobles, and laid the foundations for the traditional English belief that a strong king was the people's best protection against an oppressive nobility. At the same time he let it be known that the old laws were still in effect except when they were specifically changed. The great importance of this was that the most effective laws in England were local customs rather than national edicts. The English in each district, even on each manor, already had a very strong determination to proceed according to tradition, and the royal attitude gave them some support. There were certainly times and places where they were horribly oppressed by their overlords, but they never sank to the position of the continental peasantry. The continuance of their old traditions had its effect in aiding the preservation of their language.

There is no evidence that William's restraint was caused by any kindly feelings. He was cold, selfish, avaricious, and utterly ruthless. He could, and on occasion did, slaughter thousands to make the point that rebellion was not profitable. But he took no pleasure in cruelty, and he was too intelligent to take any action that seemed likely to stir up more trouble than it was worth. Moreover, he wanted to encourage the theory that he was a legitimate successor to the throne rather than a simple invader. Above all, now that the kingdom was his he wanted it run as efficiently and as profitably as possible.

The Organization of the Country

Naturally most of the important positions in the country went to Normans and other Frenchmen. William did not want anybody in power who was not on his side. He apparently had no prejudice against Englishmen as such, and was quite willing to leave in authority anyone who would work with him, unless he needed the position for one of his own men — which he usually did. Feudal followers had to be rewarded if they were to remain faithful. Ecclesiastical positions of importance were treated in exactly the same fashion as secular ones. This was necessary on two counts. Not only was the church a more pervasive spiritual and social influence than it is to-day, but it was in control of much land, and of the laymen who worked, and on occasion defended, that land. A bishop or abbot therefore had to be considered in his feudal as well as his spiritual functions. Also, the church had a monopoly of education, so that a country simply could not be administered without what amounted to a clerical civil service.

We don't know how many Normans and other Frenchmen William brought to England, nor what proportion of them later returned to France. One estimate, which seems as reasonable as any other, is that about 20,000 of the foreigners stayed — enough to form an adequate cadre for the organization of the country. There was not, as far as we know, any concerted effort to drive out English. It was simply that the new ruling class naturally spoke French, and saw no reason to change. A few of them, usually not on the highest levels, had to learn enough English to give orders. Aside from that, if the English wanted to learn French, let them. Some did — it was one way to get ahead. A great many more of them had to learn some French words, and these words gradually became part of English.

For some two hundred years French remained the normal language of the nobility. During this period the kings and many nobles had possessions on both sides of the Channel, and divided their time between the two. On the whole they seem to have considered themselves Frenchmen who held estates in England, rather than Englishmen. But early in the thirteenth century this condition came to an end. In 1204 Normandy was permanently lost to the English crown, and during the next half-century the nobles either had to choose between their English and French holdings, or had that choice made for them. Those who kept their English holdings soon became English because there was no longer anything else for them to be.

This development of a national feeling among the nobility was probably assisted rather than delayed by a new wave of French influence. Henry III,

King of England from 1216 to 1272, was completely French in his sympathies, and imported thousands of Frenchmen to fill most of the important positions in his administration. These were not from Normandy, but from other provinces, and their speech was closer to the Central French from which the modern standard language has developed than to Norman French — especially as that was now spoken in England. Their influence probably did something to prolong the official use of French in England. On the other hand the Norman English, especially but not exclusively those they had displaced, naturally hated them, and began to feel much more English by contrast. By the end of the century French was dying out as the primary language even of the nobility, and during the fourteenth century it lost most of its official status. About 1350 English began to be used in the schools, and by 1386 it had pretty well superseded French there. In 1362 a parliamentary statute ordered the use of English in all lawsuits. The records of guilds, of towns, and of parliament itself were kept in French until well into the fifteenth century, but it is clear that this was a matter of traditional conservatism, and no longer reflected the language in which business was transacted.

The Submergence of English

Thus during several centuries English disappeared as an official language, and for the first few generations of this period it very nearly disappeared as a written one. From the Conquest to about 1200 the only English document of much importance that has come down is the Peterborough version of the Anglo-Saxon Chronicle, which contains annual entries running down to 1154. The language of the last few years shows some differences from that of the earlier ones, so that some scholars consider it the earliest Middle rather than the latest Old English. It seems reasonable to suppose that the Chronicle was kept up by a monk who was both old and old-fashioned, and that it breaks off when he died simply because there was no one left to continue it.

We have no reason to suppose that much other writing in English during this period has been lost. With the French in control of practically everything there can have been little reason to write English. At least above the primary level (about which we know very little) the language taught in the schools was Latin, which was still regarded as the one important language of Christendom, and used for the most important documents of all kinds.

The language in which Latin was taught was French, which was used, when Latin was inappropriate or impracticable, for all important affairs, as well as the everyday affairs of practically all people of either education or position. Who was to write in English, and why?

Accordingly, if we consider only the written language for this early period, we are likely to feel that English was almost swamped out of existence, and that it made a most remarkable comeback in the thirteenth and fourteenth centuries. But the fact is that English was always the only language of the great majority of the people; and in an age when so few of them were directly affected by education there was never any real chance that it would be supplanted.

The Diversity of Middle English

It is of course possible that in the years immediately after the Conquest many of the French really expected their language to become general throughout the country, but by 1200 it seems to have been obvious to everybody that this was not going to happen. If the ordinary people were to be reached at all, they had to be reached in their own language; and a large number of works, mostly for the good of their souls, were either composed in or translated into English of various sorts.

Because Old English has come down to us almost entirely in rather late West Saxon manuscripts, it is easy to think of it as a fairly uniform language; and our whole training encourages us to think of Modern English as basically a standard language with well-codified rules, fringed with a number of dialects, inferior in kind, which for most purposes do not have to be seriously considered. In the Middle English period, on the other hand, we are confronted with such a mass of conflicting material that it is very hard to keep in mind any consistent idea of what "the language" was. We can, if we like, talk of how the four major dialects developed — Northern, East Midland, West Midland, and Southern. Or we can add Kentish and talk of the five major dialects, or split some of the others and make it nine. Whichever number we use, we should realize that until the very end of the period none of them approached the status of a standard language for the whole country; and the differences between them were so great that we find scribes translating from one to another for the benefit of their neighbors. The following excerpts from Trevisa's translation (1387) of Higden's Latin *Polychronicon* give some idea of the situation. (The forms of the words have been modernized, but the syntax has not been altered.)

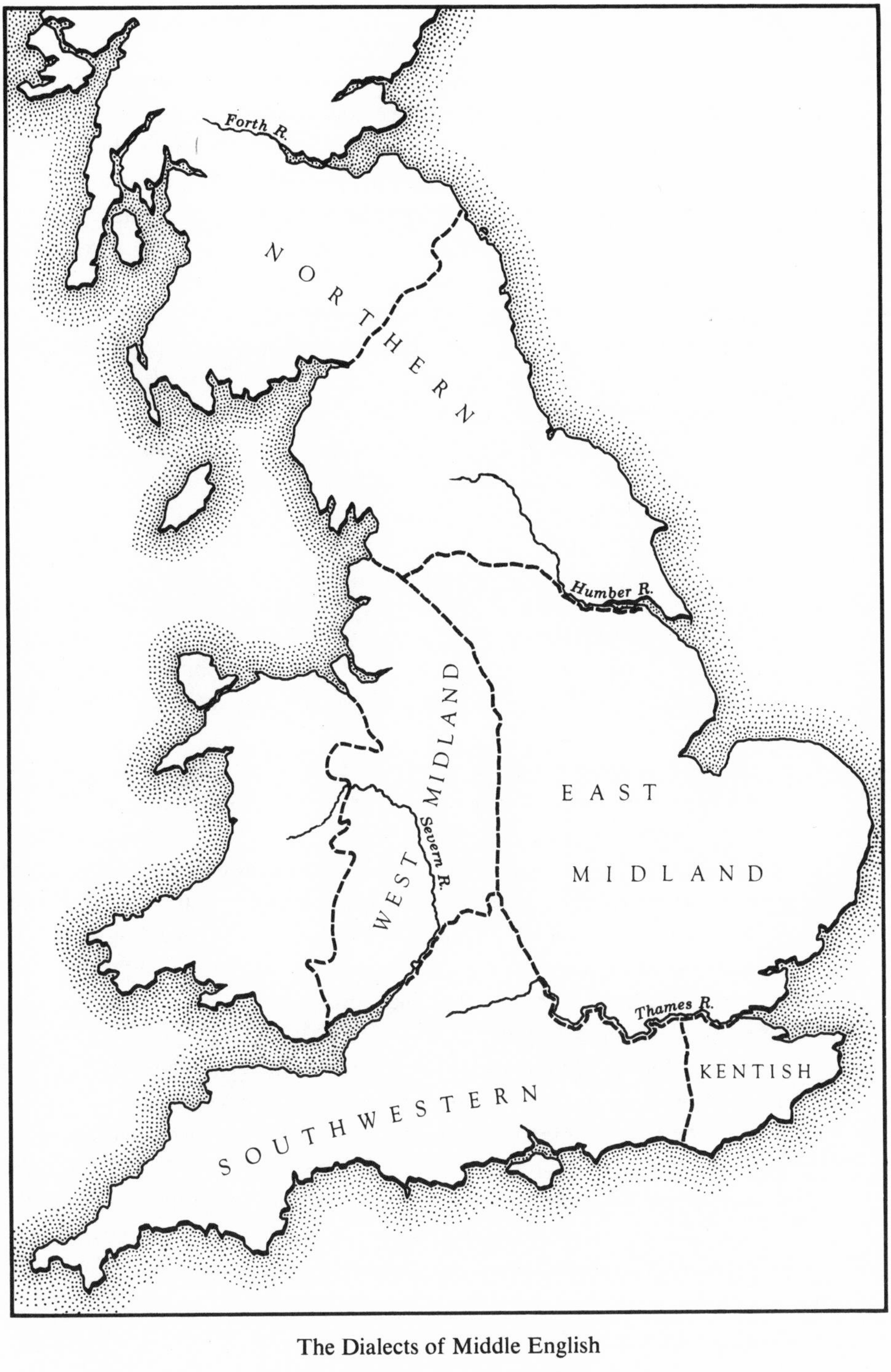

The Dialects of Middle English

> Also English men, though they had from the beginning three manner speech, southern, northern, and middle speech in the middle of the land, as they came of three manner people of Germania, nonetheless by mixing and mingling, first with Danes and afterward with Normans, in many the country language is impaired; and some use strange wlaffing, chytering, harring, and garring grisbitting. . . .
>
> . . . for men of the east with men of the west, as it were under the same part of heaven, accord more in sounding of speech than men of the north with men of the south. Therefore is it that Mercians, that be men of middle England, as it were partners of the ends, understand better the side languages, northern and southern, than northern and southern understand either other.
>
> All the language of the Northumbrians, and specially of York, is so sharp, slitting, and rasping, and unshaped, that we southern men may that language hardly understand.[1]

This passage contains some sectional bias. Those speakers who used the "strange wlaffing, chytering, harring, and garring grisbitting" might conceivably have had equally unpleasant things to say about other dialects; and the Yorkshiremen (unless they differed remarkably from their descendants) would have been very hard to convince of the superiority of Southern English. Moreover, the explanation of the origin of the differences is not quite accurate. We now trace the Northern dialect to Northumbrian, and the "middle speech" — East and West Midland — to Mercian, both of which were basically Anglian dialects in Old English times. The Southern dialect developed from the speech of the other two "manner people," though some scholars prefer to treat Kentish, which was of Jutish origin, separately. But at least the separate origins, the chief foreign influences, and the current diversity are all brought out.

Our knowledge of these dialects is far from complete, and there are differences of opinion on some points. What we think we know is based only in part on the surviving manuscripts. We also depend on forms and constructions that have persisted in the spoken dialects of Modern English. To take a very simple example, we believe that the Southern English voiced the /f/ and /s/ sounds at the beginnings of such words as *for* and *see,* as their descendants still do in some rural areas. Southern manuscripts support the

[1] Kaiser, pp. 516, 517.

voicing of the /f/ very thoroughly, because they usually spell *for* as *vor*. But they neither support nor contradict the voicing of the /s/, because most scribes did not use the letter *z* at all, but used *s* for the voiced as well as voiceless sounds, as we still do in many words today. It seems likely, however, that two such similar sound changes occurred about the same time; and because the /z/ pronunciation in Southern dialects is recorded in very early Modern English (as when Edgar poses as a peasant in *King Lear*), we have good reason to believe that it was current in Middle English.

Some Peculiarities of Middle English Manuscripts

We are so used to relying on careful editing and printing that it takes either a good deal of exposure or a strenuous effort of the imagination to realize what books were like before the new practices gradually developed. Some of the difficulties of copying long manuscripts, day after day, on very expensive material, are immediately obvious. Physical conditions did not make them easier — always a quill or reed pen, often a bad light, and little or no heat in an English winter. But we must add to these a complete lack of reference works, techniques, and above all established conventions which we now take for granted, but which took many generations after the introduction of printing to develop. During the whole of the Old and Middle English periods there was not a grammar, a dictionary, or even a spelling book of English in existence. There was not even complete agreement about the alphabet — either the letters of which it was composed or the sounds that some of these represented. And certainly nothing like the modern procedure of proofreading was in general use, for the apparently simple idea of reproducing anything with literal accuracy — that is, getting it right letter by letter — does not seem to have occurred to many people. After all, if the man you were copying spelled the same word in a number of ways, why should you be fussy? And even if he didn't, others did. An unusually careful scribe might copy word for word — or try to. A less particular one would copy sentence by sentence (if he could tell where all the sentence divisions were), introducing a good deal of variation, some of it intentional, some not. And a really broad-minded one would add, delete, or modify wherever he felt inclined to. The freedom with which even able and honorable scholars often altered their texts may seem utterly horrifying to a modern student who has been taught that it is sinful to make a silent correction of even a letter or a comma; but neither the conditions nor the traditions of modern accuracy had yet developed.

Even in Latin manuscripts of works whose text was particularly respected, and on which scholars had been busy for centuries, the variations that occur are amazing and sometimes completely bewildering. In English manuscripts all the difficulties are compounded. Consider the problems of a monk born in the north, belonging to a monastery in the midlands, and assigned to copy a manuscript composed in the south, a fairly simple case. Letter-by-letter copying would not only be painfully slow (have you ever tried to copy exactly an extensive passage in an unfamiliar dialect?), but worse than useless, because who wanted those silly southern perversions? He might try to do it word by word, but that brought up again and again and again the question of which form for each word — the one he had grown up with, the one his colleagues used, or the one he saw at the moment? Almost inevitably he would do a little of each. We may find it incredible, but there was simply no *right* way to spell anything, unless the scribe was a dogmatic reformer like Orrm (see pages 128–129), who invented his own rules — which nobody else ever followed. Otherwise each man's spelling had to be some sort of compromise between an attempt to represent the sounds he heard and a recollection of the way or ways he had most often seen a word spelled before.

And what should he do about completely unfamiliar words or forms in the strange dialect? Guess at them and substitute what seemed reasonable in his own dialect, or just copy them, rightly or wrongly (and some handwritings were hard to read even then) and leave the guessing to somebody else? Or compromise by trying to copy the word and adding a synonym or an explanation, right or wrong? We could go on with his problems, but we are trying to keep the case simple. It is easy to understand that our manuscripts seldom show any dialect in as pure a form as we should like to see it. Except for the very few autograph originals that have come down to us, any manuscript must be some kind of compromise between at least two idiolects, often separated by many miles and many years. And even an autograph manuscript is likely to reflect to some extent the author's reading in various dialects rather than simply the sounds of his own speech.

One result of this is that a student who has memorized the "characteristics" of a dialect, and then turns to a text authoritatively stated to be in that dialect, immediately finds a number of things that just shouldn't be there.

With the documentary evidence in such a confused state it does not seem useful, in an introductory book that covers as much ground as this one, to attempt a detailed account of the dialects through the centuries. To keep within reasonable bounds we are forced to discuss Middle English in general as if it were much more uniform than we know it was, with only occasional references to time and place. We can then come back to earth by examining rather casually a few assorted examples, and then quite closely a passage from Chaucer, whose dialect has three advantages: it is not far from the main line of development; it is comparatively easy to approach; and it is much the most rewarding. Finally there will be a selection from Malory, whose language, aside from the spelling and a few peculiarities of syntax, is almost modern. The *Companion* to this book has additional selections, arranged chronologically by dialect, for further study.

Sound Changes in Middle English

The most important sound changes that occurred in Middle English may be summarized as follows:

1. *Vowels.* Old English long *a* /ɑ:/ changed to long open *o* /ɔ:/ except in the Northern dialect. This open *o* changed again to long close *o* /o:/ early in the modern period. Thus *ban* eventually became *bone; ham, home;* and *stan, stone.* In each the silent final *e* is simply a spelling convention. Such forms as *bane, hame,* and *stane,* which can be found in the Border ballads and the poetry of Burns, are of course Northern. On the other hand, Old English short *a* lengthened in open syllables (that is, when followed by a single consonant followed by a vowel). This accounts for such words as *name* /nɑ:mə/, in which the *a* was originally short.

Old English *y* /y/, both long and short, unrounded to become /i:/ or /i/ except in the south, though the *y* spelling remained common.

2. *Diphthongs.* The original Old English diphthongs all simplified to become single vowels, and a new set of diphthongs developed. These changes are too complicated to be discussed here, but split development of *eo* is worth mentioning. In most of the country the second element dropped out, so that *bēo* gives us *bee* (Middle English /be:/, Modern English /bi:/),

trēo gives us *tree,* and so forth. But in the south the second element rounded the first one, so that we get such forms as *bo* and *tro,* pronounced like the German *ö*.

3. *Consonants.* Old English double consonants were pronounced as such. In Modern English the double pronunciation is used only when identical consonants are accidentally brought together in the formation of compounds, such as *bookkeeper* and *part-time*. Otherwise the double letter is used only as a spelling convention. The change occurred during the Middle English period, but cannot be precisely dated.

In the earliest English the letters *c* and *g* consistently had the "hard" values /k/ and /g/ wherever they occurred; but in West Saxon these sounds were fronted before the front vowels *e, i,* and *y*. In such positions /k/ became /tʃ/, /sk/ became /ʃ/, and /g/ became /j/. You will notice that each of these changes involves moving the tip of the tongue farther forward in the mouth to pronounce the consonant. It is thus a natural, though not inevitable, change to make in the neighborhood of a front vowel. There is a conflict of opinion (with evidence on both sides) about whether the same changes took place in Anglian territory and were later reversed under Scandinavian influence, or whether Anglian was always more like Scandinavian in this respect. But without doubt during the Middle English period the original sounds were current in the Northern dialect, and the fronted sounds were general in the rest of the country. This accounts for those contrasting pairs of words mentioned on pages 106–107, as well as for many other Northern variants found in Middle English texts.

In Old English the letter *h* was originally pronounced /χ/ in all positions. In Middle English, if not earlier, this weakened in the initial position to something like the modern /h/. Then it dropped out completely in the initial combinations *hl, hn,* and *hr*. In the south it also dropped out in the combination *hw,* but in the north it actually strengthened to a /k/ in this position.

The initial combinations *gn, kn,* and *wr* continued to be fully pronounced until the modern period.

Possibly as a result of French influence the two fricative sounds /f/ and /v/ became contrasting phonemes instead of allophones of the same phoneme; and so too did the /s/ and /z/ sounds. It seems reasonable to suppose that /θ/ and /ð/ became differentiated at the same time, though the evidence is less conclusive. This development did not spread to the south, where these fricatives were always voiced.

Loss of Inflections

On page 79 we pointed out that even before the ancestors of the English left the continent the heavy stress on root syllables characteristic of the Germanic languages had resulted in some slurring of the inflectional endings, so that originally distinct ones sometimes became identical; and that this alteration had continued throughout the Old English period. During the Middle English period it went much further. The /m/ of the dative in nouns and adjectives changed to /n/, and the vowel in all endings except the one indicating the present participle weakened to /ə/, occasionally written as *i, y,* or *u,* but generally as *e.* Later the /ən/, from whatever source, regularly (though not quite invariably) weakened to /ə/, and still later the /ə/ dropped. In early Middle English the present participle ended in *-and* in the north, *-end* in Midland territory, and *-ind* in the south. Later the modern form in *-ing* became general throughout the country, presumably by confusion with the verbal noun (gerund) in *-ing,* though the exact procedure followed is not clear. On the whole these changes took place most rapidly in the north and most slowly in the south.

Three explanations for the loss of inflections have been offered, each of which seems adequate until you think about it a little. The heavy Germanic stress must have had some effect — but look at Modern German. "Rubbing" with Scandinavian and later with French also sounds reasonable, with both sides learning root words but not bothering about endings; but in similar situations elsewhere this influence often failed to occur. And the idea that during the long period when English was spoken mainly by uneducated people the old inflections were too much of a strain to remember takes no account of the fact that they were developed and spoken for centuries by completely illiterate people. All we really know for sure about the loss is that it happened.

Borrowings from the French Vocabulary

There can, however, be no question about the influence of the French vocabulary. During the time when the invaders were in control of so many sides of life, their words for a great many things became *the* words, and were used in English as well as French. Many other borrowings, though less necessary, seem natural enough. The snobbery of the English probably accounted for some, and the laziness of the French for others. It is a very general rule that when two languages are in contact because of a conquest, the language of the conquered people is affected much more than that of the conquerors. We cannot tell how fast the French influence worked in speech. There have been studies of the rate at which French words appeared in English writing, but the picture they present must be considered very conservative. Aside from the fact that many words must have been current for generations before they happened to be used in a document that happened to be preserved, a good many Middle English authors say specifically that they are writing for people who know no French. It is reasonable to suppose that they would avoid any French words that were not thoroughly established, and perhaps many that were. For what the evidence is worth, when writings in English begin to reappear about 1200 they show no more than a sprinkling of French words. The number of new ones appearing grows steadily until about 1400, when it begins to taper off.

A good many of the words borrowed might be called technical terms in those areas where French influence was particularly strong, such as government, religion, law, and military affairs. To take just a few examples of each, we find under *government* not only that word itself but *assembly, authority, council, court, crown, empire, majesty, mayor, parliament, reign, royal, state, statute, tax,* and *treaty*. Under *religion* we have *baptism, clergy, communion, confession, creator, damnation, devotion, faith, friar, immortality, miracle, parson, pastor, reverence, saint, trinity,* and *vicar*. Under *law* (which rather curiously is not from French), we have *assault, attorney, bail, bar, bill, crime, decree, felon, fine, judge, justice, plaintiff, prison, sentence,* and *trespass*. And among our *military* terms are *arms, army, battle, captain, combat, defense, enemy, guard, lieutenant, navy, sergeant, siege, skirmish, soldier,* and *spy*. All these lists could be made very much longer, and we could add lists from other fields, such as social life and organization, food and clothing, learning and the arts. But perhaps these are enough to indicate some of the areas in which we would now be helpless without our French words. We should also notice that a large part of these are not gap-fillers, like so many of the earlier borrowings from Latin, but importations that drove out established native synonyms.

Moreover, it was not only in such special areas as these that large-scale borrowing occurred. Here are a few of the general-purpose words that came in: *able, age, aim, air, blank, brief, bucket, bushel, carry, charge, clear, cover, damage, debt, double, dozen, eager, easy, envy, error, face, fault, feeble, folly, gay, gentle, grain, grief, hardy, hasty, honor, horrible,* and so on down the alphabet. It would be hard for the most fanatical believer in "good old Anglo-Saxon" to avoid these words or a great many others just as much a part of our everyday language. But French did not, like Scandinavian, directly supply any function words. The few apparent exceptions were borrowed as full words, and only later developed their present uses. The word *cause* could be used in the phrase *by cause,* which coalesced into the new word *because;* and *during* meant *lasting* before developing the new and non-French meaning "throughout."

Irregularities in French Borrowings

Some of the borrowings listed above are spelled almost or exactly like Modern French words, although their pronunciation may be very different, because later sound changes in the two languages have not been parallel. Many other borrowings are not so easily recognizable, even in print, because Modern French spelling did not become frozen until after some changes in pronunciation, which had no effect across the Channel, occurred in France. The most useful to remember is the loss of *s* from the combination *st.* Thus initial (*e*)*st* normally became *et,* and medial or final *st* simply *t,* leaving such modern French-English pairs as *établir-establish, état-*(*e*)*state, étoffe-stuff, étrange-strange;* and *bâtard-bastard, bête-beast, côte-coast,* and *forêt-forest.* (Notice that the acute accent over the initial *e* and the circumflex accent over the medial vowel regularly though not quite invariably signal a lost *s* — often handy to know.) Most Modern French words in which the *s* remains in such positions are late borrowings from Latin.

Another cause of irregularity is that early French, like English, existed in various dialects; and the Norman one, from which most of the earliest borrowings came, had two especially important differences from Central French, the source of most of the later ones. (1) The initial Latin *ca* combination was preserved in Norman, but in Central French it changed to *ch* plus a vowel that varied according to the other sounds in the word. Often we borrowed the same word from both sources with some difference in meaning. Thus *catch, cattle,* and *cavalry* all come from Norman French, and *chase, chattel,* and *chivalry* are somewhat later borrowings from Central French. (2) Many Norman words begin with *w* and their Central equivalents begin with *gu.* Thus we have pairs like *warden* and *guardian, warranty* and *guarantee,* as well as words like *war* and *wasp* where Modern French has *guerre* and *guêpe*.

Another point to be considered is that words introduced from any other language by scholars writing or translating are often called "learned words," and those introduced in common speech are called "popular words" (the reference is to the populace, not popularity). There is no firm line between the two kinds, but a general difference is worth considering. Learned borrowings are more likely to retain their original form and meaning, because they are — as long as they remain "learned" — used mostly by people with more than an average interest in precision. Popular borrowings are more likely to be modified to resemble native words and to change with the general drift of the language. They are also likely to combine with native elements to make new compounds, and to extend their original meanings very freely.

Indirect Influence of French

Whether or not French influenced the changes in English structure, it certainly did more than add to the vocabulary. For one thing, its long use as the language of all important affairs delayed development of a standard dialect of English. In every European country regional dialects were in use more or less equally during the early part of the Middle Ages; and in every country one or another of these eventually attained the prestige of a national language. In France, the dialect of the Île de France — the country around Paris — won out quite early simply because that area became the center of power and influence, political, economic, and intellectual. It was not only the official language but the one generally adopted by influential people throughout the country. The assorted provincials brought into England by Henry III during the thirteenth century seem to have used it quite generally. But it was not until much later that the dialect of London won comparable prestige, simply because for some centuries French rather than any kind of English was the language of opportunity.

Moreover, the French borrowings were so extensive that they changed the whole balance of the language and prepared the way for the incomparable hospitality to words from other languages that English has shown ever since. The English vocabulary is now much the largest in the world, and well over half of it comes from French and Latin sources. It is often impossible to tell from which source an originally Latin word was borrowed; but even the direct Latin borrowings were certainly made easier because so many French words were already in the language.

Other Foreign Influences on Middle English

Direct borrowings from Latin not only continued but increased during the Middle English period. A list of examples would not be very informative, but they were almost entirely learned words, and the greater part came in by way of translations of Latin books. As a result, they have since undergone no such changes as affected the Old English popular borrowings. They were usually somewhat modified to make them seem legitimately English, as by changing the endings *-abilis* and *-atus* to *-able* and *-ate;* but the ease with which they could always be checked against their established Latin forms tended to prevent any further changes.

Most of the Scandinavian borrowings first appear in English documents during this period, though (see pages 104–105) they may have been in the spoken language for centuries. Moreover, their use was still spreading, so that many words found only in northern documents in the thirteenth century spread even to the London area by the fifteenth. There was also a sprinkling of words from many other languages, but not enough from any one for a sizable influence.

Loss of Native Words and Word Elements

With so many French and Latin words coming in, a considerable number of native words dropped out of use, in some instances apparently by simple cause and effect. It is easy to understand why *ætheling* gave way to *noble* at a time when almost all the nobility were French, and why the same sort of thing happened with technical terms for military affairs, the law, and so forth. It is not nearly so easy to understand why *earm* gave way to *poor* and *lyft* to *air*. In these and many other words no national principle seems to be involved. Moreover, not all the lost words were replaced by French or Latin ones. *Eek,* for instance, gave way to the equally English *also,* and *niman,* after some centuries of competition, to the Scandinavian *take*. Many of the changes can be explained only by the well-known (but itself unexplained) fact that gradual replacement of words is always occurring in every speech group, whether or not there is an outside source of supply. But the rate of turnover in England was certainly increased during this period. It is well known that more than half of our words come from French and Latin sources, but it is not generally realized that we have preserved a very much higher proportion of the Roman than of the Old English vocabulary. Something like five-sixths of the words recorded in Old English have disappeared. This figure is somewhat deceptive, because many of the lost words are recorded only in poetry and may never have had much currency in ordinary speech, but it is still impressive.

More significant than the loss of individual words is the great reduction in use of those prefixes and suffixes with which new words used to be freely made. In early Middle-English such prefixes as *be-, for-, to-,* and *with-,* and such suffixes as *-hood, -lock, -red,* and *-ship* were added to roots whenever it seemed useful and appropriate. By the end of the period these elements seem to have lost any specific, independent meaning; they were therefore seldom used in new combinations, and retained only in well-established words that were understood as wholes and not by analysis of their parts. A few clear-cut prefixes, such as *over-, under-,* and the negative *un-* remained; and so too did such suffixes as *-ful, -ish, -less, -ly,* and *-ness*. But on the whole the tendency was to use Latin rather than native elements in forming new words.

Middle English Spelling

Anything like a complete treatment of Middle English spelling would be impossibly complicated, but a few general statements will ease your approach to the selections in these sections.

1. Those words which now begin with *wh-* were spelled in Old English with *hw-,* which obviously better reflects their pronunciation. But the Old English *h,* as we have seen, was used for a stronger sound than the modern one — the fricative /χ/. Apparently this sound (in this position) was weakening in the south, but remained strong in the north. In both areas French scribes (who were not used to a strong *h*) seem to have found *hw-* an incredible combination. In the north they generally spelled the word *hwat,* for

instance, as *quat* or *quhat*. In the midlands they were likely to reverse the initial letters, as we still do; and in the south we find such spellings as *wat, ouat,* and *uat*.

2. Scribes knew that a good many words of French or Latin origin began with a silent *h,* but they didn't always know which ones. We may find *onor* for *honor* and *habundant* for *abundant*. Moreover, some scribes might pronounce an initial *h* where we do not, or vice versa. *Heten* occurs for *eten* (*to eat*), and *ost* for *host*. This procedure is therefore extremely useful: if you don't recognize a word that begins with *h,* try it without and see what you get; and if you don't recognize a word that begins with a vowel, try it with an initial *h*.

3. The letters *u* and *v* are interchangeable. We may find *uanite* for *vanity* and *vp* for *up*. Printers later tended to use *v* initially, whether for the vowel or the consonant sound, and *u* in other positions; scribes were less consistent.

4. The letter *y* had ceased to be used for the rounded front vowel (which was now generally spelled *u* in areas where it was retained), and had become simply a variant form of *i,* with which it could be interchanged in all positions. Thus *lady* may be spelled *ladi,* and *yes* may be spelled *ies*.

5. The letters *i* and *j* are also interchangeable in some positions, but not in all. Either may appear initially before a vowel, as in *iustice* for *justice* or *Iohn* for *John;* and *j* may appear in the second half of a doubled *i* (see 6.a below), or in Roman numerals. Roman seven, for instance, may be indicated as *vii, vij,* or *vjj*.

6. Long vowels may be indicated in any of three ways:

a. Not only *e* and *o* but *a* and *i* were often doubled. Thus we may find *caas* for *case* and *tiim* or *tijm* for *time*.

b. In early Middle English a final *e* indicated a pronounced syllable. In later Middle English it often indicated merely that the preceding vowel was long.

c. In the Northern dialect vowel length was often indicated by an *i* immediately after the vowel. We may find *rois* for *rose* or *maid* for *made*.

7. In diphthongs *u* and *w* were interchangeable. Thus *foul* and *fowl* were not the distinct modern words they resemble, but interchangeable variant spellings for either one.

8. The letter ȝ (yogh) was used so variously that we simply have to figure out what it must stand for in each manuscript. It may have the value of /j/, /χ/, or /z/, or substitute for *i* or *y* as the second element in a diph-

thong. There are times when it seems to have still other values, but these are enough to indicate that it should always be considered with care, to say nothing of suspicion.

9. The alternation of *g* and *y* (or ȝ) in such words as *give* or *yive* and *again* or *aȝayn* is not strictly a matter of spelling, because different dialectal pronunciations are indicated; but it is worth noticing.

The Orrmulum

In the paraphrase of the Gospels called the *Orrmulum* the modern convention of doubling consonants to indicate short vowels is used hundreds of years before it was generally adopted, and even in positions where we do not now regard it as necessary — for instance finally, and before another, different consonant. *Orrm* or *Orrmin* (he gives his name both ways) is the only Englishman before the modern period who has left us a plan for a definite system of spelling reform. Unfortunately, no evidence hints that anybody ever showed the slightest interest in following it. Possibly the reason is that none of his contemporaries or early successors ever succeeded in reading as far in his book as the explanatory passage quoted below, because his version is almost inconceivably dull. He is never contented with saying the same thing twice if he can find a way to say it three times, and he usually can. But his attempt at consistent spelling gives us some valuable information about pronunciation, and he does have the advantage of being easier to read (for a few lines) than most of his contemporaries.

Annd whase wilenn shall þiss boc   efft oþerrsiþe writenn,
Himm bidde icc, þatt hēt wrīte rihht,   swasumm þiss boc himm tæcheþþ
All þwerrtūt, affterr þatt itt iss   uppo þiss firrste bisne,
Wiþþ all swillc rīme, alls her iss sett,   wiþþ allse fele wordess,
Annd tatt he loke wel, þatt he   an bocstaff wrīte twiȝȝess,
Eȝȝwhær þær itt uppo þiss boc   iss writenn o þatt wise.
Loke he wel þatt hēt write swa,   forr he ne maȝȝ nohht elless
Onn Ennglissh wrītenn rihht te word;   þatt wite he wel to soþe.
Annd ȝiff mann wile witenn whi   icc hafe don þiss dede,
Whi icc till Ennglissh hafe wennd   goddspelless hallȝhe lare:
Icc hafe itt don forrþi þatt all   crisstene follkess berrhless
Iss lang uppo þatt an þatt teȝȝ   goddspelless hallȝhe lare

Wiþþ fulle mahhte follȝhe rihht þurrh þohht, þurrh word, þurrh dede.
Annd tærfore hafe icc turrnedd itt inntill Ennglisshe spæche,
Forr þatt I wollde bliþeliȝ þatt all Ennglisshe lede
Wiþþ ære shollde lisstenn itt, wiþþ herrte shollde itt trowwenn,
Wiþþ tunge shollde spellenn itt, wiþþ dede shollde itt follȝhenn.
To winnenn unnderr crisstenndom att Crist soþ sawle berrhless.
Annd godd allmahhtiȝ ȝife uss mahht annd lusst annd witt annd wille,
To follȝhenn þiss Ennglisshe boc, þatt all iss haliȝ lare,
Swa þatt we motenn wurrþi ben to brukenn heffness blisse.

Am[æn]. Am[æn]. Am[æn].[2]

Translation:

And whoever shall want to write this book over again
I pray him that he write it right, so as this book teaches him
All throughout, the way that it is in this first example
With all such measure as here is set down, with all so many words,
And that he look well, that he one letter write twice,
Always where it upon this book is written in that way.
Let him look well that he write it so, for he can not else
In English write the words right: let him know that well in truth.
And if anybody wants to know why I have done this deed,
Why I have turned into English the gospel's holy lore:
I have done it because all Christian folk's salvation
Depends upon that one thing, that they gospel's holy lore
With full might follow right, through thought, through word, through deed.
And therefore have I turned it into English speech,
Because I would gladly that all English people
With ear should listen to it, with heart should believe,
With tongue should pronounce it, with deed should follow it,
And win under Christianity through Christ true salvation of soul.
And that God Almighty give us power and desire and wit and will,
To follow this English book, that is all holy lore,
So that we may be worthy to enjoy heaven's bliss.

Amen. Amen. Amen.

[2] Kaiser, p. 212, ll. 48–68.

Neither this text nor this sub-dialect is a particularly rewarding subject of study except for specialists, so that no notes are given.

The Cursor Mundi

As proof that the statements on pages 117–118 about variations in manuscripts are not exaggerated, here is a selection from the *Cursor Mundi* as it appears in two manuscripts. It would be easy to find versions that differ much more; actually this is simply the first passage reproduced from two manuscripts that came to hand when an illustration was needed. A detailed analysis of the contrasting features would be out of place here; but MS *C* is closer to the Northern original, both in time and place, than MS *T*. Even a casual line-by-line inspection will show some of the things — by no means all — that could happen in copying.[3] Line 156 is particularly interesting. *Heven* (*u* and *v* were interchangeable at this time) is an old Northern verb meaning "to avenge"; but it suggested nothing but *heaven* to the Midland scribe, and so he changed the whole line to fit in with this word.

MS C	*MS T*
Þis Herods had regned thritte[4] yere,	Heroude had regned þritty ȝere,
Quen Iesus Crist vr lauedi bere;	Whenne þat Marie Iesu bere;
Siþen he regned yeres seuen.	Siþen he regned þries seuen.
His wranges godd on him sal heuen,	Fer he brouȝte him self from heuen,
Þat fals, þat fell, þat goddes fa,	Þat false feloun goddes fo
Þat soght his lauerd for to sla!	Souȝte his lord for to slo.
Hu had he hert to sced þair blod	How had he hert to shede her blood
Þat neuer did til him bot god!	Þat neuer dud but good?
Þat wili wolf, þat fox sa fals	Þat wilful wolf þat ferde so fals
Bath gain fremd and freindes als,	Aȝeynes fremde and frendes als
O carles costes al til vnknauin,	His delful dedes most be knowen;
And was manqueller til his auen.	Monqueller was he to his owen.
Þat gredi gerard als a gripe,	Þat gredy gerarde as a gripe
His vnrightes biginnes to ripe,	Now his wrongis bigonne to ripe;

[3] To facilitate this a translation of the C version (British Museum Cotton Vespasian A III; Fourteenth Century) is given. Most of the changes in the T version (Cambridge, Trinity College, R. 3. 8; early Fifteenth Century) are reasonably obvious.

[4] The spelling *thritte* is not a misprint. The scribe of MS *C* is exceptional in regularly distinguishing between the voiced and voiceless dental fricatives, using Þ for the former and *th* for the latter.

And of his seruis mani dai
Nu neghes tim to tak his lai.

And for his seruyse mony a day
Þenne coom tyme to take his pay.[5]

Translation (*C* version):

This Herod had reigned thirty years,
When Our Lady bore Jesus Christ;
Afterward he reigned seven years.
God shall avenge his wrongs on him,
That false, that wicked, that God's foe,
That sought to slay his Lord!
How had he heart to shed their blood
That never did to him (anything) but good!
That wily wolf, that fox so false
Both against strangers and friends also,
Oh churl's actions all to (those) unknown,
And (he) was mankiller to his own.
That villain greedy as a vulture,
His misdeeds begin to ripen,
And for his service of many a day
Now the time is near for him to receive his (punishment of the) law.

Alysoun

The Southern lyric "Alysoun" is here given with only a few clues rather than either a translation or an analysis on the theory that you are more likely to feel some of its charm if you miss a bit here and there than if you have to dissect it too laboriously. It is worth several readings and some discussion.

Bytuene Mersh ant Aueril — *springtime*
When spray biginneþ to springe,
Þe lutel foul haþ hire wyl — *little bird*
On hyre lud to synge. — *in her language* 4
Ich libbe in loue-longinge — *I live*
For semlokest of alle þynge, — *seemliest, most attractive*

[5] Kaiser, p. 223, ll. 153–168.

He may me blisse bringe, *"He" can mean "she" in this dialect*
Icham in hire baundoun. *captivity*
  An hendy hap ichabbe yhent, *hendy : pleasant yhent : caught*
  Ichot from heuene it is me sent, *I wot (know)*
  From alle wymmen mi loue is lent, *averted*
  Ant lyht on Alysoun.

On heu hire her is fayr ynoh, *she has blond hair*
Hire browe broune, hire eȝe blake,
Wiþ lossum chere he on me loh; *lovesome expression laughed*
Wiþ middel smal ant wel ymake. *made*
Bote he me wolle to hire take *unless*
Forte buen hire owen make, *for to be mate*
Longe to lyuen ichulle forsake
Ant feye fallen adoun. *fey : ready to die*
  An hendy hap, *etc.*

Nihtes when y wende ant wake, *wind, turn*
Forþi myn wonges waxeþ won, *my cheeks grow pale*
Leuedi, al for þine sake, *lady*
Longinge is ylent me on. *come to me*
In world nis non so wyter mon *wise*
Þat al hire bounte telle con;
Hire swyre is whittore þen þe swon, *neck*
Ant feyrest may in toune. *maid*
  An hendy, *etc.*

Icham for wowyng al forwake, *worn out by waking*
Wery so water in wore; *behind a dam (weir)*
Lest eny reue me my make *steal mate*
Ychabbe yȝyrned ȝore. *yearned a long time*
Betere is þolien whyle sore *endure*
Þen mournen euermore;
Geynest vnder gore, *fairest under apparel (gear)*
Herkne to my roun. *secret*
  An hendy, *etc.*[6]

[6] Kaiser, p. 466.

The London Dialect

The dialect from which standard Modern English is derived is basically East Midland, with a fairly strong Southern influence, and weaker influences from other parts of the country. This is the dialect of the upper classes of London and its neighborhood, and therefore of the court, the capital, the economic center, the ancient universities, the most influential public schools, and the center of the publishing business. The kind of language spoken in any of these places would have had a certain prestige, and the fact that they were all combined in one neighborhood allowed them to reinforce each other. We have seen that the inevitable emergence of this dialect as the standard language happened late because of the importance of French for several centuries. If it had happened earlier the development would certainly have been somewhat different. London itself was on the border between the southern and the East Midland territories. This location, combined with its political and economic importance, naturally resulted in some shifts in the proportions of its population, and consequently in its dialect. In the early part of the Middle English period this was distinctly Southern. By Chaucer's time it was basically East Midland, though it still preserved a number of Southern features that have since been lost.

Although this dialect was the ancestor of standard Modern English, it was not yet standardized in the way to which we have since grown accustomed. Its prestige was sufficient to make many people throughout the country attempt to comply with it, at least in writing. But nobody had yet written its rules; and though some snobs who used it undoubtedly looked down on all outsiders, many of these outsiders were happy and satisfied with their own varieties.

The Text of Chaucer

It may be well to say a few words about the nature of a modern text of Chaucer before examining a specimen. We have no manuscripts of his work from his own hand, or even from his lifetime; and the manuscripts we do have, being unusually numerous and from all over the country, show a wild variety of readings. All of them contain some obvious mistakes — which would not have surprised Chaucer in the least. Among his minor poems is one addressed to Adam, his own scribe, calling down a mild curse on him if he doesn't learn to copy more carefully, because Chaucer has to spend so much time correcting his mistakes. And at the end of *Troilus and Criseyde* he sends the book off with a prayer including the lines:

> And for ther is so gret diversite
> In Englissh and in writyng of oure tonge,
> So prey I God that non myswrite the,
> Ne the mysmetre for defaute of tonge.

We do not know whether Adam reformed, but other scribes miswrote and mismetered the poems so thoroughly that not until the present century was a reasonably satisfactory restoration of the text accomplished.

Not to be too technical, the general procedure has been to study the relations of all the manuscripts. Then the Ellesmere MS, generally accepted as the best, has been taken as the base, and corrected from other good manuscripts only when there is a very definite reason to believe that their readings are more faithful to the original. (An editor cannot simply take whichever reading he prefers, no matter where he finds it.) The spelling is not corrected simply to achieve consistency (as in the use of *i*'s and *y*'s), but only when it is obviously wrong and interferes with either the sense or the meter. This is particularly important in the matter of final *e*'s, because many that were pronounced as separate syllables in Chaucer's time became silent soon after his death. We do not know just how Chaucer spelled, but he was obviously careful. We can therefore be reasonably sure that he wrote a final *e* only when it was "organic" — that is, when it was still pronounced as a weakened form of an old inflectional ending, or when it had a syllabic value in a French borrowing. But after these organic *e*'s had all become silent, scribes who saw them in old manuscripts had no way of knowing that they had ever been pronounced, and therefore looked on them as mere spelling variants, about which there was no reason for them to be careful. A modern editor must therefore be particularly careful to remove inorganic *e*'s and to restore organic ones whenever possible.

Specimen of Chaucer

Here are the first eighteen lines of the *Canterbury Tales,* with a phonemic transcription, followed by a rather thorough analysis and some suggestions for profitable study. Lines 19 to 100 are then given with slighter notes.

Whan that Aprill with his shoures soote
hwɑn ðɑt ɑ:pril wiθ hiz ʃu:rəz so:tə

The droghte of March hath perced to the roote,
ðə dru:χt ɔf mɑrtʃ hɑθ persəd to ðə ro:tə

And bathed every veyne in swich licour
ɑnd bɑ:ðəd evəri vein in switʃ liku:r

Of which vertu engendred is the flour;
ɔf hwitʃ vertju endʒendrəd is ðə flu:r

Whan Zephirus eek with his sweete breeth
hwɑn zefirus e:k wiθ hiz swe:tə bre:θ

Inspired hath in every holt and heeth
inspi:rəd hɑθ in evəri holt ɑnd he:θ

The tendre croppes, and the yonge sonne
ðə tendrə krɔpəz ɑnd ðə juŋgə sunə

Hath in the Ram his halve cours yronne,
hɑθ in ðə rɑm hiz hɑlvə kurs irunə

And smale foweles maken melodýe,
ɑnd smɑlə fu:ləz mɑ:kən melodiə

That slepen al the nyght with open ye
ðɑt sle:pən ɑl ðə ni:χt wiθ opən iə

(So priketh hem nature in hir coráges);
so prikəθ hem nɑtju:r in hir korɑdʒəz

Thanne longen folk to goon on pilgrimáges,
ðɑn lɔŋgən folk to gɔ:n ɔn pilgrimɑdʒəz

And palmeres for to seken straunge strondes,
ɑnd pɑlmerəz fɔr to se:kən strɑundʒə strɔndəz

To ferne halwes, kowthe in sondry londes;
to fernə hɑlwəz ku:θ in sundri lɔndəz

And specially from every shires ende
ɑnd spesiɑli frɔm evəri ʃi:rəz endə

Of Engelond to Caunterbury they wende,
ɔf eŋgəlɔnd to kɑuntərburi ðei wendə

The	hooly	blisful	martir	for	to	seke,		
ðə	hɔ:li	blisful	mɑrtir	fɔr	to	se:kə		
That	hem	hath	holpen	whan	that	they	were	seeke.
ðɑt	hem	hɑθ	holpən	hwɑn	ðɑt	ðei	wer	se:kə

Chaucer's Consonants

Chaucer had one consonant that has since been lost, the palatal fricative /χ/, spelled *gh,* which is made by raising the tongue so close to the roof of the mouth as almost to make the stop /k/. The sound resulting from the friction in this narrow gap is like that represented by *ch* in German or in Scottish dialect.

His /l/ and /r/ were pronounced rather more clearly than in Modern English, and had less tendency to modify or be modified by neighboring sounds. Thus *talke* is pronounced almost like *talc* plus the schwa sound, rather than as /tɔ:kə/. In such words as *ferme, first,* and *word* the /r/ is definite and the vowels remain respectively /e/, /i/, and /o/ instead of all changing to /ə/ as in the modern derivatives.

Chaucer's other consonants apparently were identical with ours, except that he probably had no /ʒ/. The distribution of some sounds was, however, rather different. See below under *Pronunciation.*

Chaucer's Vowels

Chaucer's short vowels were approximately the same as ours, except that it is generally believed he had no /æ/ sound, but pronounced *that,* for instance, as /ðɑt/ rather than /ðæt/.

Chaucer's long vowels are pronounced more like those in Spanish or Italian than like the so-called long vowels of Modern English. As the transcription indicates, it is generally believed that they really were long vowels rather than diphthongs — that *me,* for instance, was pronounced /me:/ rather than /mei/.[7] The /ɑ:/, /i:/, and /u:/ sounds give little trouble. In Middle English generally there was a distinction between the long open and close *o*

[7] There are scholars who think that in Middle as in Old English, length was not really the distinctive feature of the "long" vowels. They may be right. But so many scribes doubled not only *e* and *o* but *a* and *i,* that they obviously thought length was significant.

sounds, /ɔ:/ and /o:/, and between the long open and close *e* sounds, /ɛ/ (a symbol we have not previously used, which stands for the vowel sound in *breath*) and /e:/.

Pronunciation

To read Chaucer as if his language were misspelled Modern English is about as satisfying as it would be to play a Beethoven sonata off-key on a tin whistle. In the first six lines of the "Prologue," for instance, none of the couplets would rhyme and no line would have a satisfactory rhythm, to say nothing of the subtler relations between sound and sense. We cannot, of course, tell precisely how Chaucer pronounced every word. He lived in a time and place where pronunciation varied a good deal, and he certainly did not always pronounce the same words in the same ways. His poetry is not so fragile that it won't stand a reasonable degree of variation, but it cannot be successfully distorted into an entirely different system.

Our aim in this section is simply to show beginning students how to make an approximation of a fourteenth-century pronunciation so that they can read Chaucer in a workable way. The differences between the open and close long *e* and *o* sounds are disregarded both here and in the transcription, not because they are not real, but because they are distracting to beginners. If you concentrate on them you are likely to lose too much of the rhythm. Moreover, they are not indicated in most texts, and Chaucer himself often disregarded them. The simplest thing is to pronounce them whichever way seems more natural in a specific word — remembering that in a word like *reed* the choice is between /re:d/ and /rɛ:d/ — it can't possibly be /ri:d/, and *rood* can be /ro:d/ or /rɔ:d/, but not /ru:d/.

1. Final *e*'s in native words represent weakened inflectional endings. In words borrowed from French they are syllabic, as they still are in French poetry, though not in prose. Both kinds of *e*'s are normally pronounced, though with the value of /ə/ rather than /e/. Failing to pronounce them when required will do more than anything else to destroy the rhythm. They are, however, light syllables, and should never be exaggerated. Moreover, they are normally elided when immediately followed by a word beginning with a vowel or an *h,* and often when followed by a word beginning with a *w*. If they occur at the end of a line they should be pronounced regardless of the sound with which the next line begins. This may sound rather complicated, but if you remember that Chaucer's verse, though not rigidly regular,

is pretty dependably rhythmical, you won't make many mistakes if you pronounce them lightly wherever they seem to fit naturally into the metrical pattern.

2. In familiar words vowels usually have the same length as in their modern form. The one important exception is that words from French are stressed on the last full syllable, as in *coráge* and *melodýe,* and the vowels in these syllables preserve a length that has been lost with the shift of the stress forward. In unfamiliar words a vowel is usually short when it is followed by two different consonants, a double consonant, or a final single consonant. It is always short when it is unstressed. Otherwise it is usually long.

3. The short *u* should be pronounced as in *put* rather than as in *but.* Moreover, an *o* was often written instead of a *u* when it came next to *m, n,* or *v,* to avoid confusion growing out of the peculiarities of medieval handwriting. Thus such words as *love, some,* and *sun* are pronounced with a *u* rather than an *o* sound, regardless of how they are spelled. Otherwise all the short vowels may be pronounced as in Modern English.

4. The long vowels are pronounced as follows:

lady	rhymes	approximately	with	modern	*body*
me	"	"	"	"	*hay*
I	"	"	"	"	*see*
good	"	"	"	"	*toad*
muse	"	"	"	"	*refuse a*

Because the Old English long *u* was already represented by the vowel-digraph *ou,* the *u* with a long sound occurs only in words from French.

5. The letters *i* and *y* are interchangeable, and so too are the letters *u* and *w* when they occur as the second element of a diphthong. *Ai* and *ei* regularly rhyme, but scholars disagree as to whether they should be pronounced as in modern *day* or *die,* or somewhere between. Without argument, but because some choice is necessary, the *day* pronunciation is used in this book.

Au normally had the value of *ow* in modern *how.* It may have had a slightly different value when followed by *n.*

Ou represents several sounds, and the best clue to its value in any word is the modern pronunciation of that word. When the modern sound is /ɑu/, as in *now* and *ground,* the Middle English sound was /u:/. When the modern sound is /ou/ as in *soul* or *grow,* or /ɔ:/ as in *thought,* the Middle

English word may be pronounced with the same value: *soule-*/soulə/, *growen-*/grouən/, *thoughte-*/þɔ:χtə/.

Eu has the value of the now unfamiliar combination /eu:/ thus *few* is pronounced /feu/ rather than /fju/.

6. Final *s* is voiceless in stressed syllables. *Was* rhymes with *glas(s)*.

7. The initial combinations *gn, kn,* and *wr* are fully pronounced.

8. Students who know French should resist the temptation to pronounce Chaucer's borrowings from that language as in modern French. The letter *j* and the combinations *ch, ge,* and *vowel plus nasal* indicate the same sounds in borrowed as in native words. French, too, has changed in the past six hundred years.

Vocabulary

Many of Chaucer's words have come down to us with no noticeable change, others with changes so slight that they are easy to recognize. Ability to see through changes and identify words varies greatly, but practice and technique will help anybody. Consider line 3:

And bathed every veyne in swich licoúr

Four of the words are identical in spelling with their modern forms, and thus easy to recognize however you pronounce them:

And bathed every ______ in ______ ______

Some students will immediately recognize two others, *veyne* and *licour*. Others will not be able to identify these words by their eyes alone; but if they take the trouble to pronounce them they will see that *veyne* might be either *vein* or *vain,* or perhaps even *vane,* and *licour* must be either *liquor* or *liqueur*.

The best way to decide between these possibilities is to pronounce the words in context rather than in isolation. It then seems obvious that *veyne* must be *vein* and *licour* must refer to the sap running through it. If you know that *liquor* was formerly used where we now use *liquid,* the problem is solved. If you don't know that, but can figure out that *liquor* is even now a more general term than *liqueur* and used to be more general still, you have learned something. Sometimes it is worth confirming these shifts in meaning by using a glossary or dictionary, but often you can be confident that a meaning you had never connected with a word *must* be intended in a passage because:

First, it seems like a reasonable variation of a familiar meaning.

Second, it is the only such variation that makes sense in the context.

Unless both these things are true, you had better look up the word. But if both *are* true, you had better *not* look it up. You are learning to react directly to the author's language, and it is better to develop confidence in your ability to do this, even if you make an occasional mistake, than to be overcautious.

The still unidentified word in line 3, *swich,* is a little harder. If you pronounce it alone you get nothing but *switch,* which makes no sense here. If you pronounce the whole line you may guess that the nearest reasonable word is *such,* which is right. If you haven't managed this guess there is no reason for shame.

The passage has a number of other words that you should have a fair chance of recognizing through the unfamiliar spellings, particularly if you read and pronounce them in context rather than in isolation. Thus *Aprill* guarantees the meaning of *shoures,* and if it is with these that the *droghte* of March has been *perced,* March must have been dry. The two words *flour* and *sonne* are worth special consideration, because our first impression is likely to be misleading, and our second may well be that Chaucer is mistakenly using the wrong homonyms. But the habit of distinguishing in spelling between such pairs as *son-sun* and *flour-flower* is not only later than Chaucer's time but a completely artificial device that we now use erratically and sparingly, though we are accustomed to think of it as very important when we do use it. *Flour* began simply as "the *flower* of the grain," just as we can still speak of "the *cream* of the crop" — and we do not use a special spelling for that metaphor. *Son* and *sun* are of different origins but have become exact homonyms, just like hundreds of other pairs that we do not distinguish in spelling. Of course we'd better follow the established conventions in Modern English, but it saves confusion if we remember that they did not exist in the fourteenth century.

With such words as *al* (all), *nyght* (night), *slepen* (sleep), and *smale* (small) simple recognition is enough, but with others some adjustment in meaning is needed. *Vertu,* for instance, is not used in its most usual modern sense, but as in the phrase "by *virtue* of." *Foweles* is not limited to barnyard birds, nor *corages* to heartfelt feelings of bravery. *Palmeres* were not card sharps, but travelers who proved they had been to the Holy Land by bringing back palm-leaf souvenirs. An Irishman would recognize *strondes* (strands) as meaning *shores* more readily than an American; and not everybody who celebrates *Halloween* knows that it means the night before All *Hallows* (Saints) Day. The clue to *kowthe* is the negative form of *uncouth* — by etymology simply "unknown," but with its original meaning now transformed by natural snobbery.

Some of the words may cause even more trouble. It is not easy to recognize *soote* as *sweet,* especially when *sweete* occurs four lines below. But if you ask the natural question, "Why did Chaucer use the two forms?" try to ask it without indignation. Indignation interferes enormously with language learning. He probably used the two forms because he heard them both every day, and he selected whichever seemed to him to sound better in a particular line. *Soote* of course rhymes with *roote;* and the repetition of vowel sounds in *sweete breeth,* while not necessary, is at least to some ears more attractive than *soote breeth.* It is really quite unlikely that Chaucer was deliberately playing a nasty trick on a later generation.

You may well find that you cannot connect *holt* (grove) and *eek* (also) with anything you know, or recognize the *Ram* as one of the signs of the zodiac, to which you have perhaps been giving little thought lately. It will be natural for you to identify *croppes* with modern *crops,* though if it occurs to you that holts and heaths are curious places for them to be growing you may look the word up and discover that it meant *shoots.* At first *yronne* may look like about the way you'd expect Chaucer to spell *iron,* but you'll soon learn that *y-, like* Old English and German *ge-,* is often a prefix indicating a past participle.

At any rate, the best way to think of Middle English is as a foreign language to which you are lucky enough to have a great many clues, rather than as English which an evil conspiracy has messed up beyond convenient recognition. You may well think that in the last few paragraphs we have been overdoing the clue business, and that it would be much easier simply to look up all the troublesome words in a glossary. This is true; but in the long run it wouldn't be nearly so profitable. To memorize the translation of a few lines is a basically childish procedure. To learn to read those same lines is a considerable step toward a worthy accomplishment. For the first few pages it is a job of considerable difficulty for almost anybody. But if you do it intelligently, so that you are learning something about the language as you go along, and not merely trying to find modern equivalents for the unfamiliar words, your speed and ease of reading will increase at a quite surprising rate. A good memory is of course most useful in language learning, but deliberate memorizing should be reserved for rather important occasions when nothing else will serve. Take the two words *eek* (also) and *holt* (grove). If you know German you can connect *eek* with *auch* and *holt* with *Holtz,* and you will probably never forget them. If you don't, you might pause to think that if you *eke out* something you do it by using something else *also.* And if this is too forced, spend a few moments trying to get it fixed in your memory, because it is a useful word that is likely to appear often. If you forget *holt,* you can afford to, because it may be quite a while before you see it again. In short,

First, try to connect every new word with something you already know.

Second, make a special effort with words that seem likely to occur frequently.

Grammatical Structure

By the fourteenth century a good many inflectional endings had either disappeared completely or had been worn down to a few blurred and often ambiguous forms. That this weakening of inflections went so far before the standard word order that was to replace them had fully developed causes some trouble, but not very often. There are, however, a few points that it is distinctly helpful to bear in mind.

Nouns

The *stān* declension of Old English became simplified and almost completely generalized during the Middle English period. Originally, as we have seen (page 81), it was declined as follows:

	Singular	*Plural*
Nominative and Accusative	stān	stānas
Genitive	stānes	stāna
Dative	stāne	stānum

By Chaucer's time it had reached its modern state except for some differences in the convention of writing. Thus:

	Singular		Plural
Common case	ston	*All cases*	stones
Genitive case	stones		

1. The long *a,* here as elsewhere, changed to a long open *o,* and somewhat later to a long close *o*. The length might or might not be indicated in the spelling.
2. The dative case dropped out of general use, and was preserved only in a few set phrases known as *petrified datives*. Thus Chaucer says *to bedde* instead of *to bed*. Perhaps the most interesting example of this construction is *on live* (meaning *in life*), from which we get the modern *alive*. The vowel of the dative is preserved, and the /f/ has been voiced to a /v/ because of its intervocalic position.
3. Because of the general weakening of the vowels in endings, *stonas* came to be pronounced, and therefore spelled, like *stones*.
4. Because both the genitive singular and the common plural form now ended in *-es,* it was natural to extend this form to the genitive plural, which had originally lacked the *s*. The convention of using apostrophes to make a visual distinction between the audially identical forms *stones, stone's,* and *stones'* did not develop until much later.

Although most of the words that had originally belonged to other declensions had been attracted to the *stone* pattern, with the *s* in both the genitive and the plural, a number still resisted. Thus Chaucer says "his lady grace" (line 88) where we should now use *lady's,* and "his hors were goode" (line 74) where we should use *horses*. He also uses many more plurals in *-en* than have survived. In some other Middle English texts these *-en* plurals are even more widespread. In fact, in early Southern texts so many nouns have this form that it, rather than the *-s* plural, might have been expected to become general.

Pronouns

Among the personal pronouns Chaucer uses *ich* and occasionally *ik* as well as *I* in the first person; *his* for *its* (which had not yet been invented); and *hem* and *hire* or *here* for *them* and *their*. He also uses a few contractions not immediately obvious. Thus *art thou* and *hast thou* may appear as *artow* and *hastow,* and *so thee ich* as *so theech* (for "so may I thrive" — *thee* here is a verb, not a pronoun). Other writers use so many forms of the pronouns that it would not be profitable to discuss them here.

Adjectives

The very highly inflected Old English adjectives had been simplified to a maximum of two forms in each degree — one with and one without a final /ə/ sound, spelled *e*. The longer form was used when the adjective was in the weak position[8] or when it agreed with a noun in the plural. In the fifteenth century the form with /ə/ dropped out of use, which was hard on Chaucer's reputation. Scribes, not knowing the *e* had ever represented a syllable, added or dropped it as they pleased, and Chaucer was unfairly accused of being very careless about his rhythm.

Verbs

Old English had ten major classes of verbs, seven strong and three weak, with variations in each class that occurred when neighboring sounds influenced each other in various ways. A natural result was that speakers often made mistakes in their use. Our grammatical habits are pretty largely based on analogy, and when too many conflicting analogies are possible, some confusion is bound to result. During the Middle English period a very considerable modification of the old inflections took place in a very irregular fashion. Because the weak verbs were much more numerous than the strong ones, and also more nearly regular, it was easier for them to survive, and this is on the whole what happened.

About half of the 312 strong verbs in Old English have completely disappeared. This loss does not prove anything, because a great many words of all sorts have given way to synonyms. But half of the remaining ones have shifted to the weak conjugation, which does show the force of the more general analogy. And many of those which are still strong do not have the forms that would normally have developed, but different ones caused by

[8] See p. 87 above.

mistaken analogy with other verbs. All these tendencies began during the Old English period and continued during the Modern period; but the confusion of forms was particularly acute in Middle English.

There was also a considerable confusion of the inflectional endings. In Chaucer's usage the *-að* ending of the present indicative plural has disappeared, and the *-en* ending, which was originally used only in the subjunctive, has taken its place. Moreover, the infinitive ending in *-an* and the past indicative plural ending in *-on* have been weakened to *-en*. And finally, this new all-purpose ending is further weakening, so that in any of its uses it can appear as either *-en* or simply *-e*. Thus we have the infinitive *to seken* in line 13, but *to seke* in line 17, and the past indicative plural as *they weren* in line 40, but *they were* in line 41. As past participles we have *holpen* (line 18), *spoken* (line 31), and *riden* (line 48) in contrast with *come* (line 23), *yronne* (line 8), and *yfalle* (line 25). And the prefix *y-* (from Old English *ge-*) which appears in the last two of these, is as optional as the final *-n*. Thus, though the form is *come* in line 23, it is *ycome* in line 77. It is perhaps worth special mention that *been* appears as an infinitive (*to been*) and indicative (*they been*) as well as a participle.

This may sound like a very confusing state of affairs, but it needn't be. After all, in Modern English we say *to put, they put* (present or past), and *they have put,* and ambiguity very seldom results. Once we realize that Chaucer's *-e* and *-en* endings are versatile, they give very little trouble.

Chaucer does, however, preserve the *-(e)st* and *-(e)th* endings in the second and third person singular of the present indicative, in contrast with the *-e* endings of the present subjunctive.

Negatives

The Middle English use of negatives is quite different from ours. In the first place, the theory that "two negatives make an affirmative" (which is reasonably true of classical Latin) had not yet been misapplied to English. As long as they were used with different words, negatives reinforced rather than canceled each other (as most of us still feel that they do, even though we have been trained not to use them that way ourselves). In lines 70–71 we find:

> He *nevere* yet *no* vileynye *ne* sayde
> In al his lyf unto *no* maner wight.

Notice also that here the simple negative is *ne,* as it usually is at this time, though the stronger *nat* is also found. *Ne* may also mean *nor,* and *ne . . . ne* regularly means *neither . . . nor.*

Chaucer also uses such forms as *nis, nadde,* and *nolde* where we use *isn't, hadn't,* and *wouldn't.* In other words, with the common auxiliary verbs beginning with a vowel or the weak consonants *h* and *w,* the contraction was formed from *ne* plus the verb rather than from the verb plus a weakened form of *not.* Thus *nis* is equivalent to *is not, nas* to either *has not* or *was not,* and *nere to were not.* The only remnant of this construction that has survived is the phrase *willy-nilly,* from *will he, nill he — whether he wants to or not.*

A change in such a fundamental construction as this is most unusual. It may be explained by the fact that *not* began as a weakened form of *naught,* which in turn is a condensed form of the phrase *ne a wiht,* meaning *not a bit.* We usually put a modifying phrase after a verb rather than before it; and even when the phrase was condensed beyond recognition, the inherited order apparently seemed more natural, just as even today *he cares not* seems more normal than *he not cares,* though neither is the usual expression.

Impersonal Constructions

These are much more common in Middle than in Modern English. Compare the following expressions:

He will do it if he pleases.
if he likes.
if it pleases him.
if it suits him.

The four *if* clauses have roughly the same meaning, but two of them have *he,* representing the person, as the subject; the other two have the impersonal *it* as the subject, and indicate the person by *him,* used as an indirect object. You will notice that *pleases* can be used either way, but *likes* can now have only the personal subject, and *suits* (in this sense) only the impersonal one.

In Chaucer's time, with the word order still unfixed and the inflections more important, it was possible to say either "If it please him" or "If him please." Anybody could see that *him* could not be the subject, and the impersonal subject *it* could be omitted. And when *ye* was strictly the subject form and *you* the object form, "If *you* please" was clearly parallel to "If *him* please." But when *you* came to be used for all purposes and the modern word order became normal, *you* looked like the subject of *please;* and a little later *him* in such a sentence began to seem unnatural, and was replaced by *he*. Now if we want to keep the expression impersonal we have to use four words instead of three and say "If it pleases him." We usually don't do this with *please;* and with *like,* and a number of other verbs, we never do; but Chaucer and his contemporaries did, and we have to be alert for such expressions as *him list* (it pleases him), *him repenteth,* and *me thinketh,* (It seems to me).

With this much general preparation it should be possible to read the next eighty-two lines with slighter notes.

  Bifil that in that seson on a day,
In Southwerk at the Tabard as I lay
Redy to wenden on my pilgrymáge
To Caunterbury with ful devout coráge,
At nyght was come into that hostelrýe
Wel nyne and twenty in a compaignýe,
Of sondry folk, by aventúre yfalle
In felaweshipe, and pilgrimes were they alle,
That toward Caunterbury wolden ryde.
The chambres and the stables weren wyde,
And wel we weren esed atte beste.
And shortly, whan the sonne was to reste,
So hadde I spoken with hem everichon
That I was of hir felaweshipe anon,
And made forward erly for to ryse,
To take oure wey ther as I yow devyse.
  But nathelees, whil I have tyme and space,
Er that I ferther in this tale pace,
Me thynketh it acordaunt to resoún
To telle yow al the condicioún
Of ech of hem, so as it semed me,
And whiche they weren, and of what degree,
And eek in what array that they were inne;
And at a knyght than wol I first bigynne.

A KNYGHT ther was, and that a worthy man,
That fro the tyme that he first bigan
To riden out, he loved chivalrie,
Trouthe and honour, fredom and curteisie.
Ful worthy was he in his lordes werre,
And therto hadde he riden, no man ferre,
As wel in cristendom as in hethenesse,
And evere honoured for his worthynesse.
At Alisaundre he was whan it was wonne.
Ful ofte tyme he hadde the bord bigonne
Aboven alle nacions in Pruce;
In Lettow hadde he reysed and in Ruce,
No Cristen man so ofte of his degree.
In Gernade at the seege eek hadde he be
Of Algezir, and riden in Belmarýe.
At Lyeys was he and at Satalýe,
Whan they were wonne; and in the Grete See
At many a noble armee hadde he be.
At mortal batailles hadde he been fiftene,
And foughten for oure feith at Tramyssene
In lystes thries, and ay slayn his foo.
This ilke worthy knyght hadde been also
Somtyme with the lord of Palatýe
Agayn another hethen in Turkýe.
And everemoore he hadde a sovereyn prys;
And though that he were worthy, he was wys,
And of his port as meeke as is a mayde.
He nevere yet no vileynye ne sayde
In al his lyf unto no maner wight.
He was a verray, parfit, gentil knyght.
But, for to tellen yow of his array,
His hors were goode, but he was nat gay.
Of fustian he wered a gypon
Al bismotered with his habergeon,
For he was late ycome from his viáge,
And wente for to doon his pilgrymáge.
With hym ther was his sone, a yong SQUIÉR,
A lovyere and a lusty bachelér,

With lokkes crulle as they were leyd in presse.
Of twenty yeer of age he was, I gesse.
Of his stature he was of evene lengthe,
And wonderly delyvere, and of greet strengthe.
And he hadde been somtyme in chyvachíe
In Flaundres, in Artoys, and Pycardíe,
And born hym weel, as of so litel space,
In hope to stonden in his lady grace.
Embrouded was he, as it were a meede
Al ful of fresshe floures, whyte and reede.
Syngynge he was, or floytynge, al the day;
He was as fressh as is the month of May.
Short was his gowne, with sleves longe and wyde.
Wel koude he sitte on hors and faire ryde.
He koude songes make and wel endite,
Juste and eek daunce, and weel purtreye and write.
So hoote he lovede that by nyghtertale
He sleep namoore than dooth a nyghtyngale.
Curteis he was, lowely, and servysáble,
And carf biforn his fader at the table.[9]

20. *Tabard:* an inn.
23. *was come:* In Middle English, as in French and German, *be* rather than *have* is the auxiliary used with verbs of motion and change of condition.
25. *aventure: chance* rather than *adventure*. Many of Chaucer's borrowings from French have meanings that have been retained in that language but lost in Modern English.
29. *atte:* a contraction of *at the.*
31. *everichon:* every one.
33. *forward:* agreement for future action.
34. *ther:* where. The originally demonstrative pronoun forms (beginning with /ð/) were all used in a relative sense before the originally interrogative forms (beginning with /hw/) took over this function.

[9] F. N. Robinson, *The Works of Geoffrey Chaucer,* 2nd Edition (Houghton Mifflin Co., Boston, 1957).

37. *Me thynketh:* not baby talk, but an impersonal construction meaning literally "it seems to me." In Old English *þencean* (think) and *þincean* (seem) were distinct verbs, but they became homonyms in Middle English.
48. *ferre:* farther.
51–66. The knight had fought in all the most distant campaigns available in Chaucer's time. Place names are among the most reasonable words to forget.
52. *the bord bigonne:* sat in the place of honor at a banquet.
54. *reysed:* traveled.
55. *degree:* rank.
60. *armee:* a military expedition rather than organization.
63. *lystes:* single mounted combat. Literally, the enclosed space in which combats took place.
67. *sovereyn prys:* a high reputation, not a prize worth a British pound.
68. *worthy:* brave; *wys:* prudent, the opposite of reckless.
69. *port:* way of carrying himself.
70. *vileynye:* churlish talk.
72. Notice the comma after *verray*. At this period *very* was simply an adjective, meaning *true*. Because it was often, as here, used as the first adjective in a series, it gradually came to be understood as an adverbial intensifier of the following adjectives.
74. *hors:* unchanged plural.
75. *fustian:* coarse cloth; *gypon:* tunic.
76. *bismotered:* besmutted; *habergeon:* coat of chain mail.
80. *lusty bacheler:* happy young aspirant for knighthood.
81. *crulle:* curly. Notice the metathesis.
83. *evene:* average.
84. *delyvere:* agile.
85. *chyvachie:* approximately "rough-riding." Like *chivalrie* this comes from a late Latin word for *horse*. The noble class did their fighting on horseback. *Chivalrie* refers to the ethical and social implications of this fact, *chyvachie* to the physical.
88. *lady grace: lady* is genitive, but this word had not yet fallen into the *stone* declension.
89. *Embrouded:* with all the bright colors of embroidery; *meede:* meadow.

91. *floytynge:* whistling, or perhaps playing the flute.
95. *make:* compose the tunes; *endite:* compose the words.
96. *Juste:* practice mounted combat with a spear.
97. *nyghtertale:* night time.
100. *fader:* not a corruption, but the original form. The /ð/ in the modern word is not a result of Grimm's Law, but of two other changes that happened to work out to the same result.

The Morte Darthur

Sir Thomas Malory's romance *The Morte Darthur* is the only long prose work in Middle English that is still widely read. The syntax is often, by modern standards, regrettably loose; but though many of the sentences would be hard to parse, their meaning is usually clear. Students may find it helpful to review the section on Middle English spelling (pages 126–127) before attempting this passage. Here as elsewhere many words that seem strange to the eye become clear when read aloud in context.

And thus they fought all the longe day, and neuer stynted tylle þe noble kny3tes were layde to the colde erthe. And euer they fought stylle tylle hit was nere ny3t, and by than was þere an hondred thousand leyde dede vppon the erthe. Than was kynge Arthure wode wrothe oute of mesure, whan he saw hys people so slayne frome hym. And so he loked aboute hym and cowde se no mo of all hys oste and good kny3tes leffte, no mo on lyve but two kny3tes: the tone was sir Lucan de Buttler and hys brother sir Bedwere; and yette they were full sore wounded.

'Jesu mercy!' seyde the kynge, 'where ar all my noble kny3tes becom? Alas, that euer I shulde se thys doleful day; for now,' seyde kynge Arthur, 'I am com to myne ende. But wolde to god,' seyde he, 'that I wyste now where were that traytoure sir Mordred that hath caused all thys myschyff.'

Than kynge Arthur loked aboute and was ware where stood sir Mordred leanyng vppon hys swerde amonge a grete hepe of dede men.

'Now gyff me my speare,' seyde kynge Arthure vnto sir Lucan, 'for yondir I haue aspyed þe traytoure that all thys woo hath wrought.' 'Sir, latte hym be,' seyde sir Lucan, 'for he ys vnhappy. And yf ye passe this vnhappy day, ye shall be ryȝt well revenged. And, good lord, remembre ye of your nyȝtes dreme and what the spyryte of sir Gawayne tolde you tonyȝt, and yet god of hys grete goodnes hath preserved you hyddirto. And for goddes sake, my lorde, leve of thys; for, blyssed be god, ye haue won the fylde. For yet we ben here three on lyve, and with sir Mordred ys nat one on lyve. And therefore if ye leve of now, thys wycked day of desteny ys paste.'

'Now tyde me dethe, tyde me lyff,' seyde the kyng, 'now I se hym yondir alone, he shall neuer ascape myne hondes! For at a bettir avayle shall I neuer haue hym.' 'God spyede you well!' seyde sir Bedyvere.

Than the kynge gate his speare in bothe hys hondis, and ran towarde sir Mordred, cryyng and saying: 'Traytoure, now ys thy dethe-day com!' And whan sir Mordred saw kynge Arthur, he ran vntyll hym with hys swerde drawyn in his honde, and þere kyng Arthur smote sir Mordred vndir the shylde with a foyne of hys speare, thorowoute the body more than a fadom. And whan sir Mordred felte that he had hys dethys wounde, he threste hymselff with the myȝt that he had vpp to the burre of kyng Arthurs speare, and ryȝt so he smote hys fadir, kynge Arthure, with hys swerde holdynge in both hys hondys, vppon the syde of the hede, that the swerde perced the helmet and the tay of the brayne. And þerewith Mordred daysshed downe starke dede to the erthe.

And noble kynge Arthure felle in a swoughe to the erthe, and þere he sowned oftyntymys; and sir Lucan and sir Bedwere offtetymys hove hym vp. And so waykly betwyxte them they lad hym to a lytyll chapell nat farre frome the see; and whan the kyng was there, hym thought hym resonabely eased. Than harde they people crye in the fylde. 'Now go thou, sir Lucan,' seyde the kyng, 'and do me to wyte what betokyns that noyse in the fylde.' So sir Lucan departed; for he was grevously wounded in many placis; and so as he yode he saw and harkened by þe moonelyȝt how that pyllours and robbers were com into the fylde to pylle and to robbe many a full noble knyȝt of brochys and bees and of many a good rynge and many a ryche juell. And who that were nat dede all oute, þere they slew them for their harneys and their ryches.

Whan sir Lucan vndirstood thys warke, he cam to the kynge as sone as he myȝt, and tolde hym all what he had harde and seyne. 'Þerefore be my rede,' seyde sir Lucan, 'hit ys beste that we brynge you to som towne.' 'I wolde hit were so,' seyde the kynge, 'but I may nat stonde; my hede worchys so. A, sir Launcelot,' seyde kynge Arthure, 'thys day haue I sore myssed the! And alas, that euer I was ayenste the! For now haue I my dethe, where-of sir Gawayne me warned in my dreame.'

Than sir Lucan toke vp the kynge the tone party and sir Bedwere the othir parte, and in the lyfftyng vp the kynge sowned, and in the lyfftynge sir Lucan felle in a sowne, that parte of hys guttis felle oute of hys bodye, and þerewith þe noble knyȝt hys harte braste. And whan the kynge awoke, he behylde sir Lucan, how he lay fomyng at the mowth and parte of his guttes lay at hys fyete.

'Alas,' seyde the kynge, 'thys ys to me a fulle hevy syȝt, to se thys noble deuke so dye for my sake; for he wold haue holpyn me that had more nede of helpe than I! Alas, that he wolde nat complayne hym, for hys harte was so sette to helpe me. Now Jesu haue mercy vppon hys soule!' Than sir Bedwere wepte for the deth of hys brothir. 'Now leve thys mournynge and wepyng, jantyll knyȝt,' seyde the kyng, 'for all thys woll nat avayle me. For wyte thou well, and I myȝt lyve myselff, þe dethe of sir Lucan wolde greve me euermore. But my tyme passyth on faste,' seyde the kynge. 'Þerefore,' seyde kynge Arthur vnto sir Bedwere, 'take thou here Excaliber, my good swerde, and go wyth hit to yondir watirs syde; and whan thou commyste þere, I charge the throw my swerde in þat water, and com agayne and telle me what thou syeste þere.' 'My lorde,' seyde sir Bedwere, 'youre commaundement shall be done, and lyȝtly I brynge you worde agayne.'

So sir Bedwere departed. And by the way he behylde that noble swerde, and the pomell and the hauffte was all precious stonys. And than he seyde to hymsellf: 'If I throw thys ryche swerde in the water, þereof shall neuer com good, but harme and losse.' And than sir Bedwere hyd Excalyber vndir a tre, and so as sone as he myȝt he cam agayne vnto the kynge and seyde he had bene at the watir and had throwen the swerde into the watir.

'What sawe thou þere?' seyde the kynge. 'Sir,' he seyde, 'I

saw nothyng but wawis and wyndys.' 'That ys vntruly seyde of the,' seyde the kynge. 'And þerefore go thou lyȝtly agayne, and do my commaundemente! As thou arte to me lyff and dere, spare nat, but throw hit in!'

Than sir Bedwere returned agayne, and toke the swerde in hys honde; and yet hym thought synne and shame to throw away that noble swerde. And so effte he hyd the swerde and returned agayne and tolde the kynge that he had bene at the watir and done hys commaundement.

'What sawist thou þere?' seyde the kynge. 'Sir,' he seyde, 'I sy nothynge but watirs wap and wawys wanne.' 'A, traytour vnto me and vntrew,' seyde kyng Arthure, 'now hast thou betrayed me twyse! Who wolde wene that thou that hast bene to me so leve and dere, and also named so noble a knyȝt, that thou wolde betray me for þe ryches of thys swerde? But now go agayn lyȝtly; for thy longe taryynge puttith me in grete jouperte of my lyff, for I haue takyn colde. And but if thou do now as I bydde the, if euer I may se the, I shall sle the myne owne hondis, for thou woldist for my rych swerde se me dede.'

Than sir Bedwere departed and wente to the swerde and lyȝtly toke hit vp; and so he wente vnto the watirs syde. And þere he bounde þe gyrdyll aboute the hyltis, and threw the swerde as farre into the watir as he myȝt. And þere cam an arme and an honde aboue the watir, and toke hit, and cleyȝt hit, and shoke hit thryse and braundysshed, and than vanysshed with the swerde into the watir.

So sir Bedyvere cam agayne to the kynge and tolde hym what he saw. 'Alas,' seyde the kynge, 'helpe me hens; for I drede me I haue taryed ouer longe.' Than sir Bedwere toke the kynge vppon hys bak and so wente with hym to the watirs syde. And whan they were þere, evyn faste by the banke hoved a lytyll barge wyth many fayre ladyes in hit; and amonge hem all was a quene. And all they had blak hoodis; and all they wepte and shryked, whan they saw kynge Arthur.

'Now put me into that barge,' seyde the kynge. And so he ded sofftely; and þere resceyved hym three ladyes with grete mournyng. And so they sette hem downe, and in one of their lappis kyng Arthure layde hys hede. And than the quene sayde: 'A, my dere brothir! Why haue ye taryed so longe frome me?

Alas, thys wounde on youre hede hath caught ouermuch coulde!' And anone they rowed fromward the londe.

And sir Bedyvere behylde all tho ladyes go frowarde hym. Than sir Bedwere cryed and seyde: 'A, my lorde Arthur, what shall becom of me, now ye go frome me and leve me here alone amonge myne enemyes?' 'Comforte thyselff,' seyde the kynge, 'and do as well as thou mayste; for in me ys no truste for to truste in. For I muste into the vale of Avylyon to hele me of my grevous wounde. And if thou here neuermore of me, pray for my soule!'

But euer the quene and ladyes wepte and shryked, that hit was pite to hyre. And as sone as sir Bedwere had loste the syȝt of þe barge, he wepte and wayled; and so toke the foreste, and wente all that nyȝt. And in the mornyng he was ware be-twyxte two holtis hore of a chapell and an ermytage. Than was sir Bedwere fayne, and thyder he wente; and whan he cam into the chapell, he saw where lay an ermyte grovelynge on all four, faste þereby a tumbe was newe gravyn.

Whan the ermyte saw sir Bedyvere, he knewe hym well, for he was but lytyll tofore bysshop of Caunturbery that sir Mordred fleamed. 'Sir,' seyde sir Bedyvere, 'what man ys þere here entyred, that ye pray so faste fore?' 'Fayre sunne,' seyde the ermyte, 'I wote nat veryly but by demynge. But thys same nyȝt at mydnyȝt here cam a numbir of ladyes and brought here a dede corse, and prayde me to entyre hym. And here they offird an hondred tapers, and they gaff me a thousande besauntes.' 'Alas,' seyde sir Bedyvere, 'that was my lorde kynge Arthur, whych lyethe here gravyn in thys chapell!'

Than sir Bedwere sowned; and whan he awooke, he prayde the ermyte that he myȝt abyde with hym stylle, þere to lyve with fastynge and prayers. 'For from hens woll I neuer go,' seyde sir Bedyvere, 'be my wyll, but all the dayes of my lyff here to pray for my lorde Arthur.[10]

1. *stynted:* stopped
5. *wode:* wild
8. *the tone:* that one

[10] Kaiser, pp. 561–563.

13. *wyste:* knew
14. *myschyff:* much stronger than the modern word
20. *vnhappy:* unlucky
27. *of:* off
29. *tyde:* betide
37. *foyne:* thrust
40. *burre:* the protective enlargement just before the grip
43. *tay:* case
45. *swoughe:* swoon
46. *sowned:* swooned
49. *hym thought hym:* it seemed to him (or perhaps *them*) that he was
51. *do me to wyte:* let me know
53. *yode:* old past tense of *go,* with the meaning *walked*
56. *bees:* armbands
61. *rede:* advice
81. *and:* if
88. *lyȝtly:* quickly
91. *pomell, hauffte:* the *pommel* is the knob at the end of the *haft* (grip)
98. *wawis:* waves
100. *lyff:* lief, synonymous with *dear*
104. *effte:* again
108. *watirs wap and wawys wanne:* waters quiver and waves turn white
110. *wene:* think
121. *cleyȝt:* gripped
125. *hens:* the final *s* is voiceless
150. *wente:* walked
151. *holtis hore:* ancient groves
152. *fayne:* glad
154. *gravyn:* dug
157. *fleamed:* put to flight
158. *entyred:* interred
159. *demynge:* judging
162. *besauntes:* gold coins

6

The English Renaissance

Early Modern English

The period from 1500 to 1650 is often called the English Renaissance, and the language of this period is known as Early Modern English. The dates are of course arbitrary, but they will do as well as any others to bound the era during which our language took on most of its present characteristics. Most modern students simply cannot read the language of 1450 without either special training or considerable editorial assistance, but before 1550 they can find a good deal of material that they can handle without difficulty. We cannot reasonably suppose that during the intervening century the language habits of the whole country changed quite so rapidly as the differences in the preserved writing seem to indicate, but a number of forces were working together to cause a rather decided break about this time. These include the rapid spread of education, a loosening in the class structure of society, the introduction of printing, and the growing belief that the development of the language could and should be controlled. The first three of these we can consider only briefly, but we must examine the last more carefully, because it added a new dimension to the language. It is not much of an oversimplification to say that during the Old and Middle English periods the language just happened, but during the entire Modern period its development has been considerably modified by efforts (sometimes misguided) at conscious direction. From this time on it is necessary to consider attitudes toward the language as a part of its functioning machinery, along with the more obvious elements such as sounds and inflections.

During this period the changes in inflections were comparatively slight, but the changes in pronunciation were considerable, and the enlargement of the vocabulary was enormous. There were also some very important developments along what might be called the borderline between grammar and rhetoric. As English became a more responsible language the habit of using more sophisticated and better articulated sentences became fairly general. It is very difficult to decide how far changes of this last sort should be attributed to the language itself, and how far simply to the skill of particular writers in using it; for habits of sentence construction are likely to vary more from person to person than any other element of a language. In order to communicate at all we have to stay pretty close together in our pronunciation, our vocabulary, and those inflections which have an actual signaling value; but the skill with which we fit our words together in order to convey the relations between ideas varies enormously — and of course depends at least as much on our ability to grasp complex relations as on our facility with words.

Another important development was the gradual emergence of a single, generally accepted system of spelling, which has remained in effect ever since with only a few slight modifications. It was a poor system at the time, and has become more and more unsatisfactory as our pronunciation has changed since; but it has had a very strong unifying effect on the language. The fact that we tend to think of the written form of a word as the real form has, as we have seen, some serious disadvantages; but it does make it easier for us to think of an unfamiliar pronunciation as a comprehensible variant rather than as something completely and arbitrarily different.

The Great Vowel Shift

The most important development in the sound system of English that took place during this period was a change in the values of all the long vowels, usually called "the great vowel shift." It is here described in a simplified form, with a footnote for those who want more details. For some reason people started pronouncing the long vowels with their tongues higher in their mouths. When the front part of the tongue was raised, /ɑ:/ changed to /e:/ and /e:/ to /i:/; when the back part was raised, /ɔ:/ changed to /o:/ and /o:/ changed to /u:/. The vowels /i:/ and /u:/ were already pronounced with the tongue so high that any further raising would have resulted in consonant rather than vowel sounds, so that people backed up and made the diphthongs /ɑi/ and /ɑu/ instead.[1] The whole process sounds most unlikely, especially the last part. Nobody knows why it happened, so that there is no use worrying about that. We have very convincing evidence that it somehow did, and at least it explains one of the main peculiarities in English spelling.

Exact dating of the shift is impossible, partly because of scanty and sometimes conflicting evidence, partly because some people were slower than others in following the new tendency. It apparently began in the fifteenth century, and is sometimes called the "fifteenth-century vowel shift." The evidence of spelling suggests that the main development was rather later. There is some doubt that the modern diphthongs in such words as *bite* and *mouse* had been fully developed in Shakespeare's time, but they must have been well on their way. The evidence for the pronunciation at various times is of several kinds, of which the most obvious are English attempts at phonetic spelling of foreign words, and foreign attempts at phonetic spelling of English words. We also have some evidence from rhymes, some from nonstandard dialects that developed differently, and a few contemporary comments.

These words indicate the changes:

[1] Actually there were two long *e*'s in Middle English: the open *e*, [ɛ:], which is a prolongation of the vowel sound in *met*, and the close *e*, [e:], which is a prolongation of the first element of the diphthong in *bait*. The open *e* sound was often spelled *ea*, and the close *e* sound *ee*, though there is a good deal of inconsistency. During the great vowel shift [ɛ:] was raised to [e:], and [e:] to [i:]. Immediately after this *clean* rhymed with *plain* rather than *keen*, and *tea* with *day* rather than *see*. This explains some of Pope's rhymes, and also the conservative pronunciation of some proper names, such as *O'Dea*. However, early in the eighteenth century the new [e:] shifted further to [i:], so that the result indicated in the text was eventually attained. The difference between the two *e* sounds in Middle English has hitherto been disregarded in this book simply because Chaucer, who is the only Middle English writer that most people are likely to be concerned about pronouncing, often rhymes with two sounds. It could not be disregarded in a more searching study of the language.

Vowel	*Word*	*Chaucerian pronunciation*	*Shakespearean pronunciation*
/ɑ:/	place	/plɑsə/	/ple:s/
/e:/	feet	/fe:t/	/fi:t/
/i:/	bite	/bi:tə/	/bɑit/
/ɔ:/	stone	/stɔ:n/	/sto:n/
/o:/	fool	/fo:l/	/fu:l/
/u:/	mouse	/mu:s/	/mɑus/

As we mentioned in Chapter 5, Chaucer's vowels had approximately the same values as those in modern Spanish and Italian, and each pair of short and long vowels had approximately the same quality. The difference between the short and long *e,* for instance, was simply in the length of time they were held, and not in a different placement of the tongue. If the shift had happened a century or two earlier our spelling would probably have reflected it; but because it occurred only after some of our spelling conventions had at least begun to solidify, it left us with our very curious habit of using the same letters to indicate phonetically unrelated vowel sounds. Our ancestors simply continued to spell with the letters they were used to, even when they had greatly changed their habits of pronunciation. The shift does not explain all our odd spellings of vowel sounds, because other factors are involved in many words; but it does account for the greatest single peculiarity.

The Short Vowels

There was no general shift in the short vowels, but /æ/ was changed to /ɑ/, and in many words /u/ was changed to /ə/. The later development of both these vowels has been so varied in different phonetic environments, however, that it is not practicable to consider them thoroughly here.

Consonants

The only general change in the consonant system during this period was that /χ/ (spelled *gh*) either changed to /f/ as in *cough* and *enough* or disappeared entirely as in *thought* and *bough.* The tendency was for it to change to /f/ when final and disappear when followed by *t;* but this tendency was often disturbed by analogies too complicated to go into here.

Toward the end of the period /i/ changed to /j/ when it was preceded by a consonant and followed by a lightly stressed vowel. This change accounts for our present pronunciation of words like *special* and *ambitious,* which often (but not always, because the change was then under way) have an extra syllable in Shakespeare.

The only other changes that need be mentioned are the shifts between /d/ and /ð/ in the neighborhood of /r/. Thus *fader* and *moder* changed to *father* and *mother,* while *burthen* and *murther* changed to *burden* and *murder.* Once again the full statement would be very complicated, and there are a number of irregularities. For most purposes it will be sufficient to remember that such changes were possible.

Changes in Inflection

The changes in inflection during this period were comparatively slight, but notice these:

1. *Nouns*

Constructions like "the King of England's crown," known as the *group genitive,* replaced the older "the King's crown of England."

The ordinary *-es* genitive ending was often written as *-is* or *-ys,* and probably usually pronounced /iz/, as it generally is today. "Charles's book" therefore sounds exactly like "Charles his book" if both phrases are pronounced casually; and the idea that the second phrase is the original one, and the first a mere contraction, became widespread during this period. (There are occasional examples of it even in Old English.) This idea has no historical justification, and could hardly explain such combinations as "the lady's dress," but it was held for centuries, and is taken for granted by many people today, though the "correct" form now seldom appears except in bookplates. The apostrophe that we still use in the genitive is due to this misunderstanding.

2. *Pronouns*

In older English *his* had been the genitive form of *it* as well as *he;* but in the neuter it was now supplanted, first by *it,* then by *its* (usually written *it's* until about 1800). The use of the forms *ye* and *you* in the singular when addressing superiors had begun in the thirteenth century. It later became normal among equals unless they were particularly intimate, and during the Renaissance the singular forms dropped out almost entirely in the standard language. Moreover, the original distinction between the nominative *ye* and the objective *you* became so blurred that either form could be used for all purposes, with *you* gradually gaining.

The use of *who* and *which* as relative pronouns became common during this period, though there are occasional examples earlier. It is generally believed that this construction developed in three stages, something like this: First, the direct question, "Who was there?" Second, the reported question, "He asked who was there." Finally, the statement, "I know the man who was there."

Because some grammarians seem to believe that the *wh-* relatives are the only fully legitimate ones, it is well to remember that "the man *that* I saw" was in use for centuries before "the man *whom* I saw." "The man I saw" is still earlier — and still good.

3. *Adjectives*

Double comparatives and superlatives (*more nobler, most unkindest*) were used freely, but not by everybody. In other words, the permissible feeling that such expressions are redundant had not been put into a rule making them criminal. Also, long adjectives were often compared by *-er* and *-est*.

4. *Verbs*

By far the most important changes in inflection took place among the verbs. The drift of the originally strong verbs into the weak class continued. Such verbs as *bide, crow,* and *dread,* among others, show the weak preterites *bided, crowed,* and *dreaded* along with the older *bode, crew,* and *drad.* In fact the drift was so strong that a number of weak forms that have since been outlawed were in respectable use, such as *blowed, growed,* and *shrinked.*

In the third person singular the -(*e*)*s* ending, which in Middle English occurred only in the Northern dialect, began to compete with the -(*e*)*th* ending that had been in use throughout the rest of the country, and eventually drove it out. Shakespeare used both, frequently in the same sentence, and presumably chose whichever form he thought sounded better in a particular place. But in the first half of the seventeenth century the -(*e*)*s* ending apparently became universal in speech, though many writers continued to spell it -(*e*)*th*. There are a number of comments on this inconsistency.

The Midland plural ending in -(*e*)*n* and the Southern one in -(*e*)*th* both dropped out of the standard language, leaving the uninflected form that we have today. But rather curiously, the -(*e*)*s* ending that had been used in the plural as well as the singular in the Northern dialect now appeared for the first time in the plural in other areas. Though it is not nearly as common as the uninflected form, it appears so often in careful writing, and in verse where the extra syllable fits the meter, that it is generally accepted as a recognized variant rather than a mistake in agreement.

The -(*e*)*n* ending dropped out completely in the infinitive, and in most past participles except those in which it is still preserved.

We may summarize by saying of inflections that most verbs had reached the forms they have now, except that the -(*e*)*th* third singular was still fairly common through most of the period, and the second singular -(*e*)*st* ending was still possible, though becoming infrequent. But our now rather rigid system of verb phrases had not fully developed. In questions Shakespeare could say "Goes he?" where we must use either "Does he go?" or "Is he going?" And in negative statements he could say either "He not goes" or "He goes not" where we have to use "He does not go" or "He is not going." On the other hand, he could say "I do go" without implying the special emphasis that such a sentence would now have.

On the whole the progressive forms (*is going,* etc.) were comparatively uncommon, partly because they were not needed in questions and negations, and partly because the simple forms could still be used to describe immediate action.

The most important difference in the "perfect tenses" is that *be* rather than *have* was used with verbs indicating change of condition or location — roughly the same kinds of verbs that require *être* rather than *avoir* in French, or *sein* rather than *haben* in German. We have preserved this tendency only very erratically. Thus in the sixteenth century the regular expressions were *is come* and *is gone,* rather than *has come* and *has gone.* We can now say either *is* or *has gone,* but only *has come.*

The Spread of Education

So far we have considered only what might be called the automatic changes in the language. Before turning to those which owe at least something to theory we must consider some of the nonlinguistic developments that made efforts at deliberate improvement far more effective than they could have been in the Old and Middle English periods.

During most of the Middle Ages education had not only been completely controlled by the church but directed very largely toward ecclesiastical ends. The language taught was Latin, and one of the chief reasons for sending boys to school was to train them to sing in choirs. The connection between the two meanings of *clerical* now found in *clerical job* as opposed to *clerical collar* was so close that anybody who could read was entitled to "benefit of clergy," which removed him from the jurisdiction of the secular courts, and was often very convenient if he didn't want to be hanged. Of course, not every student had a deep commitment to the church. Some education was obviously necessary for the law and some other careers. But on the whole even bare literacy was comparatively rare, and not universally admired. Many of the noble class clearly regarded writing as a rather menial occupation, distinctly beneath their dignity; and most of their inferiors seem to have considered it a mystery with which there was no reason for them to bother.

Both the spread and the secularization of education were gradual and complicated, but it is clear that they made considerable progress during the fifteenth century. A good many middle-class people, including women, were now learning at least to read and write English as part of the natural order of things. One result was that when printing was introduced during the latter part of the century the market for books was very much greater, especially for books in English, than it would have been even a hundred years earlier; and their effects on the language as well as the life of the times were consequently more widespread and very much faster. It has been estimated that by Shakespeare's time between a third and a half of the population of London could read — a situation that in Chaucer's age would have seemed absolutely incredible.

Weakening of Class Distinctions

One important reason for the spread of education was that hereditary class distinctions were losing some of their rigidity, so that the chance of rising in the world (as distinct from the church) was a good deal more promising than it had been. We need not here go into the causes of this change, but we should notice two of the more obvious results. The first was simply that with the possibility of rising from one class to another a great many more people found it worthwhile to educate their children in order to prepare them for the new opportunities. The same situation is paralleled on a higher level today, when the concept of a "working class" has practically disappeared, and a college education is coming to be regarded as almost indispensable for a satisfactory life. The second was more complicated. When class lines are fixed, a man might as well behave naturally, because imitating his "betters" is more likely to bring him ridicule than rewards. But when it becomes possible to move from one class to another it is important for an ambitious man to learn to behave, linguistically and otherwise, like the members of the class into which he hopes to move. At the same time there is a tendency for those in the higher orders, no longer automatically protected from invasion, to become rather more careful in their own use of language as a sign of their continued superiority. The upshot is that class dialects are likely to become both more distinct and most important just at the time when a too simple analysis of the situation might suggest that they would break down.

It apparently took the schools of England a long time to adjust themselves to the problem of teaching "good English" to everybody who wanted to learn it; but ambitious people could read as well as listen, and there is no reasonable doubt that the written form of the language began to have a stronger effect on the spoken than it had ever had before.

Introduction of Printing

William Caxton set up the first printing press in England about 1476, and others soon followed. Looking back, it would be hard for us to pick a more strategic date for the invention to have its maximum effect. Books could now be reproduced for a very small fraction of their former cost, and exact duplicates could be made in any numbers desired. The spread of education was therefore greatly accelerated, and the whole nature of the spread of knowledge — in and out of school — changed in many ways. It is easy for us to appreciate the effects of the economy brought about by printing, but it takes much more thought to realize how uniformity and immensely faster distribution affected the language.

On pages 117–118 we considered the extreme diversity of English manuscripts. An author might weep at the changes in his text made by a careless or independent copyist, but most people could not have had a very reliable idea of what the true text of even a single work was, to say nothing of an established set of conventions that should govern all works. Printing not only eliminated most of the diversity between copies but contributed greatly to the establishment of general conventions. It did not bring about any miraculously rapid change. A printer can make as many mistakes as a scribe, and it took some generations to develop the tools, the techniques, and the professional attitude that all seem so obvious once they have been achieved. But from the first, printers were forced by the very size of the audience at which they aimed to face some problems to which scribes had never had to pay much attention. And from the first the audience was presumably somewhat affected by the "authority of the printed page," which still has a powerful influence on most people — much in the way that a blueprint, which is merely an inexpensive reproduction of an architect's drawing, is likely to impress them with a feeling of inevitability that they never get from the drawing itself. The fact that London was the center of printing enormously reinforced the prestige of London English throughout the country. It no longer seemed reasonable for a northerner to translate a work from Southern English into his own dialect. Printed English was obviously for everybody.

Another effect of printing was to encourage writing as a way of making a living. Earlier authors were sometimes supported by patrons, but they could not possibly live on the sale of their work. Now printers and booksellers were willing to pay (in moderation) for copy, so that a career in letters was open to many more people than ever before. It is impossible to estimate how many books have been written primarily in the hope that they would be printed and sold, but at the most moderate guess the number is astronomical. Even if we consider only those both written and printed during the English Renaissance, the number is considerable, and many of these were either composed in or translated into English because writers and printers wanted to take advantage of the larger market in that language.

Development of Spelling Conventions

Even today English spelling is notoriously confusing. Its general inconsistencies are so well known that there is no need to go into them here. Moreover, there are a number of characteristic differences between American and British practices, some of them affecting large classes of words (*-or* and *-our, -er* and *-re,* etc.), others only specific words (*tire* and *tyre, curb* and *kerb,* etc.). And finally, there are a fair number of words in which variant spellings are current and acceptable in each country. But at least the whole subject has been thoroughly surveyed, the results published, and for the vast majority of words a definite agreement has been reached. Most of us at least try to use the spellings authorized by the dictionaries; and if we get into print our publishers take a good deal of care to see that we do.

At the beginning of the Renaissance period there was not one word with a definitely established spelling. Even the indefinite article *a* and the pronoun *I* might be spelled *o* and *y*. About the most that can be said is that words taken directly from Latin (which did, of course, have a long orthographic tradition) were spelled with a much closer approach to uniformity than those from other sources.

A good many people, naturally enough, were fairly consistent in their own habits, and a number of them proposed reformed spelling systems for general use. Some of the proposals were for purely phonetic spelling. One Thomas Smith extended the alphabet to thirty-four letters, and in addition marked the long vowels. William Bullokar, objecting to the arbitrary new symbols, took only the familiar letters as his base; but he showed variations in sound with such a bewildering collection of accents, apostrophes, and what he called "hooks and strikes" that his material is extremely hard to read even after careful study. It is too bad, however, that we could not have adopted his Rule 17, which might be called the philosopher's stone of orthography. It is given here without the diacritical markings:

> And this stryk (͵) is excepcion general
> Too spel wordz truly when thæz rulz fail al.

We haven't the faintest idea how this result was to be obtained.

Fortunately or unfortunately, such radical systems received no general support. Richard Mulcaster, in his *Elementarie* (1582), took an entirely different approach. He did not consider that truly phonetic spelling was possible, because pronunciation was constantly changing. He even doubted that it was greatly to be desired, because the use of one letter to indicate more than one sound seemed to him no worse than the use of one word to indicate more than one meaning — a variation that is inevitable unless we are to insist on a vocabulary far too large for any human memory to

THE FIRST PART OF THE ELEMENTARIE.

Cap. I.

Why I begin at the elementarie, and wherein it conſiſteth.

THere be two cauſes, which moue me to the penning of this Elementarie, whereof the one is mine own promis, the òther is the argument it ſelf. The argument it ſelf perſuades me to the penning thereof, bycauſe it is ſo fit for the training vp of childern, as nothing can be fitter: and the ſtream of diſcourſe in my former book, which I name Poſitions, did carie me on to promis it, and binds me to perform it. But for the better linkking of this book to that, ſeing this is nothing elſe, but the performing of one pece, which I promiſed in that, I muſt nedes ſhortlie run ouer the main branches of that, ear I enter into this. The matter of that book conſiſteth chefelie in two generall points, the one proper, the other proceding. I call that argument proper, which is the naturall ſubiect of that ſame book, & being once handled there deſires no further ſpeche in any other treatis. I call that proceding which being but named there as a thing moſt neceſſarie to ſom further end, requireth more handling, then it hath there, to be better fitted for ſo profitable an end. Of the firſt ſort, which is the proper inhabitant of that ſame book, and to be enquired for there, all thoſe diſcourſes be, which concern the teacher,

A ſhort repeating of the former book entitled Poſitions.

The proper argument of the Poſitions.

A

A page from Richard Mulcaster's *The First Part of the Elementarie* (London, 1582). By permission of the Folger Shakespeare Library, Washington, D.C.

master it. Moreover, he was convinced that any attempt at a wholesale revolution was so hopeless as to be a complete waste of time. He therefore wanted to start with whatever nucleus of general agreement he could find, make such minor improvements as might be accepted without too much resistance, and — above all — make the point that it is more important for everybody to spell in the same way than it is to find a theoretically perfect system.

His work was often quoted with approval and undoubtedly had some effect, though not all his specific recommendations were followed. By the end of the period most of our spellings had become pretty well standardized, and we have made few changes since except in some of the commonest endings. For instance, we now use *-y* instead of *-ie, -al* instead of *-all, -ess* instead of *-esse,* and *-ic* instead of *-ick*. Because the modern forms all remove silent letters, we may consider them improvements. At any rate, since the seventeenth century we have been spelling words borrowed (not too early) from Latin and Greek with fair consistency, though with some pedantic complications. We use the *-ant* ending for words derived from Latin verbs of the first conjugation, and the *-ent* ending for those from other conjugations. Such etymological precision probably seemed reasonable enough to a generation of Latinists; but most people today would certainly vote for the French practice of using *-ant* for them all.

A minor complication resulted from occasional efforts to bring words borrowed from French closer to the original Latin forms. Thus *debt, doubt,* and *fault* come from the French *dette, doute,* and *faute*. The restoration in the first two of the *b* from Latin *debitum* and *dubitum* did nothing but make them harder to spell, but for some reason the restored *l* in *fault* eventually came to be pronounced.

Doubtless[2] the printers had more to do with the development of uniform standards than the scholars did. As anybody who has ever had much to do with them knows, they are likely to have a passion for consistency in detail, though during the early years of printing they were tempted in the other direction. They had to "justify" their lines — that is, make them come out even at the right-hand margins. They could do this by inserting little wedges to vary the spaces between letters, but it must have been a great convenience to use a variable spelling to gain the same end even more neatly. Eventually, however, it seemed even more convenient to spell

[2] In academic writing the word *doubtless* generally means that the writer is bringing forth an opinion for which he has no real evidence.

everybody's writing the same way, and disregard the peculiar preferences of erratic authors. Nobody really knows who was responsible; but on the simple grounds that an approximate agreement was reached in only one hundred and seventy-five years, we are inclined to give most of the credit to the printers.

English and Latin in the Renaissance

We are now rather generally accustomed to thinking of English as a living language, and of Latin as not only a dead one, but one that has been dead since about the fifth century. Of course we have heard of medieval Latin, but most people seem to think of it as a comparatively small and decidedly gloomy appendix to classical Latin, consisting mostly of things like official charters and probably incomprehensible theology, all rather painfully and artificially translated from the languages in which it must have been originally conceived. It is in those languages that they expect to find all the really vivid impressions of medieval life and thought.

This evaluation would have seemed fantastic to the Middle Ages. To them Latin was, like Greek and Hebrew and a few others, a legitimate language going back to the Tower of Babel; and as the official language of Christendom it was ordained to last as long as the world. Though it was no longer the first language for anybody, educated people still spoke it as a matter of course — in casual conversation, not merely in set pieces; and much of the time they automatically thought in it. They were naturally inclined to write in it whenever they were addressing their peers, and their writing is amazingly varied, including fine drinking songs as well as magnificent hymns, and sophisticated satire along with sober history. English, on the other hand, was merely a "vernacular" — a corrupt form of speech with no particular future. A thirteenth-century scholar (or even schoolboy) would have taken the idea that it could supplant Latin for all purposes about as seriously as a twentieth-century scholar would take the suggestion that Pennsylvania Dutch would drive out Standard English as the future language of literature, learning, and government in this country.

There is some very fine Middle English poetry, but most of the prose and a great deal of pedestrian verse was written in a definitely missionary spirit, "for the common people to understand" — and to understand in a rather limited way. The laity were expected to *believe* the doctrine handed down to them rather than to analyze its structure. In other words, the audience was being talked down to — not contemptuously, but in a way that called for simplicity, and certainly discouraged any effort to "enrich and improve the language" in order to give them all the confusing details.

During the Renaissance translations and compilations from Latin sources were undertaken in a very different spirit. On one side, there was a much greater effort to give the full intellectual context; on the other, there was a growing respect for the capabilities of English, and a conscious and widespread effort to develop those capabilities. The result was an enormous increase in the vocabulary and a considerable development in the characteristic sentence structure. By the end of the period English was firmly established as adequate for all purposes.

The Debatable Importance of Authors

Because some readers will feel that in the preceding paragraph we attribute far too much importance to the efforts of individual authors, it will be well to consider the question carefully. It used to be rather generally taken for granted (by such as had any opinion at all on the subject) that a language was formed by its great writers; and Chaucer, living at a critical time, was given especial importance. As late as 1932, G. K. Chesterton began a book on this poet with an almost casual assertion that he would be writing in French if Chaucer had not chosen to write in English. It is now more usual for linguists to hold the directly contrary opinion, that language develops among the mass of the people, with writers simply using the medium as they find it, and affecting it very little. Both attitudes are exaggerated, but it is not very satisfactory to toss them aside with a sentence to the effect that "there is much to be said on both sides, and the truth no doubt lies somewhere between these two extremes." Conditions vary so much that any operating formula is hopeless, but we can occasionally learn something by considering the evidence in specific cases.

There can be no doubt of Chaucer's influence on literature. All through the fifteenth century he was widely imitated and enthusiastically praised, and the following passage from Caxton's preface to his second edition of the *Canterbury Tales* (1484) will give some idea of the esteem in which he was held:

> Grete thankes, laude, and honour ought to be gyuen vnto the clerkes, poetes, and historiographs, that haue wreton many noble bokes of wysedom of the lyues, passions, and myracles of holy sayntes, of hystoryes, of noble and famous actes and faittes, and of the cronycles sith the begynnyng of the creacion of the world vnto thys present tyme, by whyche we ben dayly enformed and have knowleche of many thynges, of whom we shold not haue knowen, yf they had not left to vs theyr monumentis wreton. Emong whom and inespecial to-fore alle other we ought to gyue a synguler laude vnto that noble and grete philosopher Gefferey Chaucer, the whiche for his ornate wrytyng in our tongue may wel haue the name of a laureate poete.
>
> For to-fore that he by hys labour enbelysshyd, ornated, and made faire our Englisshe, in thys royame was had rude speche and incongrue, as yet it appiereth by olde bookes, whyche at thys day ought not to haue place ne be compared emong ne to hys beauteuous volumes and aournate writynges, of whom he made many bokes and treatyces of many a noble historye as wel in metre as in ryme and prose, and them so craftyly made, that he comprehended hys maters in short, quyck, and hye sentences, eschewing prolyxyte, castyng away the chaf of superfluyte, and shewyng the pyked grayn of sentence, vtteryd by crafty and sugred eloquence. . . .[3]

We may cheerfully grant everything that Caxton says about the quality of Chaucer's writing; and for the sake of the argument we may even accept the contrast with all that had been written in English before as "rude speche and incongrue," though if Caxton had seen and been able to read all that is now available he might not have made his statement quite so strong. But the fact that Chaucer did wonderful things *with* the language does not in itself prove that he did anything *to* it. His influence does not, for instance, seem to have had the effect of making Caxton's own sentences particularly short and quick. It was not sufficient to keep the London dialect from changing markedly soon after his death, and losing most of the Southern forms in which his work abounds; and the best of his followers wrote in their own quite different Scottish dialect. We don't even know definitely that he added a single word to the vocabu-

[3] Kaiser, p. 566, ll. 118–136.

lary. He certainly contributed to the preservation of some that might otherwise have dropped from the language, but this was largely the result of later antiquarianism rather than of immediate contact. On the whole we must accept the belief that during the manuscript age the general drift of the language was not much influenced by literature.

But with the introduction of printing and wider education the possibility was much greater of the language changing from the top down as well as from the bottom up. From Caxton's time on we find evidence of a growing desire to improve English, and to establish it as an adequate language for all purposes, on a par with Greek and Latin. Many of the workers had contradictory aims, and much of the effort may seem misdirected, but the total effect on the language was certainly considerable. Most of us can recognize that our own usage is heavily influenced by the books we have read and the instruction we have received, and even a complete illiterate today speaks differently from the way he would if Shakespeare had never written a play or Lowth a grammar.

Increase in Vocabulary

The most conspicuous change in the language during the Renaissance was the enormous growth of the vocabulary — a growth of which the literate public was well aware, and about which writers held strong though conflicting views. Some of them were simply against it. They saw no reason why the words already in the language should not be enough for anybody who took the trouble to use them effectively, and ridiculed all innovations. The borrowings from Latin they called "inkhorn terms"; those from the other modern tongues "oversea language"; and the revivals of obsolete English words "Chaucerisms." Some of the innovators certainly gave them targets for legitimate ridicule, but the opposition to all changes now seems petty as well as absurd. Directly opposed to these conservatives was a group who believed in enriching the language by borrowing from all available sources; and in between was a third who were opposed to foreign borrowings, but believed the language could be improved not only by reviving old words but by making new compounds from native elements.

It is perhaps misleading to speak of the adherents of these three attitudes as groups. There was no movement in England with a unity or organization comparable to the school of poets known as the Pléiade, which at the same period was fighting a carefully planned campaign for enrichment of the French language. But though the debate was less thoroughly organized, it was quite as vigorous, and even more interesting because there were no party lines to tone down individual differences of opinion.

The Conservatives

A blow-by-blow account of the controversy would be long and confusing. Here we need only attempt to see the main issues in relation to their eventual effect on the language. We may begin by examining the position of a man who was quite satisfied with the language as it stood, and thought it only needed to be used more skilfully. In his *Arte of Rhetorique* (1553) Thomas Wilson has a famous passage on "Plainness what it is," which includes an imaginary "inkhorn letter" supposed to be written by a clergyman to a friend who might be able to help him get a position. It is here annotated rather thoroughly, partly because it illustrates some of the printing conventions of the times, and partly because many of the words differ from their modern equivalents either in having been formed with different suffixes from those that are now used, or in more closely preserving the literal meaning of their Latin originals. Notice that the punctuation differs from ours about as much as the spelling.

> Emong al other lessons this should first be learned, y^t we neuer affect any straũge ynkehorne termes, but so speake as is commonly receiued: neither sekyng to be ouer fine, nor yet liuyng ouer carelesse, vsyng our speache as most men do, & ordryng our wittes, as the fewest haue doen. Some seke so farre for outlãdishe Englishe, that thei forget altogether their mothers lãguage. And I dare swere this, if some of their mothers were aliue, thei were not able to tell, what thei say, & yet these fine Englishe clerkes, wil saie thei speake in their mother tongue, if a mã should charge thẽ for coũterfeityng the kynges English. Some farre iorneid ientlemẽ at their returne home, like as thei loue to go in forrein apparell, so thei wil pouder their talke w^t ouersea lãguage. He that cometh lately out of France, wil talke Frẽche English, & neuer blushe at the matter. Another choppes in with Angleso Italiano: the lawyer wil store his stomach with the pratyng of Pedlers. The Auditour in makyng his accompt and rekenyng, cometh in with sise sould, and cater denere, for vi. s. iiij d. The fine Courtier wil talke nothyng but Chaucer. The misticall wise menne, and Poeticall Clerkes, will

speake nothyng but quaint prouerbes, and blynd allegories, delityng much in their awne darkenesse, especially, when none can tell what thei dooe saie. The vnlearned or foolishe phantasticall, that smelles but of learnyng (suche felowes as haue seen learned men in their daies) will so latine their tongues, that the simple cannot but wonder at their talke, and thynke surely thei speake by some Reuelacion. I know them that thynke Rhetorique, to stande wholy vpon darke woordes, and he that can catche an ynke horne terme by the taile, hym thei compt to bee a fine Englishe man, and a good Rhetotician [*sic*]. And the rather to set out this folie, I will adde here suche a letter, as Willyam Sommer himself, could not make a better for that purpose. Some will thinke and swere to, that there was neuer any suche thyng writtẽ, well I wil not force any man to beleue it, but I will saie thus muche, and abide by it to, the like haue been made heretofore, and praised aboue the Moone.

An ynkehorne letter

Pondering, expẽding, and reuoluting with my self your ingent affabilitie, and ingenious capacitee for mundane affairs: I cannot but celebrate and extolle your magnificall dexteritee, aboue all other. For how could you haue adepted suche illustrate prerogatiue, and domenicall superioritee, if the fecunditee of your ingenie had not been so fertile, & woũderfull pregnaunt. Now thefore beeyng accersited, to suche splendent renoume, & dignitee splendidious: I doubt not but you will adiuuate suche poore adnichilate orphanes, as whilome ware cõdisciples with you, and of antique familiaritie in Lincolne shire. Emong whom I beeyng a Scholasticall panion, obtestate your sublimitee to extoll myne infirmitee. There is a sacerdotall dignitee in my natiue countrey, contiguate to me, where I now contemplate: whiche your worshipfull benignitee, could sone impetrate for me, if it would like you to extend your scedules, and collaude me in them to the right honorable lorde Chauncellor, or rather Archigrãmacian of Englande. You knowe my literature, you knowe the pastorall promocion, I obtestate your clemencie, to inuigilate thus muche for me, accordyng to my confidence, and as you knowe my condigne merites, for suche a compendious liuyng. But now I relinquishe to fatigate your intelligence with any more friuolous verbositie, and therefore he that rules the climates be euermore your beautreux, your fortresse, and your bulwarke.

Amen[4]

1. *y^t:* that. A carelessly made thorn (þ) looked rather like a *y*, and early printers often abbreviated *the* as *y^e* and *that* as *y^t*. The pronunciation of this *y^e* as *ye* is a purely modern error.
1. *neuer.* The letters *u* and *v* were originally merely different forms of the same letter, which could be used to indicate either the vowel or the consonant sound. Printers generally adopted the practice found here, of using *v* for either sound initially, and *u* for either sound in all other positions.
2. *straũge.* In manuscripts a macron (¯) or tilde (~) over a vowel indicated that a following *m* or *n* had been omitted to save space. This practice is followed rather erratically here, and in many other early books.
6. *mothers.* The convention of using an apostrophe to indicate the genitive had not yet been developed.
10. *iorneid ientlemẽ:* journeyed gentlemen. The practice of using *i* for initial *j* is very common. It is not so often used instead of *g*, as here.
12. *w^t:* with. This abbreviation is not nearly so common as *y^t*.
15. *pratyng of Pedlers.* Underworld slang.
17. *vi. s. iiij d. Six sous and four deniers* (French coins) for six shillings and fourpence. The modern abbreviations for English money, £–s–d, are from the same source, with £ standing for *livres* (pounds).
20. *awne:* own.
29. *Sommer.* Author of a Saxon-Latin-English dictionary, and thus well supplied with all sorts of words if he wanted to use them.
36. *expẽding:* weighing out. The modern meaning skips to the logical next step of paying out.
36. *reuoluting.* Many Latin verbs had in the past participle an *-at-*, *-et-*, or *-ut-* element which did not appear in the infinitive. French verbs are regularly taken from the infinitive

[4] J. L. Moore, *Tudor-Stuart Views on the Growth, Status, and Destiny of the English Language* (Halle, 1910), pp. 91–93.

form, and many English verbs are taken from the French. But English verbs borrowed directly from the Latin are regularly based on the past participle. Thus we say *celebrate* and *contemplate* (both of which occur in this passage) where the French have *célébrer* and *contempler. Revoluting* is thus as reasonable a form as *revolving,* though it does not happen to have survived (except as a playful expression for "making a revolution").

36. *ingent:* enormous. Probably dropped because it didn't sound big enough.
38. *magnificall.* After all, we say *beneficial* as well as *beneficent.*
39. *adepted:* attained. An *adept* has obtained a good deal of skill.
40. *domenicall: Lordly,* though we now use this word only in connection with the Lord's day (*dimanche* in French).
40. *ingenie:* intellect. From *ingenium,* and better etymology than our *ingenuity.*
42. *accersited:* brought.
43. *adiuuate:* aid. From the past participle *adiuvatus.*
43. *adnichilate:* reduced to nothing. A variant (on good authority) of *annihilate,* though here not quite as strong in meaning. Here, as in a few other words, the implication of the past participle is preserved without the addition of the *-d* ending. Compare *finite, destitute,* and so forth.
46. *panion.* From *panis,* meaning *bread.* We now say *companion,* or fellow bread-eater.
46. *obtestate:* call upon for testimony.
47. *sacerdotall dignitee:* priestly position.
47. *contiguate.* Change *-ate* to *-ous.*
49. *impetrate:* obtain by request.
50. *collaude.* The prefix omitted from *companion* is added here to *laud.*
53. *inuigilate:* look out for.
54. *condigne:* worthy.
55. *compendious.* Here, simply *convenient,* because so close at hand.
57. *beautreux:* buttress.

The gist of his argument is the sound Aristotelian advice that we should depend on our brains and skill rather than on our vocabularies for rhetorical effect; and it is presented so skilfully that unless we are very careful we may overlook its two serious defects. The first is that it simply assumes that the language is already completely adequate for all purposes; the second, that it considers only the practices of fools and a straw man set up to be conveniently demolished, and makes no attempt to consider what might be done by sensible men using the practices it opposes.

Obviously anybody who seriously wrote such a letter as the one presented would be an ass (unless he happened to know that the man he was addressing was one, and proceeded accordingly). But possibly he would have been an ass in any language, and a good many of the words that Wilson ridicules have not only passed into everyday use, but would be very hard to do without today. We may grant Wilson's principle that it is always bad to use a fancy word when a simple one will do the job as well; but we shall soon find evidence that some of the new words were being introduced because they could demonstrably do the job better. Wilson does go on to say that some borrowings are legitimate "either for lacke of store, or els because wee would enriche the language"; but because he excepts them from the charge of affectation only when "all other are agreed to folowe the same way," it is hard to see how anybody could legitimately introduce them.

Nearly forty years later (1592) Thomas Nash echoes Wilson, offering a "patheticall posie" of inkhorn words and phrases, including such (to him) obvious absurdities as *conscious mind, ingenuity, rascality, artificiality, addicted to theory, perfunctory discourses, amicable terms, extensively employed, notoriety,* and *negotiation.* But perhaps the most delightfully innocent summary of the conservative position is this sentence from Samuel Daniel's *A Defence of Ryme* (1603):

> And I cannot but wonder at the strange presumption of some men that dare so audaciously aduenture to introduce any whatsoeuer forraine wordes, bee they neuer so strange; and of themselues as it were, without a Parliament, without any consent, or allowance, stablish them as Free-denizens in our language.

It would be nice to know what past *Parliament* he thought had had the *strange presumption* to give *consent* or *allowance* to such *forraine* words as *stablish, audaciously,* and *aduenture,* and to *introduce* them as *denizens* in our *language.*

The Enthusiasts for Native Resources

Wilson's remark that "The fine Courtier wil talke nothyng but Chaucer" is tantalizing. We don't know how much exaggeration it contained, nor how long the fad lasted. The movement to revive old terms, and to make new combinations of old elements, had a much slighter permanent effect on the language than borrowings from outside sources; but courtiers were not the only ones engaged in it. A number of poets, with Spenser as the most determined as well as the most distinguished example, were naturally enough delighted with Chaucer, and felt free to reintroduce any words that he had used — or that they thought he had or might have used. (It is quite unreasonable but almost inevitable for a student of Middle English to wish that Spenser had been a better linguist. Obviously false antiques have a singular lack of charm for anybody who recognizes their synthetic quality.) And finally there were scholars like Sir John Cheke, interested not so much in the flavor of antiquity as in the theoretical purity of the language. In a letter to a friend (1557) he says:

> I am of this opinion that our own tung shold be written cleane and pure, vnmixt and vnmangeled with borowing of other tunges, wherein if we take not heed bi tijm, euer borowing and neuer payeng, she shall be fain to keep her house as bankrupt. For then doth our tung naturallie and praisablie vtter her meaning, when she bouroweth no conterfeitness of other tunges to attire her self withall, but vseth plainlie her own with such shift, as nature craft, experiens, and folowing of other excellent doth lead her vnto, and if she want at ani tijm (as being vnperfight she must) yet let her borow with suche bashfulnes, that it mai appeer, that if either the mould of our own tung could serue vs to fascion a woord of our own, or if the old denisoned wordes could content and ease this neede we wold not boldly venture of vnknowen wordes. . . .[5]

Whatever we may think of the argument as a whole, the paragraph is a beautiful example of the difficulty of expressing a puristic attitude without doing violence to it in the very expression. We should write English clean and pure, unmixed and unmangled. Good enough. But while *cleane* and *vnmangeled* follow the precept in which they appear, *pure* is not pure in

[5] Moore, p. 94.

this sense, and *vnmixt* is decidedly mixed, containing a Latin root and an English prefix. In fact a sixth of the words in the paragraph have foreign roots, which seems rather a high proportion for the "bashful" borrowing that Cheke condones because the language is "vnperfight." A great many later objections to borrowings, whether of Latin words, Americanisms, or slang terms, have been marked by the same kind of inconsistency.

Cheke did follow his expressed principles to the extent of coining such words as *hundreder* for *centurion* and *gainrising* for *resurrection;* but most of them failed to stick, and it seems likely that similar ones would fail in the same way today. It is a very curious fact that we seem to regard the roots and prefixes of Greek and Latin as the natural building blocks of new words, to be used with complete freedom, but are extremely conservative about making any combination with their English equivalents that are not already authorized by the dictionary. In this respect English is in strong contrast with German, which still compounds native elements so freely that no dictionary pretends to list all the legitimate combinations.

But curiously enough there was not in the Renaissance, and there is not now, any hesitation about the use of native suffixes, inflectional or otherwise, to shift borrowed words to new functions. As Richard Carew points out:

> For our owne partes, we imploye the borrowed ware soe far to our advantag that we raise a profitt of new woordes from the same stock, which yeat in their owne countrey are not merchantable; for example, wee deduce diuers wordes from the Latine which in the Latyne self cannot be yealded, as the verbes To *Aire, beard, cross, flame,* and their deriuations *ayring, ayred, bearder, bearding, bearded,* &c., as alsoe *close, closely, closenes, glosingely, hourely, maiesticall, maiestically.* In like sort wee graffe vpon Frentch wordes those buddes to which that soyle affordeth noe growth, as *cheifly, faulty, slauish, precisenes.* Diuers wordes alsoe wee deriue out of the Latyne at second hand by the French and make good English, though both Latyne and French haue their handes closed in that behalfe, as verbes *Praye, Pointe, Paze, Prest, Rent,* &c., and alsoe in the aduerbs *carpingly, currantly, actiuely, colourably,* &c.[6]

Half a century later Richard Verstegan was carrying on Cheke's argument, and showing the same sort of inconsistency. He tells us that English

[6] From *The Excellency of the English Tongue* — Moore, p. 114.

is a branch of Teutonic, and traces Teutonic back to the Tower of Babel, thereby putting it on a par with Latin, Greek, and Hebrew. He even finds etymological evidence that Teutonic rather than Hebrew (as was generally believed) was the original, pre-Babelian language of all mankind. The argument is that the name *Adam* is cognate with the Teutonic word for breath (German *atem*), and *Eve* with *even,* as in "even the same" — Adam having been changed from clay to man by the Lord's breath, and Eve having been made even the same as her husband. Verstegan does not insist on this theory, taking the stand that its originator's "opinion exceeded his proofs"; but he puts it in for whatever it may be worth. After several pages of demonstration that a language of such antiquity needs no help from strangers, he sums up his argument in these words:

> For mine owne part, I hold them deceived that thinke our speech bettered by the aboundance of our daily borrowed words, for they being of an other nature, & not Originally belonging to our language, do not neyther can they in our tongue, beare their naturall, and true derivation. . . .[7]

Counting the Scandinavian pronoun forms, exactly one-fourth of these words are of foreign origin.

The Travelers: Oversea Language

Foreign travel was very fashionable, and apparently most of the travelers thought it was worth advertising. The young man who returned from the continent wearing strange clothes and filling his talk with foreign phrases is a popular object of Elizabethan ridicule. Borrowing from French, of course, was nothing new, and most of us would find it impossible to distinguish between the words taken in at this time and those imported earlier, though contemporaries could recognize their novelty. Italian and Spanish words had a much more exotic flavor, especially in their *-a* and *-o* endings (which the Elizabethans frequently confused). Many of these other words have now lost their endings, and their flavor with them. *Barricade, cavalier, duel,* and *grenade* have nothing like the exotic effect of *barricado, cavaliero, duello,* and *grenado.* Other words have retained their endings but become common-

[7] From *A Restitution of Decayed Intelligence* — Moore, p. 128.

place through everyday use — *banana, potato, tobacco,* for instance. But we still have many that retain some of their original tang, though we might disagree about just which these are. *Bastinado, bravado, cupola, desperado, embargo, peccadillo,* and *sombrero* are examples.

Scholarly Innovators: Inkhorn Terms — and Others

Much more important than either the Chaucerisms or the oversea language were the thousands of words taken from the classical languages. Some of these were taken directly from Greek; but because many Greek words had already been borrowed by Latin, and reached English through this language, they will here be lumped together as Latin borrowings. They differed from earlier ones from the same source in two important ways. In the first place, a much higher proportion of them were learned rather than popular, because learned borrowings now had a much better chance of becoming permanent. A word borrowed earlier in a manuscript might easily be replaced the first time that manuscript was copied, if the scribe happened to dislike it or fail to understand it; and in any case its spread into general use was necessarily slow — often a matter of generations. But a word borrowed in print could get to thousands of readers in a very short time, and therefore had an excellent chance of being used again and again until it was generally accepted, and used in speech as well as in other books. The delight in words, of which we find so much evidence in Elizabethan literature, made the chances of survival greater than they would have been somewhat earlier. This delight was not, as we have seen, shared by everybody; but the general climate was decidedly favorable to rapid growth. No impersonal way of evaluating this growth is possible. An inkhorn term might be defined as a newly imported polysyllable that you don't happen to like. There is therefore no reliable way of determining exactly which of the new words could legitimately be called inkhorn, but we should all now agree that at least a good many of the imports were valuable.

In the second place, many of the new additions were the result of a conscious, and to some extent concerted, effort to improve the language. The Renaissance had made available a great many Latin works that had been unknown in England during the Middle Ages, and the spread of education had created a large new class of readers who knew no Latin, or at least not enough to allow them to use it with comfort. Both writers and publishers were tempted by this public. As a result there was great activity in both translation and the compilation of new works based largely on Latin sources. Translators and compilers almost inevitably borrowed freely. Often there were no English words in existence that could render a technical term or an unfamiliar shade of meaning. Even if such words existed, they might not occur to the writer who had the Latin words right before his eyes, or might not seem to him either sufficiently precise or sufficiently dignified. Intellectual snobbery, on the part of authors and readers alike, certainly played its part, but many of the new words were so useful that we can now hardly imagine being without them.

Perhaps the most interesting of these innovators was Sir Thomas Elyot. In the "proheme" to *The Knowledge that Maketh a Wise Man* (1533) he says:

> His highnesse benignely receyuynge my boke which I named the Gouernour, in the redynge therof sone perceyued that I intended to augment our Englyshe tongue, wherby men shulde as well expresse more abundantly the thynge that they conceyued in theyr hartis (wherfore language was ordeyned) hauynge wordes apte for the pourpose: as also interprete out of greke, latyn or any other tonge into Englyshe, as sufficiently as out of any one of the said tongues into an other. His grace also perceyued that through out the boke there was no terme new made by me of a latine or frenche worde, but it was there declared so playnly by one mene or other to a diligent reder that no sentẽce is therby made derke or harde to be understande.[8]

Some examples of the ways in which he "declared" his new terms:

> to *deuulgate* or sette fourth some part of my study
> shulde *animate* or gyue courage to others
> the beste fourme of *education* or bringing up of noble children
> shall be *appoynted* or chosen by the soueraigne gouernour
> without *adminiculation* or aid
> made his exile to be more *facile* and easy
> *inclination* and towardnes to vertue
> *agilitie* and nymblenesse
> *Affabilitie* . . . where a man is facile or easy to be spoken unto

[8] Moore, p. 82.

> *Metamorphosios,* whiche is as moche to saye as, chaungynge of men in to other figure or fourme
>
> Wherefore I am constrained to usurpe a latine worde, calling it *maturitie* . . . that word *maturitie* is translated to the actis of man . . . reseruyng the wordes rype and redy to frute and other thinges
>
> wisdome, in a more elegant worde called *Sapience*[9]

These examples have been chosen to illustrate the whole range from those like *devulgate* and *adminiculation,* which are likely to strike us as purest inkhorn, to ones like *appoint* and *education,* which we can hardly imagine doing without. It is just as well to bear in mind that our immediate reactions to strange words are not necessarily sound. *Devulgate* — to make common — has not stuck, possibly because *divulge,* with a somewhat different implication, has; but the word itself seems in no way inferior to *popularize. Adminiculation* for *aid* (presumably only a little of it) strikes us as ridiculously overanalytical; but no more so than thousands of words that are current today — and perhaps a few that we ourselves use.

Another comment in much the same spirit as Elyot's is this from Richard Eden (1562):

> And whereas the Master of Savoye tolde me that your Honour sumwhat Doubted that the booke coulde not be translated into the Englysshe toonge, I assure your Honour that this I Dare saye without arrogancie, that to translate the variable historie of Plinie into our toonge, I wolde be ashamed to borowe so muche of the Latine as he Dothe of the Greke, althowgh the Latine toonge be accompted ryche, and the Englysshe indigent and barbarous, as it hathe byn in tyme past, muche more than it nowe is, before it was enriched and amplified by sundry bookes in manner of all artes translated owt of Latine and other toonges into Englysshe.[10]

Copiousness

One of the particular aims of the borrowers was to make English *copious* — that is, to provide it with a wealth of approximate synonyms that would express exact shades of meaning. Elyot's *maturity* is an obvious example of

[9] Moore, pp. 83–86.
[10] Letter to Sir W. Cecil-Moore, pp. 94–95.

this effort. He wants to use this word for a distinctly human quality, confining *ripeness* to things like fruit. There can be no doubt that a high degree of copiousness was obtained. It is often said that no other language is as rich as English in the ability to express fine distinctions; and it is sometimes added that there are no exact synonyms in the language.

The first of these statements is, to the best of our knowledge, true. The second is a half truth. There is probably no word that can satisfactorily be exchanged for any other in all positions; but it certainly cannot be proved that one of a set of synonyms is inevitably best in any position, and that the substitution of any other will necessarily take something from the sentence. Any word that we encounter often will build up a set of associations; and if we attempt to communicate above a very simple level we must gamble that our audience will have a fairly similar set. But, as in any gamble, we will sometimes lose. The distinction that Elyot makes between *ripe* and *mature,* and their corresponding nouns, is of course sometimes followed today. We are probably more likely to speak of *ripe fruit* and a *mature man* (or *plan*) than the other way around. But we can also speak of *mature fruit;* and (in spite of Elyot) we can speak only of a *mature tree,* not a *ripe* one. On the other hand, a man may be either *ripe* or *mature,* with or without an intended difference of meaning. If Shakespeare had said "maturity is all" the line would probably never have been quoted — except perhaps by psychologists.

Compendiousness

Another aim often expressed was to make English *compendious* — that is, compact and economical. If we tried to write English now without using any of our Latin borrowings, we would often have to use four or five words in place of one. To consider only a few of the words introduced at this time, take *absurdity, analogy, compatible, contradictory, democracy,* and *education.* If we tried to paraphrase a passage containing several of these words, using only native words to do so, the result would inevitably be much longer than the original, and would probably seem almost childish in its simplicity. (And if we tried to write that last sentence without using *paraphrase, native, result, inevitably, original, probably,* and *simplicity* we would have another — well, *task* is not quite as good as *problem* here, but it will have to do.)

We have all been advised so often to write simply and use concrete terms whenever we can that we may be tempted to think that all polysyllables are always inferior, but this is not so. It is a sound rule never to use a long and comparatively fancy word when it says no more than a short, everyday one (unless you are saying so little that you have to depend on sound rather than sense to make any impression at all). In most sentences, and to most people, *remuneration* means no more than *pay*. The language could spare it without much loss. But when a long word not only takes the place of several short ones, but sums up their relationship in a familiar arrangement that can be grasped as a unit, it can be very useful.

Such words, sensibly used, are abstractions in the best sense, because they abstract the particular features of a complicated situation that we want to consider at a given time. They have the same sort of value as the simple symbols mathematicians use to sum up complicated equations when they want to move into still higher orders of complexity; or that the term *field army* has to a soldier, who knows that it means an organization composed of several corps, each composed of several divisions plus supporting artillery, and so on all the way down the line. The advice so often given to young writers to "avoid abstractions" would, if taken literally, reduce us all to a kindergarten level. It actually means something like this: "Avoid using abstract terms unless you have a very clear idea of what they stand for, and can convey that idea to your intended audience."

The two preceding paragraphs may seem to belong to a freshman English text rather than a history of the language; but it is impossible to consider Renaissance borrowings intelligently without giving some thought to their possibilities, both good and bad. The translations and much of the new literature needed many new abstract terms unless they were to be intolerably wordy.

Other Reasons for Borrowing

The workmanlike and demonstrable qualities of copiousness and compendiousness were not the only ones sought in developing the vocabulary. Such terms as *choice, sweet,* and *elegant* occur again and again in the discussions. It would be silly to deny the importance of the qualities indicated by these words; but it would be just as silly to pretend that we can examine them with impersonal accuracy. They did not mean the same thing to everybody, and we can never be sure that we know exactly what they meant to anybody. Our esthetic reactions to words are based on a mixture of immediate sense-impressions and past associations that it is simply impossible to separate. Even when we hear a word for the first time, the effect it has on us depends partly on the way we subconsciously associate it with other words we have known.

Of course many people have complete faith in the absolute validity of their own reactions, and we hear confident assertions that such and such words are "the most beautiful in the language." But beauty contests among words are no more conclusive than they are among women. We guarantee the story of a student who was perfectly sure that she reacted simply to the sounds, not to the associations, but believed that it was a natural, if somewhat mysterious, process for us to give beautiful names to beautiful objects. For her prize example she chose *ermine,* a word as lovely as the fur it names. To prove that this was not an accident, she pointed out that the French word for the mysterious medieval fur, *vair,* was equally beautiful. She repeated both words aloud, several times, and they certainly sounded fine. But when it was suggested that an even more beautiful word, combining the qualities of the first two, was *vermin,* we had to change the subject.

It is natural that some of the words borrowed for esthetic reasons have not pleased enough people to remain in the language. Even when the aim was copiousness or compendiousness it often happened that competing words or competing forms of words were borrowed by different people to meet the same purpose. Sometimes these were later differentiated in meaning, to give a still more copious effect, as in the pairs *continuous-continual* and *beneficial-beneficent,* but naturally some of the words simply dropped out of use. Thus *obtestate* seems to have gone completely, *splendent* has given way to *splendid* (though we still have *resplendent*), *magnifical* to *magnificent,* and *contiguate* to *contiguous.* No principle of choice in such cases seems to be discoverable.

Many borrowings from Greek and Latin have lost much of their effectiveness with the general decrease in the knowledge of these languages. *Conflagration,* for instance, conveys to a ready Latinist the idea of a number of fires burning together and reinforcing each other. It is thus a fine term, significant as well as resounding, when used among Latinists. But to most people now it means simply "big fire"; and though it has the apparent advantage of being one word against two, it has the more important disadvantage of being four syllables against two, and those syllables less meaningful. Nobody ever seems to speak of the "San Francisco conflagration," or even "the great conflagration of London." It therefore seems to be approaching the end of its usefulness. Perhaps the moral is that we can afford to be compendious only about situations that arise again and again.

It is easier to be a little diffuse now and then than to control too enormous a vocabulary.

Considered simply as a debate, the long argument about improving the language did not get anywhere in particular. At the very end of the period we still find adherents of the three main theories — for enrichment, for purification, and for a more careful use of the language as it was — stating their positions as strongly as ever. As Edward Phillips wrote in *The New World of English Words* (1658): "Whether this innovation of words deprave, or enrich our English tongue is a consideration that admits of various censures, according to the different fancies of men." But when we turn from theoretical discussions to observable facts, there can be no doubt that the vocabulary was enormously increased during the period, and that the methods of addition were so well established that it has been increasing on the same lines ever since. It is also clear that much of the enlargement was due to conscious effort rather than passive absorption, and that far more people than ever before developed a lively interest in the quality of the language, and took pride in trying to use it well.

Men still have different fancies, but now that three centuries have passed since Phillips wrote, very few of them would argue that this issue "admits of various censures." Most of us would agree with what George Pettie wrote in the preface to a translation in 1581:

> There are some others yet who will set light by my labours, because I write in English: and those are some nice Trauailors, who retourne home with such queasie stomachs, that nothing will downe with them but French, Italian, or Spanish, and though a worke bee but meanelie written in one of those tongues, and finelie translated into our Language, yet they will not sticke farre to preferre the Originall before the Translation. . . . For the barbarousnesse of our tongue, I must likewise saie that it is much the worse for them, and some such curious fellowes as they are: who if one chance to deriue anie word from the Latine, which is insolent to their eares (as perchance they will take that phrase to be) they forthwith make a iest at it, and tearme it an Inkhorne tearme. And though for my part I vse those wordes as little as anie, yet I know no reason why I should not vse them, and I find it a fault in my selfe that I do not vse them; for it is in deed the readie waie to inrich our tongue, and make it copious, and it is the waie which all tongues haue taken to inrich themselues; For take the Latine wordes from the Spanish tongue, and it shall

bee as barren as most part of their Countrie; take them from the Italian, & you take away in a manner the whole tongue: take thẽ frõ the French, & you marre the grace of it: yea take from the Latine it selfe the wordes deriued from the Greeke, & it shall not be so flowing & flourishing as it is. Wherefore I meruaille how our English tõgue hath crackt it credit, that it may not borrow of the Latine as wel as other tongues: and if it haue broken, it is but of late, for it is not vnknowen to all men, how many wordes we haue fetcht from thence within these few yeeres, which if they should be all counted inkpot tearmes, I know not how we should speak anie thing without blacking our mouths with inke: for what word can be more plaine thã this word (plaine) & yet what can come more neere to the Latine? What more manifest than (manifest)? & yet in a manner Latine: What more commune than (rare), or lesse rare thã (commune) & yet both of them comminge of the Latine? But you will saie, long vse hath made these wordes currant: and why may not vse doe as much for these wordes which we shall now deriue? Why should not we doe as much for the posteritie, as we haue receiued of the antiquitie? and yet if a thing be of it selfe ill, I see not how the oldnesse of it can make it good, and if it be of it selfe good, I see not how the newnesse of it can make it naught: wherevpon I infer, that those wordes which your selues confesse by vse to be made good, are good the first time they are vttered, and therefore not to be iested at, nor to be misliked. But how hardlie so euer you deale with your tongue, how little so euer you esteeme it, I durste my selfe vndertake (if I were furnished with learning otherwise) to write in it as copiouslie for varietie, as compendiouslie for breuetie, as choicelie for words, as pithilie for sentences, as pleasantlie for figures, & euerie waie as eloquentlie, as anie writer should do in anie vulgar tongue whatsoeuer.[11]

Renaissance Neglect of Grammar

In an age like ours, when "good grammar" and "good English" are generally regarded as synonymous, it may seem curious that grammar got so little attention during a period so greatly concerned with the language; but

[11] Moore, pp. 103–104.

there seems to have been quite general agreement with the famous remark of Sir Philip Sidney which has convinced so many modern students that he was indeed the flower of his age:

> Nay truly, it [English] hath that prayse, that it wanteth not Grammer; for Grammer it might haue, but it needs it not; being so easie of it self, and so voyd of those cumbersome differences of Cases, Genders, Moodes, and Tenses, which I thinke was a peece of the Tower of Babilons curse, that a man should be put to schoole to learne his mother-tongue.[12]

This is of course a naive statement. The fact that English is comparatively "voyd of those cumbersome differences" does not mean that English has less grammar than more highly inflected languages, but only that its structural patterns are of a different sort; and Sidney found it "easie of it self" simply because he had grown up with it. No Frenchman forced to learn the language would have agreed with him. Communication is possible only when a group of speakers have a similar reaction to patterns of arrangement as well as to individual words. Whether these patterns have been explicitly described and formally taught is a secondary, though not a trivial, matter.

Nevertheless, Sidney had a point that is worth emphasizing because it is hard for most people today to believe that the situation he took for granted could ever have existed. In matters of syntax and accidence the "don't do this" age had not yet arrived. Toward the end of the period we find a few attempts to explain the structure of English to foreigners, and a few others aimed at teaching children, in English, those principles of grammar which they would later need in studying Latin; but it is not until a century later that we find any serious efforts to teach native speakers the grammar of English for its own sake. Those critics who accuse Shakespeare of being ungrammatical are a trifle anticipatory, because the rules he broke had not yet been either formulated in books or arrived at by tacit agreement.

Development of Sentence Structure

But even without a formal theory there was a remarkable change in the standards of sentence construction. It seems to have come mostly from an

[12] Moore, pp. 105–106.

increased respect for the language and a greater sense of responsibility about using it. Here again the influence of Latin was of great importance. It cannot be proved by any such definite evidence as we have for the borrowing of words, and the opinions expressed in this section are certainly open to argument. But the matter is too important to be passed over, and they are given for whatever they may be worth.

For centuries students had been trained in the exact analysis of Latin sentences, as some are still being trained today. They were required to identify the precise form in which each word appeared, explain why it was in that form, and exactly what function it performed. It was assumed that any sound sentence could meet the test of such analysis — that its total meaning was the inevitable result of all the detailed interrelations within it. The structure of most Classical Latin sentences can, in fact, be analyzed as definitely and finally as algebraic equations — though it is not unlikely that this is true of some of them only because they have been emended by centuries of scholarship. And students were sternly encouraged to compose sentences of their own that could meet the same tests.

It is only since the middle of the eighteenth century that any such analysis has been applied to English. Its value is open to question, and will not be debated here. The point we are considering is that though in Old and Middle English comparatively short grammatical patterns were as definite and significant as ours, there were no strict and generally recognized standards for combining them. There was a tendency to join the clauses of a long sentence loosely by a series of *and*'s, rather than precisely by the appropriate subordinating conjunctions. It was very common to change the construction in the middle — to start out in one person and finish in another, to shift from one number or tense to another, or to mix direct and reported statements. The result is that many sentences are ambiguous. And often even when we are quite sure, from the context or by intuition, that we know what an author meant by a sentence, we can't prove it — or anything else — by the most careful analysis. The sentence simply does not hang together as we have been taught that it should.

As we have seen, one reason for the lack of discipline in English sentences was that so many books were composed in an effort to meet uneducated people on their own ground. A writer was likely to take the attitude expressed in the explanation of why *The Castle of Love* (which is moralistic rather than romantic) is put in English for those who know no other language:

Þauh hit on Englisch be dim and derk
Ne nabbe no sauur bifore clerk,
ffor lewed men that luitel connen
On English hit is þus bigonnen.[13]

If this attitude seems curious, we must remember that in the Middle Ages the laity were often asked to believe rather than understand, and it may have seemed more important to address them in the comfortable rhythms of familiar speech than to confuse them with exact reasoning. But a Renaissance man, writing for his peers and taking pride in his language, was naturally inclined to attempt a higher standard of performance. Translators and compilers, for instance, were no longer content to make the English a loose equivalent of the Latin; they felt responsible for preserving the precise relations between ideas. There was a good deal of difference of opinion as to how far this was possible. Even at the beginning of the period we find some writers arguing that the language is already fit for the highest tasks. Even at the end we find others scorning its attempts to compete with its natural betters. But all the way through we find still others holding the view that it can be made better than it is, and working to make it so. Some would be content to put it on a par with the other modern or "common" languages; others saw no reason why it should not rival or even surpass the classical or "learned" languages. Among them, they established the English sentence as a solid and coherent unit.

This is not to argue that the basic structure of the language was changed because a few writers were handling it more carefully. The point is rather that the whole literate population was exposed to more carefully constructed English than their ancestors could have encountered, and that this exposure had a very perceptible effect on their own use of it.

The Status of Local Dialects

The spoken language of the uneducated classes still varied greatly in different parts of the country, as this quotation from Richard Verstegan's *A Restitution of Decayed Intelligence* illustrates:

> . . . in some severall parts of *England* it selfe, both the names of things, and pronountiations of words are somewhat different,

[13] Kaiser, p. 243, ll. 21–24.

> and that among the Country people that never borrow any words out of the *Latin* or *French,* and of this different pronountiation one example in steed of many shall suffice, as this: for pronouncing according as one would say at London *I would eat more cheese if I had it,* the Northern man saith, *Ay sud eat mare cheese gin ay hadet,* and the Westerne man saith, *Chud eat more cheese an chad it.*[14]

But although such departures from the London usage had once been perfectly respectable, they were now regarded as "uplandish" or countrified. Sir Walter Raleigh, in spite of his learning and position at the court, is reported to have spoken broad Devonshire to his dying day. The interesting thing about this is not that it shows his independent spirit, but that it was considered worth mentioning as something remarkable.

In written, or at least in published English, all the local dialects practically disappeared except for the Scottish. This had once been simply a subvariety of the Northern dialect; but its use had gradually become a national rather than a geographical habit, and its distinct qualities were patriotically preserved.

The Quality of Renaissance English

An adjective often applied to Renaissance English is *luxuriant* — a term that suggests both the richness of the language and its freedom from the sorts of restrictions that later came to be applied to it. Although Court English had become a national standard, it was in itself not nearly so rigid as it later became. Grammarians and schoolmasters had not yet begun the attempt to "ascertain" it — that is, to decide which of the various ways of saying anything was right, and to outlaw all the others. The general feeling of guilt about the language that has plagued most educated speakers for the past two hundred years had not yet been aroused. Some people had strong objections to borrowing words from other languages, but everybody seems to have felt free to use whatever words he regarded as English however he liked — with reasonable attention to their meaning, of course, but with no fear of misusing a part of speech, and little concern about

[14] Moore, p. 126.

which was the accepted idiom. Among the unsettled questions that are likely to strike us most forcefully were the forms of many verbs and the idiomatic uses of prepositions and the articles.

As for the richness of the language, we have been talking about it ever since; and in spite of those traveled show-offs who sneered, it seems to have been quite generally appreciated at the time. Choosing from the many glorifications of the state of the tongue, we may close the chapter with this from William L'Isle:

> . . . our language is improued aboue all others now spoken by any nation, and became the fairest, the nimblest, the fullest; most apt to vary the phrase, most ready to receiue good composition, most adorned with sweet words and sentences, with witty quips and ouer-ruling Prouerbes: yea able to expresse any hard conceit whatsoeuer with great dexterity; waighty in weighty matters, merry in merry, braue in braue. Tell me not it is a mingle-mangle; for so are all: but the punishment of confusion we marke not so much in other tongues, because wee know not them and their borrowing so well as our owne; and this also is delightfull to know.[15]

[15] Moore, p. 139.

7

The Authorities Step In

The Desire to Regulate the Language

The exuberant English Renaissance ended in eighteen years of exhausting struggle, running from the first Civil War in 1642 to the Restoration in 1660. It was followed by an age of more orderly and much more regulated progress, which it is convenient to call the eighteenth century. The period from 1660 to about 1800 was by no means uniform. There was a considerable difference in tone between the Restoration and the Age of Johnson, not to mention the intervening Age of Pope and the succeeding Age of the Precursors of Romanticism, or whatever we choose to call these generations. And in each of these ages, of course, strong differences of opinion were heard on practically all important questions, including the nature of language and what should be done about it.

Grammarians and pedagogues have never been able to establish the complete control over the language that some of them have wished, but for the past two centuries they have exerted at least a modifying influence of a kind that was previously lacking. Throughout the Old and Middle periods English had developed with practically no attention to academic theory, partly because it had always been overshadowed by Latin, and for several centuries by French as well. During the next century and a half it had come to be recognized as the primary language of England, and the feeling had grown that it was adequate for all purposes. We find different degrees of enthusiasm for its new status expressed — that it could at last hold its own with the other modern languages (all, by nature, inferior to the classical ones); that it was comparable to Latin and Greek themselves; and even that it was — or could be made — the finest language ever known. There had been a definite movement to enrich it by systematic borrowings and coinings, but comparatively little interest in regulating it.

Some progress toward regularity in the conventions of writing had certainly been made, and there had been some tentative efforts to set up guides in the way of dictionaries and grammars. But the dictionaries were merely lists of "hard words" — recent borrowings, technical terms in special fields, and puzzling archaisms; and the grammars, mostly intended either to introduce foreigners to English or to prepare schoolboys for the later study of Latin, had made practically no impression on the general public. Most people seem to have felt (like Sidney) that they could use their mother-tongue without instruction. A writer might criticize the vocabulary or the rhetorical taste of another writer, but he was no more likely to find fault with the other man's "grammar" than to doubt the soundness of his own.

Shortly after the Restoration we find a very different atmosphere. It was generally agreed that the resources of English were up to any demands that could be made on them; but a feeling was growing that even "the best authors" were often regrettably deficient in their practice, and that explicit guides were needed to help them out. Thus John Dryden complains that "we have as yet no prosodia, not so much as a tolerable dictionary, or a grammar"; and in another place, "I am often put to a stand, in considering whether what I write be the idiom of the tongue, or false grammar." Having no English grammar to help him, he sometimes solved a problem by translating a sentence into Latin, and then putting it back into English in the light of what he had discovered. He was particularly shocked to find that he (like practically all writers of English up to his time) was in the habit of using prepositions at the ends of sentences — a practice that conflicted both with the habits of Latin authors and with the etymology of the word *preposition,* which means something placed before. He not only revised some of his own writings to remove this supposed fault but established a shibboleth that has been bedeviling the language ever since. Of course terminal prepositions are sometimes awkward; but to change a sentence like "You are just the man I am looking for" to "You are just the man for whom I am looking" is, to put it mildly, very dubious progress. Unfortunately, Dryden's rule is exactly the sort that delights a certain kind of pedant. After all, there is not much satisfaction in being able to recognize and correct mistakes that educated people seldom commit. To make a really pleasurable career of your superiority it is necessary to find something wrong with their habitual practices.

It was to be a long time before the effective guides that Dryden wanted were to be produced, but the feeling that they were needed was widely shared. It was quite generally accepted (in some circles) that Man, after a long struggle through the hopeless valley of medieval ignorance, had finally reached the plateau on which he was henceforth to dwell. There was still work to be done in order to make this plateau a second Eden, but not a great deal, and the blueprints for it were pretty well in hand. Thus we find Dryden writing in his "Essay of Dramatic Poesy":

> Is it not evident, in the last hundred years, when the study of philosophy has been the business of all the Virtuosi in Christendom, that almost a new nature has been revealed to us? That more errors of the school have been detected, more useful experiments in philosophy have been made, more noble secrets in optics, medicine, anatomy, astronomy discovered, than in all those credulous and doting ages from Aristotle to us? — so true it is, that nothing spreads more fast than science, when rightly and generally cultivated.[1]

Dryden's uncertainty about his own grammar is an unhappy portent of a kind of anxiety that has afflicted many if not most educated speakers of English (and particularly American English) ever since, though it seems to be almost unknown among their opposite numbers in other countries. Most of us take it for granted that a French doctor speaks "good French," and a German banker "good German" — and the doctor and banker agree with us completely. But American doctors, bankers, and even university professors in other departments are very likely to confess (often quite cheerfully) that "good English" is beyond them. Because there is no particular reason to believe that we are the most modest of all nations, the likeliest explanation is that the gulf between school theory and normal

[1] Ed. Thomas Arnold (1903), p. 18.

usage is greater here than elsewhere. It is in the period we are now studying that this gulf developed. Caxton's uncertainty, expressed nearly two centuries earlier (see page 8) was natural enough, for he was a businessman who had grown up in Kent, and then spent most of his life abroad before he began his literary career. But Dryden was the most distinguished professional man of letters of his time; and the fact that he felt uncertain foreshadows the belief that good English is not a normal practice but a sort of Holy Grail, to be pursued but not attained.

"Universal Grammar"

Dryden's trick of translating an English sentence into Latin to find its true structure was based on a belief in universal grammar. This is a question on which the linguists of today are sharply divided. Some of them hold that behind the obvious diversity of known languages are some basic similarities, and that these must be accurately charted before we can make really adequate analyses of the structure of individual languages. Others believe that each language must be studied in and for itself, and that any resemblances in structure are best considered simply as coincidences. Bloomfield, for instance, says: "The only useful generalizations about language are inductive generalizations. Features which we think ought to be universal may be absent from the very next language that becomes accessible." [2] Both sides, however, now believe that differences in structure should be considered impartially, and that changes are both inevitable and legitimate. The eighteenth-century idea was rather that all changes were corruptions of the original true structure, which was pretty well preserved in Latin but badly eroded in most modern languages, particularly English. This theory crops up again and again throughout the period, sometimes explicitly stated, more often apparently assumed; and it brought into our grammatical tradition a number of concepts from Latin grammar that could never have been derived from the study of English alone.

Even in the eighteenth century the theory was by no means universally accepted. There was much support for the contrary "doctrine of usage," which held that the only reasonable criterion of language is simply the established "custom" of its speakers, and that any theoretical considerations which conflict with this custom are nonsensical. And finally, because

[2] Leonard Bloomfield, *Language* (New York, 1933), p. 20.

usage on many points was so obviously divided that no simple description of it seemed possible, plenty of people were willing to accept any set of rules, even perfectly arbitrary ones, in the hope that they would settle matters once and for all.

The Idea of an Academy

In 1635 Cardinal Richelieu had founded the French Academy, a self-perpetuating group of forty members charged with the tasks of compiling an official dictionary, grammar, rhetoric, and prosody, and in general with assuming control of the language. Shortly after the Restoration the idea of founding a somewhat similar institution in England received a good deal of support. We do not know who first proposed it, but Dryden was its most important advocate up to the time of his death in 1700. Thereafter Dean Swift headed the movement, and an English Academy might indeed have been established had Queen Anne not died in 1714. But the German George I, who succeeded her, was not sufficiently interested in the English language even to learn to speak it himself. The movement accordingly died, and it has never been seriously revived since.

The Incubating Period

The aims proposed for the abortive academy had been to "ascertain" the language by settling all disputed questions; to free it from all impurities (which might be defined as those features to which any particular pundit particularly objected); and to stabilize it so as to prevent any future changes. Even after the idea of an academy had died there was a great deal of interest in attaining the same ends by unofficial means; and a modern writer is under a strong temptation to "trace the development of the eighteenth-century tradition" as if this had been an orderly, cumulative process. Actually it was nothing of the sort. It is true that the makers of dictionaries generally used and enlarged upon preceding efforts, but the growth of such works was influenced at least as much by commercial as by intellectual considerations; and theorists about the structure of the language for the most part beat their own lonely drums and got nowhere in particular. As an active force, our grammatical tradition began in 1762 with Lowth's *Short Introduction to English Grammar* — a book that could just as well have been written, with little change except in the illustrative quotations, at least a century earlier. What had happened in between was not the development of a foundation on which he could build, but simply a growing demand for some guiding authority. There were now millions of people who wanted (though perhaps not very badly) to be told how to use the language correctly; and there were thousands of schoolteachers who wanted a basis for telling them — definitely and without hesitation or qualification. Our opinion, though we can't prove it, is that the thousands were more influential in this respect than the millions. A teacher of Latin knew exactly where he stood. There was a definite rule for everything, and anybody who questioned it could be smacked. Those who had to teach English — and there were more of them every year — must have longed for comparable security.

The Earliest English Dictionaries

Most of us seem to have grown up with a vague but nonetheless powerful idea that The Dictionary was somehow dictated shortly after the Ten Commandments, and with approximately the same moral authority. It must therefore contain all the legitimate words in the language, with their pronunciation, spellings, grammatical classifications, and exact meanings, along with a little etymology that it is usually convenient to skip. If anybody uses a word that we cannot find in the sacred list we say it is not a real word; and if anybody questions any of the dictionary's statements we are likely to regard him as either intolerably conceited or a dangerous radical.

Now, a good dictionary is an extremely valuable as well as interesting work; but anybody who regards it with superstitious veneration not only loses much of its usefulness but puts an unnecessary obstacle in the way of his own understanding of the language. To get the full benefit from such a work it is necessary to understand its limitations as well as its achievements; and the best way to do this is to consider both the gradual steps in the development of lexicography and some of the conflicting demands making anything like a perfectly satisfactory all-purpose dictionary impossible even today. The first steps were taken before the period we are now discussing, and very important advances have been made since the end of it. But because it was in the eighteenth century that dictionaries first became a really important influence on the development of the language, it seems reasonable to discuss them here.

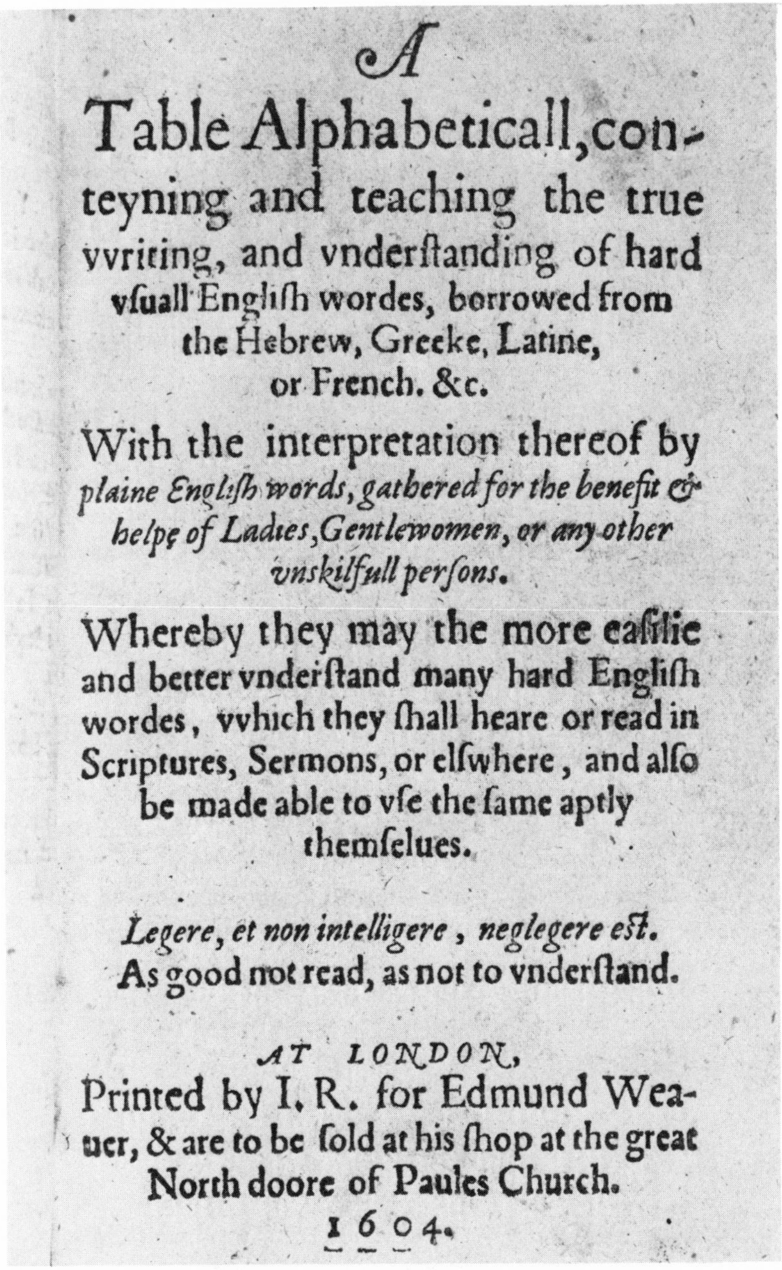

A

Table Alphabeticall, conteyning and teaching the true vvriting, and vnderſtanding of hard vſuall Engliſh wordes, borrowed from the Hebrew, Greeke, Latine, or French. &c.

With the interpretation thereof by *plaine Engliſh words, gathered for the benefit & helpe of Ladies, Gentlewomen, or any other vnskilfull perſons.*

Whereby they may the more eaſilie and better vnderſtand many hard Engliſh wordes, vvhich they ſhall heare or read in Scriptures, Sermons, or elſwhere, and alſo be made able to vſe the ſame aptly themſelues.

Legere, et non intelligere, neglegere eſt.
As good not read, as not to vnderſtand.

AT LONDON,
Printed by I. R. for Edmund Weauer, & are to be ſold at his ſhop at the great North doore of Paules Church.
1604.

Title page of Robert Cawdrey's *A Table Alphabeticall* (London, 1604). The Bodleian Library, Oxford, England.

During the medieval period a reader who found an unusual word in a manuscript might write an explanation of it, called a *gloss,* in the margin — a practice most students will recognize as natural. Eventually it occurred to somebody that it would be convenient to collect all the glosses in his small library into a single list, called a *glossary.* The next step was to combine several glossaries into a longer list. When such lists became too long to be scanned at a glance it seemed helpful to group the words by subjects. Then some unknown genius decided it would be still more convenient to put together all those which began with the same letter. It took a surprisingly long time for the completely alphabetical order we now take for granted to develop.

The earliest glossaries were in Latin. Next came bilingual ones — Latin-English, English-Latin, and so forth. These tended to be more inclusive than the older type, because even the simplest words in one language might be unfamiliar to a speaker of the other. Not until 1604 was the first attempt at a purely English dictionary published. This was Robert Cawdrey's *"A Table Alphabeticall,* conteyning and teaching the true writing, and vnderstanding of hard usuall English wordes, borrowed from the Hebrew, Greeke, Latine, or French, &c." Though a step forward in one way, this is obviously a step back in another; only the "hard" words are included. Cawdrey's book was soon succeeded by others of the same sort, each claiming to have longer and more complete lists than any of its rivals.

Next to the hard words derived from foreign languages perhaps the most obvious sources of difficulty are archaic words and the array of technical terms we encounter in fields with which we are not familiar; and such words were soon added, by no means silently. The blurb on the title page of Blount's *Glossographia* (1656), though comparatively short and modest, may be taken as sufficiently illustrative:

GLOSSOGRAPHIA
OR A
DICTIONARY
Interpreting all such
HARD WORDS,

Whether *Hebrew, Greek, Latin, Italian, Spanish, French, Teutonick, Belgick, British* or *Saxon;* as are now used in our refined *English Tongue.*

Also the Terms of *Divinity, Law, Physick, Mathematicks, Heraldry, Anatomy, War, Musick, Architecture;* and of several other *Arts* and *Sciences* Explicated.

With *Etymologies, Definitions,* and *Historical Observations* on the same.

Very useful for all such as desire to understand what they read.

There is of course a sort of superficial logic in limiting a dictionary to the hard words. You explain them by the easy ones — and if the reader doesn't already know *them,* he can't use the book anyhow. Even the simplest words do bring up a number of questions, however, and it eventually became obvious that a dictionary including the ordinary basic vocabulary would be very useful. The first considerable attempt in this direction was made in 1706, in John Kersey's edition of Edward Phillips' *The New World of English Words,* the best of the hard-word dictionaries. By adding ordinary words chosen from "the best authors" Kersey increased the vocabulary of this work from 17,000 to 38,000 words. In 1721 Nathan Bailey published *An Universal Etymological English Dictionary.* This work was carefully compiled from most of its best predecessors, and remained popular, in many editions, throughout the century. It is, on the whole, a very competent work, considering the state of linguistic knowledge then available; but a modern schoolteacher might be shocked to discover that in the most authoritative work of the time a good many of the definitions begin "is when."

Up to this point the growth of dictionaries had been largely a matter of what might be called incremental plagiarism. Each compiler took what he wanted from his predecessors, often verbatim. He might or might not acknowledge these debts. Then he added something of his own, either additional words or special features, from common proverbs to mythology, to support his claim that his was the best dictionary yet offered to the public. Such a procedure involved perpetuating many errors, and particularly encouraged the continual listing of words that had never been used enough to have any reasonable claim to be considered as being in the language. In fact, it has often been suspected that some of them had never been used at all, but were simply borrowed or adapted from foreign sources to increase the lists.

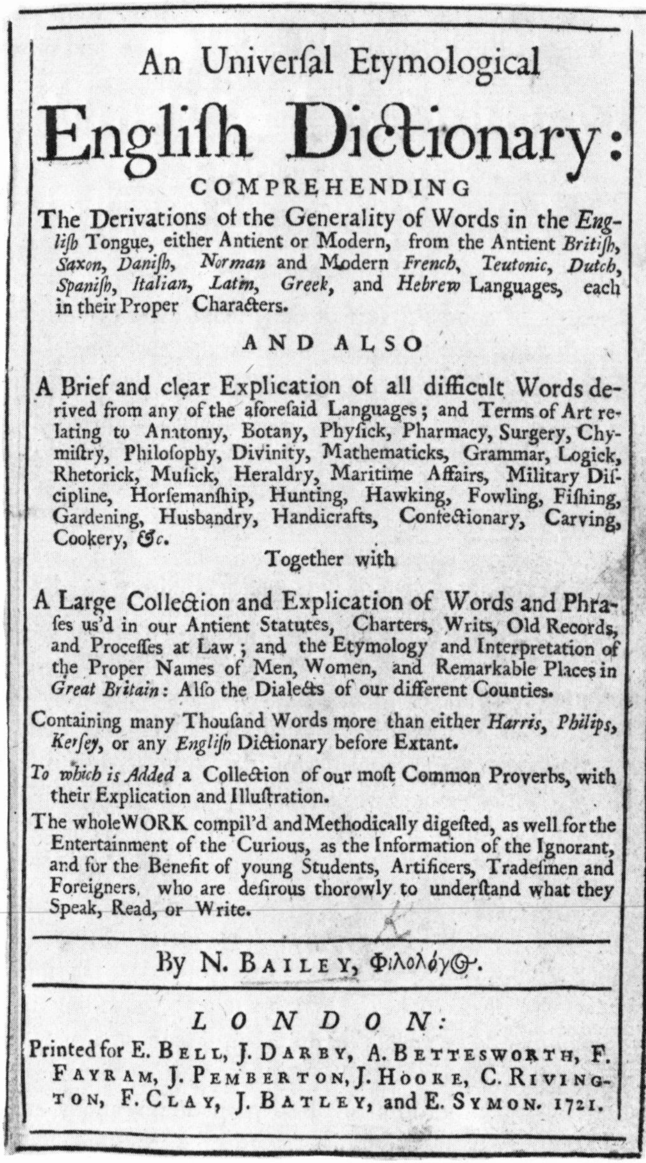

An Univerſal Etymological

Engliſh Dictionary:

COMPREHENDING

The Derivations of the Generality of Words in the *Engliſh* Tongue, either Antient or Modern, from the Antient *Britiſh*, *Saxon*, *Daniſh*, *Norman* and Modern *French*, *Teutonic*, *Dutch*, *Spaniſh*, *Italian*, *Latin*, *Greek*, and *Hebrew* Languages, each in their Proper Characters.

AND ALSO

A Brief and clear Explication of all difficult Words derived from any of the aforeſaid Languages; and Terms of Art relating to Anatomy, Botany, Phyſick, Pharmacy, Surgery, Chymiſtry, Philoſophy, Divinity, Mathematicks, Grammar, Logick, Rhetorick, Muſick, Heraldry, Maritime Affairs, Military Diſcipline, Horſemanſhip, Hunting, Hawking, Fowling, Fiſhing, Gardening, Husbandry, Handicrafts, Confectionary, Carving, Cookery, *&c.*

Together with

A Large Collection and Explication of Words and Phraſes us'd in our Antient Statutes, Charters, Writs, Old Records, and Proceſſes at Law; and the Etymology and Interpretation of the Proper Names of Men, Women, and Remarkable Places in *Great Britain*: Alſo the Dialects of our different Counties.

Containing many Thouſand Words more than either *Harris*, *Philips*, *Kerſey*, or any *Engliſh* Dictionary before Extant.

To which is Added a Collection of our moſt Common Proverbs, with their Explication and Illuſtration.

The whole WORK compil'd and Methodically digeſted, as well for the Entertainment of the Curious, as the Information of the Ignorant, and for the Benefit of young Students, Artificers, Tradeſmen and Foreigners, who are deſirous thorowly to underſtand what they Speak, Read, or Write.

By N. BAILEY, Φιλολόγος.

LONDON:

Printed for E. BELL, J. DARBY, A. BETTESWORTH, F. FAYRAM, J. PEMBERTON, J. HOOKE, C. RIVINGTON, F. CLAY, J. BATLEY, and E. SYMON. 1721.

Title page of Nathan Bailey's *An Universal Etymological English Dictionary* (London, 1721). By permission of the British Library Board.

Johnson's Dictionary

In 1747 Samuel Johnson, whose reputation in the world of letters was already considerable, was engaged by a group of booksellers to undertake preparation of a new dictionary. He completed the task in eight years, with no other help than that of half a dozen copyists who transcribed passages that he had marked in books. When we compare this with the seven hundred fifty-seven editorial years needed for the preparation of Webster's Third, the accomplishment seems almost incredible; yet during these same years Johnson found time for other work which so increased his reputation that he came to be regarded as a sort of semi-official one-man academy who should be entrusted with the regulation of the language. His preface suggests that he began the work with very much this idea. What he learned convinced him that prevention of change was impossible, and that established customs must be respected even when they were not reasonable; but he retained a firm belief that a lexicographer (at least one named Johnson) had a definite responsibility for improving the language, and the authority to do so.

This preface should, emphatically, be read as a whole, both as admirable prose and as one of the most enlightening discussions of the language ever published;[3] but the paragraphs quoted here will give some indication of the task that he saw confronting him and the way he proposed to go about it.

> When I took the first survey of my undertaking, I found our speech copious without order, and energetick without rules: wherever I turned my view, there was perplexity to be disentangled, and confusion to be regulated; choice was to be made out of boundless variety, without any established principle of selection; adulterations were to be detected, without a settled test of purity; and modes of expression to be rejected or received, without the suffrages of any writers of classical reputation or acknowledged authority.
>
> Having therefore no assistance but from general grammar, I applied myself to the perusal of our writers; and noting whatever might be of use to ascertain or illustrate any word or phrase,

[3] It is most readily available in *Johnson's Dictionary: A Modern Selection,* E. L. McAdam, Jr. and George Milne (New York, 1963). The page references are to this book.

accumulated in time the materials of a dictionary, which, by degrees, I reduced to method, establishing to myself, in the progress of the work, such rules as experience and analogy suggested to me; experience, which practice and observation were continually increasing; and analogy, which, though in some words obscure, was evident in others.[4]

An incredibly difficult job could hardly be described more modestly. Johnson proposed to list the words of the language as he found them in his enormous reading; to define them as he found them actually used; and to support his definitions by actual quotations from his sources. Thus his book would be derived directly from the language rather than from earlier compilations that, whether good or bad, offered no evidence in support of their statements. He was prepared to use earlier dictionaries as checklists to make sure that he did not leave out any important words, but not as reliable sources. This is essentially the system that was followed, more than a century later, in the making of the Oxford English Dictionary; and which then required nearly seventy years and hundreds of skilled workers. Johnson, working with only half a dozen copyists, soon had to modify his plan, but with characteristic honesty he made his deviation from the ideal clear:

Many words yet stand supported only by the name of Bailey, Ainsworth, Phillips, or the contracted *Dict.* for Dictionaries subjoined: of these I am not always certain that they are read in any book but the works of lexicographers. Of such I have omitted many, because I have never read them; and many I have inserted, because they may perhaps exist, though they have escaped my notice: they are, however, to be yet considered as resting only upon the credit of former dictionaries. Others, which I considered as useful, or know to be proper, though I could not at present support them by authorities, I have suffered to stand upon my own attestation, claiming the same privilege with my predecessors of being sometimes credited without proof.[5]

It is so easy to miss the significance of this paragraph that a rather insistent repetition may be forgiven. It implies that a dictionary is primarily a record of the language — a list of the words actually used, and an ex-

[4] Ibid., p. 4.
[5] Ibid., pp. 12–13.

planation of the meanings actually intended by the users. The statements of the lexicographer are properly based simply on his understanding of what past usage was, not on any theory of what it should have been; and they should be supported as far as possible by actual examples of usage, which the reader can examine for himself. Anything other lexicographers have said should be repeated only with an appropriate warning, so that possible errors may not be reinforced and perpetuated; and unsupported opinions should be given only as a last resort.

Johnson thus laid the foundation for the "dictionary on historical principles," which (in theory) aims simply to record usage, not to judge it; but he obviously did not feel that a simple record of past events would entirely fulfill his duty. The following sentence occurs in a paragraph describing his treatment of spelling, but is a fair description of his attitude toward every aspect of language:

> Every language has its anomalies, which though inconvenient, and in themselves once unnecessary, must be tolerated among the imperfections of human beings, and which require only to be registered, that they may not be increased, and ascertained, that they may not be confounded; but every language has likewise its improprieties and absurdities, which it is the duty of the lexicographer to correct or proscribe.[6]

The debate on whether it really is the duty of a lexicographer to correct or proscribe has been extremely lively in this country since publication by the Merriam-Webster Company of the third edition of *Webster's New International Dictionary*. We shall not attempt to settle that debate here; but point out that most dictionaries are intended to perform two not entirely compatible functions, and that their compilers almost inevitably aim directly at only one, and treat the other as secondary. To oversimplify somewhat, we may say that a dictionary must be aimed either at readers or at writers.

A reader's main interest is in knowing what the words he encounters mean. If he meets one that he doesn't know, he looks it up. If he is a good reader and has a good dictionary, he will not be satisfied with the most obvious or common meaning, but will want to find out what the writer probably meant in the sentence he is investigating. On the same

[6] Ibid., p. 4.

principle, he will often look up words which are quite familiar in some meanings, but which do not seem to fit the sentences in which they occur. Suppose he encounters the word *disinterested* used in a sentence where there seems to be no implication of lack of bias. He looks it up, finds it can also mean *uninterested,* decides that that is what it means here, and goes on with his job. He does not particularly care whether the word in this sense is used "loosely" or even "erroneously." He simply wants to understand the sentence. Maybe he is a Frenchman, and feels no responsibility toward English.

On the other hand, a writer wants to use words that will not only express his meaning, but impress his readers favorably. If he has heard both *uninterested* and *disinterested* used to express boredom, he wants to know (even if he is a Frenchman) which one he should choose; and he will be grateful for any labels indicating that one is better for his purpose than the other.

Of course, with the cost of bookmaking what it is, all dictionaries aim at both readers and writers, and all lexicographers must make some kind of choice (which will not please everybody) about how far they should go in indicating the status of words, and how insistent they should be. If they go lightly they will be accused by some critics of abdicating their responsibilities. If they take a strong stand they will be accused by others of assuming a kind of authority to which they have no right whatever. It seems rather silly to be dogmatic in either direction about what all dictionaries should do. There are now a number of good dictionaries, and they vary. The best way to use them is to find out what each one attempts, and make allowances.

Because Johnson does not point out the exact borderline between anomalies which must be tolerated and improprieties which should be proscribed, we may assume that he located it about where most of us do — between those irregular expressions we happen to use ourselves, and those we have somehow been trained to avoid. His division is likely to strike us as especially arbitrary in his assignment of such classifications as *low, cant, burlesque language,* and *not used* to words he felt to be less than standard. Thus he doubly condemns *fun* and *stingy* as both low and cant, though he lists a number of well-known four-letter words with no suggestion that they are not respectable. To *progress* is "not used," though *myropolist* ("one who sells unguents") apparently is. But if we are tempted to make too much of these and many similar peculiarities, we may be restrained by rereading the sentence in which he remarks that "a few wild blunders, and risible absurdities, from which no work of such multiplicity was ever free, may for a time furnish folly with laughter, and harden ignorance in contempt."

A dictionary more than two hundred years old is bound to be hopelessly out of date. Many of Johnson's definitions have been invalidated by later changes either in the language or in the world and our knowledge of it, though they were judicious, concise, and accurate at the time. But, by an irony that he would have appreciated, his Dictionary is now treasured particularly for occasional exceptions when he permitted prejudice, resentment, or his full-blooded sense of humor (especially at his own expense) to lead him cheerfully astray. Here are a few examples:

> *excise.* A hateful tax levied upon commodities, and adjudged not by the common judges of property, but wretches hired by those to whom excise is paid.
>
> *grubstreet.* Originally the name of a street in Moorfields in London, much inhabited by writers of small histories, dictionaries, and temporary poems; whence any mean production is called grubstreet.
>
> *lexicographer.* A writer of dictionaries; a harmless drudge, that busies himself in tracing the original, and detailing the signification of words.
>
> *oats.* A grain, which in England is generally given to horses, but in Scotland supports the people.
>
> *patron.* One who countenances, supports, or protects. Commonly a wretch who supports with insolence, and is paid with flattery.
>
> *pension.* An allowance made to any one without an equivalent. In England it is generally understood to mean pay given to a state hireling for treason to his country.

There are many more, and perhaps they are the best reason for reading the book now; but we should remember that Johnson not only made a better dictionary than had ever existed before, but gave it a new status. Chesterfield had suggested that Johnson should be accepted as the dictator of the language. This could hardly be done officially, but to a very considerable extent it was done unofficially. It seems quite clear that our tradition of reverence for "the dictionary" goes back to Johnson's work, and no further.

LIB LIB

Before they did oppreſs the people, only by colour of a *lewd* cuſtom, they did afterwards uſe the ſame oppreſſions by warrant. *Davies on Ireland.*

3. Luſtful; libidinous.

He is not lolling on a *lewd* love bed,
But on his knees at meditation. *Shakeſpeare's Rich.* III.
Then *lewd* Anchemolus he laid in duſt,
Who ſtain'd his ſtepdam's bed with impious luſt. *Dryden.*

LE'WDLY. *adj.* [from *lewd.*]

1. Wickedly; naughtily.

A ſort of naughty perſons, *lewdly* bent,
Have practis'd dangerouſly againſt your ſtate. *Shakeſp.*

2. Libidinouſly; luſtfully.

He lov'd fair lady Eltred, *lewdly* lov'd,
Whoſe wanton pleaſures him too much did pleaſe,
That quite his heart from Guendeline remov'd. *Spenſer.*
So *lewdly* dull his idle works appear,
The wretched texts deſerve no comments here. *Dryden.*

LE'WDNESS. *n. ſ.* [from *lewd.*] Luſtful licentiouſneſs.

Suffer no *lewdneſs*, nor indecent ſpeech,
Th' apartment of the tender youth to reach. *Dryd. Juv.*

Damianus's letter to Nicholas is an authentick record of the *lewdneſſes* committed under the reign of celibacy. *Atterbury.*

LE'WDSTER. *n. ſ.* [from *lewd.*] A lecher; one given to criminal pleaſures.

Againſt ſuch *lewdſters*, and their lechery,
Thoſe that betray them do no treachery. *Shakeſpeare.*

LE'WIS D'OR. n. ſ. [French.] A golden French coin, in value twelve livres, now ſettled at ſeventeen ſhillings. *Dict.*

LEXICO'GRAPHER. *n. ſ.* [λεξικὸν and γράφω; *lexicographe*, French.] A writer of dictionaries; a harmleſs drudge, that buſies himſelf in tracing the original, and detailing the ſignification of words.

Commentators and *lexicographers* acquainted with the Syriac language, have given theſe hints in their writings on ſcripture. *Watts's Improvement of the Mind.*

LEXICO'GRAPHY. *n. ſ.* [λεξικὸν and γράφω.] The art or practice of writing dictionaries.

LE'XICON. *n. ſ.* [λεξικὸν.] A dictionary; a book teaching the ſignification of words.

Though a linguiſt ſhould pride himſelf to have all the tongues that Babel cleft the world into, yet if he had not ſtudied the ſolid things in them as well as the words and *lexicons*, yet he were nothing ſo much to be eſteemed a learned man as any yeoman competently wiſe in his mother dialect only. *Milton.*

LEY. *n. ſ.*

Ley, lee, lay, are all from the Saxon leaȝ, a field or paſture, by the uſual melting of the letter ȝ or g. *Gibſon's Cam.*

LI'ABLE. *n. ſ.* [*liable*, from *lier*, old French.] Obnoxious; not exempt; ſubject.

But what is ſtrength without a double ſhare
Of wiſdom? vaſt, unwieldy, burthenſome,
Proudly ſecure, yet *liable* to fall
By weakeſt ſubtleties. *Milton's Agoniſtes.*

The Engliſh boaſt of Spenſer and Milton, who neither of them wanted genius or learning; and yet both of them are *liable* to many cenſures. *Dryden's Juvenal.*

This, or any other ſcheme, coming from a private hand, might be *liable* to many defects. *Swift.*

LIAR. *n. ſ.* [from *lie.* This word would analogically be *lier*; but this orthography has prevailed, and the convenience of

LI'BBARD. *n. ſ.* [*liebard*, German; *leopardus*, Lat.] A leopard.

Make the *libbard* ſtern,
Leave roaring, when in rage he for revenge did yearn.
Spenſer's Fairy Queen, b. i.
The *libbard*, and the tiger, as the mole
Riſing, the crumbled earth above them threw. *Milton.*

The torrid parts of Africk are by Piſo reſembled to a *libbard*'s ſkin, the diſtance of whoſe ſpots repreſent the diſperſneſs of habitations, or towns of Africk. *Brerewood.*

LI'BEL. *n. ſ.* [*libellus*, Latin; *libelle*, French.]

1. A ſatire; defamatory writing; a lampoon.

Are we reproached for the name of Chriſt? that ignominy ſerves but to advance our future glory; every ſuch *libel* here becomes panegyrick there. *Decay of Piety.*

Good heav'n! that ſots and knaves ſhould be ſo vain,
To wiſh their vile reſemblance may remain!
And ſtand recorded, at their own requeſt,
To future days, a *libel* or a jeſt. *Dryden.*

2. [In the civil law.] A declaration or charge in writing againſt a perſon in court.

To LI'BEL. *v. n.* [from the noun.] To ſpread defamation; generally written or printed.

Sweet ſcrauls to fly about the ſtreets of Rome:
What's this but *libelling* againſt the ſenate? *Shakeſpeare.*
He, like a privileg'd ſpy, whom nothing can
Diſcredit, *libels* now 'gainſt each great man. *Donne.*

To LI'BEL. *v. a.* To ſatiriſe; to lampoon;

Is then the peerage of England any thing diſhonoured when a peer ſuffers for his treaſon? if he be *libelled*, or any way defamed, he has his ſcandalum magnatum to puniſh the offender. *Dryden.*

But what ſo pure which envious tongues will ſpare?
Some wicked wits have *libelled* all the fair. *Pope.*

LI'BELLER. *n. ſ.* [from *libel.*] A defamer by writing; a lampooner.

Our common *libellers* are as free from the imputation of wit, as of morality. *Dryden's Juvenal.*

The ſquibs are thoſe who, in the common phraſe, are called *libellers* and lampooners. *Tatler.*

The common *libellers*, in their invectives, tax the church with an inſatiable deſire of power and wealth, equally common to all bodies of men. *Swift.*

LI'BELLOUS. *n. ſ.* [from *libel.*] Defamatory.

It was the moſt malicious ſurmiſe that had ever been brewed, howſoever countenanced by a *libellous* pamphlet. *Wotton.*

LI'BERAL. *adj.* [*liberalis*, Latin; *liberal.* French.]

1. Not mean; not low in birth; not low in mind.
2. Becoming a gentleman.
3. Munificent; generous; bountiful; not parcimonious.

Her name was Mercy, well known over all
To be both gracious and eke *liberal.* *Spenſ. Fa. Queen.*
Sparing would ſhew a worſe ſin than ill doctrine.
Men of his way ſhould be moſt *liberal*,
They're ſet here for examples. *Shakeſp. Henry* VIII.
Needs muſt the pow'r
That made us, and for us this ample world,
Be infinitely good, and of his good
As *liberal* and free, as infinite. *Milton.*

There is no art better than to be *liberal* of praiſe and commendation to others, in that wherein a man's ſelf hath any perfection. *Bacon's Eſſays.*

The *liberal* are ſecure alone;

An excerpt from Samuel Johnson's *A Dictionary of the English Language* (London, 1755). By permission of the Folger Shakespeare Library, Washington, D.C.

The Beginnings of Our Traditional Grammar

The first attempt at an English grammar of which we have any record was the *Bref Grammar* of William Bullokar, printed in 1586. During the next hundred and seventy-five years about twenty others appeared, varying greatly in purpose, quality, basic assumptions, and methods of analysis. The one valid generalization that can be made about them is that they had very little influence either in their own time or on the later development of grammatical theory. The most convincing testimony on this point is that of Samuel Johnson, who certainly knew the field as well as any man of his time. Presumably at the insistence of his publishers, he preceded his dictionary with what he called a grammar. He begins with this statement: "Grammar, which is *the art of using words properly,* comprises four parts: *Orthography, Etymology, Syntax,* and *Prosody.*" His treatment of all four is contained in thirteen pages (admittedly large ones), and is divided as follows: orthography, four pages; etymology, seven; prosody, two pages; and syntax, twenty-three lines, including the following paragraph:

> The established practice of grammarians requires that I should here treat of syntax; but our language has so little inflection, or variety of terminations, that its construction neither requires nor admits of many rules. Wallis therefore has totally omitted it; and Johnson [*sic,* but he is referring to Ben Jonson], whose desire of following the writers upon the learned languages made him think a syntax indispensably necessary, has published such petty observations as were better omitted.[7]

His own observations can hardly be considered a step forward. He does not, for instance, formally list the parts of speech, though he makes a few comments about some of them. Perhaps his most significant sentence is the one concluding his treatment of adjectives:

> Some comparatives and superlatives are yet found in good writers formed without regard to the foregoing rules; but in a language *subjected so little and so lately to grammar* such anomalies must frequently occur.

[7] This and the following quotation are taken from the eighth edition (1790), in which the grammar has no pagination.

The italics are added. It is not clear whether Johnson intended the phrase to mean that the true rules of grammar had not been adequately discovered and stated, or that arbitrary ones had not been invented and accepted. Possibly he had not made up his mind. In any case, he obviously felt that it was not worth his while to make any serious attempt to fill the gap.

The Lowth Tradition

Not all of Johnson's contemporaries were so willing to accept "anomalies" cheerfully. In an age so devoted to reason and authority there were strong theoretical reasons for organizing the language. Moreover, the rise of a new middle class and the trend toward universal education were proceeding simultaneously. One of the principal reasons for going to school was to learn to talk, not like your old neighbors, but like the new ones you hoped to acquire. It would be convenient if they could be persuaded to talk with some regularity. In any case, definite and dependable rules were needed.

Under these circumstances it was inevitable that systematic grammars designed for school use should be written and adopted; but the question of what form they would take was still open. In 1761 Joseph Priestley, better known as a chemist, published an English Grammar that, if it had been successful, might have given us a very different tradition from that which actually developed. It was based quite consistently on actual usage, allowed for a reasonable degree of variation, and insisted throughout that there were many more important things in life than a pedantic concern with trifles. Perhaps it was these virtues that prevented its academic success. The demand was for yes-or-no answers.

The man who did most to meet the demand was Robert Lowth, who published his *Short Introduction to English Grammar* in 1762. At this time he had already been a professor of Hebrew poetry at Oxford for many years, and he was later to become Bishop of London, and to be offered (though he declined it) the archbishopric of Canterbury. With such a background he naturally had a strong belief in order and authority — not to mention a reasonable confidence in the soundness of his own opinions.

It would be unfair to imply that he had no basis for his confidence. He was a competent scholar in Hebrew and the classical languages, at home in several modern languages, and had a surprising (for his time) knowledge of Old English. It would be hard to find a man of his period whose knowledge better qualified him for the task of "ascertaining" English grammar. But his authoritarian attitude and his concern for regularity set an unfortunate tone, which was exaggerated by some of his much less qualified followers. His book was immediately successful in the schools. More than twenty editions appeared during the eighteenth century; and simplifications, modifications, and expansions began to appear almost at once. The most influential was that of Lindley Murray, a retired Philadelphia lawyer who happened to be bed-ridden in England. He was approached by the headmistress of a girls' school who wanted a text for her pupils and convinced Murray that he had nothing better to do than to write one. The work he produced, which might be described as the logical expansion of Lowth worked out by a well-informed but petty mind, became the bible of most schools in both England and America for several generations.

Lowth's Preface

Lowth's grammar is such a pivotal document that it is worthwhile examining in some detail the preface in which he gives his view of the state of the language and explains what he proposes to do about it. A condensed version is therefore given here:

> The English language hath been much cultivated during the last two hundred years. It hath been considerably polished and refined; its bounds have been greatly enlarged; its energy, variety, richness, and elegance, have been abundantly proved, by numberless trials, in verse and prose, upon all subjects, and in every kind of style; but, whatever other improvements it may have received, it hath made no advances in Grammatical Accuracy. . . .
>
> The Construction of this Language is so easy and obvious, that our Grammarians have thought it hardly worth while to give us anything like a regular and systematic Syntax. The English Grammar, which hath been last presented to the public, and by the person [Johnson] best qualified to have given us a perfect one, comprises the whole syntax in ten lines. . . .
>
> It doth not then proceed from any peculiar irregularity or difficulty of our Language, that the general practice both of speaking and writing it is chargeable with inaccuracy. It is not the Lan-

guage, but the practice, that is in fault. The truth is, Grammar is very much neglected among us . . . . a faculty, solely acquired by use, conducted by habit, and tried by the ear, carries us on without reflection; we meet with no rubs or difficulties in our way, or we do not perceive them; we find ourselves able to go on without rules, and we do not so much as suspect, that we stand in need of them.

A Grammatical Study of our own language makes no part of the ordinary method of instruction, which we pass through in our childhood; and it is very seldom that we apply ourselves to it afterwards. Yet the want of it will not be effectually supplied by any other advantages whatsoever. Much practice in the polite world, and a general acquaintance with the best authors, are good helps; but alone will hardly be sufficient. . . . Much less then will what is commonly called Learning serve the purpose; that is, a critical knowledge of antient Languages, and much reading of antient authors. . . .

But perhaps the Notes subjoined to the following pages will furnish a more convincing argument, than anything that can be said here, both of the truth of the charge of Inaccuracy brought against our Language, as it subsists in Practice; and of the necessity of investigating the Principles of it, and studying it Grammatically, if we would attain to a due degree of skill in it.

It will evidently appear from these Notes, that our best authors have committed gross mistakes, for want of a due knowledge of English Grammar, or at least of a proper attention to the rules of it. The examples given . . . might easily have been increased in number. . . . However, I believe they may be sufficient to answer the purpose intended: to evince the necessity of the Study of Grammar in our own language; and to admonish those, who set up for authors among us, that they would do well to consider this part of Learning as an object not altogether beneath their regard.

The principal design of a Grammar of any Language is to teach us to express ourselves with propriety in that Language; and to enable us to judge of every phrase and form of construction, whether it be right or not. The plain way of doing this is, to lay down rules, and to illustrate them by examples. But, beside shewing what is right, the matter may be further explained by pointing

> out what is wrong. I will not take it upon me to say, whether we have any Grammar, that sufficiently instructs us by rule and example; but I am sure we have none, that, in the manner here attempted, teaches what is right by shewing what is wrong; though this may perhaps prove the more useful and effectual method of instruction.[8]

It does not seem quite just to call the views here expressed "the eighteenth-century attitude," because Lowth is obviously dissatisfied with his century and wants to change its ways. But they are the very fountainhead of a schoolroom attitude that is still common, particularly in the patronizing admonishment to "those who set up for authors among us" that they would do well to pay less attention to earlier authors, even the best of whom have committed gross mistakes, and more to the teacher and the text. There is (he says) absolutely no substitute for a formal study of grammar, which alone can teach us to express ourselves with propriety, and "to judge of every phrase and form of construction, whether it be right or not." Possibly by this last Lowth meant "whether it be right *for us to use* or not"; but the other possible interpretation has proved more attractive. Only by studying grammar can we prepare for a lifetime of pleasure in pointing out the mistakes of practically everybody else. Unfortunately, we may have to pay for this pleasure by a tense and defensive concern about our own use of language.

Lowth's Grammar

When we turn from Lowth's preface to his text we find on the first page two definitions that neatly conceal a basic paradox:

> Grammar in General, or Universal Grammar, explains the principles, which are common to all languages.
>
> The Grammar of any particular Language, as the English Grammar, applies those principles to that particular language, according to the established usage and custom of it.

This pair is easy enough to swallow if we take it fast; but if we stop to wonder just how far the usage and custom of two languages may diverge without either one of them doing violence to the "common principles," a definite answer is hard to find, and "universal grammar" becomes a rather vague

[8] Edition of 1775, pp. viii–xi.

term. On the other hand, if we try to base our grammar simply on established usage, we are immediately faced with the question of "whose usage?" It can't be everybody's usage, because the reason for writing the grammar is a conviction that much usage is wrong. The best usage, then — but whose usage *is* best? A conscientious grammarian may find a temporarily satisfactory answer in "the usage of our best authors." But when he examines these authors more carefully, he finds "gross errors" even in them. For a really satisfactory standard he has to look higher — not at the sentences the authors wrote, but at the sentences they would have written if they had understood grammar better, and practiced it more carefully — if they had, in fact, studied and followed the book he is composing. To a nongrammarian this reasoning may seem a little peculiar, but neither Lowth nor his followers seem to have been bothered by it.

In laying down his rules Lowth did not ordinarily pay much attention to universal grammar, which was usually believed to be best exemplified in Latin. Thus (unlike most of his successors) he rejected Dryden's theory that terminal prepositions were basically incorrect. On the contrary, "This is an idiom, which our language is strongly inclined to: it prevails in common conversation, and suits very well with the familiar style in writing. . . ." And on various other attempts to model English grammar on Latin we find such comments as "This comes of forcing the English under the rules of a foreign language, with which it has little concern. . . ."

But he likewise had some reservation about accepting "custom" as a satisfactory basis. Complaining about the corruption by which the past tenses of some strong verbs were substituted for the past participle, he says: "And in some of these, Custom has established it beyond recovery: in the rest it seems wholly inexcusable. The absurdity of it will be plainly perceived in the example of some of these Verbs, which Custom has not yet so perverted." The *yet* in the last clause is most revealing. In fact, his whole book is quite as much an attempt to reform custom as to expound it.

On the whole he seems to have depended largely on his own ear and judgment — the latter sometimes expressed modestly, sometimes simply announced as absolute. (Remember, he was already a professor, and was soon to become a bishop.) Thus he says, simply and firmly: "Two negatives in English destroy one another, or are equivalent to an affirmative." He illustrates by a quotation from Milton:

> *Nor* did they *not* perceive the evil plight
> In which they were, or the fierce pains *not* feel.

This might strike some of us as a rather cloudy way of explaining that "they" really suffered, while the five examples he gives of incorrect usage all seem perfectly clear; the negatives obviously enforce rather than cancel each other. Yet his statement was quite generally accepted as revelation, and most educated people have been carefully avoiding double negatives from this time on.

Lowth either invented or gave general currency to a number of other shibboleths that have been taking up a great deal of time in schools ever since, such as the distinction between *will* and *shall,* the proper use of *who* and *whom* in the most complicated situations, the theory that *as* and *than* should never be used as prepositions, the distinctions between *lie* and *lay,* the theory that adjectives with an absolute meaning (such as *extreme* and *straight*) can have no comparative or superlative degrees, and so forth. His followers sometimes rejected some of his rules; more often they expanded them to cover finer and finer points, or made new ones in the same spirit. The result was that in many schoolrooms the study of grammar became an exercise in fault-finding; and a great many of the people who had suffered through it became so nervous about possible criticism that their own writing became labored and colorless.

Nevertheless, the tradition that Lowth founded had a distinct value. The time had come when the English-speaking world badly needed school grammars of some sort; and if Lowth's analysis was not entirely satisfactory, it was more usable than any that had been available before. Many of the constructions he criticized were in fact awkward or ambiguous; and most of the rules he laid down are reasonably sensible if not pushed too far. The main trouble with our traditional grammars is not so much in the books themselves as in the way they are often used. This subject will be discussed in Chapter Nine.

Sound Changes

During the eighteenth century, as in all other periods, some developments simply happened with no guidance from academic theory. Changes in the sound system were few. The long vowels /e:/ and /o:/ became the diphthongs /ei/ and /ou/ as they are today. The /w/ disappeared from the initial combination /wr/, so that originally contrasting pairs like *wring* and *ring, wreak* and *reek* became homonyms. In some dialects /r/ disappeared finally and before consonants. Americans are likely to consider this feature as a characteristic of the "southern accent," but it appears also in the Received Pronunciation of Britain and in the dialect of Eastern New England. And a large number of words in which the spelling *ea* represents an original long open *e* changed their vowel sound from /ei/ to /i:/. Pope, for instance, is very consistent in rhyming words like *tea* and *obey, ear* and *repair;* but by the end of the century such rhymes have practically disappeared, and the modern phonemic system is pretty well established.

There have, of course, been many changes in the pronunciation of individual words, but these are very hard to date, because different pronunciations often compete for a long time; and even the most careful poets are likely to take advantage of them. Thus Pope rhymes *none* with *own* and *alone,* but also with *sun* and *upon;* and he shows the same sort of variety in his treatment of many other words.

Development of Progressive and "Emphatic" Constructions

One of the most unusual features of contemporary English is that we can use expressions like *I am going* (often called the progressive form) and *I do go* (often called the emphatic form) along with the simple *I go*. Most languages have only the equivalent of *I go* for all purposes. We can find examples of both the other types in earlier English; but the extensive and fairly systematic use of them is an eighteenth-century development. As late as Shakespeare's time *do go* is used simply as a variant of *go,* with no suggestion of emphasis; and *go* is often used where we should now expect *are going*.

Though *going* in such constructions is now considered a participle, it was originally a verbal noun. In its earliest stage the expression was *he was on going* — that is, in the act of going. This shortened first to *he was a going,* then to *he was going. Is going* and *was going* appear with increasing frequency during the Middle English period, but such combinations as *will be going, had been going,* and *will have been going* are not found until much later, and it is only at the very end of the eighteenth century that the "progressive passive" appears in such phrases as *is being built*. For many years this was criticized by purists as an unnecessary complication, on the grounds that the active construction meant the same thing, and was both older and simpler. Like most puristic theories, this works only on selected samples.

Dinner is cooking is, indeed, equivalent to *dinner is being cooked;* but *he is being cheated* means something quite different from *he is cheating.*

It has often been pointed out that "emphatic" does not indicate the most important uses of the *do* phrases. In expressions like "I *did* finish it" it is not the word *did* but the heavy stress that makes the emphasis, and the result is no more emphatic than "I *have* finished it," or even "I *finished* it," though the implications may be slightly different. Though Shakespeare could use such expressions as "Goes he?" and "He goes not," we must now say "Does he go?" and "He does not go." The most reasonable explanation of these new constructions is that verb phrases gradually became so common in questions and negations that they, rather than simple verbs, eventually came to be regarded as the typical pattern. Our ears have grown used to expressions like these:

Will he go?
Can he go?
Has he gone?
Is he going?

Consequently the old expression "Goes he?" seems to lack something, and we supply the deficiency by saying "Does he go?" In the same way we say "He does not go" to be consistent with the pattern of "He will not go" and so forth.

8

English Spreads Out

The Double Expansion of English

In 1800 the population of the British Isles was about fifteen million, but nearly a third of them, including most of the Irish and many of the Scotch and Welsh, spoke little or no English. The combined population of the United States and Canada (both much smaller in area than they are now) was between five and six millions, and many of their inhabitants had their roots in France, other European countries, and Africa. None of the other British colonies had yet attracted much emigration. Altogether there were perhaps fifteen million native speakers of English; but a good many of them knew only their local dialects, some of which differed enough to interfere drastically with mutual understanding. At this time horses and sailing vessels were still the fastest means of communication as well as travel. Steam had not yet been put on wheels or keels, and the practical uses of electricity and electronics were not yet dreamed of. Even newspapers and the postal service were still too expensive to be parts of the lives of most people.

Today there are more than three hundred million native speakers, much more widely distributed over the earth, plus a good many more millions who use English in their daily work; and practically all of them are exposed, by modern communications if not personal contact, to the main stream of the language. Dialectal differences still persist, but for the first time in history they seem to be getting weaker instead of stronger.

The expansion of the English vocabulary has proceeded at least as fast as the expansion in the number of speakers. Johnson's dictionary contained about fifty thousand entries, and was as complete as he could make it. He even included a few words at whose meaning he could not even guess, simply to record their existence. By contrast Philip B. Gove, the editor of *Webster's Third New International Dictionary,* claims for his book a vocabulary of more than 450,000 words, and specifically denies that the coverage is complete. He says in the preface: "The number of words available is always far in excess of and for a one-volume dictionary many times the number that can possibly be included."

Trade and the British Empire

The two kinds of expansion were of course closely related. As the British people spread over the world they came into contact with all sorts of things their ancestors had never encountered at home, and they needed new words to designate them. The goods they brought home, the new foods they learned to eat, the new plants, animals, geographic features, and customs they encountered — all these things inevitably made their contributions. And the fact that English was already a decidedly mixed language seems to have made it more hospitable to additional foreign words than more homogeneous languages such as French and German. New words do not stand out so strongly against the already patchwork background, and therefore are more readily acceptable. All the European languages were borrowing, but none — not even those of the other powers that were competing for world trade and dominion — nearly so freely as English.

It is rather curious that words borrowed from distant parts of the world were more completely naturalized than those from European neighbors. They were spelled more or less phonetically and took on the regular English inflections. But European borrowings usually retained their original spelling, and often developed a curious pronunciation, which might not be comprehensible in their land of origin, but at least marked them as expensive imports. (A Frenchman might shudder at our/tæbəl dout/ — if he suspected that it meant *table d'hôte* — but at least we don't say /teibəl də hout/. The same Frenchman, if he has honored the English word *shocking* by admitting it to his language, spells it *schocking,* pronounces it — approximately — as *show can,* and is quite prepared to criticize an Englishman for getting it all wrong.) There was also a strong tendency, fortunately now diminishing, to insist on such foreign plural forms as *tableaux, banditti,* and *seraphim,* not to mention the even more confusing Latin and Greek ones.

The Influence of American English

The British colonies that contributed most to the expansion of the language were of course the ones that broke away and became the United States. By 1840 the population of this country had passed that of England, and at present about two-thirds of the native speakers of English are Americans. Their numbers alone would have made a sizable contribution inevitable. In addition there was a new continent that invited new ways of living, and an enormous polyglot immigration.

No attempt will be made here to consider in detail the differences between the British and American varieties of English, or the specifically American contributions to the common language. There is a fascinating treatment of these subjects in H. L. Mencken's *The American Language,* admirably abridged and revised by Raven I. McDavid, Jr. The point we want to emphasize is that English is no longer the language of part of an island, with somewhat debased extensions in other parts of the world. It is now the established language of one entire continent, most of another, and considerable areas in other parts of the world, as well as all of the original island. And in spite of all local differences, it is used with an amazing approach to uniformity throughout this enormous territory. If the colonization had taken place a few centuries earlier, American might well have become as different from English as French is from Italian. But the earliest settlements were made well after the invention of printing, and the growth took place through a period when the idea of educating everybody was making rapid progress. For a long time most of the books in America came from England,

and a surprising number of people read those books, in or out of school. Moreover, before the Revolution most of the colonists felt a strong tie with England. In this they were unlike their Anglo-Saxon ancestors, who apparently made a clean break from their continental homes.

Nevertheless, some differences did develop. The earliest settlers borrowed from the Indians words like *hickory, moccasin, moose, opossum, powwow,* and *wigwam* — all (except possibly *powwow*) new and strange things for which they had no words. A little later they were borrowing from other colonists: words like *chowder, levee,* and *portage* from the French, *boss, cookie,* and *sleigh* from the Dutch. At the same time they were making new combinations of English words, such as *backwoods, bullfrog, catbird,* and *eggplant;* and using old words in new ways, such as *creek* for a running stream instead of a tidal inlet, and *lumber* for timber rather than miscellaneous junk. The same sort of thing was happening in the other colonies; but because their ties with England were more enduring, their population much smaller, and their political and economic influence less significant, their influence on the whole language was much weaker.

There was little objection in England to borrowings for entirely new things — after all, what can you call a moose but a moose? But all the other kinds of change were frequently and bitterly criticized. A good many conservative Englishmen felt that Americans were debasing the language; and — above all — that any Americanisms which showed any signs of taking root in England should be resisted with all necessary violence. Their attitude was perfectly natural, if not entirely reasonable. They considered that colonials were, in the nature of things, an inferior class of people, who should at least have the decency to try to preserve the traditions of their homeland. And ungrateful colonials who rebelled and broke away were essentially traitors as well as barbarians. Nothing good could come out of Nazareth. Of course this attitude was far from universal, as the continual and still growing influence of American on British English clearly shows; but the opponents of change were much more vocal than the receptive ones, who simply took what they wanted.

Not all the conservatives lived in England. Many Americans (there are still a few) believed that "Americanisms" were somehow inferior, even in America. Undoubtedly the name of the language is an important factor in this belief. If we called it something else — say, *Jutish* — there would be no reason to feel that the variety spoken in Ohio was inferior to that spoken in Devon. But the name *English* powerfully suggests that the English people still own the language, and have the exclusive right to guide its development. One interesting result is that many speakers of other languages, though they learn English primarily because of its importance as the language of America, would be shocked at the idea of learning it from American teachers, who could give it to them only in a corrupted form. They are, of course, no sillier than the Americans who insist on learning the "pure" Castilian Spanish in school, though their only reason for learning it is to do business in Latin America.

Thousands of differences in detail distinguish British from American English, and occasionally they crowd together enough to make some difficulty. If you read that a man, having trouble with his *lorry,* got out his *spanner* and lifted the *bonnet,* you might not immediately understand that the driver of the *truck* had taken out his *wrench* and opened the *hood.* And because such differences stand out, while similarities remain unnoticed, their importance is often greatly exaggerated. Actually it is often very hard to decide whether a book was written by an American or an Englishman; and even in speech typically national differences are no greater than some local differences in either country. Moreover, the language habits of the two countries are clearly growing more rather than less alike, although some differences will undoubtedly remain, and some new ones will develop.

The comparative uniformity is of course much greater in the written than in the spoken form of the language, and greater still when written English is edited and printed. Differences in pronunciation are eliminated, and differences in vocabulary and construction greatly reduced, except when there is some special reason for preserving a local or distinctly personal flavor.

But radio, moving pictures, and television have also greatly reduced, though not eliminated, regional and other differences in speech. The desire for enormous audiences has tempted them to homogenize the language; and because a great many people spend much more time listening to electronics than to their neighbors, the effect has been powerful, and has been reinforced by greater mobility. Perhaps the differences between "pure" dialects are as great as they ever were, but it has become virtually impossible to live in a single one. A group of farm workers from Alabama and a group of factory hands from Yorkshire might sit for some time at adjoining tables in a restaurant without either party suspecting that the rather noisy conversation of the other was in English; but if they were introduced and found interests in common they would have no great difficulty in talking to each other.

Other English-Speaking Countries

The other countries and regions in which English came to be either the principal language or the language of an important and powerful section of the population all developed additions to and changes in the kinds of English spoken locally; but the sum total of all their contributions to the general language was very small compared to that of the United States. Most of them are simply nouns for things not previously encountered elsewhere — nothing to alarm even the most conservative purist.

But two quite unrelated developments deserve special mention. The first is Pidgin English, consisting mostly of English words, often mutilated (*pidgin* itself is said to be a Chinese mispronunciation of *business*), supplemented by others of Portuguese and Malay origin, and arranged more or less according to the patterns of Chinese grammar. It began in the seaports of southern China as a means of communication between natives and foreigners, and spread widely over the Pacific area and sometimes beyond, with local variations and sometimes local names — a lingua franca spoken by many traders and settlers who knew none of the languages of which it was composed. The other is the use of English as the official language of both India and Pakistan — both countries of many languages that could neither function as Towers of Babel nor agree to use any one of their diverse languages to the disadvantage of the others.

The Expansion of Knowledge

The development of modern science and technology has resulted in a much more detailed analysis of the universe, and a greatly increased ability to manipulate it. We need words for a great many things that our ancestors never heard of; and we meet this need partly by giving new meanings to old words, partly by creating new ones. Even those branches of knowledge which have not resulted in new inventions or physical discoveries have contributed great numbers of words for new, or at least newly defined, ideas — some of them useful, some merely pretentious. We can read a fair proportion of eighteenth-century books with little trouble; but an eighteenth-century reader would find in our books — even those dealing quite simply with everyday affairs — innumerable words that would either mislead him or mean nothing to him; and no dictionary could explain to him their meaning. He would need, at the very least, an encyclopedia to give him some idea of what they were about. Some examples of the scope of this development are given at the end of the next section.

The Oxford English Dictionary

In 1858 the British Philological Society adopted a proposal for a "New English Dictionary" that would record the complete history of every word in the language from about 1000 A.D. to the present. Every English word that could be discovered was to be listed with all its forms, spellings, functions, and meanings. The project took seventy years to complete. In 1928 the final section of *A New English Dictionary on Historical Principles,* edited in turn by Sir J. A. H. Murray, Henry Bradley, and (jointly) Sir W. A. Craigie and C. T. Onions, was issued by the Oxford University Press.

In 1933 it was reprinted as *The Oxford English Dictionary,* with the original ten volumes rebound as twelve, and a supplementary volume consisting mostly of new words and meanings that had developed during the long course of production. The first volume, from A to G, of a three-volume second supplement, was printed in 1972. Even before the publication of this the "OED" claimed about fifty million words, providing 414,825 definitions and 1,827,306 illustrative quotations. These quotations were selected from more than five million gleaned from thousands of texts by hundreds of scholars and assembled over a period of about fifty years by a permanent staff of some 1,300 workers. The quotations are given chronologically under each meaning of every word (at the rate of at least one quotation per century, but usually more) with date, author, title, chapter, and page (or act, scene, line). Partly to make possible adequate quotations from medieval English, the Early English Text Society was founded in 1864 and has published several hundred volumes, mostly of Middle English sources. These statistics, selected from a recent advertisement for the OED by the Oxford University Press, give some idea of the thoroughness of the dictionary:

"There are 57,428 words under the entries beginning in 'S' alone.[1] Defini-

[1] This rather clumsy and ambiguous statement should be corrected to read "57,428 entries." More than 2,400 pages are devoted to "S," with an average of about 25 entries to a page.

tions and other material on the word 'set' cover more than 18 pages and extend to 154 main divisions; the verb 'go' fills 35 columns; 'get' requires 22 columns and is divided into 73 senses."

Without question, this is the greatest dictionary of any language ever produced. It provides the student of English language and literature with an inexhaustible mine of information. Here is a sample of an OED definition, followed by a brief explanation of its arrangement.[2]

Earth (ɜːɹþ), *sb.*[1] Forms: α. 1–4 **eorðe**, 1– *Northumb.* **eorðu**, **eorðe**, 2 **horðe**, 3–6 **erð(e**, 4–5 **irthe**, **urth(e**, 4–6 **yerth(e**, **herthe**, 5 **ȝerþ**, **yorth**, 6 **earthe**, **yearth(e**, (**erith**), 8–9 *Sc.* **yirth**, 9 *Sc.* and *dial.* **yearth**, **orth**, 6– **earth**. β. 3–5 **erd(e**, 6 **eard**, **eird**, 8 **yird**, 9 *Sc.* and *north. dial.* **yird**, **yeird**, **eard**. [Common Teut.: OE. *eorþe*, wk. fem., corresponds to OS. *ertha* wk. fem. (MDu. *aerde*, *erde*, Du. *aarde*), OHG. *erda* str. and wk. fem. (MHG., mod.G. *erde*), ON. *iǫrð* (Sw., Da. *jord*), Goth. *airþa* str. fem.:—OTeut. **erþâ*, (? WGer.) *erþôn-*; without the dental suffix the word appears in OHG. *ero* earth, Gr. ἔρα-ζε on the ground; no other non-Teutonic cognates are known to exist, the plausible connexion with WAryan root **ar*, to plough, being open to serious objection.

With the northern and Sc. forms with *-d* cf. ME. *dede* for *death*; the change of *-þ* into *-d* is rare at the end of a word, though in medial positions it is frequent in Sc. The northern forms of the present word were in the early ME. period graphically coincident with those of ERD, and in some phrases the two words seem to have been confused.]

(Men's notions of the shape and position of the earth have so greatly changed since Old Teutonic times, while the language of the older notions has long outlived them, that it is very difficult to arrange the senses and applications of the word in any historical order. The following arrangement does not pretend to follow the development of ideas.)

I. The ground.

1. Considered as a mere surface. † ***To win earth on***: to gain ground upon; ***to lose earth***: to lose ground.

Beowulf 1533 Wearp ða wunden mæl..þæt hit on eorðan læȝ stið and styleċȝ. *c* **1000** ÆLFRIC *Hom.* in Sweet *Ags. Reader* (ed. 5) 85 Iohannes..astrehte his lichoman to eorðan on langsummum gebede. *c* **1200** ORMIN 8073 Forr he [Herod] warrþ seoc, and he bigann To rotenn bufenn eorþe. **1330** R. BRUNNE *Chron. Wace* (Rolls) 13860 Þey wyþ-drowen hem, & erþe þey les. **1375** BARBOUR *Bruce* IV. 284 The Kyng.. Wes laid at erd. *c* **1400** *Destr. Troy* 6817 Sum [he] hurlit to þe hard yerth. *c* **1435** *Torr. Portugal* 657 Twenty fote he garde hyme goo, Thus erthe on hym he wane. **1611** SHAKS. *Wint. T.* v. i. 199 They kneele, they kisse the Earth. **1664** EVELYN *Kal. Hort.* (1729) 192 Let your Gardiner endeavour to apply the Collateral Branches of his Wall-Fruits..to the Earth or Borders. **1847** TENNYSON *Princ.* v. 486 Part roll'd on the earth and rose again.

2. Considered as a solid stratum.

a **1300** *Cursor M.* 4699 Þe erth it clang, for drught and hete. *c* **1340** *Ibid.* (Fairf.) 16784 The day was derker then the night Þe erthe quoke with-alle. **1562** BULLEYN *Bk. Simples* 57 a,

[2] This part of the definition of *Earth* from *The Oxford English Dictionary* is reproduced by permission of the Oxford University Press, Oxford.

a. The entry itself, in **boldface type,** shows the present form of the word.

b. The pronunciation is indicated by parenthesized phonetic characters. They are different from those used in this book and its *Companion,* because they were chosen long before the IPA was invented, and naturally represent British pronunciation.

c. The abbreviation *sb.*[1] indicates that the word is here discussed as a substantive or noun, with the superscript[1] signaling that at least one other entry as substantive will follow. (The OED lists this word also as a verb [*v*.].)

d. All the forms in which the word has ever been recorded are given for each century of the Middle and Modern English periods. Words not known to have been used after 1150 are omitted entirely. The symbol 1 indicates use before 1100, 2 indicates the twelfth century, 2–5 twelfth to fifteenth centuries, etc.

e. The etymology of the word is given in square brackets. *Earth* is a Common Teutonic word, represented in Old English by *eorþe,* a weak feminine noun equivalent to Old Saxon *ertha,* Dutch *aarde,* Modern German *erde,* Old Norse *iǫrð*, Swedish and Danish *jord,* Gothic *airþa* (a strong rather than weak feminine noun in this language), etc. All these cognate words are descended from an Old Teutonic word **erþâ.* (The asterisk indicates that this form has been hypothetically reconstructed by linguists; there is no written record of its existence.) Finally we are told that the word appears without the dental suffix (*þ* or *d*) in Greek as well as Old High German, suggesting that it is of Indo-European origin, though no other non-Teutonic cognates are definitely known.

f. A series of definitions follows, arranged under Arabic numerals grouped under Roman numerals. Each major definition is illustrated by a series of quotations (at least one per century). The earliest date indicates the first recorded written use of the word in English. We have no way of tracing earlier spoken uses.

You may very reasonably feel that this is more than you really care to know about one word, especially all at once. And if you turn to the OED itself and find that this is less than a tenth of what is said about *Earth* as *sb.*[1], you may wonder just where scholarship ends and insanity begins. But once you learn to use the book you can find out a great many things more quickly and accurately than you could anywhere else.

There is no doubt that the OED is the best dictionary ever compiled in any language; and it may well be, as some of its admirers claim, the greatest work of scholarship ever published in any field. Nevertheless, it falls considerably short of the original plan to "record the complete history of every word in the language from about 1000 A.D. to the present." In 1858 the approximate accomplishment of such a plan — allowing a little leeway for inevitable imperfections — did not seem impossible. Today, largely because of what the OED workers found out, no experienced lexicographer would dream of attempting it.

The first modification was to omit all words not recorded in use after 1150, because a starting date in the Old English period would have forced inclusion of "an immense number of words, not only long obsolete, but also having obsolete inflections, and thus requiring, if dealt with at all, a treatment different from that adapted to words which survived the twelfth century." [3] Later the workers discovered that the expression "every word in the language" was meaningless, because "the circle of the English language has a well-defined center but no discernible circumference." Out from the central group of literary and colloquial words (overlapping but not identical) are extensions in various directions of international scientific words, words from other individual languages that may be used in English, technical terms, dialect, slang, and cant, and "there is absolutely no defining line in any direction." Yet a lexicographer must draw the line somewhere, and must eventually be satisfied to "exhibit the greater part of the vocabulary of *each* one, which will be immensely larger than the whole vocabulary of *any* one."

Thus the number of words that may be legitimately used in English sentences is enormous (there are said to be nearly a million scientific names for insects alone). But the question about how many of them are "really" in the English language is utterly meaningless; and questions about when particular words from outlying areas become sufficiently "common" to merit inclusion cannot be settled on any one fixed principle. A dictionary must simply draw up a set of house rules.

The second supplement to the OED just published gives impressive evidence of how greatly the expansion of knowledge mentioned in the preceding section has affected the growth of our vocabulary. Although there are new words and new uses of old words throughout, two samples

[3] All the quoted material in this paragraph is from the "Historical Introduction" to the OED, p. xxvii.

will do. The original OED, covering more than seven centuries of use, devotes three columns to the root *bio* and compounds beginning with this element. We learn that *biotic* appeared once in 1600, but not again until 1874; that *biographer, biographic, biographical, biographically, biographist,* and *biography* all date from the seventeenth and eighteenth centuries; and that none of the other compounds, not even *biology,* is recorded before 1800. The 1933 supplement has two and a half columns on the same area — a little less space, but a much greater proportion of the whole work. And the 1972 supplement has eleven columns. A few lines in both supplements are given to occurrences previously missed, but most of them deal with new creations traceable to the growth of knowledge and more and more refined specialization. Already in the OED are *biochemical, biophysiological,* and *biostatical.* In the first supplement are (among others) *biolysis, biomolecule,* and *bionomic.* And in the second such words as *biospelaeology* and *bioluminescence.*

We find a similar development for *electro* and its compounds. Only *electrophorus* (an instrument to develop static electricity by induction) and its anglicized form, *electrophore,* appear before 1800; but of later compounds there are five columns in the OED, two in the first supplement, and fifteen in the second.

Making Compounds

The most obvious way of forming new words is to take old words or parts of words and put them together in new combinations, preferably self-explanatory. This method has always been used freely in English, but has become even more common in the past two centuries. In some of the sciences, particularly chemistry, new words are literally formulated, so that a competent analyst can recognize the composition of a new substance by inspecting its name. The *-ide* ending in such words as *oxide* and *chloride* indicates the presence of a simple element in a compound, and the *-ate* ending indicates the presence of a salt or ester of that element. Even a layman can recognize that *carbon tetrachloride* must consist of molecules containing one atom of carbon combined with four of chlorine, and is perfectly willing to believe that an expert can do equally well with *dichlorodiphenyltrichloroethane,* though he probably restricts himself to calling it DDT and hoping it will merely get rid of mosquitoes, not people.

Ordinary citizens follow the same general process in making compounds like *workmanship* and *unavailability,* but their methods are less precise, and both the choice of affixes and the exact meaning assigned to them are often a matter of chance. We may carefully observe the distinction between *continual* (occurring with great frequency) and *continuous* (going on without interruption); but the two words could just as well have been reversed, and there is no obvious reason why we say only *contiguous* and *residual* instead of *contigual* and *residuous.* The availability of both native and borrowed affixes of parallel meaning makes for a very large number of variants, some of which are not demonstrably useful. It is possible to argue that any two competing forms *should* be used with some distinction in meaning; but it is not possible to prove that they always are so used, and it would take a good deal of ingenuity even to recommend a distinction between some pairs that exist simply because they were brought into the language independently by different people. What is the useful distinction between *incontrovertibility* and *incontrovertibleness?* For that matter, what is gained by listing either word? Our vocabulary has been enormously swollen — and our dictionaries too — by the convention that all legitimate compounds are permanent. In German, compounds are made even more freely than in English; but many of the self-explanatory ones are regarded as temporary creations, almost like sentences, and no lexicographer dreams of trying to list them all. Thus you can start out with an already compound word like *Gesellschaft* (company), combine it with another for insurance to make *Versicherungsgesellschaft,* limit it to fire insurance as *Feuerversicherungsgesellschaft,* and designate its chief executive *Feuerversicherungsgesellschaftpräsident.* There does not seem to be any particular place to stop. Dictionaries list only those compounds which either occur very frequently or have a special meaning which a reader might not be able to get by examining the component parts. In English, however, the feeling is that a word is a word, and that any new compound should either be denounced as incorrect or listed for all to share.

Shortenings

Because compounds are often inconveniently long, we often shorten them in various ways. Thus *automobile* is often reduced to *auto,* and *aeroplane* was first simplified to *airplane,* and then shortened to simple *plane.* Such abbreviations are often denounced as undignified, but many of them have become so well established that they have practically superseded the original words. Even people who insist on *telephone* rather than *phone* usually ride on a *bus* rather than an *omnibus.* The shortened form may, as in *auto* and *plane,* be one of the original elements of a compound; or it may be either more or less than an independent element.

Another way of shortening words is by using the initials of their component parts, or of the words in a phrase. If the result is pronounced like an ordinary word, it is called an *acronym.* Thus *NATO* is an acronym for *North Atlantic Treaty Organization, radar* (with an extra letter to make it pronounceable) is formed from *r*adio *d*etection *a*nd *r*anging, and so forth. There is no special name for terms like DDT and c.o.d. In fact, the question of whether such combinations are really words is usually silently avoided.

Then there are blends like *smog* from *smoke* and *fog, pulmotor* from *pulmonary* and *motor,* and so forth; somewhat mangled abbreviations like *bike* from *bicycle* and *pram* from *perambulator;* back-formations like *opine* from *opinion* and *enthuse* from *enthusiasm.* These last are presumably formed by mistake, and so are often denounced; though a few, like *beg* from *beggar,* have been established for centuries.

Other Sources

Two other common sources are proper nouns and brand names, both of which are often extended beyond their original application. Thus *Stetson* is often used to indicate the shape rather than the make of a cowboy hat, and a macadam road need not exactly follow the design of its long-dead originator. *Coke,* beginning as a shortening of Coca Cola, is often used for any cola drink, and Kodak for any small camera, though both these extensions are resisted by the patent holders. *Kodak,* incidentally, is a pure coinage — a word with no etymology, simply invented by somebody who liked the sound or appearance. Such words are very rare — *gas* is about the only other one in common use.

Changes in Meaning

Along with the creation of new words there has been at least as important a change in the meanings of old ones. This process, sometimes called "semantic shift," has always occurred in all languages and will continue, in spite of objections. Those people who tell us we should use words only in their "true" meanings seem to have logic on their side — how can we communicate effectively unless words stay put? But they have all history and human nature against them. They are also likely to suffer from the delusion that the earliest meanings with which they happen to be acquainted are the original ones. The fact is that nobody knows the original meaning of any of our really old words. An etymologist can tell us that *digit* meant a finger or toe before it meant an Arabic numeral, but if he calls this the original meaning of the word he is simply guessing. We know quite well that *tête,* the normal and entirely respectable French word for *head,* began to be used in its present sense as a bit of slang; an earlier meaning was *pot,* and before that there may or may not have been others. We can trace the English word *head* to a hypothetical Indo-European form, from which Latin *caput,* French *chef,* Anglo-Norman *chief,* German *Haupt,* and other cognates were derived by quite regular though complicated processes; but for all we know this hypothetical form may itself have been a slang or metaphorical transfer from a still earlier meaning.

The four kinds of semantic shift most frequently discussed are *specialization, generalization, elevation,* and *degeneration* (other terms, such as *narrowing, broadening, amelioration,* and *pejoration* are sometimes used). Thus *deer,* which used to mean any wild animal, has been specialized to mean only the kind that produces venison; and *hound,* originally any dog, no longer includes such breeds as setters and spaniels. *Horse,* on the other hand, has been generalized to designate a mare or gelding as well as a stallion; and *pig* and *pigeon* no longer refer only to the young of these species. A *governor* used to be a man who steered a ship. Now it may be a man who steers the ship of state. (Of course it may also be a mechanical gadget that keeps an engine from running too fast — some words move in all directions.) An Old English *hūswīf* was presumably a respectable woman; but by the time the form of the word had contracted to *hussif* and then to *hussy* its meaning had become so uncomplimentary that the original elements in a later form had to be recombined to make *housewife.*

The four kinds of shift mentioned in the preceding paragraph are not the only ones that occur; in fact their neat symmetry probably does more to conceal than to explain the ways in which words change their meaning. In general, a word may be shifted from one meaning to another whenever there is a resemblance between two things. To go back to the word *head,* its first known use is to name a part of the body. But it has been extended to other things that resemble this part in shape, as a *head of lettuce;* in position, as the *head of the stairs;* or in function, as the *head of the company.* Sometimes the resemblance is at two or more removes. Because the top part of almost anything can be called a head, the water kept high in a dam to supply power may be called a *head of water;* then steam, ready to work regardless of its position, may be called a *head of steam.* Such an expression as "the dispute *came to a head*" would be meaningless if we were not familiar with boils and pimples forming a recognizable head as they are about to pop.

Of course it could be argued that any extension of meaning is simply a kind of generalization, but sometimes the earlier meaning drops out of use, leaving a complete transfer. Very few people now use *digit* to refer to a finger, and no Frenchman uses *tête* to refer to a pot. And *silly* and *nice* have virtually swapped places since Chaucer's time. His *"sely"* could mean "innocent" or "kind" as well as "happy," and his *nice* regularly meant "ignorant" or "foolish."

We sometimes call the supposedly original meaning of a word its *literal* meaning, and all derived meanings *figurative;* but until we all become profound etymologists, such a distinction is not very useful. If the *head of a pin* is a metaphor, how are we to express the same idea literally? Our language is full of frozen metaphors. Many of them were deliberately created, proved attractive, and thus came into common use. Others came about simply because there are more things in the world than there are words in any conceivable human vocabulary. When we meet a new thing we have to call it something, and it is usually more convenient to modify the meaning of an old word than to invent a new one.

Changes in meaning are so fascinating that there is a strong temptation to go on discussing them for dozens or hundreds of pages, and to revel in all their historical, philosophical, and psychological implications; but in this chapter we have room for only two more points. First, semantic shift has been unusually active during the past two centuries simply because our environment, both physical and intellectual, has been changing more rapidly than ever before. The "natural" meaning of the word *car,* for instance, has shifted from a small horse-drawn vehicle to a railroad coach, to a streetcar, to an automobile; and the automobile is most likely to be a *sedan,* though it weighs a good deal more than the original sedans, and rides on rubber tires rather than human shoulders. And it is full of working parts that did not exist a century ago, though they are mostly designated by words that did. And although most Americans continue to believe in the *rights of man,* the *principles of democracy,* and the advantages of a *liberal education,* their interpretation of these terms might surprise their great-grandfathers a good deal.

Second, the development of euphemisms has been particularly extensive, though not always in the same direction. The tendency to avoid the direct naming of things felt to be offensive, unpleasant, or dangerous has always existed, but has probably never been quite so strong as during the "Victorian" period. (In this respect Victoria's reign lasted to about 1950, and was even more effective in the United States than in Britain. Her subjects could at least eat a chicken's breast or thigh, while we had to be content with white or dark meat.) The "four-letter words" dealing with sex and elimination became so disgraceful they were dropped even from dictionaries, though most of them managed somehow to survive; and even their polite replacements soon became too strong for the more sensitive ears. Thus *rest room* or *powder room* came to be substituted for *toilet,* which was originally of about the same degree of delicacy. This procedure could go on forever, and perhaps it will; but the direction veers from time to time.

Current taboos seem to have mostly a sociological rather than a biological basis. We can now be as explicit as we like about organs and their functions, but should be careful to speak of *senior citizens* rather than *old people,* change the *poor* to the *underprivileged,* and designate special parking spaces for the *handicapped*. There is nothing either new or unreasonable about women objecting to such terms as *poetess* and *aviatrix;* but insistence on words like *chairperson* suggests some rather frightening complications. It is too bad we can't revive the archaic *wight* as a natural word for a member of either sex; and maybe we could if it didn't sound so much like *white,* which would suggest unfairness in another area. The objection to uncomplimentary names for races and nations seems admirable, and perhaps people who use the less popular hand are justified in resenting such terms as *left-handed compliment* or the fact that *sinister* has a less complimentary meaning than *dexterous*. But the idea that we can keep any set of words permanently free from connotations is rather naive; and it does sometimes happen that a poor old crippled man is as cheerful and contented as his neighbor, an underprivileged and handicapped senior citizen.

Varieties of English

Not all the differences in English can be assigned to geography. Varieties and subvarieties are based on social status, education, occupation, and a number of other things; and the differences intersect in such a complicated way that complete analysis of them is utterly hopeless. We cannot even agree on the meanings of the terms used to designate different kinds of "nonstandard" English, as this excerpt from *Webster's Seventh New Collegiate Dictionary* shows:

> *dialect* . . . . *1 a:* a regional variety of language distinguished by features of vocabulary, grammar, and pronunciation from other regional varieties and constituting together with them a single language (the Doric *dialect* of ancient Greek) *b:* one of two or more cognate languages (French and Italian are Romance *dialects*) *c:* a regional variety of a language usually transmitted orally and differing distinctively from the standard language (the Lancashire *dialect* of English) *d:* a variety of a language used by the members of an occupational group (the *dialect* of the atomic physicist) *e:* the customary language of a social class (peasant *dialect*) . . .
>
> *syn* DIALECT, VERNACULAR, LINGO, JARGON, CANT, ARGOT, SLANG mean a form of language that is not recognized as standard. [But dialect obviously does not mean that to everybody — see definitions *a, b,* and *d* above.]
>
> DIALECT applies commonly to a form of language persisting regionally or among the uneducated; VERNACULAR applies to the everyday speech of the people in contrast to that of learned men; LINGO is a mildly contemptuous term for any language not readily understood; JARGON applies to a technical or esoteric language used by a profession, trade, or cult; it may also be a stronger designation than LINGO for language or usage that sounds outlandish; CANT is applied derogatorily to language that is both peculiar to a group or class and intrinsically lacking in clarity or precision of expression (journalistic *cant*); ARGOT is applied to a peculiar language of a clique or other closely knit group (thieves' *argot*); SLANG designates a class of mostly recently coined and frequently short-lived terms or usages informally preferred to standard language as being forceful, novel, or voguish.

It is obvious that the terms overlap, that they are used differently by different people, and that it would be hard for even one man to use any one of them with complete consistency. To simplify matters we may now disregard the five synonyms and concentrate on *dialect* itself, which is given a sixth definition to contrast it with *vernacular,* etc., and *standard,* which is not defined here, but is defined under the adjective Standard in the same book as "*5:* substantially uniform and well-established by usage in the speech and writing of the educated and widely recognized as acceptable and authoritative English."

Fifty years ago this would have been generally accepted as sound, and even today many people consider the two terms mutually exclusive — standard as the "good" English used by educated people (people who use good English) everywhere, whereas dialects "persist" (revealing word) only "regionally or among the uneducated." But now many linguists consider that even the best-educated people must speak one dialect or another, and that a dialect may therefore have both standard and nonstandard forms. Other linguists consider standard to be merely one dialect, enjoying greater prestige than the others, but not intrinsically better. And still others say that there is obviously a standard written English used throughout the world, but that it is absurd to talk of standard spoken English, because there is no accepted interregional standard to which people can even try to conform.

We can't hope to settle all the issues in such a complicated disagreement, but the weight of the evidence is sufficient to establish three points:

1. No dialect is "ungrammatical," because no human being is bright enough to learn and use a kind of language without systematic regularities. Dialects simply have different grammars.
2. All dialects deserve full respect. Condescension about any of them is a sign of ignorance, not of superiority.
3. But anybody who doesn't learn to use standard English when he wants to is likely to be building a low ceiling over his future.

Changes in the Verb System

The principal structural changes that have taken place since the eighteenth century affect verbs, and are of three sorts. In the standard language the tendency toward simplification of inflections was arrested, and in a few cases reversed. Lowth's campaign to prevent any more verbs from shifting to the regular conjugation, or losing the old distinction between the past tense and past participle, has proved more successful than he would probably have thought possible, so that some of the forms to which he says regretfully that "our ears have grown accustomed" would now strike most educated people as impossible, though they continue to be heard in popular speech. And we have come to insist on "you *were*" for both numbers, though "you *was*" in the singular seemed to be well established a hundred and fifty years ago.

The development of perfect and progressive systems has continued, so that now it is at least theoretically possible to say something like "By next month he *will have been being treated* for three years," and call it "third person singular future perfect indicative passive." Such expressions are fortunately rare, but we do frequently use combinations that would not have occurred to our ancestors. We have also extended the use of some additional auxiliaries, in such constructions as *got hurt, got moving, kept* (*on*) *doing it,* and so forth. In fact our system of verb phrases has become so complicated that few grammarians have even attempted a systematic study of it, and no analysis has been generally accepted. The usual practice is either to oppose or ignore those which cannot be readily explained; but they continue to gain ground.

There has also been a great increase in what are now usually called verb-adverb combinations, such as *put away, put by, put down, put in, put off, put on, put out,* and *put up*. Many of us used to be taught that these were deplorable, and that it was much better to use a specific word for each purpose, and not to overuse the common ones. This advice ignored the fact that the preferred words were usually Latin compounds of no greater variety — *appose, compose, depose, expose, impose, interpose, oppose, propose,* and so forth (the two lists are typical rather than parallel). The fact that the Latin compounds have the modifying element first and are written solid, while the English ones have it second and after an intervening space, is interesting, but hardly proves that the English ones are inferior. At any rate, we may rejoice that we are not afflicted with the German mixture of the two systems, which calls for saying "Wollen sie hereinkommen?" (Will you enter?), but "Er kam herein."

9

"Traditional" Grammar — and Some Early Reactions

Some General Remarks about Grammar

It is now time to shift from the development of the language itself to the development of our knowledge of it, and some of the theories that have affected our treatment of it in our schools. The widespread and deeply rooted dislike of grammar, at least in English-speaking countries, has long been notorious. Several reasons, each containing at least some truth, have been advanced to explain the aversion. One is that the kind of grammar that has been traditionally taught in our schools is based on Latin, and fits English so loosely that considerable parts of it can be understood only as acts of faith, with a distinct element of mysticism. Another is that the subject is often taught not as a body of information but as a system of morals, toward which we often have a split reaction. While one side of our mind tells us that we ought to obey the rules because they must somehow be right, the other tells us that if we do we'll lose many of our friends, and feel like prigs as we do it. And finally there is the widespread suspicion that the whole subject is unnecessary — an imposition foisted on us by schoolteachers and their ilk. If somebody would just shoot all grammarians, honest men could live in peace. "Why," asks young Tommy, "have any parts of speech at all? What are they good for? Why don't they just let us talk sense?"

Such questions are often dismissed as silly or rebuked as impertinent, but they are important and deserve honest and careful answers. If we are to continue to insist that everybody study grammar, we ought to be able to explain clearly what it consists of, and how it can be profitably used.

One reason for the general confusion is that we use the term *grammar* in a number of incompatible ways, and we often shift from one meaning to another without realizing that we are changing the subject. We cannot solve this problem by defining the term to indicate that only one meaning is legitimate; but we can clarify it by getting a firm grasp of the more important meanings, and keeping them distinct in our own minds.

1. The *study* of the structural patterns that are used to put words or morphemes together into meaningful sentences. The exact boundaries of this study have never been settled, but this meaning causes comparatively little trouble.

2. The *patterns themselves*. Here we run into a very real difficulty that is often disregarded. We are tempted to say that *the* grammar of a language is the set of patterns that actually exists in it, built into the minds of the speakers, and that *a* grammar is a particular attempt to describe them. But if the language is composed of dialects, subdialects, and finally idiolects, no two quite alike, the "set of patterns that actually exists" becomes a rather vague (though impressive) term. A grammarian can describe only those patterns which he has observed — inevitably a limited sample, seen from a particular point of view. Conceivably the time may come when all competent grammarians will agree on at least the major points of their descriptions. At present they do not.

3. A *set of rules* that everybody ought to follow. Grammars that lay down such rules are called *prescriptive* or *normative,* and many linguists feel that they are illegitimate — that a grammarian has no more right to legislate about his phenomena than a chemist has; his "laws" should be merely generalizations about what he has observed. Most laymen, on the other hand, think of prescriptive grammars as the only possible kind. Some of them assume that the rules are based on the same sorts of inevitable relations as those which underlie the rules of arithmetic; others, that they are an arbitrary set of regulations, like traffic laws, but that they are necessary to make accurate communication possible. In either case, they consider that any utter-

ance that does not comply with the rules is ungrammatical, though by definition (2) above it would be simply based on a different kind of grammar.

It would be a waste of time to argue about which of these two attitudes is correct, because they are based on such different premises that they are not comparable. But we can probably agree that if we are to use prescriptive grammars in our schools they should be based on the best descriptive ones now available; and we should know what we are using them for. The idea that nobody can learn to handle a language competently without a thorough knowledge of grammatical theory, though firmly believed by many teachers, simply will not stand investigation. Grammars appeared so late in history that the authors of much of the great literature of the world could not possibly have been acquainted with any systematic descriptions of the structure of the languages in which they wrote. The first Greek grammar, for instance, was not composed until long after the great age of Greek literature. Dante could not possibly have seen an Italian grammar. Shakespeare could have seen an English grammar, composed by a crackpot named Bullokar; but it is hard to see how he could have profited by it, and there is certainly no evidence that he or anybody else ever did.

In fact, there is a great deal of evidence to indicate that anybody who grows up thoroughly immersed in *one socially satisfactory and fairly homogeneous dialect* can learn that dialect by simple exposure quite as well as he is at all likely to do by any system of structural analysis. But today few people in America are in a position to do this. How often do we hear mothers complain, "Rick used to talk so nicely until he went to school, and now he is an absolute barbarian"? For anybody who grows up in a socially unsatisfactory dialect, or in a confusing mixture of competing but not clearly differentiated dialects, a systematic description of how standard patterns differ from others can be very useful in saving time and increasing confidence — provided, of course, that the description is reasonably accurate, and is not offered for more than it is worth.

If it is offered and accepted as gospel it can lead to its own kind of trouble. People who have always received A's in grammar courses are often handicapped in a way of which they are quite unaware. Having accepted a particular set of conventions as universal truths, they are very comfortable in certain situations, but rather helpless in others, and the mixture of smugness and irritation that they often develop is not particularly attractive. And they may be in for a severe shock when they are forced to realize that people they had thought stupid for saying "I don't see it" were on sounder ground than those who had accepted everything the books and teachers had said.

Structural Patterns

Speakers of any language somehow develop by tacit agreement (but never quite uniformly) a set of structural patterns; and the organization of these patterns, even in languages that we are likely to think of as primitive, can be amazingly complex. Students who find the subjunctive mood confusing may be interested in learning that the Cree Indians in Canada have verbs with fifteen moods; and a Turkish verb is said to have more than three thousand possible terms. Moreover, recent investigations have shown that the structural differences among languages are far greater than used to be believed. Some languages do not have the subject-predicate sentences that are so important in our structure. Some do not even have permanent words, but rather word-sentences composed of such shifting arrangements and modifications of elements that at first meeting we find them absolutely incredible. These and other differences are so fundamental that we cannot satisfactorily treat them as variations within a single system, but as representing utterly different systems, each of which must be studied in and for itself.

We have no reason to believe that any of the speech communities who developed these amazing complications were more consistent than their descendants, nor can we reasonably assume that in the ages before written grammars the learning of any language was a systematic mastery of a completed structure. Presumably most people gave the patterns no particular thought, but simply assumed that they were among the laws of nature. Each speaker absorbed what he could of the conventions in which he was immersed, and perhaps made a few small contributions or modifications of his own. The language was therefore gradually but continually changing in its patterns as well as its vocabulary, and at no time was it ever quite uniform.

To suppose that behind this ever-shifting collection of imperfectly consistent habits there is somehow a "true" and logically consistent grammar now seems a little unreasonable; and such a supposition certainly cannot be proved. With a few million people talking as fast and as variously as they do, the obvious fact is that anybody who tries to make a comprehensive description — any grammarian — must first select a sample of language small enough for him to have time to examine and consider it carefully. He must then find some way to classify his material — a task that involves a number of arbitrary decisions about which similarities and differences are significant and which are negligible. And when he finds inconsistencies and outright contradictions, as he surely will if his sample is large enough, he must either find ingenious ways of fitting them into his system or throw them out as illegitimate. In other words, there is an element of invention as well as of discovery in his grammar. There is nothing shameful about this, and his grammar may be valuable and useful; but it is inevitably limited. Some grammarians are abler and more sensible than others, but none of them can approach the impersonal accuracy of physicists, because the speech acts of people are more complicated and less regular than the movements of particles. And even in physics it is now realized that any description is an interaction between the observer and what he observes.

We shall no doubt continue to talk about *the* grammar of a language, but we should realize that this is a convenient rather than a precise use of the word. *A* grammar is an attempt to describe the patterns that a particular student, called a grammarian, has observed in a particular language, usually with the aid of some earlier attempts, and necessarily from a particular point of view. The enormous array of facts is always somewhat contradictory, and different analyses and descriptions are always possible. This statement annoys a few of the more zealous linguists, who are quite sure that they have found the one true road to the truth. But they disagree forcefully about which road is this true one. At least three approaches (each with variations) are being used by able scholars in studying the patterns of English. Some features of the oldest one will be considered in this chapter, and of the two newer ones in the next.

Variations in Traditional Grammar

Two things must be emphasized here: First, that the word "traditional" is not used as a term of reproach; second, that the tradition has never been either static or uniform. Admirable scholars as well as bigoted pedants have used the traditional approach, modifying it in the light of new knowledge. Once we recognize that it is an analysis based on certain assumptions and not a moral code, we can use it for what it is worth — which may be a good deal in certain circumstances. But the schoolroom version of it did, as it developed, become more and more Latinized, and this during a period when fewer and fewer students had any real knowledge of Latin. The result is that even people who have mastered the rules are often oppressed by a sense of mystery about the whole thing. It therefore seems worthwhile to run through the traditional parts of speech in an effort to show how certain concepts that are quite comprehensible when applied to Latin become almost mystical when transferred to English. The result is comparable to what we might get if we tried to indicate the political geography of Africa on an outline map of South America. The picture would not be utterly useless. After all, both continents are roughly triangular, and much wider at the top than at the bottom, so that the sizes and relative positions of the countries could be indicated after a fashion. But a good deal of distortion would be necessary — and instruction based on such a map would be better if this fact were continually borne in mind. Detailed argument about the exact and true locations of all the boundaries would be rather pointless.

Nouns and Adjectives

Latin nouns are inflected much more fully than Modern English ones; and Latin adjectives have the same kinds of inflection as nouns. In fact the resemblance between Latin nouns and adjectives is so great that until the nineteenth century they were not usually classified as separate parts of speech. When a noun was used to name something it was called a *noun substantive;* when used to modify another noun it was called a *noun adjective.* (In both these phrases the second noun modifies the first.) Some nouns could be used either way. Others were restricted by their meaning (not by rule) to one function or the other. Nouns adjective could also be inflected in degrees comparable to our *big, bigger, biggest.* There doesn't seem to be any temptation to speak of *wolf, wolfer, wolfest.*

A noun is now usually said to be the name of something, and an adjective to be a word that modifies a noun. These two definitions carry the seeds of confusion, because nouns are defined in relation to the things of which we talk, but adjectives in relation to other words rather than to things. They still work well enough in simple cases, but lead to endless argument in others. Consider the word *green* in these sentences:

Green is my favorite color. (Noun)
The *green* grass grows all around. (Adjective)
The grass is *green.* (Adjective)
The color is *green.* (Debatable)
I like *green* better than red. (Noun)

I like the *green* better than the red. (Highly debatable. Is *green* an adjective modifying "a noun understood," an adjective used in place of a noun, an adjective that has become a noun by its use in the sentence, or a noun in its own right? And does it make any difference whether we are talking about two tubes of paint or two sweaters?)

Or consider the phrase "a stone fence." Is *stone* an adjective modifying *fence* or is it an attributive noun, the phrase being "a fence made of stone," and its real structure remaining unchanged in spite of the quite perceptible difference in form?

The fact that such questions have been argued with much heat for many generations suggests that they cannot *within this system* be settled by an appeal to evidence. They should therefore be classified as a philosophic diversion rather than linguistic analysis. To provide a tangible basis for more limited discussions we will now look at the forms of a Latin noun. Five of the original eight cases of Indo-European are still in common use, and their forms are still fairly, though not perfectly, distinct. This is the Latin noun for *wolf:*

	Masculine	
	Singular	*Plural*
Nominative	lupus	lupī
Genitive	lupī	lupōrum
Dative	lupō	lupīs
Accusative	lupum	lupōs
Ablative	lupō	lupīs
	Feminine	
Nominative	lupa	lupae
Genitive	lupae	lupārum
Dative	lupae	lupīs
Accusative	lupam	lupās
Ablative	lupā	lupīs

1. The set of forms of a noun is called its *declension* — an apparently mysterious term with a simple origin. In some early grammars the forms were shown in a diagram like the one on page 246.

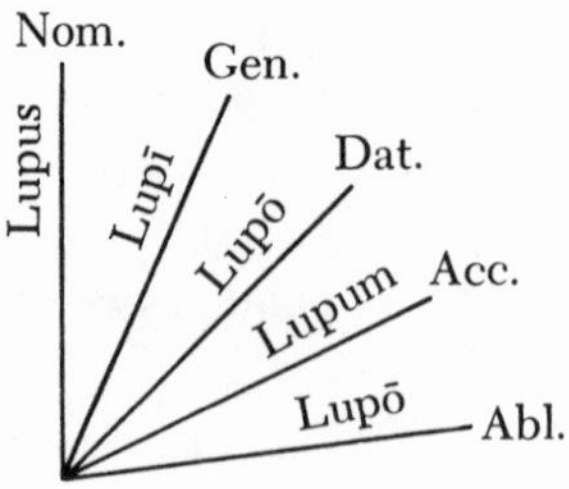

Here all cases but the nominative "decline," or fall away, from the vertical. They are therefore still often referred to as "the oblique cases."

2. There are five declensions in Latin. Nobody knows why. *Lupa* belongs to the first and *lupus* to the second. The others are not illustrated here.

3. We believe that originally all twenty of the forms listed above (as well as some others long lost) were different, but keeping them all straight had apparently been too much of a strain, and some of them had run together. Thus in the masculine singular the dative and ablative forms had both become *lupō,* and in the feminine singular the genitive and dative had both become *lupae*. In the plural the dative and ablative forms are not only identical with each other but are the same in both genders. Altogether we have only thirteen forms where there ought to be twenty — the smallest number that could unambiguously indicate the three "properties" of gender, number, and case. *Property* is another term that often carries an aura of mystery. Its only discoverable meaning in grammar is a *restriction in use imposed by a certain form*. Modern English adjectives have completely lost these three properties, because one form can now be used for all purposes; and Modern English nouns have lost more of the properties than authors of some grammars admit.

There is no justification for the idea that these properties are somehow inherent in all nouns, whether or not there is any tangible evidence of them. None of these limitations is necessarily shown by the forms of nouns, because other devices are available. And when any one of them is not shown by the form of a noun it ceases to be a property of that noun. Thus our word *sheep* has neither gender nor number, and the only limitation on its case is that it is not genitive. It is a reasonable, though not a necessary, fiction to consider it as sometimes singular and sometimes plural, because it can thus be treated as resembling most other nouns. But it is a completely useless fiction to consider it as sometimes nominative and sometimes objective, because no English nouns are now limited in this way.

Number

The easiest of the three "properties" for us to grasp is number because, like the Romans, we not only think of things as being either singular or plural, but we indicate which almost every time we use a noun. This is not a matter of course. Some languages have more than two grammatical numbers: for instance, one, two, and more than two. Other languages do not bother with grammatical number at all, but use the equivalent of *one man, two man, many man* with all nouns, whereas we do it with only a few, like *sheep*. And many languages show number in their adjectives as well as their nouns. The French, for instance, call a little boy *un petit garçon;* but two little boys *deux petits garçons*. In other words, although arithmetical numbers are international, grammatical number is an arbitrary device in a given language. You will notice that in Latin number is not expressed either separately or consistently by anything equivalent to the modern *-s* ending. Instead, number, gender, and case are all indicated (though sometimes ambiguously) by a single ending. This seems so complicated that we wonder how illiterate people, including their small children, could have practiced it for centuries, but they somehow managed, at least after a fashion.

Gender

Gender is a grammatical device, very useful in such synthetic languages as Latin because it helps to show which adjectives modify which nouns, and which nouns particular pronouns refer to. In analytic languages, where these relationships are indicated by a dependable word order, it is a complicated and almost completely useless nuisance inherited from the past. In speaking French we must be careful always to call an old man *vieux* and an old woman *vieille,* though one form would do for both exactly as well as *old* does in English.

Some languages have as many as a dozen genders, which may be based on any kind of distinction, such as animate against inanimate, or even small against large; but the best-known genders are based, though far from reliably, on sex. Thus both Latin and Old English have three genders — masculine, feminine, and neuter. Male beings are likely to be referred to by masculine nouns, and female beings by feminine nouns, but there are some conspicuous exceptions. It is hard to think of anything more professionally female than a prostitute, yet the Latin word *scortum,* which means one, is neuter. So was the Old English *wīf* (woman, later wife); and the Old English *wīfman* was masculine, because *man* was masculine, and remained so even in a combination that meant *woman.*

We can see gender in action by examining the French translations of three sentences:

I saw the king, and he was happy.
J'ai vu le roi, et il était heureux.

I saw the queen, and she was happy.
J'ai vu la reine, et elle était heureuse.

I saw his majesty, and he was happy.
J'ai vu sa majesté, et elle était heureuse.

It seems natural enough to use the feminine pronoun *elle* in the second sentence, because it is here the equivalent of our *she.* Using *la* and *heureuse* instead of *le* and *heureux* for *the* and *happy* may strike us (reasonably enough) as an unnecessary complication, but we can accept it without much concern. Most Americans do find ridiculous at first meeting the feminine forms in the third sentence. Why call a king *she?*

The answer is that although *elle* is often equivalent to *she,* there is an essential difference between the two words. In languages having gender, pronouns must be selected to agree with their antecedents. In English, pronouns must simply be appropriate to the people or things to which they refer. We call a woman *she* not because *woman* is a feminine word — it never has been — but because a woman is female.

It is often said that Modern English has "natural gender," but this curious statement only complicates the problem. Gender is a purely grammatical convention, and there is nothing natural about it. We can understand it more easily if we don't extend the term to cover something quite different. The fact that we use *cow* to refer to a female bovine has no more grammatical consequence than the fact that we use *calf* to refer to a young one.

Case

A case is a special form used to show the noun's relation to other words in the sentence. To see how it works we can consider these simple Latin sentences:

1. a.	Lupus videt Marcum.	The wolf sees Marcus.
b.	Marcum videt lupus.	"
c.	Marcum lupus videt.	"
d.	Lupus Marcum videt.	"
e.	Videt lupus Marcum.	"
f.	Videt Marcum lupus.	"

Lupus is in the nominative case and is therefore the subject. *Marcum* is in the accusative case and is therefore the direct object. The different word orders give slightly different emphases, but cannot change the basic relations.

2. Lupum videt Marcus. — Marcus sees the wolf.

Now the cases have been reversed, and so has the meaning. Here again six word orders would be possible.

3. Lupō Marcus carnem dedit. — Marcus gave the wolf meat.

Lupō is in the dative case, and is therefore the indirect object. *Marcus* is the subject and *carnem* (from a different declension) is the direct object.

4. Lupī Marcus carnem surripuit. — Marcus stole the wolf's meat.

Lupī is in the genitive case, which shows that the meat was already the wolf's.

An English-speaking child, meeting structures like this for the first time, finds them not only confusing but ridiculous. Take sentence 1b. If *Marcum* means *Marcus, videt* means *sees,* and *lupus* means *wolf,* how in the world can "Marcum videt lupus" mean anything but "Marcus sees the wolf"? The people who say it does — Romans and teachers alike — must be crazy, and the subject is obviously not worth pursuing. As a matter of fact a good many children give up the subject right here, and even if they are forced to sit in Latin classes for some years, and to memorize some words and some rules, they never learn anything of the slightest importance about the language.

Other children, with slightly more flexible minds, are willing to accept the rules, and to treat all Latin sentences as something like algebraic equations — puzzles which can be solved by applying the proper techniques, but which obviously have to be torn apart and reassembled before they can be understood. Such children usually consider Latin a very learned subject, of which only the bare elements can be learned in high school. The idea that rather stupid children used to learn to prattle Latin quite accurately before they were five seems absolutely incredible — yet they did.

Naturally, these Roman five-year olds had never heard of a direct object or an accusative case. They had simply learned by continual exposure that the *-um* form showed that the wolf didn't do anything, but had something happen to him, and that the *-us* form would be used to indicate the actor. They knew these things just as an American child knows the difference between "My father is taller than *John*" and "My father is taller than *John's.*"

Of course these are very simple examples. This is no place to go into detail about Latin grammar. The important point is simply that the basic signalling system of Latin was quite different from that of English. It is useless to argue about which is better. Opinions differ and proof is impossible. Whether they were moved by intelligence or pure laziness our ancestors somehow drifted away from using cases to a combination of position and prepositions.

Even the Romans had begun this drift, as you can see by the duplications in the declension of *lupus.* This occasions some difficulty in reading Latin. We have to depend on cases to understand the meaning, and the case forms are sometimes ambiguous. In Old English the drift had gone much further, and the ambiguity was proportionately more serious. To make up for the losses in distinct inflections we have gradually developed a standard word order that indicates meaning by position rather than cases. We often call this word order "normal," which has the unfortunate effect of suggesting that any other order is silly; ours is normal only in the sense that it has become habitual for us. The Spanish, for instance, habitually put an adjective after a noun instead of before it, and get along just as well.

A great deal of unnecessary confusion has been caused by some grammarians who have shifted the meaning of *case* from the form used to show a relation, and use it to indicate the relation itself. Thus many grammarians say that whenever the word *wolf* is used as the subject it is in the "nominative" case, and whenever it is used as the object it is in the "objective" case — a combination of the old accusative and dative cases. A few conservative grammarians even talk about separate dative and accusative cases in Modern English. Thus we have these three competing declensions of the noun *wolf* in the singular.

Common case	wolf	*Nominative case*	wolf	*Nominative case*	wolf
Possessive	wolf's	*Possessive*	wolf's	*Genitive*	wolf's
		Objective	wolf	*Dative*	wolf
				Accusative	wolf

Aside from mere differences in nomenclature we have from two to four cases postulated. Of course it is obvious that *wolf, wolf,* and *wolf* look and sound a good deal alike. If you made a mistake and used a nominative *wolf* where you were supposed to use a dative one, it would be a little hard to check up on you. The existence of three or four cases in Modern English nouns is therefore not a fact that can be proved by evidence, but a purely arbitrary convention which is worth adopting only if it can be shown to be useful — and which has been dropped as useless by most contemporary grammarians, though it is still often found in school texts.

Naturally, the convention is not utterly without foundation. If you will examine the declension of *lupus* you will notice that the dative and ablative cases are shown as identical in the masculine singular and in the plural of both genders. If it were not for the feminine singular (and if all nouns were declined like *lupus*) we could say that the ablative case has disappeared in Latin, as it has in Greek and German. And with the facts as they are we could say that this case has disappeared in the plural of all Latin nouns, and in the singular of a great many. This would be quite as accurate as what we do say, but without some years of experimenting we can't determine whether the new statement would be more or less convenient than the old. It can at least be argued that it is easier to make and apply rules that treat the dative and ablative as different, even though they are often identical, than rules that call for the use of the ablative of some nouns but the dative of others.

But we cannot apply this sort of argument to Modern English without stretching it much too far. Not a single noun has preserved more than two cases; and the only reasonable thing to do is to stop talking about those which were dropped six or seven hundred years ago as well as those which were dropped even earlier. Or else we should be really consistent and talk about the vocative, locative, and instrumental cases as well as those already discussed, and attribute them to adjectives as well as nouns.

Pronouns

The traditional definition of a pronoun is "a word used in place of a noun." Unfortunately, the definition works only if we are careful to consider only such examples as support it. Otherwise it misses badly in both directions.

You and *I,* for instance, are not substitutes for some other words; they are the most natural words to use when referring to *us* — and try to find a good noun for that one. And on the other hand a great many words that *are* used in place of nouns are seldom called pronouns. For instance:

The *poor* are suffering.
The doctors were busy with the *wounded.*
To drive so fast is dangerous.

We may argue about whether *poor* is an adjective used as a noun or one that has actually become a noun, but we never call it a pronoun, any more than we do the participle and infinitive that are used in place of nouns in the next two sentences.

Actually the words that have traditionally been called pronouns in English are simply the words normally used to translate the words called pronouns in Latin; and these Latin pronouns are a group of words used very much like nouns but inflected a little differently. Probably the most nearly reliable definition of a Latin pronoun is "a noun that has a genitive case ending in *-ius.*" By this definition *aliquis,* a Latin word for *anybody,* is a pronoun, because its genitive case is *alicuius*. But the English word *anybody* is obviously a compound form of the noun *body*. It can just as well be called an indefinite noun as an indefinite pronoun.

The personal pronouns *I, he, she, it, we, you,* and *they,* along with *who,* are the only English pronouns that have preserved case inflections different from those of nouns, and many modern grammarians accordingly consider them to be the only pronouns left in the language. Old English had some other words that can be classified as pronouns because of their inflections, but not nearly so many as Latin.

Much of the confusion about the classification as well as the use of pronouns is the result of a more deep-seated confusion between *antecedents* and *referents*. A referent is the person or thing to which a word refers. An antecedent is a word to which a later word called a pronoun is grammatically related. Suppose you have a cousin, five foot ten, weighing a hundred and sixty-two pounds, named Rick, and you happen to say "Rick asked me to have lunch with him tomorrow." The actual boy, all those inches and pounds of him, is the referent for both *Rick* and *him;* and the word *Rick* is the antecedent for the word *him*. Obviously both nouns and pronouns need referents, unless we want to talk about nothing at all. And pronouns sometimes, but by no means always, need antecedents. Suppose you added to the sentence just quoted: "I told him I was just too busy to get away." Here *I* and *him* both have referents, and *him* has its antecedent in the previous sentence; but *I* neither has nor needs one.

In no language known to us does a pronoun always have an antecedent; but in most highly inflected languages if a pronoun does have one it must agree with it in gender, number, and person. We have seen one example in the French sentence quoted above:

J'ai vu sa majesté, et elle était heureuse.

Since *majesté* is feminine, the pronoun *elle* is required, even if the majesty referred to is a king rather than a queen. In other words, the pronoun disregards the sex of the referent to agree with the gender of the antecedent. This at first seems unreasonable to most speakers of English because, as inflections have become less important, we have tended to use the pronoun most appropriate to the referent, regardless of the antecedent. Thus we may say "I want every one of you to do *your* best," though agreement in person would require *his*. Or "The class decided to invite *their* parents to a party," though agreement in number would require *its*.

Verbs

Much the greatest contrast between the Latin and Modern English structures is in the verb systems. In spite of some duplications the Latin *vocō* has more than a hundred physically different forms, indicating its *person, number, tense, mood,* and *voice*. The word *vocāvissēmus,* for instance, is first person, plural, pluperfect, subjunctive, active. It cannot possibly be anything else, and it cannot be adequately distinguished from all other possible forms without all five of the terms above. The complete set of forms is called the *conjugation,* which means "yoking together," or showing what verb forms agree with what subjects — though, as we have just seen, the forms actually indicate three other things as well as those (person and number) necessary for agreement.

The English *call* has only four forms: *call, calls, called,* and *calling*. Moreover, the use of two of these is a matter of etiquette rather than of communication. We don't need a special third-singular form in the present any more than we do in the past; and the absence of a distinctive past form in such verbs as *put* and *set* does not seem to cause any confusion. Only the two forms *call* and *calling* are consistently useful in our system.

Person and Number

There are three grammatical persons, defined as follows: *first,* the person speaking; *second,* the person addressed; *third,* the person or thing spoken of. These are grammatical, not natural, distinctions. Thus if Private Jones says to his captain, "I would like your permission to leave the area," *I* is in the first person, *your* in the second, and *permission* and *area* in the third. But if he says (as he is supposed to), "Private Jones requests the captain's permission to leave the area," the third person is used throughout. Except for *am* and the *-s* forms, English verbs have lost all traces of person, but Latin verbs preserve it throughout. Latin verbs also show either singular or plural number throughout; but in English number is shown only in the forms that also show person.

Tense

The word *tense* is derived from the Latin word *tempus,* which means *time;* but *tense* is no more a synonym for *time* than *gender* is a synonym for *sex.* Rather, tense is a grammatical device that is one of the possible ways of indicating time, and by no means a completely reliable one. Suppose you say, "We play them next month." *Play* is in the present tense. It is *next month* that indicates future time. And if you say, "If you tried in Phoenix tomorrow you could probably find one" you are quite correctly using the past tense to refer to future time.

Some languages do not have tenses, but always indicate time by words other than verbs. Latin has six tenses, which indicate (roughly) action going on in the present, past, and future, and action already completed in these three divisions of time. Some languages have more. Long before English developed, the Germanic branch of Indo-European lost all but two of its original tenses — the present and the past.

To replace the lost tenses English has developed a number of verb phrases such as *I was calling, I used to call, I have called, I had called, I shall call, I will call, I am going to call,* and so forth. Grammarians disagree as to which, if any, of these combinations constitute tenses. In this book none of them are so called.

Mood

The forms of the *indicative mood* (or *mode*) are used principally for definite statements and direct questions. In four of the six tenses Latin has another set of forms called the *subjunctive mood* that are used to express wishes, fears, contrary-to-fact conditions, and a few other things. A few modern English expressions, such as "If he were here" and "God bless him" contain verb forms different from those which would be used in statements, and are often said to be in the subjunctive mood; but not a form left in the language is in itself a subjunctive.

Some grammarians speak of infinitive and imperative moods in English. Others add the conditional, the optative, or both. For a reasonable fee we would guarantee to invent nine more, putting us on a par with the Cree Indians. But this would, of course, be simply a metaphysical complication. There are no discoverable mood-forms in English.

Voice

Such constructions as *I call* are said to be *active,* and such constructions as *I am called* are said to be *passive.* In Latin there is one set of active inflections called the *active voice,* and an incomplete set of inflections, such as *vocor,* pieced out with verb phrases such as *vocatus sum,* called the *passive voice.* We have no idea why the term *voice* was chosen, but they had to find some term. English does not have two comparable sets of inflections, but the term *voice* is still used.

Latin and English Systems Compared

Because most of our verb forms no longer indicate person and number, we have developed both a stable word order and a greater use of pronouns. For instance, we say "you call" where the Latin equivalent is simply, *vocātis.*

And to make up for the other lost inflections we have developed an extensive system of auxiliary verbs, supplemented by adverbial expressions of time and by such conjunctions as *if* and *though*. But it should be clearly understood that we have not replaced the lost elements by any system of one-for-one substitution. Much of the mystery of traditional grammar is caused by failure to realize this fact.

To anybody who is thoroughly familiar with the organization of a Latin verb, and who has never studied an independent analysis of any other kind, it may seem perfectly natural to assume that a verb is a verb in any language. If he makes this assumption he will look for an active and a passive voice, from two to four moods (depending on whether or not he has been taught to consider the imperative or the infinitive or both as moods in Latin), and exactly six tenses; and he will take it for granted that any finite verb must somehow agree with its subject in person or number, even when there is no physical sign of agreement. Naturally, he will find what he looks for — or, to be more accurate, he will find things that he can, with a little juggling, call by the familiar names. He can then display the four forms of *call,* accompanied by pronouns, auxiliaries, and a few conjunctions, over anything up to ten pages of rather small print, giving each recognized combination an analytic name. Thus *if he had been called* may be described as third person singular, pluperfect, subjunctive, passive — though neither *if* nor *he* is part of the verb phrase, which in itself has no indication of person, number, or mood. But *he is to call,* though quite as legitimate an expression, is usually left unmentioned, because it has no exact Latin equivalent.

This sort of analysis is of course clear to anybody who knows Latin, and it may seem easy to a student who does not, if his mind works in a certain way. But a good many people, not necessarily stupid, instinctively reject it.

There are people who admit that the traditional analysis is arbitrary, but who believe that it ought to be taught because it is useful as an approach to Latin or to such other languages as French or Spanish. These people may be right, but there are at least three reasons to hesitate before accepting their opinion:

1. Most Americans (regrettably, of course) never learn enough about any other language to make it worthwhile to befuddle them about their own.

2. The idea that it is easier to learn this system in English before getting entangled with the other difficulties of a foreign language is decidedly open to question. Students have been saying for generations "I never really understood English grammar until I studied Latin (or French or Spanish)."

What this amounts to is that the system is reasonably clear when it is used to explain inflections that are still in existence. When it is applied to the ghosts of inflections long dead, it strains some minds.

3. A good deal of evidence indicates that students could learn the other languages more easily if they were told at the outset that these languages have a radically different structure, instead of being given to understand that they have basically the same structure with what seem like completely unnecessary complications.

It is my (LMM) experience that most teachers of foreign languages immediately and haughtily reject these reasons. I can only reply that I have been in their position, and they have probably not been in mine. It happens that I taught French in college for three years before shifting to English. During those years I made the traditional assumptions, and took a smug pleasure in the statements of students that they were for the first time really beginning to understand English grammar. There I was, just incidentally and by the way, doing a better job than the people who got paid for concentrating on it.

This pleasant illusion disappeared completely during my first semester of trying to teach the English language directly. In the first place my students didn't seem to be learning English grammar any faster under me than under those instructors whom I had previously scorned. In the second, I soon realized that much of what I thought they should learn was of no conceivable value in their handling of English. I could pretty well boil down my treatment of the subjunctive to the single sentence, "Don't say *he was* when you know he wasn't — and the same goes for *I was*." If they asked why, I could tell them that such expressions as *If he were here* were idioms— fossil remnants of a time when there really was a discoverable subjunctive mood in English. This not only saved a good deal of time, but reduced their mystification and consequent resentment.

Adverbs

The identifying of adverbs and adverbial elements, and their subclassification as referring to time, manner, degree, concession, and what not, is probably at once the most difficult and the most useless practice in the teaching of traditional grammar, because it usually has little to do with either the constructing of sound sentences or the understanding of sentences already written.

The words traditionally called adverbs vary greatly in both their origins and their uses. The greater number are formed from adjectives by a sort of converter — usually *-iter* in Latin, *-ly* in English. Many of the most common ones, however, are simply prepositions, conjunctions, nouns, pronouns, or adjectives used in new ways. They are most often defined as "words used to modify verbs, adjectives, or other adverbs," and it is easy enough to find sentences in which they clearly do such things. But there are a great many sentences in which this definition does not work very convincingly.

Some grammarians therefore extended it. They point out that adverbs often modify nouns (the man *upstairs*), prepositions (*nearly* in), or whole phrases, clauses, or sentences. Other grammarians disagree, sometimes violently — not usually about the classification of the words, but about what they do. Perhaps the most useful definition would be "an adverb is any word that cannot readily be fitted into any other part of speech."

Prepositions and Conjunctions

Prepositions and conjunctions are both uninflected classes of connectives, easier to illustrate by example than to distinguish by precise definition. We are not likely to confuse prepositions such as *at, by, from,* and *under* with conjunctions such as *although, and, because,* and *however;* and the fact that such words as *after, before, but,* and *for* can be assigned to both classes causes little difficulty in constructing sentences, though it bewilders many students in parsing them. In Latin both classes need careful attention because it is necessary to learn which prepositions are followed by the accusative case, which by the ablative; and which conjunctions are followed by the indicative mood, which by the subjunctive — not to mention the fact that some members of each class can be used both ways, but with different meanings. In English most of the trouble is caused by the placid acceptance of two completely inconsistent rules:

1. The part of speech to which a word belongs is determined by its use in the sentence.
2. A word must never be used in a part of speech to which it does not belong.

The first is a reasonable statement of the fact that in English (unlike Latin) words shift their functions very freely — a fact that is usually mentioned with great pride. The second is not a statement of fact, but an expression of determination to keep a very few words from doing this — because somebody once said they shouldn't. Anybody who objects to such sentences as "He is older than me" and "It looks like he will be the next governor" may reasonably correct his students for using them on the grounds that they will be criticized as incorrect by a good many people. But before he complicates his students' approach to the language with a confused and indefensible theory he really should check a few dictionaries — unless, of course, he is a bishop as well as a professor.

Interjections

An interjection is a word "thrown into" a sentence for its emotional force, rather than structurally connected with the other words. Such words as *oh* and *ouch* are regularly interjections, and many other words may be so used: *Well,* I suppose so; *Now,* John, don't act that way; *Holy cow!*

A Few Roman Ghosts

An educated Frenchman who had studied Latin for years before approaching English might find a grammar embodying all the concepts we have just discussed consistently intelligible and occasionally useful. An American schoolboy who knows no Latin is likely to find it bewildering; and even if he accepts it without protest and masters all the rules, much of what he learns leads only to saying unnecessary things about the language, and is of no value in either understanding sentences or writing sound ones of his own. It does him no good to learn that the nominative case is required for direct address, because if he wants to say "John, come here," or even "You, come here," there is no possible alternative; and he can't possibly say "He, come here." In the same way, he can say "We made him the leader" without thinking about the case of *leader,* and he will never have to choose between "We made the leader *he*" and "We made the leader *him.*"

To the Frenchman the subjunctive mood is a fact of life, and knowledge that it has left only a few traces in English comes as a relief — there is that much less for him to learn. But the simplest way to teach an American child to say "If I were you" is simply to insist on his saying that instead of "If I was you." Call it an idiom, if you like. To insist on an elaborate treatment of the subjunctive mood is to parade our own knowledge rather than to increase his.

The earliest division of Latin words into parts of speech is that of Varro, who found four classes: *nouns,* which are inflected to show case; *verbs,* which are inflected to show time; *participles,* which are inflected to show both case and time (Latin participles are much more complicated than English ones); and *particles,* which are not inflected at all. This is an oversimplification that has long since been abandoned, but it is useful in indicating that the parts of speech were once based on observable physical characteristics of words. Donatus later doubled the number of categories, adding *pronouns,* and dividing particles into *prepositions, conjunctions, adverbs,* and *interjections.* During the eighteenth century this classification was transferred to English with only one change — the substitution of adjectives for participles as a more useful category in English.

In either language each of the eight parts has its own characteristic functions, and in Latin the classification is something like 95 per cent reliable. If you cut a Latin paragraph into its individual words, paste these words separately on cards, and then shuffle the cards, you can still classify nineteen out of twenty words confidently and accurately. But if you tried to do the same thing with an English paragraph you would find that only about a third of the words could be assigned to any class. This is partly because we have lost so many inflectional endings that a good many words that used to be different are now identical; and partly because, no longer relying much on endings, we can shift words from one function to another far more readily than the Romans could.

In other words, the relation between form and functions was so reliable in Latin that you would get very nearly the same result no matter which you used as a basis for classification. In English the relation is very much looser, and when this fact is not realized absurdities often result. If you tell a class that the part of speech to which a word belongs depends on its use in a sentence, you can justify your statement by one kind of grammar. If you tell them that "He worked good" is wrong because *good* is not an adverb and therefore can't modify a verb, you can justify your statement by another kind. But if you make both statements to the same class, they can be forgiven for being confused. You are.

"Formal English"

The kind of English generally taught with normative traditional grammar was usually called "formal English." It differed from any of the definitions of standard English discussed in Chapter Eight, for it was based not so much on the way even the "best" people actually used the language as on some rather peculiar theories about how they ought to use it. Logic — or what passed for logic — was often considered more important than even the most thoroughly established custom, so that schoolroom English became a somewhat artificial jargon. Students were brought up to believe that all contractions and other short cuts (such as incomplete comparisons) were essentially sinful; that *colloquial* was practically equivalent to *illiterate;* that correctness was more important than force, grace, or even intelligibility; and (perhaps most unreasonable of all) that whoever had written "the book" knew what he was talking about. Parsing and diagramming became ends in themselves. Students spent month after month learning to distinguish not only between adjectival and adverbial clauses, but between adverbial clauses of time, manner, condition, concession, and a number of other things. Shibboleths multiplied and were almost never abandoned. The "bad grammar" of Shakespeare was notorious, and most of our other authors were found guilty in some degree. Students who wanted to know why *they* couldn't indulge in similar freedom with the language were told that such liberties were justified only if you really knew better.

We don't wish to imply that all instruction based on traditional grammars — even bad ones — was wasted. But it is easy to understand why, early in this century, a good many people were thinking "There must be a better way," and attempts were made to find it.

"Functional Grammar"

Early in this century a nationwide (but far from unopposed) movement set out to drive "formal grammar" out of the schools and put "functional grammar" in its place. The reformers did not dispute any statements of the traditional grammarians; they simply wanted to teach "correct" practices without wasting any time discussing why (or even if) they were correct. Their announced aim was to "eradicate the most common errors" by allotting class time in proportion to the frequency with which those were found to occur. Unfortunately (as they cheerfully admitted) they did not feel up to deciding what usages actually were errors. They therefore accepted the decisions of the very grammars they wished to discard as useless, and did not even consider the possibility that when an error is made by most of the speakers of a language it ceases to be an error and becomes standard practice.

The "Doctrine of Usage" Reappears

Another movement, sometimes confused with the "functional" approach but actually quite different, was a revival of the "doctrine of usage" just after World War I. Few of its adherents were any more interested in "formal grammar" than the functionalists. Instead of saying "the theory is useless, but we should insist on the rules derived from it," they said in effect: "Let's find out how the 'best' people actually talk and write, and encourage others to do the same." They condemned the usual "normative" school grammars not simply as time-wasting, but as illegitimate, holding that a grammarian's function was not to prescribe, but to describe. And though they were usually careful to say a few words of praise for "scholarly" grammars that stuck to description, they gave little evidence of knowing much about them. Instead they also concentrated on the "most common errors," not (like the functionalists) to eradicate them, but to find out if they really were errors. They demonstrated that a good many of them were thoroughly established in the usage of the "best-educated" and "most-cultivated" people they could find.

Their principal conclusions were:

1. Nobody has a right to legislate about language, and neither history nor logic is a legitimate court of appeal.
2. When an established usage violates a rule of grammar, it is not the usage but the rule that is wrong. A grammarian ought to know what he is talking about.
3. *Formal* is not on the same scale as *good*. Instead of using *colloquial* as virtually a synonym for *illiterate*, teachers should encourage the use of good, colloquial English on all but the most formal occasions.

Such "liberalism" was widely regarded as inherently immoral, and newspaper editorial pages, magazines, sermons, and cocktail parties were full of warnings that "letting down the bars" would result not only in ruination of the language but in total collapse of all morality.

Structural Linguistics

Though the early liberals questioned both the authority and the accuracy of the usual school grammars, they would on the whole have been satisfied with more carefully composed and less dogmatic books of the same general nature. But Leonard Bloomfield's *Language* (1933) attacked the whole framework of traditional grammar as essentially false. The work of his followers, for some years proudly hailed as "linguistic science," is now called "structural linguistics" to distinguish it from several later approaches, some of which will be discussed in the next chapter.

The brief treatment of the structural approach on pages 14–18 indicates that it had worked well in analyzing the languages of small groups of illiterate people in out-of-the-way corners of the world, but that it was not entirely appropriate for languages used by millions of widely scattered people with centuries of literate tradition behind them. For one thing, insistence on purely inductive methods, which had some value in combatting the natural tendency to warp the description of little-known languages to fit the Indo-European mold, proved to be a disabling handicap in the new task. Then there was the slogan, "Writing is not language, but merely a way of recording language by means of visible marks." [1] Aside from being a little captious (we already have the word *speech*) this conceals a wild and by no means inductive generalization. An investigator's transcript of Klickitat *is* "merely a way of recording language," and presumably has no effect on either the language or the lives of the native speakers. But written English — not only in literature but in laws, contracts, directions, prescriptions, and a thousand other forms — affects every detail of our lives, including the way we speak. Centuries of feedback cannot be wiped out by the word "merely."

The emphasis on speech did produce an analysis[2] of and a notation for the "suprasegmental" elements of pitch, stress, and juncture that have proved useful. It also helped pave the way for studying dialects (and not only regional ones) as respectable variants of, rather than quaint departures from, the main stream of the language. But structuralist work in syntax seems likely to be soon forgotten. The appearance of Noam Chomsky's *Syntactic Structures* in 1957 turned the main stream of linguistic investigation in a new direction, which will be discussed in Chapter Ten.

[1] Bloomfield, p. 21.

[2] George L. Trager and Henry Lee Smith, Jr., *An Outline of English Structure,* 1951.

10

Contemporary Developments in America

by Samuel R. Levin
and Constantine Kaniklidis

Introduction

The developments we write of here are not those which have been undergone by the *language* — so that the appearance of "hopefully" as a sentence adverb would be the sort of thing to be discussed — but those which have affected how one approaches the *study* of language. In other words, we will focus on recent developments in linguistics, particularly on the adequacy of linguistic theories in accounting for the facts of English grammar. Further, in conformity with our view of the most significant developments, we will give most time to fundamental aspects of transformational-generative (TG) grammar, will also study case grammar, and will briefly describe several other recent matters in linguistic theory.

To set the current developments in a proper framework, we will sketch the assumptions that underlie two of the approaches to linguistic analysis that preceded TG grammar, the so-called traditional and structural approaches to linguistic analysis. The traditional approach is embodied in the work of such eminent grammarians as Otto Jespersen, Henry Sweet, George Curme, and H. Poutsma. The works of these men are extensive and full of important information about the grammatical structure of English. Moreover, they have frequent and penetrating insights into interesting parts of that structure, revealing features of the language that are not obvious on cursory examination. The work of these scholars, in short, exhibits many and considerable virtues. The major deficiency alleged against them is that they make little or no attempt to justify *in a formal way* their analyses.

Traditional grammars are very useful for people who already know the language, who, when a fact about English structure is pointed out, can see that English indeed works this way. The knowledge this reader gains, however, comes about not because the grammarian has provided analytic techniques or deductive rules which lead to that result; instead, the reader of the grammar already knows that fact about English structure — implicitly — and the explicit statement of the fact is enough to make that knowledge self-evident. Traditional grammars can thus be said to give an account of a language, but they do so primarily for a reader who already has a tacit knowledge of the language.

Structural linguistics brought a new conception of linguistic analysis — how it should proceed and what it should accomplish. Ideally, a grammar in this view should be constructed exclusively with facts that could be deduced from a linguistic corpus. This body of facts might consist of utterances transcribed from the speech of a native informant, written sentences from some text or collection of writings, or some comparable form. It would have to be quite extensive to be adequate. The criterion for adequacy would be occurrence in the corpus of all the grammatical constructions comprised by the language. In practice, this meant that examination of additional utterances or sentences did not turn up any constructions or sentence types not represented in the material already collected. When this stage had been reached, the corpus was held to be adequate, representative of the grammatical constructions in the language. To this corpus the techniques and methodology of structural linguistics were applied to construct the grammar of the language from this body of concrete material. In theory, nothing was to figure in arriving at the grammar but the objective data in the corpus and the analytic techniques employed by the investigator. In particular, no knowledge that either the investigator or the informant might have about the language was permitted to influence in any way the results of the analysis. The grammar of the language had to be "discovered" in the data; it was not to be sought in the understanding that the informant or analyst might have about the sentences in the corpus or the relation between those sentences and any others that the informant or analyst might know of.

The virtue of the structuralist approach lay in developing rigorous analytic techniques, with which claims about structural relationships could be thoroughly checked to see whether the techniques were properly and consistently applied. A constraint on this approach — later counted a limitation — was that native-speaker intuitions about the structure of the language were intentionally excluded from the analysis. In extreme cases what the analysis claimed about a linguistic structure might not agree with what a native speaker would say about it from his knowledge of the language.

A new conception of grammar and a new focus were introduced by the work of Noam Chomsky. He claimed that the grammar of a language was not the result of applying analytic techniques such as segmentation, substitution, and classification to a body of concrete manifestations, spoken or written. A grammar, rather, is a system of rules whose function is to explicate the body of knowledge that native speakers have about their language. This body is sometimes called linguistic competence, the knowledge on the basis of which communication between speakers of a language is made possible. To the conception that a grammar should explicate linguistic competence — a conception shared, as we have seen, by the traditional grammarians — Chomsky added the requirement that this competence must be explicated formally, by explicit rules.

At the heart of the new approach is the distinction Chomsky drew between linguistic competence and linguistic performance. Competence is the linguistic knowledge of native speakers; among other things it is the set of rules and principles with which speakers produce and understand the sentences of their language. Performance means the motor, mental, and perceptual capacities implemented in the actual production and comprehension of language; under performance *constraints* are such features as memory limitation, attention span, and subpar physical condition. A person may fail properly to implement his linguistic competence because of fatigue, distraction, anxiety, inebriation, or other factors. Any such shortcoming, if occasioned by such a factor, would not reflect on the speaker's linguistic competence but would indicate the difference between that competence and its implementation on that occasion, a difference caused by something interfering between what the speaker was capable of and what he performed.

Competence includes various kinds of knowledge about the sentences of one's language. One function of a speaker's competence is to know the difference between grammatical and ungrammatical sentences, not in the prescriptive sense that forbids some usages, but in regulating some constructions. We apply our linguistic competence to these sentences:

1. The cat drank the milk.
2. The cat arrived the milk.
3. The milk drank the cat.

We know that 1 is grammatical, whereas 2 and 3 are not. Moreover, our competence tells us that the problem with 2 is different from that in 3. In 2, we might say, the problem is with the construction; in 3, on the other hand, the construction seems all right (it is, after all, like the first), but something is anomalous about the juxtaposition of lexical items.

The approach to grammar that sees it as inhering somehow in a corpus of sentences would not be likely to bring to light considerations like the preceding. The linguistic deviance in sentences 1 to 3 is an issue that any native speaker of English will be aware of (perhaps on a little reflection). Inasmuch as sentences like 2 and 3 will hardly occur in any corpus, that issue would probably not appear on that approach. Generalizing, we see that in this approach native speakers may know some things about their language that will not be reflected in the grammatical account that is given of it.

Our linguistic competence also tells us that the sentences

4. Visiting relatives can be boring.
5. I met him at the bank.

are ambiguous and in different ways — syntactically in 4 and semantically in 5.

Furthermore, our competence tells us that although two sentences like

6. I persuaded John to wash his shirt.
7. I expected John to wash his shirt.

are superficially alike in grammatical form, these are to be analyzed somewhat differently. Here again the account given in a grammar written by analyzing a linguistic corpus would differ from one meant to explicate linguistic competence.

This different approach to grammatical analysis is paired with a new conception of the form a grammar should take. Instead of describing the sentences of a corpus, it is required to generate the sentences of a language, along with their structural descriptions. This task is achieved with rules that produce grammatical sentences plus accompanying structural descriptions. A grammar of this sort — a transformational-generative grammar — has three components: syntactic, phonological, and semantic. We will describe the first two of these components.

Transformational-Generative Syntax: The Standard Theory

A transformational-generative (TG) grammar is designed to account for what the native speaker implicitly knows about his language — for native-speaker competence.[1] Among other things, it must specify precisely and explicitly the relationship between sound and meaning. To reach this goal, a TG grammar is built of syntactic, semantic, and phonological components. The semantic and phonological components are purely interpretive — operating on structures produced outside themselves — by the syntactic component. Because of their different functions, however, the structures upon which these two components operate must be different. For this reason the syntactic component is divided into base and transformational components. The output of the base component is a set of deep structures, for these serve as the input to the semantic rules. The output of the transformational component creates a set of surface structures; these serve as the input to the phonological rules. What results from the application of the rules of a component *is* the output. This result may then be introduced (be the input) to another component for the latter's rules to apply to it.

Categorial component of the base

The base component consists in its turn of the categorial component and the lexicon. The categorial component provides the constituent structure of a sentence in a way much like that of the Immediate Constituent (IC) analysis developed by American structuralists. The latter was essentially a segmentation or analysis into the syntactic or grammatical constituents of the sentence considered as a unit given in advance; the categorial generates

[1] Our discussion of transformational-generative grammar in this section is based on the model presented by Noam Chomsky in *Aspects of the Theory of Syntax* (1965). To simplify the discussion, we have modified some of the original notation. We have also not described the complex organization and operation of the semantic component and its rules: such a description cannot be entered into here. For further discussion of transformational-generative syntax and semantics, consult the references in the bibliography.

or builds up that constituent structure. This generation or building up is accomplished through rewrite or phrase structure rules, which this simplified sequence illustrates.

Phrase structure rules of the categorial component

1. S → NP Aux VP
2. VP → V (NP) (PP)
3. $\text{VP} \rightarrow \textit{be}\begin{Bmatrix} \text{Adj} \\ \text{NP} \\ \text{Adv} \end{Bmatrix}$
4. NP → (Det) N (S)
5. Aux → T (M) (have + en) (be + ing)
6. PP → Prep NP
7. $\text{T} \rightarrow \begin{Bmatrix} \text{Pres} \\ \text{Past} \end{Bmatrix}$
8. N → Δ
9. V → Δ
10. Adj → Δ
11. Adv → Δ
12. Det → Δ
13. Prep → Δ
14. M → Δ

You may be pleased to have these rules explained. Rule 1: a sentence is composed of, or its constituents are, a noun phrase (NP), followed by an auxiliary element (Aux), followed by a verb phrase (VP). Rule 2: a verb phrase must contain at least a verb (V) as a constituent, and also *may* (the option is indicated by parentheses) contain a following noun phrase or prepositional phrase (PP) or both. Rule 3: the possible structures of verb phrases containing the verb *be*. The braces indicate an alternation: one of the elements, an adjective, a noun phrase, or an adverb must be chosen. (Rules 2 and 3 share the same element (VP) to the left of the arrow; they could be collapsed into one rule.) Rule 4 indicates the structure of noun phrases: a noun is obligatory, a preceding determiner is optional, and a sentence following the noun is optional (this rule is designed to handle some complex structures in English that we will discuss briefly below). Rule 5: the auxiliary element must be rewritten at least as Tense (T), and this obligatory tense marker may be followed optionally by a modal (*can, will,* etc.), and by two other elements that we will explain further. Here rules 6 and 7 should be self-explanatory. Rules 8 to 14, however, require additional discussion.

In TG grammars of the sort we are considering, the actual words or morphemes of English are not introduced directly by categorial (phrase-structure) rules such as

N → *boy, man, hill. . . .*
V → *run, hit, throw. . . .*

although this was indeed the way in which words were introduced in the earlier *Syntactic Structures* (1957) model of a TG grammar. Rather, all grammatical categories for which actual lexical items can be substituted **(lexical categories)** are rewritten as or are replaced by abstract dummy symbols (Δ's), which act as place holders for the later insertion of the actual lexical entries by different types of rules. That is how categorial rules are *interpreted.* How are such rules actually *applied?*

In a TG grammar it is always stipulated that the categorial component starts with the symbol S (for sentence). Now as we have seen, all categorial rules are of the form in which some symbol on the left is said to be rewritten as a **String** (a linear sequence) of the symbol or symbols to the right of the arrow. The formal interpretation is that *wherever* we find an occurrence in a derivation (this notion will be explained below) of the symbol on the left side of a rule, we may substitute for it (rewrite it as) the symbol(s) on the right of the rule, for any rule. Any instance of NP can be replaced *anywhere* it occurs in a derivation by (Det) N (S), where this is to be understood as explained above. *Grammatically,* however, the interpretation is that the string (Det) N (S) *is* a noun phrase — or, alternatively, that a noun phrase has the *constituents* (Det) N (S) — so that from the grammatical point of view such rules express the fundamental facts of English constituent structure.

The sequence of structures resulting from the proper successive application of these rules, starting with the symbol S, is a **Derivation**. Thus we say that during the derivation a sequence of **Phrase Markers** (PM's) are generated. It is in these markers that the grammatical (categorial) relations are represented.

With S as the initial or start symbol, we can represent application of rule 1 as shown in Figure 1.

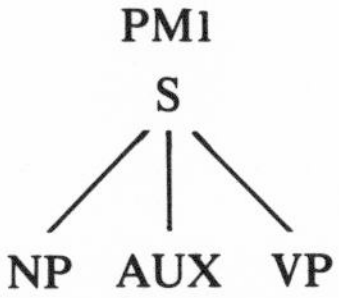

Figure 1

Now we can rewrite any or all the elements NP, Aux, VP according to the categorial rules: NP by rule 4, Aux by rule 5, and VP by either rule 2 or 3. Suppose that we decide to: (1) rewrite NP as Det N (optionally including Det but excluding S in this instance); (2) rewrite Aux as simply T (optionally omitting the modal and aspectual elements); and (3) rewrite VP by rule 2 rather than 3, and, using rule 2, rewrite VP as V NP PP (optionally including all the possible elements). Applying the rules in this way converts PM1 (phrase marker 1) above into PM2 in Figure 2.

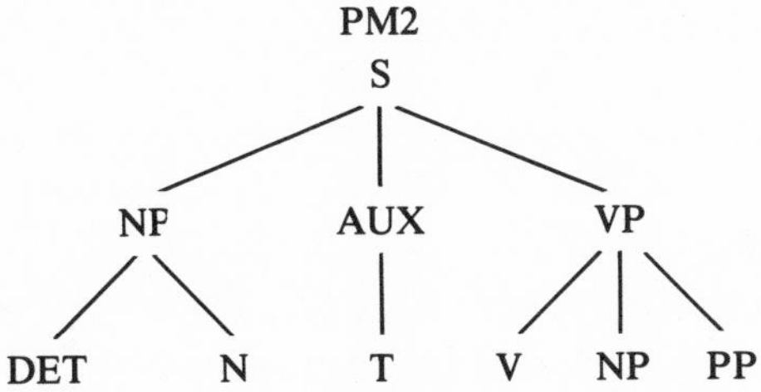

Figure 2

Now, we can continue to apply categorial rules wherever possible, including those rules which expand the lexical categories, until we obtain PM3 in Figure 3 (page 272).

As indicated, such successive application of the categorial rules, beginning with the start symbol S, is called a derivation (or, more precisely, a **base derivation,** to distinguish it from an application we will later refer to as a **transformational derivation**), and we say that phrase markers PM1, PM2, PM3 are generated or derived by the categorial component whose rules are given above. Notice that now it is not possible to apply any further categorial rules; no categorial rules are available for expanding the dummy element or the element *past* (named a grammatical formative). When a derivation reaches this point — when the PM cannot be converted any further into a different PM because no categorial rules are any longer

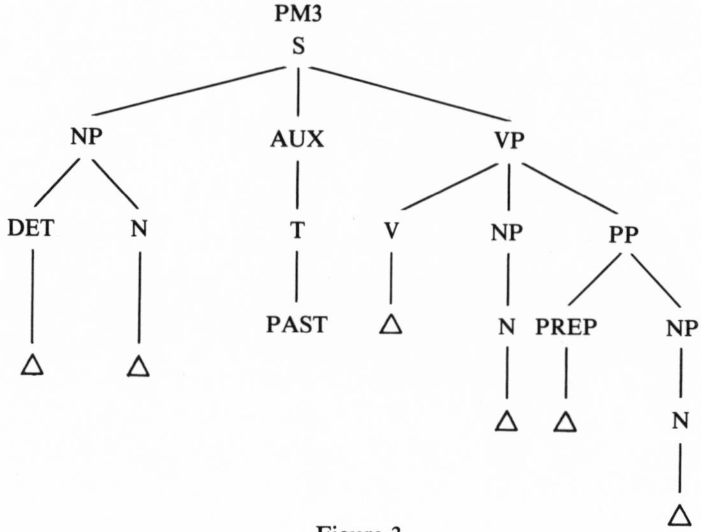

Figure 3

applicable, then that PM is called a **pre-terminal PM.** Thus PM3 is a pre-terminal PM.

It is customary to say of any PM whatever, whether pre-terminal or not, that any node (label of a PM) that branches (or is expanded) into some one or a set of further nodes *immediately dominates* these nodes; and, conversely, that the latter nodes are *immediately dominated* by that (parent) node. Of PM3, we can say that node VP immediately dominates the V, NP, and PP nodes into which it branches. It is also said to *dominate* in addition all nodes into which the three nodes V, NP, PP (its daughters, so to speak) branch. In the latter branching the domination is not *immediate* or direct. Thus, Aux immediately dominates only T, but (generally) dominates both T and *past.*

In sum, therefore, the categorial component generates or derives phrase markers by successive application of its categorial rules, and we distinguish pre-terminal PM's from all others as those whose final nodes cannot be further rewritten by any categorial rules. In this sense, we say that the *output* of the categorial component is a set of pre-terminal PM's (such as PM3 above). But by definition the final nodes of a pre-terminal PM are dummy symbols and grammatical formatives, which have no intrinsic meaning or content of their own, so that we must inquire exactly how meaningful elements are inserted into such pre-terminal PM's so that the resulting structure can be properly interpreted. This problem is dealt with in TG grammar by having the categorial component supplemented by a **lexicon.**

Lexicon of the base component

The lexicon is the stock of **lexical entries,** one for each morpheme or lexical item of the language. Each lexical entry is a written or printed representation of the syntactic, phonological, and semantic features of the item represented. We will pass over the phonological and semantic features of lexical items to study how the syntactic features of lexical items are coded into the associated lexical entries, and how the lexicon, as part of the base component, provides for proper insertion of these lexical entries into the pre-terminal PM's generated by the categorial component of the base.

The general types of syntactic features are *category features, inherent features,* and *contextual features.* **Category features** simply represent the grammatical class or category a lexical item belongs to. The item *boy,* being a noun, will have in its lexical entry the category feature [+ N]; the verb *give* will be represented in the lexicon by an entry marked [+ V]. As the base component as a whole works, these category features function in lexical insertion in this way: any lexical entry with some particular category feature, say [+ N], can be substituted for a dummy symbol of a pre-terminal PM just where that dummy symbol is immediately dominated by a node of the same grammatical class or category; here the lexical entry for *boy,* containing the category feature [+ N], can be substituted for any of the three dummy elements dominated by node N in the pre-terminal PM, PM3 above, generated by the categorial component. Similarly, the lexical entry for *give,* being marked [+ V], can be substituted for the single dummy symbol PM3 dominated by the V node. Thus, all lexical items will have appropriately marked lexical entries to ensure proper lexical insertion according to grammatical class.

The second type of syntactic feature — **inherent features** — is meant properly to subclassify lexical items. A noun may be either *abstract* or *concrete,* countable or mass, animate or inanimate, human or nonhuman, or many others. The lexical entry for the item *boy* would contain the inherent feature specifications of [+ Concrete], [+ Count(able)], [+ Animate], [+ Human]. But note that if you have the feature [+ Human] then the features [+ Concrete], [+ Count], [+ Animate] are redundant; that is, predictable. **Redundancy rules,** whose form we will not consider, can supply these redundant markers into any lexical entry which omits them but which contains the inherent feature [+ Human]. In the model of a TG grammar we are considering, inherent features are associated with nouns only.

Finally, there are **contextual features** for lexical entries specifying more precisely the environment or context of a PM into which an entry may properly be inserted. The major types are **strict subcategorization features** and **selectional features.** To understand the first, consider these sentences:

1. *The boy frightened.
2. The boy frightened the cat.

The verb *frighten* is syntactically transitive, requiring a direct object, so that 1 is ungrammatical (marked by *) and 2 is grammatical. To capture this syntactic property of the lexical item *frighten,* we include in its lexical entry the strict subcategorization feature [+ ____ NP]. (We simplify the notation used by Chomsky.) Thus, the lexical entry for *frighten,* marked [+ ____ NP] for strict subcategorization features and [+ V] for category features, can be substituted for the dummy element dominated by the V node in the pre-terminal PM labeled PM4a below, but not for the same element in PM4b in Figure 4 (omitting much inessential detail of the PM's). Strict subcategorization features specify only the permissible syntactic con-

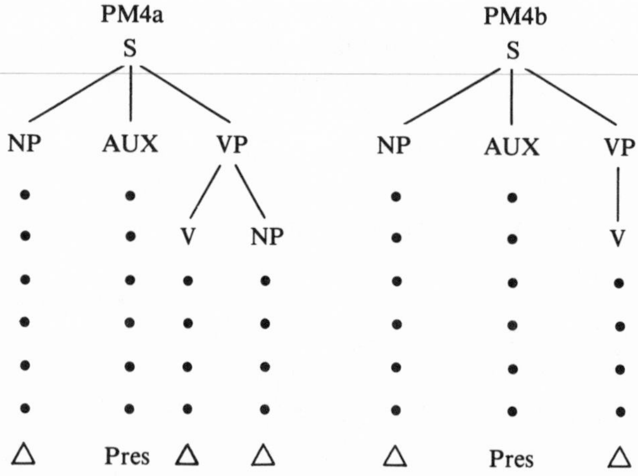

Figure 4

text into which lexical entries can be inserted (a preceding determiner, a following noun phrase, etc.).

Other restrictions are shown by selectional features:

3. The boy frightened the cat.
4. *The boy frightened the table.
5. *The boy frightened the idea.
6. *Sincerity frightened the boy.

The fact that 4 to 6 are ungrammatical and only 3 is grammatical indicates that the verb *frighten* requires both a nonabstract (concrete) subject *and* an animate object. (Notice that we judge 5 ungrammatical. Others may decide it grammatical, making the verb *frighten* unrestricted in object.) This type of restriction on verbs for co-occurrence with nouns of particular *inherent features* is known as **selection restriction;** for the verb *frighten* this restriction is represented by a selectional feature, which may be specified by the notation [+ [+ Concrete] ___ [+ Animate]], and included in the lexical entry for *frighten*. Notice that selectional features restrict the permissible contexts for proper insertion of lexical entries for verbs *by the inherent features* ([+ Animate], [+ Human], etc.) of surrounding nouns, not — as opposed to strict subcategorization features — the category features of the surrounding elements (NP, PP, etc.).

A partial lexicon for a few lexical items might look something like Figure 5 on page 276 (omitting semantic and phonological features).

Therefore, in the operation of the entire base component, the categorial component generates — as we have seen — a set of pre-terminal PM's, containing dummy elements and grammatical formatives as final nodes. Then the dummy elements are replaced in these pre-terminal PM's by entries from the lexicon, in accordance with the category, inherent, and contextual (both strict subcategorization and selectional) features that make up the syntactic specification of the entries. As we have described insertion, nouns would have to be inserted before verbs, because verbs are selections dependent on the inherent features of surrounding nouns. (We will not justify this order, or consider the order of insertion for other lexical categories. Notice also that grammatical formatives, such as *past,* are not replaced; we will later comment briefly on their fate.) The PM that results after all dummy elements of a pre-terminal PM are replaced by appropriate lexical entries is named the **deep** (or **underlying**) **structure** of the sentence being generated. Thus, the output of the full base component (categorial component + lexicon) is a set of such deep structures. These, as we indicated

boy: [+ N
+ DET ___
+ Human
+ Male
+ Young]

sincerity: [+ N
+ ___
+ Abstract
− Count]

book: [+ N
+ DET ___
+ Count
− Animate]

frighten: [+ V
+ ___ NP
+ [+ Concrete] ___ [+ Animate]]

put: [+ V
+ ___ NP PP
+ [+ Animate] ___ [+ Concrete]]

Figure 5

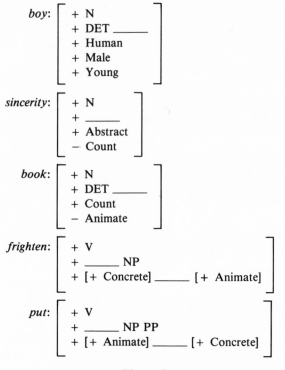

earlier, will be taken as input to two other components of a TG grammar. On the one hand, deep structures will be interpreted by the **semantic component,** yielding **semantic representations** that specify the meaning of the sentences. On the other hand, these same deep structures are converted by the **transformational component** into **surface structures** that are then interpreted by the **phonological component,** yielding **phonetic representations** that specify the sound of the sentences. We can therefore represent the overall structure of a TG grammar in Figure 6.

In this treatment we do not offer a full account of how the semantic component operates on deep structures to provide them with interpretations. We wish, however, to call your attention to an aspect of deep structures significant in the semantic interpretation of sentences; this aspect involves their role in defining **grammatical functions.**

In TG grammar, grammatical functions such as "subject of," "object of" are defined *configurationally* at the level of deep structure. The subject of

Diagram A

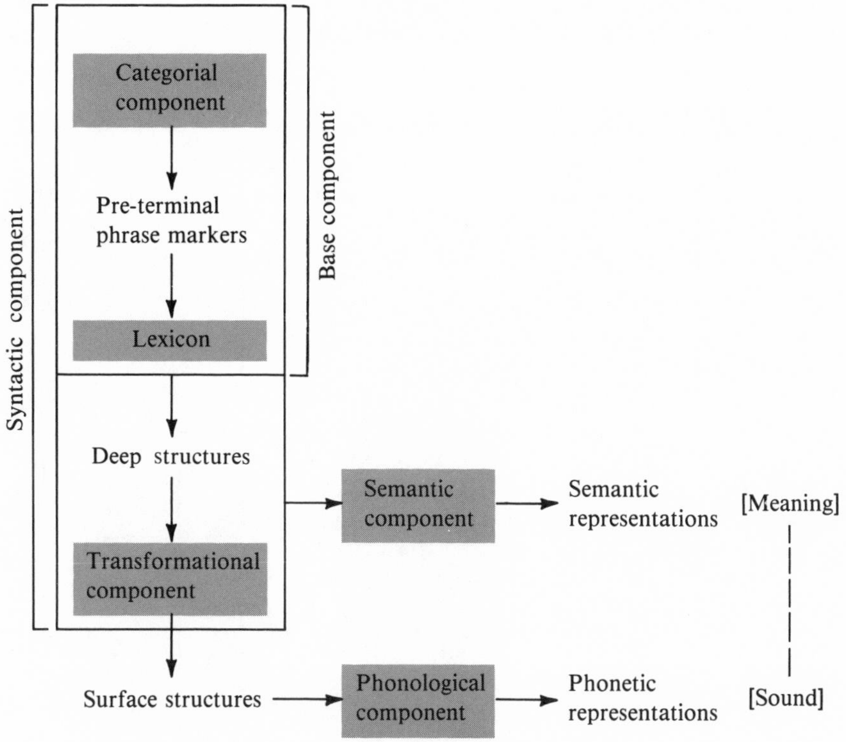

Figure 6

the sentence, for example, is defined as that NP which is immediately dominated by an S node in deep structure; thus, if we were to convert the preterminal PM, PM3, into a deep structure by substituting for the dummy elements appropriate lexical entries from the lexicon, then one of the possible resulting deep structures would be DS1 in Figure 7 (on page 278).

Notice that no actual lexical *items* occur in deep structure: only the lexical *entries* as a bundle of features that *represent* the lexical item. The actual English lexical items in parentheses at the bottom of phrase marker DS1 are for convenience only, abbreviations for the full set of features. Let us take DS1 as the deep structure for the sentence

7. The boy gave candy to Mary.

In DS1 the NP that ultimately would be realized as *the boy* is the one immediately dominated by S, so that *the boy* is the subject of 7 in its deep structure DS1. Similarly, the direct object of the verb is defined in deep

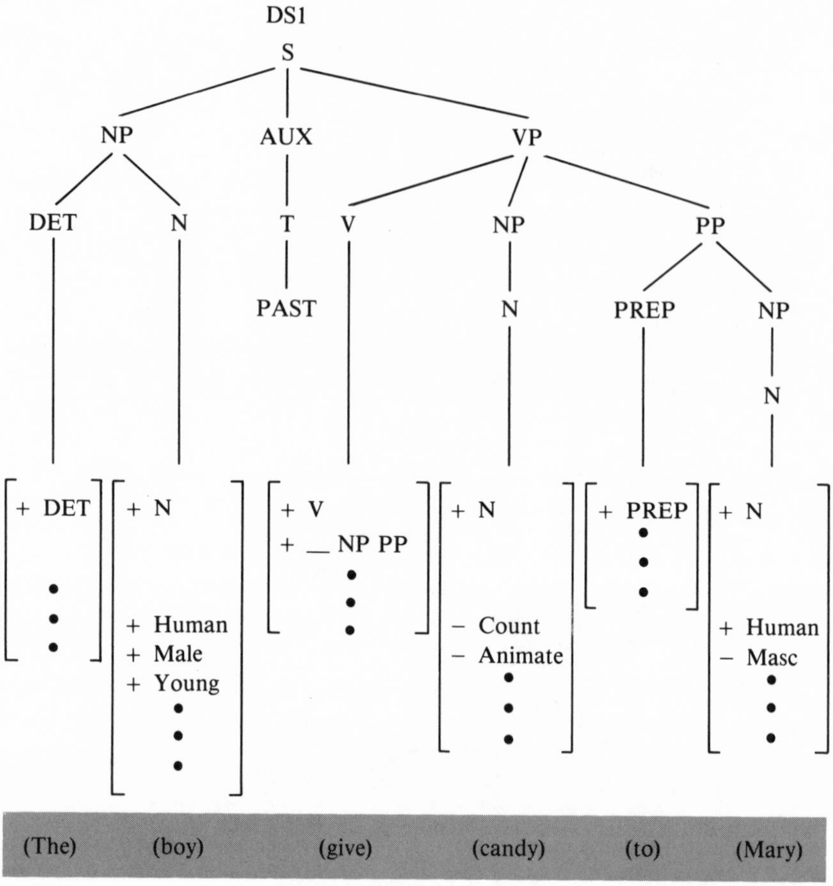

Figure 7

structure as that NP which is immediately dominated by the VP that is itself immediately dominated by S. For DS1, therefore, the NP that ultimately would be realized as *candy* is the direct object of the verb (here *gave*). Such grammatical functions must be definable in this configurational manner as deep structure in order for the semantic component properly to interpret deep structures. In these sentences,

8. Linda hit Peter.
9. Peter hit Linda.

the semantic component must be able to determine the subjects and objects for the two sentences, because if we merely used their lexical items there would be no difference in meaning.

We have examined the structure and operation of the base component of a TG grammar in its two parts, the categorial component and the lexicon. The categorial component, consisting of a set of phrase structure or categorial rules, begins with start symbol S (for sentence) and, by successive application of the rules as illustrated (see the derivation of PM1 to PM3), generates as output pre-terminal phrase markers containing dummy elements and grammatical formatives as final nodes. These pre-terminal PM's then function as input to the lexicon, which replaces the dummy elements by appropriate lexical entries in accordance with the syntactic properties (coded as sets of features) of the lexical items represented by these entries. The PM resulting after all such **lexical insertion** of entries has been completed for a pre-terminal PM is a deep structure and is ready for interpretation by the semantic component, and conversion by the transformational component.

The transformational component

We turn now to the remaining part of the syntactic component — the transformational component. It has the task of converting deep structures into well-formed surface structures of the language, using a set of **transformations.** Let us examine what "conversion into well-formed surface structures" means, what transformations are, and how they work. Consider again the deep structure DS1 above, which was generated by the base component. We reproduce that structure here; but again, for simplicity, we omit actual representation of lexical entries and use instead the abbreviations for such entries offered by the orthographic shape of the lexical items themselves. (When we appear to be manipulating mere lexical items, it is shorthand for manipulation of the lexical entries that represent these items as sets of features.) We will refer to the abbreviated deep structure as DS1′ (see Figure 8 on page 280).

The linear sequence of final nodes of any deep structure is a **terminal string;** for DS1′ above the terminal string (bearing in mind the abbreviation mentioned above) is

10. The boy *past* give candy to Mary.

Now consider this phrase marker in Figure 9 on page 281 (we will explain where it comes from in a moment).

The major difference between DPM1 (Derived Phrase Marker 1) and the phrase marker of DS1′ is that in DPM1 the T(ense) element *past* has been shifted around the verb *give* and is attached to it to form the single verbal unit *give* + *past* (the Aux node is removed by a principle that we

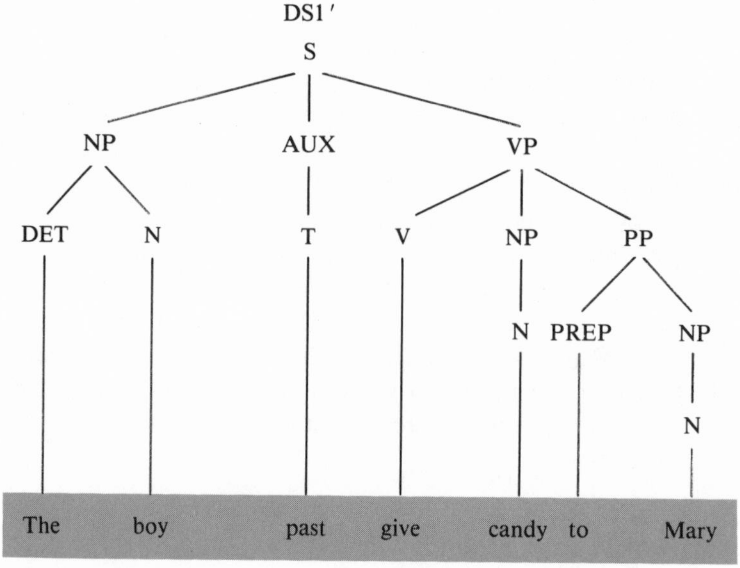

Figure 8

cannot go into here). The sequence *give + past* is ultimately realized as *gave,* so that the surface structure will finally be

11. The boy gave candy to Mary.

We now have to explain how the phrase marker DPM1 can be derived from the deep structure DS1′. In other words, we need some formal operation that can take one PM as input and modify it structurally to form another PM. A formal operation that converts or maps one PM into another is a **transformation** and is specified or defined by a **transformational rule.** We say that two PM's that stand to each other in this manner are *transformationally related* by the rule. Further, any PM that has been converted or structurally modified by a transformational rule is a **derived phrase marker.**

Let us now see exactly what the form or structure of such a transformational rule is and how it operates, using as our first example the rule that is needed to convert DS1′ into DPM1. A transformation consists of two fundamental parts: a structure index (SI) and a structural change (SC). The structure index of a transformation (also known as the **structural analysis** or **structural description)** specifies the structure a PM must have to be a permissible input to that transformation, and the structural change describes the modification that the transformation effects on the input PM. We will illustrate with a relatively simple transformation that, in its fully developed

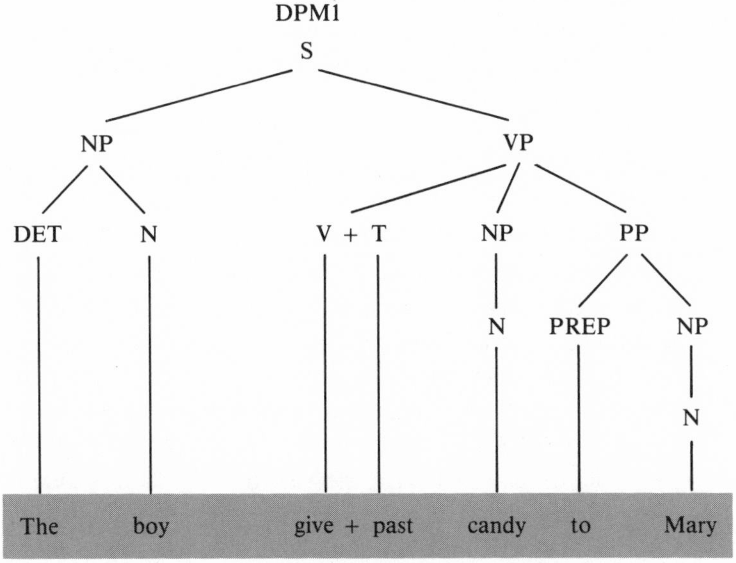

Figure 9

form, is known as *affix-hopping*. Consider this preliminary version of that transformation in Figure 10.

The part of the rule above the arrow (double-shafted for transformational rules) specifies the structure into which a PM must be analyzable to qualify as an input to that transformation. The part of the rule below the arrow describes that change. The transformation T1 states that if a PM is analyzable into category T followed immediately by category V, those two elements may be permuted, the second one being attached to the first. The symbols X and Y (in transformational rules) are variables; they stand for

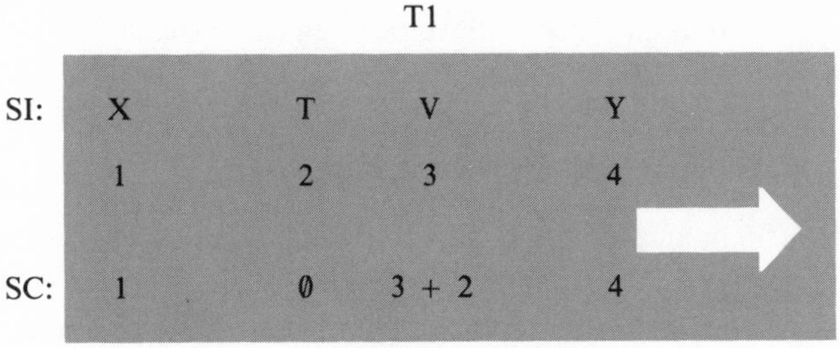

Figure 10

anything (or nothing) and are used when it is immaterial for the transformation what structures, if any, occur in those positions.

Rule T1 may seem to involve a lot of machinery to accomplish relatively trivial results. But when generalized, it accomplishes a good deal more than we have indicated so far. If we look at categorial rule 5, we see that it contains, in addition to T, also the elements (*have* + *en*) and (*be* + *ing*). The two latter elements are used in forming past and present participles in English and represent the verbal aspects *perfect* and *durative* (*progressive*), respectively. The analysis in categorial rule 5 claims in effect that in a sentence like *John has eaten his lunch,* the element that signals past participiality is actually discontinuous, comprising a form of *have* and of the suffix *-en* on the verb. A similar analysis applies to the present participle in a sentence like *John is eating his lunch.* The rule expanding Aux thus expresses in very concentrated form the structure of phrases auxiliary to the main verb in English. It is an important observation about English that verbal aspects like perfective and durative are in fact expressed by complex (discontinuous) constituents. What is more, by casting the Aux element in the form of rule 5, it is possible to generate with a minimum of categorial rules the entire range of verb phrases in English, many of them quite complex, as in *John might have been eating.* To accomplish this, however, we must cast Aux in the form of rule 5, where this has the effect of generating deep structures with terminal strings like these:

12. John past may have + en be + ing eat.

If the base rules will generate structures like 12, then the elements of those structures will have to be rearranged to assume their proper surface order, and some sort of transformational rule is needed. This fuller version of the transformational rule of affix-hopping is necessary here (see Figure 11).

By successive applications of this revised affix-hopping transformation, we can convert 12 to 13:

13. John may + past have be + en eat + ing.

which will ultimately yield the well-formed surface structure

14. John might have been eating.

You may question the decision implicit in categorial rule 5 to have the elements of T(ense) and the suffixes *-en* and *-ing* first precede the verb only to be 'hopped' subsequently to a post-verbal position: TG grammarians have presented syntactic evidence for such an approach, but it is beyond

Affix-hopping

X	{Pres, Past, -en, -ing}	{M, V, have, be}	Y
1	2	3	4
→			
1	∅	3 + 2	4

Figure 11

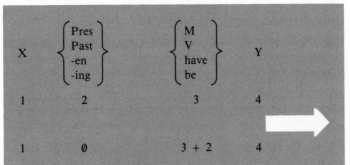

considering here; primarily we want to exhibit *how* transformational rules operate.

It is clear that deep structures may undergo transformations and yield derived PM's. But transformations are not limited in their inputs to deep structures; being essentially mappings of PM's to PM's, they may operate also on derived structures themselves. Structure DPM1, which we derived (transformationally) by the rule of affix-hopping from the deep structure DS1′, is itself a PM and therefore can itself form the input to another transformational rule to yield still another derived PM. Transformations simply map PM's into other PM's in accordance with their SI and SC — the input PM is not required to be a deep structure (although in our example it was). For further clarity, let us use the derived PM, DPM1, as input to another transformational rule, the *dative movement* transformation, a version of which is shown in Figure 12.

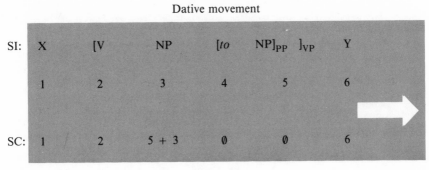

Dative movement

SI:	X	[V	NP	[*to*	$NP]_{PP}$ $]_{VP}$	Y
	1	2	3	4	5	6
→						
SC:	1	2	5 + 3	∅	∅	6

Figure 12

The interpretation of the SI and the SC is along the same lines described for affix-hopping. The SI here is simply more refined, stating that the terminal string of a permissible input PM must be analyzable into six factors, the first and last of which can be any sequence of elements at all; the second, third, and fifth must be dominated by (belong to the categories of) V, NP, and NP respectively; and the fourth must be the lexical constant *to*. It also requires that the sequence of fourth and fifth elements (*to* NP) be dominated by node PP, and the entire sequence of the second through fifth elements (V NP *to* NP) must be dominated by node VP. All is represented in the SI above by labeled bracketing notation: $[\text{to NP}]_{PP}$ states that the sequence *to* NP inside the brackets is of the category of the label on the bracket, namely PP; and in general, $[\ldots]_L$ indicates that any material inside the brackets is dominated by the node or category label L, where L is any grammatical category at all. To simplify the exposition, we have merged the *give* + *past* sequence of DPM1 into the single element *gave* without discussing the type of rule that accomplishes this. The sixth term, the variable Y, is simply null (Ø): as we have said, such variables may correspond to any sequence of elements, including the null sequence.

If we now consider the SC of this transformation, we see that in essence it deletes the preposition *to* and shifts indirect object NP to the left of direct object NP. The result of this SC is a new derived PM whose terminal string is

15. The boy gave Mary candy.

(We omit detailing the entire PM itself.) Both sentences 11 and 15 were transformationally derived from the same deep structure, DS1′. In deriving 11 from DS1′ only the rule of affix-hopping applied, but in deriving 15 from the same deep structure we first applied affix-hopping (to get DPM1, which yielded 11) and then applied dative movement to the output of affix-hopping to get 15. For any well-formed surface structure, such as 11 or 15, the sequence of transformational rules applied to the appropriate deep structure to derive or generate that surface structure is its **transformational history.** The sequence of PM's involved makes the first the deep structure and the last the surface structure, with each intermediate (non-deep structural) PM being derived from the preceding PM by the appropriate transformational rule; this is its **transformational derivation.** The latter notion includes that of the former, of a transformational history, because not just any sequence of PM's that begins with a deep structure is a valid transformational derivation, but only those PM sequences which have also been properly generated by the appropriate transformational rules. Thus, for the well-formed surface structure 15, its transformational history involved the rules of affix-hopping and dative movement (in that order) and its transformational derivation involved the sequence of PM's comprising the input and output PM's of these two rules. We say then that the transformational component, by such derivations, maps deep structures into surface structures. Notice further that in the model of TG grammar we are describing, two sentences which have identical deep structures (like 11 and 15), but which differ in their transformational histories (the sequence of transformations applied), have the same meaning; they are paraphrases. The fact that 11 and 15 mean the same is reflected in TG grammar by having them share the same deep structure (but differ in their transformational histories).

Two major differences distinguish transformational rules from categorial rules of the base component. First, the categorial rules (technically known as context-free phrase structure rules, or simply CF rules) simply expand individual categorial symbols: if such a symbol appears at a specific place in the derivation of a PM, then the categorial rule that has the *single* symbol on its left may be applied to rewrite the symbol into the sequence of symbols on the right of the rule. Input to categorial rules are thus category symbols. Transformational rules, on the other hand, operate on entire phrase markers. Their input is any PM which satisfies or meets — which can be analyzed in conformity with — the SI of the transformational rule. And where the output of a categorial rule is a string or sequence of symbols, the output of a transformational rule is another PM. Second, transformational rules have the power of **variable reference:** the SI of a transformational rule may contain variables (like X and Y above) which may refer to any structure. Categorial rules, however, are restricted to *particular* single-category symbols. These two properties, the ability to operate on entire PM's (converting them to other PM's) and the power of variable reference, make transformational rules much more general and powerful than categorial rules. There are other less radical differences between these two types of rules, but they are highly technical.

The transformational component comprises a set of transformational rules. Transformational rules are designed to apply in a specific order, however, during a derivation, and they must be tried (tested for applicability) in that order. Roughly, this is the procedure: beginning with a deep structure generated by the base component, the transformational rules are examined in some prescribed order, one by one, for their applicability. Some rules are *obligatory* — they must be applied if their SI is met by a PM (otherwise an ill-formed structure results) — and some are *optional* and may or may not be applied, either choice yielding a well-formed structure. Therefore not every rule will apply in every derivation even if the SI is met, because with optional rules we may choose not to apply them. The affix-hopping rule is obligatory. If it is not applied, the T(ense) element and other auxiliaries will not be correctly placed with respect to the verbal element, and no grammatical output can be derived. On the other hand, the dative movement rule is optional: notice that whether we apply it or not, a grammatical output is derived (both *The boy gave candy to Mary* and *The boy gave Mary candy* are grammatical).

Transformational rules can of course be applied to structures more complex than those we have dealt with so far. In the model of TG grammar we are considering, transformations may operate on PM's that contain more than a single S node: this possibility arises for categorial rules like 4, where for certain types of subordinate structures (those with **embedded sentences**), the optional S is chosen. **Generalized PM's** contain multiple S nodes and rules that allow for such generalized PM's to be generated by the base component are **recursive rules.** Relative clause structures and various forms of complement constructions, for example, would involve deep structures with one or more embedded S nodes (in addition to the highest, or so-called *root* (S) node). But the generation of such generalized PM's raises the question of just how transformations are to apply to these structures. In TG grammars of the type we are examining, transformations must apply to such structures in accordance with the *cyclic principle,* or the *principle of the transformational cycle*. The set of transformational rules must be applied first to the structure dominated by the lowest or most deeply embedded S node, one after the other, in whatever fixed order the rules have been given; after all rules of the set have been tested for applicability in this order (and applied or not, according to the form of the rules), the entire set of rules is retested for application to the entire structure dominated by the next highest S node, in precisely the same order. This successive testing of the full set of rules to successively higher S-dominated structures is continued until the set has been gone through once for each embedded sentence structure and also, finally, for the highest or root S of the generalized PM. For a sentence like *John knew the man who burned the house that stood on the corner,* we would have a deep structure in the form of a generalized PM that would contain three S nodes — one each for the two embedded relative constructions, and one for the root S of the PM. In this case, therefore, the cyclic principle requires that the entire set of transformations of the grammar be tested for application three times, first for the two embedded clauses (from lower to higher), then for the root S structure, each such scan of the full set of transformations within any one structure dominated by the node S constituting a *cycle*.

Now let us take a concrete example of applying transformations to generalized PM's in accordance with the cyclic principle. Consider the sentence

16. The boy wants to give Mary candy.

It should be clear from the meaning that the subject of the object complement of the verb *want* is the NP *the boy:* that is, 16 is generally understood as meaning that what the boy wants is for *himself* to give Mary candy. For sentence 16, the proper interpretation is that the subject NP of *want* and the subject NP of *give* (in the complement construction) are the same, namely *the boy*. Therefore, a simplified version of the deep structure of 16 would be (ignoring tense and other syntactic detail irrelevant here, and using a labeled bracketing notation):

17. [The boy want [the boy give candy to Mary]$_{S_2}$]$_{S_1}$

S_2 is the embedded sentence that forms the object complement of the verb *want,* and S_1, which contains S_2, is called the matrix S(entence). The surface structure 16 contains only one instance of the NP *the boy,* but its deep-structure source 17 has two such instances (the second explicitly marking the understood subject of the embedded sentence). Therefore to derive 16 from 17 we require some sort of transformational rule that deletes the subject NP of an embedded S when that NP is identical to the subject NP of the matrix sentence (which contains the embedded sentence). The transformational rule known as *equi-NP deletion* performs precisely this operation. But notice first that the surface structure 16 contains the sequence *give Mary candy* but the embedded S of the deep structure 17 for this sentence contains the sequence *give candy to Mary.* As we have seen, however, the former sequence is the result of applying the transformational rule of dative movement to a construction with the latter sequence. Therefore, at least two transformational rules are involved in deriving 16 from 17: equi-NP deletion and dative movement. Furthermore, it is generally assumed that these two rules are so ordered in the set of all transformational rules of the grammar that equi-NP deletion precedes dative movement (possibly with some other rules intervening). The derivation of 16 from 17 would proceed as follows: The first cycle involves the entire structure under domination of S_2, namely the embedded sentence (but no part of matrix S, by definition, because we are working from bottom to top and must start with the lowest sentential structure). On this cycle we must first test the rule of equi-NP deletion for possible application. But this rule cannot apply on this cycle because it requires two identical NP's in *different* S-dominated structures (one in the embedded, and one in the matrix S), and we are now examining only a single S-dominated structure, that of S_2. Passing over equi-NP deletion as inapplicable, we proceed to test (ignoring any intervening rules) dative movement for possible application. For S_2 the SI of dative movement is satisfied and we choose to apply it (it is an optional rule) here. This converts S_2 from [*the boy give candy to Mary*] to [*the boy give Mary candy*]. Other rules, irrelevant to this derivation, would then be tested in the order prescribed for the grammar, completing the testing of each rule in the ordered set of all rules. This done, we proceed to the next (second) cycle and begin testing the rules for applicability in precisely the same order. We must test equi-NP deletion before dative movement (again) on this higher cycle, where this second cycle involves all the structure under the domination of the matrix S, S_1 (which includes S_2, as modified by dative movement on the first cycle). Thus, on this cycle we are dealing with this intermediate structure:

$$\text{[The boy want [the boy give Mary candy]}_{S_2}]_{S_1}$$

But equi-NP deletion does indeed apply on this second cycle to the above structure, because this structure contains a subject NP of an embedded S (here *the boy* in S_2) that is identical to the subject NP of the matrix S (S_1) containing that embedded sentence (*the boy* in S_1). Equi-NP deletion therefore applies, deleting the instance of subject NP of the embedded S to yield this structure:

$$\text{[The boy want [}\emptyset\text{ give Mary candy]}_{S_2}]_{S_1}$$

(The null symbol ($\emptyset$) marking the site of the deletion is purely for convenience of exposition.) This structure, after suitable adjustments for tense and the complementizer element *to,* gives us the surface structure 16. (Notice that dative movement is inapplicable on this second cycle.)

This is a purposely simple case of transformational rules applying to generalized PM's according to the cyclic principle, but it illustrates the essential aspects of such complex transformational derivations without obscuring the discussion with purely technical problems. With this ability of transformations to apply (cyclically) to generalized PM's, a TG grammar can in principle generate any surface structure, no matter how complex, and hence can be used to account for virtually all syntactic constructions of English. Much work, of course, still needs to be done to arrive at a well-motivated and precisely formulated set of rules of such a grammar, but already much valuable insight has been gained by the TG approach to syntax.

Generative Phonology[2]

As part of their lexical representation, entries are listed in the lexicon in the form of a matrix, each column of which represents a segment and each row a **distinctive feature.** The lexical entry for *pin* would include this matrix:

1.

	p	i	n
consonantal			
syllabic		+	
sonorant			
nasal			+
high		+	
low			
back		−	
anterior	+		+
coronal	−		+
voice	−		

Matrix 1 is redundancy-free. Only those features are specified — by a plus or a minus — which are necessary to distinguish *pin* from, say, *bin, pen,* or *pit.* The blanks (sometimes zeros are used) indicate where feature values are predictable because of the positively marked features and can be filled in by general **redundancy rules.** From the fact that *p* is specified for anteriority (similarly for coronality), it is redundant [+ cons, − syll, − son, − high,

[2] The following sketch of generative phonology is necessarily brief and selective. It is based primarily on Chomsky and Halle's *The Sound Pattern of English* (1968), from which also most of the examples are drawn. Among the other limitations on this account is the lack of space to describe the distinctive features employed in generative phonology. Anterior sounds are produced by an obstruction in front of the alveolo-palatal region of the mouth, and coronal sounds are produced with the blade of the tongue raised from the neutral position. Thus: the labial and alveolar (dental) consonants are [+ anterior], and the alveolar (dental) and palato-alveolar consonants are [+ coronal]. So that /p/ is [+ ant, − cor], /t/ is [+ ant, + cor], /k/ is [− ant, − cor]. For other questions on distinctive features, refer to the items on generative phonology in the bibliography.

− low, − back]. From the fact that it is specified [− voice] it follows that it is [− nasal] (in English). Similar considerations apply to the other two segments.

When the redundancy rules have been applied to matrix 1 (plus "readjustment rules," which we can overlook), it becomes a **phonological** (otherwise, **systematic phonemic, morphophonemic**) **representation** and serves as input to the phonological rules. An item like *pin* will emerge from the phonological rules essentially unchanged. It does so because *pin* is invariant phonetically, assuming the same (**systematic**) **phonetic** form whether it occurs in *pins, pinwheel, safety pin,* and others. The phonological rules are of limited interest for invariant items. The fact is, however, that a great many lexical items in English do not have the property of **invariance.** Furthermore, the variant forms that such items assume in different linguistic contexts are not random or accidental but are quite systematic, hence predictable. For such items, then, passage through the phonological rules is not routine; it results in significant modifications.

Consider an item like *vain.* The phonetic form depends on whether it occurs alone, or in *vanity.* If vain were the only lexical item that manifested such variants, the simplest procedure would be to list *vain* and *vanity* separately in the lexicon — each, that is, with its own matrix. But in addition to *vain/vanity,* we have such pairs as *sane/sanity, profane/profanity,* and *inane/inanity.* Moreover, the same type of alternation between a tense, diphthongal vowel nucleus and a lax simple vowel occurs at other phonetic levels in pairs like *divine/divinity, sublime/sublimity; serene/serenity, extreme/extremity.* Because the phonological processes that result in the variation are regular, a single form may be listed in the lexicon (in each case), and the variants may be derived by general (phonological) rules. Furthermore, to account most efficiently for the variants, the basic lexical entry must be designed in optimally general form. For this reason the lexical representation may at times assume an "abstract" character. Thus *vain* will be listed in the lexicon (with a matrix that we will abbreviate) as

2. vǣn

where the vowel segment in 2 is neither that of *vain* nor that of *vanity,* and is "abstract" to that extent. Depending on the context in which 2 appears, (in isolation or preceding the suffix *-ity*), the phonological rules will derive [ēy] or [æ] as the vocalic nucleus.

Notice that in all the pairs given above, the alternation is not correlated with a difference in stress placement, as it is in pairs like *derive/derivation;*

redeem/redemption; explain/explanation. We may therefore in this case omit discussion of the rules that would assign stress to those forms.

To account for our variants *vain/vanity,* we set up these rules:

3. $\emptyset \rightarrow y / \bar{V}$ ____

4. $\bar{V} \rightarrow [-\text{low}] / \begin{bmatrix} \underline{\quad\quad} \\ -\text{high} \\ -\text{back} \end{bmatrix}$

5. $V \rightarrow [-\text{tense}] / \underline{\quad\quad}\, C \begin{bmatrix} -\text{stress} \\ V \end{bmatrix} C_o V$

Rule 3 says to rewrite zero as *y* in the context of a preceding tense vowel; in type it is an insertion rule. It forms a diphthong from simple vowel nuclei. Rule 4 says that a tense vowel that is also [− high, − back] must be [− low]. The horizontal line within the square brackets stands for the place occupied by the tense vowel; in other words, the rule states a kind of environment in which the rule applies, but the environment is stated according to the co-present features in a segment, not the features of adjacent segments. As formulated, rule 4 will affect only the vowel *æ,* raising it to *ē.* Rule 5 states that vowels must be lax when they occur before a consonant followed by an unstressed vowel followed by zero or more consonants followed by a vowel. It is designed to make vowels lax when they occur before a suffix like *-ity*.

To derive [vēyn] from /vǣn/ we apply rules 3 and 4; to derive [væn-] (in *vanity*) we apply rule 5.

Rules 3 to 5 are oversimplified and somewhat ad hoc. In particular, rule 4 must be generalized to account for all the alternations in the preceding paragraph. The phonological representations also, drawn from Chomsky and Halle (1968), may be inconsistent with other systems of representation with which the reader may be familiar. Our purpose so far, however, has been merely to show in a general way how the rules of the phonological component derive the phonetic forms of English; for fuller and more detailed analyses, consult the sources in the bibliography.

We said above that to analyze pairs like *vain/vanity,* stress assignment was of little interest inasmuch as the vowel alternations took place independent of stress. In deriving many forms, however, it turns out that stress assignments are integrally related to vowel quality. It is therefore necessary to know something about the way in which stresses are assigned to words. In a generative phonology this — as well as all other aspects of phonological derivation — is done by rules. Developing adequate rules, which will automatically and correctly assign stresses to all the words of English, is a complicated and extensive affair; even with much elaboration it leaves quite a residue of problematic cases. Such a development cannot be gone into here. We will describe a few relatively simple cases to indicate how the system works.

For demonstration we will describe how compound words and noun phrases are allocated their correct stress contours (the numeral 1 represents loudest or strongest stress; 2, 3, 4, etc., lower stresses in descending order of loudness). Compounds in English have the stress contour 13 — $\overset{1}{\textit{black}}$-$\overset{3}{\textit{board}}$; noun phrases the contour 21 — $\overset{2}{\textit{black}}$ $\overset{1}{\textit{board}}$. Before considering how the rules assign stresses to such strings, let us examine more closely the form those strings assume as they come from the syntactic component of the grammar and present themselves as input to the phonological rules. Syntactic rules we have not treated earlier provide each syntactic surface structure with two types of boundary symbol. The symbol # is a boundary that appears between words, + a boundary that appears essentially between stems in morphologically complex words. This is how the word boundary symbol appears in terminal strings: Each lexical category (N, A, V) and each category that dominates a lexical category (S, NP, VP) assigns the boundary symbol # to the left and to the right of the string that it dominates. Further, in syntactic derivations compounds are dominated by a node labeled N, noun phrases by one labeled NP. These facts are illustrated in these partial trees (and their equivalent labeled bracketings):

6.

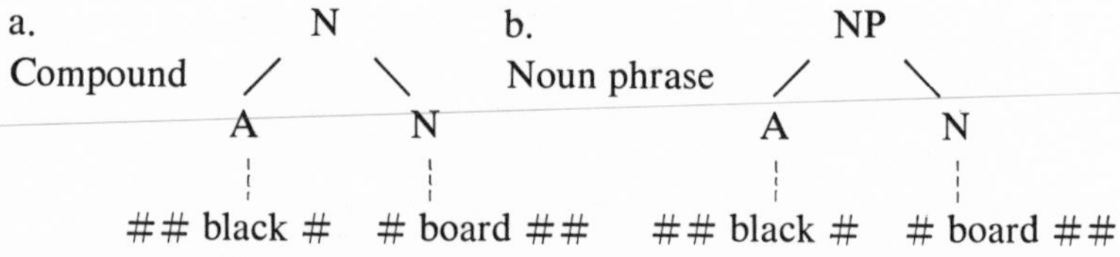

[N #[A # black #]A [N # board #]N #]N

[NP #[A # black #]A [N # board #]N #]NP

In 6b *black* has two occurrences of # to its left and one to its right. The one to its right and the inner one to its left derive from node A, which immediately dominates *black*. The one to the left of and the inner one to the right of *board* derive from node N, by which it is immediately dominated. Finally, the two outermost occurrences of #, the outer one to the left of *black* and the outer one to the right of *board* derive from node NP, which immediately dominates A and N. The same analysis applies to 6a.

Proceeding to the stress assignments, we assume first that all monosyllabic words (of the lexical categories) are assigned primary stress, a rule we will label 7. Consider now this rule (in simplified form):

$$8.\quad \overset{1}{V} \rightarrow [1\ \text{stress}] \;/\; \left\{\begin{array}{ll} \text{—}\ldots\overset{1}{V}\ldots\quad N \\ \overset{1}{V}\ldots\text{—}\ldots\quad NP \end{array}\right\}\begin{array}{l}\text{a.}\\ \text{b.}\end{array}$$

The rule collapses two — the Compound Rule 8a and the Nuclear Stress Rule 8b. Subrule 8a directs that any string which is a noun and which consists of two words both of which have primary stress (by rule 7) shall have primary 1 stress reassigned to it on the vowel of its first syllable; 8b is the same except that 1 stress is reassigned to the vowel of the second syllable. We now introduce a convention:

9. When primary stress is reassigned to a syllable, all other stresses in the string are automatically reduced by one degree.

With rule 8 and convention 9, *bl*$\overset{1}{a}$*ckbo*$\overset{1}{a}$*rd* becomes *bl*$\overset{1}{a}$*ckbo*$\overset{2}{a}$*rd* and *bl*$\overset{1}{a}$*ck bo*$\overset{1}{a}$*rd* becomes *bl*$\overset{2}{a}$*ck bo*$\overset{1}{a}$*rd*. The noun phrase now has its correct stress contour. For compounds an additional rule is required:

$$10.\quad \overset{1}{V} \rightarrow [1\ \text{stress}] / \;\text{——}\;\#\#\;\overset{2}{V}\;\#\quad N$$

On reassigning 1 stress to the first syllable of *blackboard* by 10, Convention 9 will reduce the 2 stress to 3 and we obtain *bl*$\overset{1}{a}$*ckbo*$\overset{3}{a}$*rd*.

Like the transformational rules, the rules of the phonological component that we have been describing here apply cyclically. They are arranged in linear order in a block, and on each cycle of their application all are applied in succession until the last rule in the block has applied. Each rule, in its application, applies to the longest string that contains no internal brackets. In some cases the string to which the rules are being applied does not meet the structural description of one or more rules in the block. Then a rule is said to apply vacuously — it is recurred to in the passage through the rules, but it has no effect, produces no alteration, in the string being processed. When all the rules in the block have been recurred to in turn, a cycle has been completed. The last rule in the block is the instruction to erase innermost brackets.

In our derivations of *blackboard* and *black board,* we did not — so as to keep the discussion at that early stage relatively simple — introduce the notion of the cycle. We now do so, and at the same time illustrate that the utility of rules like 7 and 8 is not limited to simple strings like *blackboard* and *black board.* Let us then consider how the correct stresses are to be assigned to a string like *black board-eraser,* which must be stressed $\overset{2}{black}$ $\overset{1}{board}$-$\overset{3}{eraser}$. The string has this labeled bracketing:

11. [NP [A black]A [N [N board]N [N eraser]N]N]NP

In 11 *black board-eraser* is analyzed into an adjective, *black,* and a compound noun consisting of the nouns *board* and *eraser,* the entire string being a noun phrase.

We might begin the derivation of $\overset{2}{black}$ $\overset{1}{board}$-$\overset{3}{eraser}$ by applying rule 7. This would correctly assign primary stresses to *black* and *board; eraser,* however, because it is not monosyllabic, does not satisfy the structural description of 7 and therefore that rule cannot determine on which syllable of *eraser* to assign the stress. *Eraser* has something like this analysis:

12. [N # [V # erase #]V r #]N

and we want the stress to be assigned to the second syllable of *erase*. Let us now formulate a rule:

13. $V \rightarrow [1 \text{ stress}] \ / \ X \text{ —— } C_0]NAV$

where X stands for any string (or null) and C_0 stands for zero or more consonants. Rule 13 will assign the stress correctly on the second syllable of *erase*. We can see, however, that 13 not only assigns the stress correctly on words like *erase,* but will also correctly assign stresses to all monosyllabic words. Our earlier rule 7 is now superfluous and may be dropped. Notice also that 13 is now not limited to nouns (as 7 was) but has been extended to apply equally to adjectives and verbs. Rule 13 thus is a significant generalization over 7 and so is to be preferred.

Resuming our description of how the cycle works in the derivation of $\overset{2}{black}$ $\overset{1}{board}$-$\overset{3}{eraser}$: on the first cycle only rule 13 applies to the representation 11, assigning primary stress correctly to each of the three words in the string. The other rules that we have introduced do not apply on the first cycle (they apply vacuously) because their structural descriptions are not met. We said that each rule applies to the longest string that contains no internal brackets. Thus rule 8a is blocked from application by the presence in 11 of the innermost brackets that the representation [N [N board]N [N eraser]N]N contains in the derivation — on the first cycle. The same considerations block the application of 8b on the first cycle.

At the end of the first cycle innermost brackets are erased. Thus the string as input to the second cycle is in form 14:

14. [NP bl$\overset{1}{\text{a}}$ck [N b$\overset{1}{\text{o}}$ard er$\overset{1}{\text{a}}$ser]N]NP

On the second cycle rule 13 cannot apply; it applies only to words that have no stresses. Rule 8a can apply, however, because we have a string labeled N that contains a $\overset{1}{V}$ following another $\overset{1}{V}$. Primary stress is thus reassigned to the first $\overset{1}{V}$, after which the second $\overset{1}{V}$ is reduced to $\overset{2}{V}$ by convention 9. On the second cycle 8b cannot apply because, although there is a string labeled NP, it contains internal brackets. At the end of the second cycle innermost brackets are again erased, yielding 15:

15. [NP bl$\overset{1}{\text{a}}$ck b$\overset{1}{\text{o}}$ard er$\overset{2}{\text{a}}$ser]NP

On the third cycle 8b applies, reassigning primary stress to *board* and yielding, with convention 9, *bl$\overset{2}{a}$ck b$\overset{1}{o}$ard-er$\overset{3}{a}$ser*. The same general procedure can be used to derive *bl$\overset{1}{a}$ckb$\overset{3}{o}$ard er$\overset{2}{a}$ser, J$\overset{2}{o}$hn's bl$\overset{1}{a}$ckbo$\overset{4}{a}$rd er$\overset{3}{a}$ser*, and so on. Notice that the cyclic application of the rules as we have described it obeys the principle that the block of rules is applied first to the most deeply embedded structure(s), then on each succeeding cycle to the next most deeply embedded structure, and so on, until on the last cycle it applies to the highest or most dominating structure.

Although rule 13 appears well-motivated, a problem is associated with its use. Because the solution to the problem involves boundary symbol #, let us reconsider how that symbol is introduced into and carried along in derivations.

If we look at the form of rule 13 we see that it directs the assignment of primary stress on the final vowel in the context of a preceding X, where X is not specified as to what or how much linguistic material it may represent.

Earlier we saw that this nonspecificity was an advantage, in that monosyllables turned out to be automatically taken care of by rule 13. Now, however, the nonspecificity threatens to pose problems. Consider form 14. As that form stands, rule 13 would be applicable to the N *board eraser,* assigning primary stress to the vowel of the suffix *-er,* with the previously assigned primaries weakened by one degree. Obviously we do not want this to happen, so that rule 13 must be constrained in some way to prevent such consequences. We can do it by adding to rule 13 the condition that it applies only if the X in its structural description contains no internal occurrences of #. If we go back now to representation 14 and formulate it in its full form, with the boundary symbols that would be generated in its derivation, it would appear as

16. [NP ## black # [N ## board ## eraser ##]N #]NP

With this form of the string and the condition on applying rule 13, that rule would not be applicable. And of course it is in form 16, not 14, that the string passes through the phonological rules.

You may wonder why we have not developed this section more directly and uniformly — why we did not introduce rule 13 at the outset rather than rule 7, why we postponed stating the condition on rule 13, and why we did not begin analyzing *black board-eraser* with a representation in which all boundary symbols were included instead of with representation 11. We felt that proceeding as we did — moving back and forth between sections, instead of starting off with our conclusions — would give you a sense of how an adequate set of phonological rules is actually developed — beginning with hypotheses designed to account for a restricted amount of data and then, as more and more data are introduced, having to modify and tighten the analysis.

Trager-Smith (1951), an outstanding example of structural linguistics, provided phonemic analyses that, particularly about stress, yield much the same results as do those of Chomsky and Halle (1968); thus compounds are marked as in *bláckbòard,* noun phrases as in *blâck bóard,* more complex strings as in *blâck bóard-eràser,* where the symbols ´, ˆ, ` mark primary, secondary, and tertiary stresses and correspond, respectively, to Chomsky and Halle's 1, 2, and 3 stresses. You may therefore feel like asking what difference there is between the two systems. The answer apparently is not to be sought in descriptive results. The difference is, rather, in approach. We have indicated something of that difference.

Case Grammar

The rules of a transformational-generative grammar make use of elements like S, NP, V, which stand for grammatical *categories* (see page 270). Further, some grammatical *functions* can then be defined by the way in which these categories are distributed in phrase markers, the relations between these categories. Among the grammatical functions we have mentioned are subject of the sentence, main verb of the sentence, and direct object of the verb. Of course there are a good many such grammatical functions, like indirect object, subject complement, and object of the preposition. We could try to be exhaustive and specify all such functions as dominance relations among grammatical categories, in the way sketched in our discussion of TG grammar (page 269). We would, however, run into technical problems beyond the scope of this book. Quite apart from these technical difficulties is the question of whether analysis by grammatical function reveals as much about the structure and content of a sentence as does some other type of analysis. We suggest that the approach taken by **case grammar** may provide a more refined analysis of how sentences are constituted and how their parts function.

Let us notice first that both grammatical categories and grammatical functions are properties of sentences (or parts of sentences). We speak about the noun phrase *of a sentence* and the subect *of a sentence*. Consider these examples:

1a. Sue opened the door.
 b. The key opened the door.

Both *Sue* and *the key* are NP's in the sentences of 1; also both sequences function as subjects of those sentences. Knowing this much about the similarities between the two sequences, however, we feel that something remains to be said about the differences between them. Of course, we could point out that in 1a it is Sue and in 1b it is the key that is said to be opening the door. But this is obvious and does not account for our intuition that the difference should be statable in general words. Consider these sentence pairs:

2a. The boy broke the window.
 b. The hammer broke the window.
3a. The butcher sliced the salami.
 b. The knife sliced the salami.

In 2 and 3 we find the same general similarities and differences between the a and the b sentences as in 1a and 1b. Suppose we say that in the a sentences of 1, 2, 3 it is an *agent* that is performing the action, whereas in the b sentences an *instrument* is responsible. We have now moved from an analysis by grammatical function (subject of the sentence) to one by **semantic roles;** the semantic role represented by *Sue, the boy, the butcher,* is "agent performing the action," that represented by *the key, the hammer, the knife* is "instrument by which the action is performed." We notice among other things that the *agents* are all animate, the *instruments* all inanimate objects. There does appear to be something general that analysis into semantic roles can capture. Moreover, if we reflect on the shift represented by case grammar, we see that we have moved from an approach considering the sentence as a *grammatical structure* and now consider it a *description of some action or event,* a description in which the participants in that action are identified not so much by their grammatical as by their semantic function.

So far we have mentioned just two cases: **Agent** and **Instrument.** Among the other cases are **Patient, Location, Experiencer, Goal, Result, Benefactive, Stative,** and **Cause.** These cases are illustrated respectively by the italicized NP's in these sentences:

4a.	Ted hit *the ball.*	(Patient)
b.	Ted slipped on *the rug.*	(Location)
c.	*Ted* became angry.	(Experiencer)
d.	Ted went to *the store.*	(Goal)
e.	Ted built *a house.*	(Result)
f.	Mary made a doll for *Ted.*	(Benefactive)
g.	Ted is *a farmer.*	(Stative)
h.	*The rain* wet the streets.	(Cause)

In the lexicon verbs are represented in **case frames** or **role structures.** These frames indicate the case or roles of the NP's that do accompany or may accompany those verbs in sentences. Each of the verbs in 4a to 4h would contain in its case frame at least the semantic role represented by the NP's italicized above. The verb *hit* would contain in its case frame at least **Patient.** Moreover, to take account of the fact that *Ted* in 4a stands for an **Agent,** the case frame for *hit* would include that case also. Because we can also say "Ted hit the ball with a bat," the case **Instrument** must also be represented. Finally, because we can say "The ball hit the bat," where neither NP stands for an **Agent** — both represent **Patient** — this possibility must also be indicated in the lexical entry for *hit*. To take account of all these possibilities, the case frame for *hit* in the lexicon is this:

5. *hit:* Agent, Patient $\left\{ \begin{matrix} \text{(Instrument)} \\ \text{Patient} \end{matrix} \right\}$

Case frame 5 indicates that *hit* may occur in two case relations. In one of these relations it must be accompanied by NP's in the **Agent** and **Patient** cases, and it may but need not be accompanied by an NP in the **Instrument** case. In the other relation it must be accompanied by two NP's, each in the **Patient** case.

Let us now return to consider sentences like those in 1 and add a sentence to them:

6a. Sue opened the door with a key.
  b. The key opened the door.
  c. The door opened.

In a TG grammar the NP's *Sue, the key,* and *the door* of 6a to 6c would be analyzed as the Subject in the deep (as well as in the surface) structure. In case grammar, although they would be the subject at the surface level, they perform quite different functions, different semantic roles, in deep structure. Thus in the deep structures of 6a to 6c: *Sue* is the **Agent** in 6a, *the key* is the **Instrument** in 6b, and *the door* is **Patient** in 6c. Moreover, *the key* has the same semantic role in 6a and 6b, despite the fact that it is the object of a preposition in 6a and the subject in 6b; finally, *the door* has the same semantic role in 6c as in 6a and 6b, despite the different surface functions. These regularities of semantic roles are not captured by the formal machinery that defines the grammatical functions in TG grammar.

To see the differences between TG grammar and case grammar still more clearly, consider these sentences:

7a. Ted emptied the bucket.
  b. Ted underwent surgery.
  c. Ted heard the thunder.

In a TG grammar *Ted* has the same grammatical function, that of Subject, in each sentence of 7. In a case grammar analysis, however, *Ted* is the **Agent** in 7a, the **Patient** in 7b, and the **Experiencer** in 7c. An analysis that assigns different roles or functions to the three occurrences of *Ted* in the sentences of 7 is in keeping with our intuitions, which tell us that Ted's participation in the activities expressed by the three verbs in 7 differs from sentence to sentence. We understand that Ted, in emptying something, in undergoing something, and in hearing something, stands in different and varying relations to those somethings, and the case analysis reveals those differences. On the other hand, to say that *Ted* is the Subject in all three sentences of 7, though correct, is not very revealing. Charles Fillmore has pointed out that the notion of Subject does not have "semantic constancy," which means simply that NP's which occupy the subject position in surface structure play all sorts of semantic roles — as we have seen.

The same situation (lack of semantic constancy) afflicts the grammatical function of Direct Object. Consider these sentence pairs:

8a. Ted made *the cabinet.*
b. Ted polished *the cabinet.*
9a. Ted wrote *the letter.*
b. Ted burned *the letter.*

All four of the italicized NP's in 8 and 9 are Direct Objects, but here again to say just that much about them would be to overlook and leave unmentioned a distinction of some importance. In the b sentences the semantic role of the Objects is that of **Patient;** the cabinet and the letter undergo the activity of polishing and burning. To do so, of course, they must exist before the respective acts are performed on them. But it would be counterintuitive to say of the Objects in the *a* sentences that they similarly have the role of **Patient,** inasmuch as before the action expressed by the verb is performed on them no object is there to serve as **Patient;** the object comes into existence only *in consequence* of the action expressed by the verb. The semantic role of the italicized NP's in 8a and 9a is therefore that of **Result.** It is interesting that the same considerations which lead to our assigning different semantic roles to the Objects in the *a* and *b* sentences were recognized in traditional grammar, where they were accounted for by distingiushing between *affected* and *effected* Objects; thus the Objects in 8a and 9a are effected, those in 8b and 9b are affected.

An important bonus carried by the theory of case grammar is that inspection of the case frames or role structures by which verbs are accompanied as part of their lexical representation can reveal significant similarities and differences in their semantic force or potential. Consider the verbs *like* and *please* in these sentences:

10. I like music.
11. Music pleases me.

I in 10 and *me* in 11 are in the same conceptual relation to the respective verbs; they are both **Patient.** As to the role of the other NP, *music,* suppose we call it **Actuator.** The basic case frames for both *like* and *please* will then contain the roles **Patient** and **Actuator:**

12. *like:* Patient, Actuator
    please: Patient, Actuator

The representation in 12 reflects the fact that the two verbs implicate the same set of roles and, to that extent, may be said to have the same semantic force. Form differs between sentences 10 and 11 because in 10 the **Patient** role is selected to serve as Subject, whereas in 11 it is the **Actuator** role that is selected to perform that function.

The same set of semantic roles as in 12 will also be contained in the case frames for the verbs *fear* and *frighten:*

13. I fear lightning.
14. Lightning frightens me.

where *I* and *me* are **Patient** and *lightning* is **Actuator.** The case frame for *frighten* must also, however, contain the role **Agent,** inasmuch as we have sentences like

15. My sister frightened me.

where my sister is **Agent.** Now consider a sentence like

16. Snakes frighten Ted.

Sentence 16 is ambiguous between a sense in which it means that snakes perform acts that frighten Ted and a sense in which it means that the mere presence (or thought) of snakes frightens Ted. To account for these facts the case frame for *frighten* would contain (at least)

17. *frighten:* Patient $\left\{\begin{matrix}\text{Agent}\\ \text{Actuator}\end{matrix}\right\}$

One of the virtues of case grammar analysis, as we can see from the preceding discussion, is that it picks out functions of NP's that are in a way deeper, more "semantic," than the grammatical functions. A syntactic consideration which is automatically accounted for by case grammar analysis and which thus adds to its explanatory power is our last subject. Consider these sentences:

18. The boy broke the window.
19. The rock broke the window.
20. The boy broke the window with a rock.
21. *The boy and the rock broke the window.

Sentence 21 must somehow be blocked — as ungrammatical. Case grammar provides a simple and obvious means. It lays down as a principle that two NP's cannot be conjoined if they have different semantic functions. In 21 *the boy* is **Agent** and *the rock* is **Instrument.** The principle mentioned above, stated in semantic roles, accounts for the ungrammaticality of 21, and such a sentence would not appear in the output of a case grammar.

Post-Standard Theory Developments

We have described (page 268) the general structure and operation of the model of TG grammar in Chomsky's *Aspects of the Theory of Syntax* (1965), which has since come to be known as the **Standard Theory.** It is so called primarily because: (1) that theory dominated much of the post-1965 linguistic research, and (2) subsequent alternative theories took the Standard Theory as the point of departure, modifying and extending it. Although for many people transformational-generative grammar implies the Standard Theory, few linguists today accept any but the most general of its main assumptions — indeed, Chomsky himself has explicitly rejected the approach as inadequate and has formulated a significantly different theory intended to address a number of difficulties he felt inherent in the original model. Furthermore, the alternative theory advanced by Chomsky is only one of a number that have been proposed, and linguistics currently has a somewhat disconcerting number of rival approaches, each of them undergoing extension and revision. We will present merely in outline three of the most influential of these post-Standard Theory developments: **Generative Semantics, Extended Standard Theory,** and what we will here call **Variation Theory.**

You may remember that one of the most important concepts of the Standard Theory (hereafter ST) is deep structure, defined in that approach as that level which has these properties:

1. It is the level of structure arrived at after all lexical entries are inserted into pre-terminal phrase markers and before operation of any transformations.

2. It is the level that contains all the information necessary for the semantic component to impose an interpretation on that structure and yield as output the appropriate semantic representation or meaning of the sentence.

3. It is the level containing all the information necessary for the transformational component to convert it into the grammatically well-formed sentences of the language (the surface structures).

Deep structure was thus a level characterized as post–lexical-insertion, and serving as input both to the *interpretive* semantic component and the *generative* transformational component.

One of the most radical challenges to ST came from Generative Semantics (GS) (a movement most closely associated with the linguists Lakoff, McCawley, Ross, and Postal), which denied that any level of structure in a grammar possesses the three properties cited above — therefore denying the existence of deep structures. Of number 1, proponents of GS argued that lexical insertion does not occur in a "block" before any transformational rule is applied, but that it takes place at many points of a derivation (subject to constraints), some before any transformations have applied and some after at least specified transformations have already applied. The GS linguists assert, therefore, that at least some lexical entries cannot be inserted before application of certain transformations.

As for numbers 2 and 3, taken jointly, they entail a conception of grammar in which transformational rules can be said to be *meaning-preserving* and one in which the level of semantic representation and that of surface structure are not directly connected in any way. First, if all aspects of semantic interpretation can be successfully developed from the level of deep structure, then transformations, in converting those structures into surface structures, must not change meanings. If they did, it would be necessary to consult the structures resulting from the application of transformations in order to obtain the new meanings introduced by their application, and the semantic component would now have to be modified or supplemented so that it could account for these altered meanings. Second, the levels of semantic representation and surface structure must be distinct, because the former results from the application of interpretive rules of the semantic component, and the latter from the generative (transformational) rules of the transformational component.

Now the theory of GS accepts the first concept in the preceding paragraph as entailed by 2 and 3, namely that transformations are meaning-preserving, but it rejects the second — that semantic representations and surface structures are not directly connected. In the GS view the rules map semantic representations directly into surface structures *without* any intermediate level of deep structure. Now transformations operate on structures that already directly represent the meaning of sentences, as contrasted with the ST view in which transformations operated on structures that had to be *interpreted* by the rules of a separate semantic component to arrive at that meaning. In a GS grammar the transformational rules apply to structures that *in the first instance* are designed to represent meaning and, as meaning-preserving rules, they convert those structures (which *are* semantic representations) into the grammatical sentences (the surface structures). The theory, therefore, can dispense with a semantic component in the form of distinct interpretive rules and requires only what proponents of GS describe as a single *homogeneous set of generative rules* (transformations) which map semantic representations into surface structures, so that no notion of a deep structure level as mediating between these two levels is needed. Hence the name *Generative* Semantics because all the rules are generative (transformational) rules, and no (semantic) interpretive rules exist. A great deal of the analysis that would be necessary to enrich the phrase structure rules enough to generate initial phrase markers that in fact represented the semantic structure of sentences was never really carried out.

In contrast to the GS approach, Chomsky's **Extended Standard Theory** (EST) appears (at least on the surface) to be a less radical modification of the ST that he originally formulated. The EST theory accepts the existence of a deep structure and employs distinct interpretive semantic rules for producing semantic representations, in addition to transformational rules that map deep structures into surface structures; this is the same as in the ST approach. The first major difference is in the rejection by EST of the claim that transformations are meaning-preserving. Chomsky argues that at least some transformations *do* change meaning in significant ways and if they do, then, although a level of deep structure is accepted that has properties 1 and 3, EST must deny that such a level has the second property listed. For if transformations change meaning, then we must consult the structures built by applying transformations to obtain the new meanings introduced by their application. Therefore, deep structure cannot contain *all* information sufficient for semantic representation. And this leads us to the second major departure of EST from ST: although EST still employs distinct interpretive rules for deriving meanings, these rules must now refer not only to the level of deep structure but also to later stages of a transformational derivation — to surface structures — for at least part of the meaning of some sentences (and possibly also to structures intermediate between deep and surface structures). Thus, under the EST model the interpretive rules may have as input, in addition to deep structures, any other intermediate or surface structures. As we have said, this follows from the fact that transformations may effect changes in meaning. Because of this extended power of the interpretive rules, EST is sometimes referred to as **Interpretive Semantics** (as opposed to Generative Semantics).

At present, after a good deal of relatively inconclusive debate between proponents of GS and EST, interest (at least in America) in GS has declined considerably. On the other hand, EST has not been abandoned but has been extended and enriched — once again by Chomsky himself — into the **Revised Extended Standard Theory** (REST) or, because of a device called a trace, **Trace Theory.** The principal departure of REST from the EST approach described above is that now *all* semantic interpretation is done at a non–deep-structure level, namely, surface structure. Notice how radical a change this is from the original ST model: there all semantic interpretation was accomplished in deep structure; now, in REST, no level other than surface structure is considered necessary for proper semantic interpretation. Because REST is relatively recent, some time must pass before its validity can be evaluated. Nevertheless, it is the major current model of grammatical analysis.

All the theories discussed here share with the Standard Theory at least one main assumption about a linguistic rule: rules are *categorial;* they either apply or do not apply depending only on whether the string satisfies or does not satisfy the structural description of the rule. The work of sociolinguist William Labov, however, has suggested that linguistic theory must be extended to include a rule of a wholly different sort, the **variable rule.** It may apply a different *percentage* of times depending on the context. Labov presents evidence that there is a rule of final consonant deletion for speakers of the Black English (BE) dialect of many urban American communities: words such as *bold, find, fist* are pronounced by many speakers of BE as if no final *t* or *d* were present (it occurs in white Standard English too, although less often). But in the application of this rule there is true (Labov calls it inherent) variation: no speakers always drop such consonants in BE and no speakers of BE always retain them; rather, the rule is variable in that it is applied more frequently when the following word begins with a consonant than with a vowel, in sequences like *sand castle* or *fast car* more often than in *lift it* or *wild elephant*. Notice that the speech of a single speaker is not necessarily uniform on all occasions of its use; it may vary with different extralinguistic settings. This then is a source of variation.

Let us now consider how such a state of affairs would be handled within TG phonology as described on page 291. Because the rule does not always apply, it would have to be optional, something like:

1. $C' \rightarrow \emptyset \ / \ C \ \rule{2em}{0.4pt} \ \#$

where C′ stands for the consonants *t, d,* and # for word boundary. But rule 1, although it is optional, is still categorial; *every* form that undergoes it loses its final consonant. The rule thus fails to reflect the facts on the variability of the rule's application: that it does not always apply in the environment stated, and that the frequency of its application when it does apply varies relative to the phonological environment: it occurs more frequently in the environment C —— # C than in C —— # V. To reflect the facts about the variability of the rule, Labov would reformulate it somewhat like this:

2. $C' \rightarrow (\emptyset) \ / \ C \ \rule{2em}{0.4pt} \ \# \ (-V)$

The parentheses around ∅ in 2 mean the rule is not categorial, like 1, but variable in the sense that even in the environment indicated the rule will not always be applied; the parentheses around − V remind us that the absence of a vowel favors application of the rule.

We may call a theory designed to account for facts about the variability of rule application under well-defined conditions **Variation Theory.** This theory is being extensively developed, and a number of innovations have appeared. Variable rules are an extremely powerful device. Where there are a number of variable conditioning factors, each favoring the application of some rule in different degrees, we can rank the factors along some quantifiable scale and code the *relative order* of such effects in the rule itself. Indeed, the concept of a conditioning factor (a *variable constraint* in the theory) is not restricted to purely linguistic factors as it was in 2. Labov has demonstrated that many rules are variably conditioned for application by socioeconomic, ethnic, dialectal, and stylistic factors. Rule 2 is favored (applied with greater frequency) in less formal contexts, within lower socioeconomic groups and elsewhere — and factors of these kinds can be incorporated within the general framework of variable rules.

Select Bibliography

This bibliography is limited to two kinds of books: first, those of which considerable direct use has been made in the preparation of this text; second, those likely to be particularly useful to students beginning to explore various areas of the language. Many of the books listed contain much more detailed bibliographies.

Allen, Harold B. *Linguistics and English Linguistics*. New York, 1966.
Bach, Emmon. *Syntactic Theory*. 2nd ed. New York, 1974.
Baugh, Albert C. *A History of the English Language*. 2nd ed. New York, 1957.
Bloomfield, Leonard. *Language*. New York, 1933.
Brook, G. L. *A History of the English Language*. London, 1958.
Bryant, Margaret M. *Current American Usage*. New York, 1962.
———. *Modern English and Its Heritage*. 2nd ed. New York, 1962.
Chomsky, Noam. *Syntactic Structures*. The Hague, 1957.
———. *Aspects of the Theory of Syntax*. Cambridge, Mass., 1965.
———. *Studies on Semantics in Generative Grammar*. The Hague, 1972.
———. *Reflections on Language*. New York, 1975.

———, and Halle, Morris. *The Sound Pattern of English.* New York, 1968.

Conner, Jack E. *A Grammar of Standard English.* Boston, 1968.

Curme, George O. *A Grammar of the English Language,* Vols. II and III. Boston, 1931, 1935.

———. *Principles and Practice of English Grammar.* New York, 1947.

Emerson, Oliver Farrar. *A Middle English Reader.* New and rev. ed. New York, 1948.

Fillmore, Charles. "The Case for Case" in Bach, E. and Harms, R. T. eds. *Universals in Linguistic Theory.* New York, 1968.

Francis, W. Nelson. *The Structure of American English.* With a chapter on American English dialects by Raven I. McDavid, Jr. New York, 1958.

Fries, Charles Carpenter. *American English Grammar.* New York, 1940.

———. *The Structure of English.* New York, 1952.

Gleason, H. A., Jr. *An Introduction to Descriptive Linguistics.* Rev. ed. New York, 1961.

———. *Linguistics and English Grammar.* New York, 1965.

Jesperson, Otto. *Essentials of English Grammar.* New York, 1933.

———. *Growth and Structure of the English Language.* 9th ed. Oxford, 1954. (Originally pub. 1905.)

———. *Language: Its Nature, Development and Origin.* New York, 1922.

Jones, Daniel. *The Pronunciation of English.* 4th ed. Cambridge, Eng., 1958.

———. *The History and Meaning of the Term "Phoneme."* University College, London, 1957.

Kaiser, Rolf. *Medieval English.* Berlin, 1961.

Krapp, George Philip. *The English Language in America.* 2 vols. New York, 1925.

Labov, William. *Language in the Inner City.* Philadelphia, 1972.

Laird, Charlton. *The Miracle of Language.* New York, 1957.

Lakoff, George. "On Generative Semantics" in Steinberg, D. D. & Jakobovits, L. A. eds. *Semantics.* Cambridge, 1971.

Leonard, Sterling A. *Current English Usage.* NCTE Monograph, No. 1. Chicago, 1932.

———. *The Doctrine of Correctness in English Usage, 1700–1800.* University of Wisconsin Studies in Language and Literature, No. 25. Madison, Wis., 1929.

Long, Ralph B. *The Sentence and Its Parts.* Chicago, 1961.

Lowth, Robert. *A Short Introduction to English Grammar.* London, 1775. (First ed. 1762.)

Marckwardt, Albert H. *American English.* New York, 1958.

———. *Introduction to the English Language.* New York, 1942.

———, and Fred G. Walcott. *Facts About Current English Usage.* New York, 1938.

———, and James L. Rosier, *Old English Language and Literature*. New York, 1972.

McAdam, E. L., Jr., and George Milne. *Johnson's Dictionary, A Modern Selection*. New York, 1963.

Mencken, H. L. *The American Language: The Fourth Edition and the Two Supplements*. Abridged and ed. Raven I. McDavid, Jr. New York, 1963.

Moore, J. L. *Tudor-Stuart Views on the Growth, Status, and Destiny of the English Language*. Halle, 1910.

Moore, Samuel. *Historical Outlines of English Sounds and Inflections*. Rev. ed. by Albert H. Marckwardt. Ann Arbor, Mich., 1964.

Ogg, Oscar. *The 26 Letters*. New York, 1948.

The Oxford English Dictionary. 13 vols. Oxford, 1933. (Originally pub. 1884–1928 as *A New English Dictionary on Historical Principles*, reissued with Supplement in 1933. Second supplement in progress. Volume A-G published in 1972.)

Potter, Simeon. *Our Language*. London, 1950.

Pyles, Thomas. *Words and Ways of American English*. New York, 1952; London, 1954.

———. *The Origins and Development of the English Language*, 2nd ed. New York, 1971.

Roberts, Paul. *Understanding English*. New York, 1958.

———. *English Syntax*. Alternate ed. New York, 1964.

Robertson, Stuart. *The Development of Modern English*. 2nd and rev. ed. Frederic G. Cassidy. New York, 1954.

Rogovin, Syrell. *Modern English Sentence Structure*. New York, 1965.

Sapir, Edward. *Language: An Introduction to the Study of Speech*. New York, 1921.

Saussure, Ferdinand de. *Course in General Linguistics*, ed. Charles Bally and Albert Sechehaye in collaboration with Albert Reidlinger, trans. Wade Baskin. New York, 1959.

Starnes, DeWitt T., and Gertrude E. Noyes. *The English Dictionary from Cawdrey to Johnson, 1604–1755*. Chapel Hill, N.C., 1946.

Trager, George L., and Henry Lee Smith, Jr. *An Outline of English Structure*. Studies in Linguistics: Occasional Papers, 3. Norman, Okla., 1951.

Webster's Third New International Dictionary. Springfield, Mass., 1961.

Webster's Second New International Dictionary. Springfield, Mass., 1934.

Index